The Price of Inefficiency

Frank Koester

Alpha Editions

This edition published in 2019

ISBN : 9789353975098

Design and Setting By
Alpha Editions
email - alphaedis@gmail.com

"The true measure of a man's success is the service which he renders, not the pay he exacts for it. The true measure of a man's ability is the power to help others and to contribute to their advancement. The effort to make money is an important incentive to social service and industrial progress; but the amount of wealth each man acquires is no accurate indication of the service he has rendered or the progress he has made possible."

PRESIDENT HADLEY of Yale.

PREFACE

THE great burden of inefficiency, with its terrible cost, is a burden that is carried on the shoulders of each and every one of us. Whatever your income may be, much or little, increasing or decreasing, you are paying your full share in one form or another of the waste, which amounts to over ten billions of dollars annually; a waste that means that forty cents of every dollar you earn goes for nothing.

You are paying this, the price of inefficiency, in a thousand different ways for your personal negligence in not taking the interest that you should in the business and governmental affairs of the country and in your own private concerns.

What it is possible for you to do to reduce the frightful costs of inefficiency, what you should do and what you must do, is a question the responsibility for which you cannot escape. If you remain merely neutral, you bear the loss just as surely, since the government, city, state and national, your employer, your employees, and your friends will be all the more active in their work of reducing your resources, cheating or robbing you, both directly and indirectly, and adding to the costs due to your inefficiency as a recreant member of a government, the individuals of which must rule themselves as a body, if they are not to be ruled by bosses, minorities and combinations.

A little well directed individual effort, which will become a matter of habit, will suffice to effect vast reductions in the price of inefficiency. Even the knowledge of where the waste is, will in many cases call forth the remedy, though in other cases entirely new principles must be called into action.

It is the purpose of this book to show where the frightful wastes are being incurred, in governmental, and industrial, social and educational affairs, to point out remedies for reducing them to a minimum or eliminating them entirely, and to indicate new principles which may often operate not only to reduce and eliminate inefficient methods, but to leave the field clear for efficiency.

It is of tremendous importance to the nation to take a stand for betterment. Conditions will grow worse unless they are made to grow better, and the problems which are so acute and pressing cannot be solved by parties or by statesmen, by legislators or committees, but must be solved by the spontaneous and irresistible effect of public sentiment and individual action. There is something for everyone to do, and when the extent and gravity of the situation is understood, no one will hesitate to do his part. It is the duty of those who are acquainted with the facts to make them more widely known, and in this respect the influence of the press is of the greatest consequence, and a patriotic and non-partisan espousal of the cause of efficiency on their part and a genuine and persistent attention to the subject cannot fail to be reflected in increased prosperity for all concerned. Newspapers should devote their attention systematically to the matter, treating every phase of it in a constructive way, pointing out how efficiency is to be obtained and how much it means.

Not alone will the interests of the public be served but their own as well, by increased circulation and increased advertising and by the influx of new firms with new advertising. The propaganda of efficiency will mean increased prosperity for every paper and every reader, and no editor can serve his country, his public and his paper better than by a thorough and persistent attention to efficiency.

Efficiency is not a thing reserved for the comprehension of the elect. It is not a thing to be called "scientific management" and used as a bug-a-boo; it is, on the contrary, nothing but common sense applied to every day affairs, the doing of a thing in a better, quicker and more economical way than at present, the doing of a thing in the right way, the easy, the adept, the direct and natural way, rather than in the careless, the slovenly, the wrong and the round-about way.

Efficiency has a widespread application and may be practiced in a widespread manner and by every one, in some form or another. Efficiency is the duty, not only of every man to himself, but of every man to his neighbor. It is a slogan that means prosperity and a watchword of honest effort and well directed energy.

If a hundred men have a certain work to perform, week in and week out, a few of them will presently be found to execute the work with greater ease and dispatch than the rest, and of these few, one will be found who, with less expenditure of energy and time than any of the others, accomplishes the work better. That man is the efficient man, and he has evolved the efficient method. That method should be made known to all and followed by all, and a high degree of efficiency will be the result for all. The inferior methods of the others are costly and should be discarded without delay. Those who are willing to learn will progress, but those who cling to their old methods and refuse to learn will fail.

This is true not only of individuals but of nations as well, and it is a criminal waste of time and resources not to adopt methods which have proved themselves the right ones elsewhere, but instead either to stick to old methods or experiment along lines which have already been gone over.

Every possible improvement should be known and considered instead of being ignored until it forces its way into use. Instead of the ready excuse when a new thing comes out elsewhere, that it is not applicable to our conditions, it should be made applicable. Merit should be sought out wherever it may be found, instead of being choked off and forced to fight its half starved way to the front.

As long as a man is satisfied that he has nothing more to learn, he will learn nothing more, but when he realizes that he is not yet the master of the accumulated knowledge of the world on his subject, he will progress. Once in the swing and step of progress, he can readily keep abreast of his competitors and apply to his own problems the results which have been and are constantly being achieved by others.

It was, at the outset, the intention to make this volume a brief exposition of certain of the more noticeable phases of inefficiency, but in compiling the data and in seeking out the underlying causes for inefficiency, new and more profound causes appeared.

It was as if an underground city of decay had been entered, avenue after avenue of inquiry presented itself and at every turn new and greater vistas of crumbling walls and tottering pillars appeared. Overhead the world takes its way, with here and there a sinking of the street or an upheaval of the surface. Beneath, the foundations are undermined by neglect, carelessness, graft, self-satisfaction, disrespect of authority, lack of discipline, faulty education, lawlessness, suspicion, waste, squandering of resources, extravagance, crooked dealing, monopoly, indolence, superficiality and politics; a stupendous labyrinth of destructive forces, which mean national disaster if fundamental and comprehensive measures for correction are not undertaken at once.

As in the design and construction of a great engineering work, where the whole and its various components must be suited to the requirements to be met, so the governmental, social, economical and business organization of a country must be suited to conditions if disaster is not to be encountered.

Like a great dam which conserves enormous resources of energy in storing millions of gallons of water, so must the social structure conserve the energy of humanity and utilize it for the benefit of humanity.

Unless the dam be properly calculated, and of the right design; constructed of the best materials and erected on a firm foundation, it will soon begin to show evidence of failure; crevices will appear, the true alignment be lost and the relief gates jammed. Although expedients be adopted, crevices patched and reënforcements applied, if the weakness is in the original design the time will come when nothing further will avail, when the dam cannot be saved and when it is destined to carry death and destruction in its final collapse.

So with the social machinery of a country. If it be not rightly constructed, if the attitude of the individuals to each other and to the government, and the attitude of the government toward the individual be not properly founded in mutual respect and self respect, no amount of patching can save the structure. And though the disaster may be far reaching, it will, as in the case of the failure of the dam, at least wipe out old mistakes and makeshifts, and leave the ground clear for the work of new engineers, who, profiting from experience of the past, and with sounder theory and more thorough practice, will erect a structure capable of withstanding the stresses to which it will be subjected and capable of utilizing the accumulated forces to the greatest possible advantage.

Such an improved social structure once established will, like a dam using the energy of the stored water to turn a multitude of generators, distributing energy in other forms throughout the surrounding country and stimulating its production similarly, infuse a new stimulus to the whole life of the nation, both in the present and in the future.

The great extent and deep-rootedness of the evils of the situation cannot be comprehended by the individual who does not take a broad and public-spirited view of conditions. It is indeed appalling when seen as a whole, and the lack of real patriotic interest in the country, taken by its citizens, is a reproach and a menace of impending disaster.

The neglect of the individual extends not only to the nation's affairs, but to his own, and it is only after a realization of how general is this condition, that the individual can be expected to see that only by a thorough readjustment of his own attitude and affairs, can he do his part in the new scheme of things that must come into existence, if we are not to descend to far more serious conditions.

That a grave situation exists cannot be denied, but that conditions may be improved is equally patent, as shown by what exists abroad, where a more advanced and efficient public opinion has found a means of enforcing itself.

It would be impossible for any one person to speak with authority on subjects so complex and varied as must go to make up a broad review of national conditions, but in every department the situation has been analysed by experts, and wherever, herein, conclusions have been advanced, they are based on accumulated experience and fortified by the highest authorities. The reports of the federal government, census reports, state and national authorities and specialists have been freely quoted, so that it is believed that in every important particular, corroboration will be found for any statements advanced.

Although it might appear that much of the matter is of a negative or critical nature, there will be found no small amount of constructive criticism, that is to say suggestions for actually remedying conditions. Americans are, unfortunately, not prone to criticism, and are much imposed upon in consequence. Their proverbial generosity and magnanimity are too much taken advantage of. A more critical spirit could not fail to have a stimulating effect, and while many of the criticisms here made might appear antagonistic if from the pen of a passing visitor, yet as the author has been a resident of some ten years' standing, continually active in business and professional life, and has become a citizen and cast his fortunes here permanently, it will be seen that the criticisms are as of one member of a family to another, intended for the common good and for the remedying of conditions from which we all suffer alike.

The volume is not intended, however, in any way to be a comprehensive resumé of American life or institutions, and any general conclusions should not be attempted to be drawn from it, for the many admirable, not to say unparalleled, activities of American life are but seldom referred to. The purpose of this book is not to praise nor sit in judgment nor to attempt a broad summary, but to point out defects and shortcomings which are much more apparent to one with foreign experience than to one to the manner born, defects and shortcomings which perhaps on that account have gone if not unnoticed, at least unremedied.

For the quotations made throughout the book, the author begs to acknowledge the courtesy extended by the several authors and publishers. It is through this courtesy that the author hopes to have made the book an authoritative presentation of the various subjects.

It is hoped that the work will be received in the spirit intended, that of helpful and constructive criticism, and that it will be of assistance in promoting a better understanding of the great cohesive force of social life, the fuller co-operation of individuals with each other and with the state, of the state with the individual, and of the states of the world with each other.

F. K.

March, 1913,
New York City.

CONTENTS

INTRODUCTION

UNREST and turmoil are the order of the times, protest and animosity show themselves at every hand, and hatred and hopelessness, bitter distrust and denunciation govern our relations as classes and as individuals.

We are facing an acute but intensely complicated crisis in the existence of the nation, and the contributing causes are numerous and grave, with remedies difficult to understand and more difficult to apply. The country is like a giant, bound hand and foot and tormented on every side, in an intolerable situation but hopeless of any relief.

We confront conditions, not theories. Familiar with great prosperity and accustomed to the swing of progress, there seemed no bounds which we might not permit ourselves; and thus the awakening is all the more abrupt and severe, and the present stagnation all the more keenly felt.

A young nation with vast natural resources, the fair way ahead was free and clear, but suddenly we find that our resources have been squandered and are approaching exhaustion, that we have been betrayed by our financiers and politicians and led into the blind alley of disaster.

Though being a self-satisfied people, we are yet unable to assert ourselves at the right juncture in our own interests. We cannot kick and kick vigorously enough at the right time and place, and we are continually getting deeper and deeper into trouble. In a national crisis of this kind, the statesmanship of a country should be its guiding light, but where are our statesmen to be found? Where are our leaders who are not chiefly concerned with their own political interests. A government should be an inspiration and a guiding force, an encouragement for industry and business, but instead of exhibiting such a firm and fruitful policy, our administration is one of waste and gross inefficiency.

With statesmanship such as America should command, the dangerous shoals we are now encountering, would long ago have been avoided. With patriotic and disinterested hands at the helm of state, such dangers would have been clearly seen and avoided, whereas now the vessel of government is crushing first against Scylla on one side and tossed by Charybdis on the other.

The government may be charged and unanswerably charged with:

Ruining of prosperity for petty partisan advantage;

Creating industrial unrest and turmoil;

Destruction of confidence of the public in the state;

Unexampled waste of natural resources;

Gross administrative inefficiency and incompetency;

Restriction of industrial development;

Crippling business enterprises;

Neglect of agricultural needs and a failure to check enormous waste of farm products;

Sacrifice of countless lives in unregulated industrial establishments;

Negligence in combatting industrial diseases;

Administrative self interest, waste and graft;

Inadequacy and insufficiency of the law;

Failure to cope with monopolies;

Failure to prevent adulteration of foods;

Continuance of a deceptive and destructive patent system;

Autocratic administration of the post office;

Continuance of shameful pension frauds;

Promoting the spirit of lawlessness and disrespect for law;

A wrongful immigration policy.

While these are among the principal items directly chargeable to the government, a more considerably responsibility is chargeable to its failure to take constructive action. The government is negligent in that it

Fails to modernize the constitution;

Fails to provide an adequate and proper educational system;

Fails to link the educational system with practical life through not compelling the learning of a means of livelihood on the part of every citizen;

Denies the right to work;

Fails to protect small industries from the aggression of monopolies;

Neglects to provide a national testing plant for the promotion of manufacture;

Fails to provide industrial insurance systems for accident, sickness and old age.

Improperly develops waterways;

Does not cause the administration to command the respect of the public;

Does not obviate mismanagement of railway and industrial plants;

Does not cause the servants of the public to realize that they are the servants of the public;

Fails to prevent the congestion of wealth in the hands of the few;

Fails to diminish the controversy between capital and labor;

Fails to command the respect and good will of foreign commerce;

Fails to promote our merchant marine;

Fails to adopt a constructive diplomatic policy.

The machinery of the government and the personnel which has been evolved to administer its affairs is incompetent and inefficient. It is in a state of break down, is unable to cope with conditions which it has created and its deplorable and destructive and desperate activities are like a huge machine grinding itself to pieces. The situation is acute and demands the careful thought and vigorous action of every citizen.

Incompetency and inefficiency are not alone confined to high places; they take their noisome course through the whole body of the government.

As Superintendent of Insurance, William H. Hotchkiss of New York, in a recent newspaper interview said: "The times are out of joint.

"Never before was enlightened public service more in demand. Indeed, may we not well turn aside from insurance problems and for the moment glance at the problems with which all Americans are now concerned? Whither are we of a great republic drifting? Labor glowers and threatens an industrial war. Big business shakes with ague. Capital is dissatisfied, prosperity is checked. The people call loudly for retributory law against manager and magnate. Strong arm methods toward great corporations are in full operation in nation and state. Commercially speaking our times are out of joint. Likewise our politics. The people's legislators long since lost the people's confidence. Their executives must now exceed the written law or lose in power and usefulness. Their judges even are threatened with recall.

"Parties once potent are going to pieces as the voters rightfully gain the power to nominate their public servants. Socialism—of the right or of the wrong sort—is winning converts every day. The cloistered citizen of the kid gloved wards is beginning to have his say, while the horse block orator is haranguing an audience that may any moment become a mob.''

The government, which includes not only the ever changing federal administration, and its legislative and judicial branches, and the governments of the states as well, are as open to criticism as the most outrageous of the trusts. The ensemble governments of the United States, in their mountebank struggle with conditions passed some 44,000 laws in 1910.

In the words of ex-Governor Herrick of Ohio, there were:

''Laws to regulate everybody and everything except the public expenditures of the law-makers themselves and of the various departments of the government. The great majority of men sitting in our legislative bodies are lawyers, whose natural tendency is to attempt to remedy every ill by a statute.

''The oversight of business enterprises by the government has placed on the government payrolls a vast number of officials; it has necessitated the establishment of new departments, the keeping of a mass of records and the compilation of a great quantity of statistics. All this has been done with no serious attempt to reform the antiquated expensive methods prevailing in all departments of the government.

''The people have been so intent on placing the corporations under governmental control that they have overlooked the additional burden they are putting on their own shoulders by placing this work in the hands of officials who, handicapped by bad methods, are rendered powerless to do little more than swell the payrolls.

''It goes without saying that predatory corporations either should be brought within the law or put out of business. It is doubtless true that salutary laws have been passed regulating other corporations, but we should also apply ourselves, as a condition precedent to the government's further controlling and managing these corporations, to reforming the administration of the government. Otherwise the burdens of taxation will become unbearable, intolerable, and in the reaction which will surely follow, much of the good of the progressive legislation of recent years will be undone.''

The great majority of the 44,000 laws referred to will undoubtedly be dead letters in a short time, if they ever have any effect. As dead letters they only serve to clog the administration of justice and encourage disrespect for the law. Any one of them, however, may be utilized at any moment as a means of creating confusion and for political effect, as has been the case with the Sherman law.

To such conditions, to inefficiency in office, to corruption, to graft, to neglect of the preservation of natural resources, to failure to encourage industry and agriculture, to the throttling of business, to utter disregard of public welfare we have been brought by our statesmen in their wisdom.

What it all means in dollars and cents alone may be computed, but what it means in unrest, distress, discouragement and misery is beyond any human calculation.

The principal items in the indictment of inefficiency, costs which could not be charged against an efficient government, quickly total an appalling figure, a figure which concerns vitally not alone every citizen of the country, but the world at large, for the prosperity of all civilized nations is vitally connected.

We waste $50,000,000 and sacrifice fifty lives a year in forest fires, and have been doing it for over a generation, while in some years the loss amounts to $200,000,000 in money. In addition the young growth destroyed by fire is far more valuable than the merchantable timber burned.

We waste a billion cubic feet of natural gas daily, the most perfect of fuels; enough to supply every city of over 100,000 population in the United States.

We waste $22,000,000 a year in the manufacture of coke in lost gases; 540,000 tons of ammonium sulphate of similar value and nearly 400,000,000 gallons of tar worth $9,000,000, a total with other wasted by-products of $55,000,000.

We waste a vast sum yearly in not utilizing our deposits of peat as fuel. The value of available peat beds is estimated at thirty-nine thousand millions of dollars.

We waste 30,000,000 horsepower every year, by failure to utilize our water power. At $20 per horse power per annnum, which is below the average price, being less than one cent per horse power per hour, this waste amounts to $600,000,000. This is far in excess of the value of all coal used annually, and if this power were utilized, coal could be conserved for future uses, for heating and purposes where the power would not be serviceable.

We waste $238,000,000 in losses through floods and freshets. The most of this could be prevented by proper engineering in the erection of levees and dams.

We waste $500,000,000 a year in soil erosion. Through the neglect of farmers to properly work their land and to prevent the formation of gullies, the fertility of the soil is washed into the lowlands and seas.

We waste vast land resources by failure to drain swamps and overflowed areas. These lands could be reclaimed at small expense, increasing the value of the land three fold, and supplying homes for 10,000,000 people.

We waste $659,000,000 a year through losses to growing crops, fruit trees, grain in storage, etc., by noxious insects, whose multiplication is largely due to careless methods of agriculture.

We waste $267,000,000 a year through the attacks of flies, ticks, and other insects on animal life. A greater loss is caused by the enormous sacrifice of human life due to mosquitoes, flies, fleas, and other germ carrying insects.

We waste $100,000,000 annually in losses to live stock and crops by wolves, rats, mice and other depredatory mammals.

We waste $93,000,000 a year in losses of live stock due to disease, of which $40,000,000 is chargeable to Texas fever, while tuberculosis, scabbies and cholera are next in importance, all of which are largely preventable if not eradicable.

We waste $772,000,000 annually in losses of income, due to industrial diseases; that is diseases which attack workers on account of the nature of their employment and the unsanitary conditions in which the work is carried on.

We waste $1,500,000,000 a year through loss of life and illness to industrial and other workers, through preventable disease, accidents and carelessness. The truth of this is corroborated by the fact that the expectation of life in Germany is ten years longer than in America.

We waste $2,503,900 a year, in the form of 1465 human lives, (using the figure $1700 as the economic value of a human life, the governmental estimate later referred to) in coal mine accidents, which are almost wholly preventable.

We waste 10,585 lives and the cost of 169,538 injuries in railroad accidents.

We waste $300,000,000 annually in the lax administration of the government itself. This is equivalent to the economic value of 176,470 lives.

We waste a considerable proportion of our vast pension expenditures of $173,000,000 due to fraudulent and undeserved pensions granted. The cost of the pension armies of Germany,

France, England and Austro-Hungary is less than $100,000,000.

We waste $25,000,000 a year in handling the mails, while the German government makes a net profit of $28,000,000 on a much smaller gross business.

The foregoing are only a few of the principal items in the price we pay for the inefficiency of our federal and state governments, as with proper administrative efforts, an enormous part of the total would be saved. There are in addition countless important items of loss, which cannot be definitely ascertained, as many unknown factors enter into them, though the losses are no less because of not being determinable in dollars and cents. The foregoing figures are the result of careful and frequently repeated estimates by conservative governmental experts, and are in each case in accord with the observations of intelligent farmers and other interested persons acquainted with conditions.

Nor do these items aggregate the principal part of the losses of inefficiency. In other branches of activity over which the federal and state governments have no control, the losses are even greater.

We waste $250,000,000 annually in fire losses to buildings and other structures.

We waste $400,000,000 a year in the expense of the portion of city water supply used for fire fighting, in fire department charges and in distribution charges, all of which makes the loss per capita in this country ten times that of European countries, showing the grossest waste and inefficiency.

We waste $650,000,000 annually in mismanagement of railroads, of which $300,000,000 is due to personal services, $300,-000,000 in fixed charges and $150,000,000 in supplies.

We waste perhaps a greater sum in private manufacturing establishments. While this has not been estimated by experts, yet since the railroads of the country are valued at eleven thousand million of dollars, while the value of manufactured products exceeds seven thousand millions, and since railroad efficiency is 70% while manufacturing efficiency is but 60%, the loss in manufacturing is probably greater than in railroad inefficiency.

We waste in the careless handling of eggs, $40,000,000 a year, largely due to breakage in transportation. What the vast waste of careless freight, express and baggage handling amounts to in actual damage, besides the increased cost of packing to guard against it, it is impossible to estimate.

We waste an enormous amount, which has not yet been made the basis of a comprehensive examination, in losses due to improper and antiquated methods of mining; in coal, copper, gold, silver and other metals and in metallurgical processes of various kinds.

We waste not less than one third of all the coal used for power purposes and vastly a larger proportion in heating through failure to adopt modern machinery and methods.

We waste $25,000,000 a year by failure to adopt the potato drying process used in Germany, that proportion of our potato crop rotting unnecessarily.

We waste $12,000,000 in failure to utilize the leaves of potato and other plants, a source of profit in Germany but a total loss with us.

We waste sums which though immense, are not capable of being computed, in our slowness to adopt a great number of improvements which are available and in daily use in Europe. Potato drying is only an insignificant example of this waste.

We waste $702,000,000 a year at the lowest estimate in the failure of our workmen and manufacturers to adopt common sense practice in daily operations, a method of working the introduction of which is being greatly hampered by being called by the high sounding name of "scientific management" or "motion study."

We waste 350 lives and the cost of 2700 accidents in transportation in New York City alone, with a proportionate loss in other cities throughout the country. These losses involve, in addition, great expenditures in litigation, the total of which is probably not less than $25,000,000 annually.

What we waste in losses through inefficiency of administration in cities and towns, losses due to crooked and ill-considered contracts, and the great wastes of graft of all kinds are beyond computation.

These figures, although startling, are only a part of the staggering price of inefficiency. A multiplicity of additional researches in all industries would be necessary to ascertain the entire amount of waste.

Making due allowance in the items enumerated, where saving could not be effected; where the waste though great may be termed unavoidable; the total remaining constitutes a frightful indictment of American extravagance, waste and carelessness. It amounts to more than ten thousand millions of dollars annually, a per capita loss, assuming the smaller figure, with our population, of not less than $100. For the 33,000,000 wage-earners of the country, it amounts to not less than $300 per year or a minumum of $5.75 per week, since the burden is concentrated on their shoulders. As the average wage of wage-earners is under $10 a week, the crushing weight of inefficiency, of the venomous graft and criminal waste which pervades our national life from government to individual, is understood, and the necessity of prompt, thorough and vigorous efforts at remedying conditions is appreciated.

Among the principal causes of these conditions is the fact that everybody is looking out for himself too much and too ruthlessly; seeking with too much energy the immediate "practical" advantage, and ignoring the fact that his own welfare is indissolubly bound up with the welfare of his neighbor. A vicious circle is set up in that the citizen lacks respect for the employer and the government, and the government is not primarily concerned with the welfare of the citizen. Everyone is working at loggerheads and the result of this condition is seen in the establishment of trusts and their consequent train of evils, through the impossibility of the business man surviving in the conditions of fierce competition which ordinarily prevail. Had fair competition been assured by law, trusts could never have overcome the independence of business men and forced them into consolidations.

In seeking remedies for the conditions which have been created, it is the part of wisdom to draw comparisons with other countries in which similar conditions have been met.

Owing to certain advantages in inherited policy and characteristics, as well as from natural causes, one of the countries which has solved many of the problems which are obstacles to general prosperity and progress in America to-day, is Germany; and in considering American conditions, many comparisons will be made with German conditions, where efficiency has reached the highest point of development yet achieved; since the author, being of German birth and training, is familiar with those conditions, as well as with American conditions through citizenship and an active participation in American business and engineering undertakings during the past ten years.

Of the great benefits that are to be derived by individuals as well as countries, from the study of conditions in other countries, there can be no doubt.

Mr. Herman Ridder, the eminent editor, in the American Travelers' Edition of "Deutschland," an official journal for the promotion of international intercourse, writes under the title "The United States and Germany" as follows:

"Any move which tends to stimulate international intercourse is conducive to universal welfare. For upon the shaping of the relations between the civilized nations of the earth, depend its future destinies, and these relations are seldom strained, but, almost unexceptionally, improved by mutual acquaintance. Let the people—mind you, the real people, and not the fortuitous exponents of their dispositions or customs or policies—the people of two nations, like the United States and Germany, once grow to understand and know one another thoroughly, and they will be apt to rule the world. Not as allied conquerors by the strength of arms, but as joint leaders in the material and intellectual development of the human race. Then there would be no need of a formal alliance secured by convention or treaty, for as soon as either nation becomes convinced that there is no elementary antagonism of interests, and that, on the contrary, their interests are reciprocal, a co-operation along the whole line of human development will be the perfectly natural result. This is, in the case of Germany and the United States, no idle vision of a desirable future status. For there exists between the American and German peoples a closer community of interests, a truer identity of national endeavor and a nearer relationship of national consciousness than may be obvious to the casual observer.

"When more than fifty per cent of the population of the United States have German blood in them—a fact established by the Federal census returns—the German influence upon the forming of the character of the American nation cannot be ignored. True, the German vein current within the national American body is less pretentious than those inoculated by the Puritan, or the Scot or the Celt, but when we analyze the product of the mixture and weigh its component values, we find some of its best qualities traceable to German origin: Thoroughness, endurance, reliability in the pursuit of live tasks; aspirations for ideals; artistic sentiment and the zest for mind culture.

"Many of the great inventions which have in the last century revolutionized the world, have rooted in German inventive spirit, while American pluck and enterprise have perfected them. On the other hand, Americans engaged in gigantic financial, com-

mercial or industrial occupations are wont to look to Germany
for methods to give them economic strength.

"The interdependence of the two nations is well understood
and appreciated by all thoughtful and instructed men. With
so much in common in the past and so many ties in the present,
an earnest collaboration in the work of civilization, education
and training,—to quote the words of a prominent American—
'Germany and America may well move forward in harmony,
each maintaining all its independence of method and thought
and action, yet both gaining strength from a better understanding and mutual self-help by which each may supplement the
needs of the other.' "

Germany herself, a generation ago, was an inefficient and exhausted nation, and her progress and prosperity have been due
principally to sound statesmanship and the recognition the
country over of what could be learned from other countries.

The great lessons to be learned, especially from America, were
appreciated, and this policy is vigorously continued. German
students are sent the world over and return home with new
ideas to the great benefit of the country. For example, fourteen hundred Germans came over during the St. Louis exposition
in 1904 to study American methods, customs and business, to
be applied to German conditions wherever an advantage could
be found in doing so.

The enormous strides which Germany has made in the last
twenty years have served to place her in a position of leadership
among the nations of the world, and in making comparisons of
efficiency it will be necessary to draw a picture by no means
favorable to other countries, especially our own, not so much on
account of their lack of progress as on account of their failure
to progress at the rapid rate which Germany has maintained.

Frequent references to German accomplishments will thus
throughout be necessary even to the point of over iteration, but
they will be necessary in order to furnish a basis of comparison;
for efficiency is not an absolute quality, but rather one that is
always relative and therefore one which must employ the most
efficient unit as the basis of comparison.

As has been pointed out by prominent English statesmen in
criticizing Germany, the German mind is of a certain robust
quality that thrives on criticism and consequently the Germans
are preferably engaged in energetic criticism of each other rather
than in criticism of outsiders. A criticism that is well taken is

consequently regarded as an asset rather than an affront as it points out a possible place where improvement may be made. Thus every knock may be regarded as a boost. The tone of the present work in its freedom of criticism is not, therefore, other than of the most friendly character, and if it succeeds in indicating only one point at which improvement may be effected, it will certainly have justified itself in every respect by the value which will accrue in the effecting of such improvements.

The enormous progress of Japan has been due to following the example of Germany, and the Japanese found their most valuable lessons in Germany, where the experience of the world had been accumulated.

To-day Argentina and China are carrying out the same policy, while even England is waking up. The movement in America to take advantage of foreign conditions, though slow, is of considerable extent. It must necessarily, however, be carried out on a more elaborate and vigorous scale, and a thorough reorganization of internal conditions effected, if we expect to keep abreast of the times.

THE PRICE OF INEFFICIENCY

THE PRICE OF INEFFICIENCY

CHAPTER I

THE SITUATION

National unrest—False conception of public duty—Public indifference to official neglect—Bismark's remedy—Its stimulation of German progress—Political isolation of the United States—Neglect of the value of the experience of other countries—The duty of Americans to America—Monopoly and progress in Germany—Co-operative nationalism—Fundamental alteration of the attitude of the state towards the individual.

THE causes of the unrest which is the dominant motive in American life to-day; of the social unrest, economic unrest and the unrest of the losing struggle for existence; and the question of remedies, if they are to be found, is forcing itself to the attention of everyone; artisans and students, farmers and professors, laborers and corporation managers alike. It is the principal problem of government itself.

The question is continually arising; is this a government of the people for the people by the people, or is it a government of the indifferent and uninformed for and by the incompetent and venal?

The dissatisfaction of the public extends from municipal government and local business affairs to the management of the great trusts and the conduct of congress.

The distrust so evident is founded on the belief that public officers and the managers of the great corporations, who are also, in effect, public servants, have not as a class sought the truth with a determination to act upon it for the public welfare, but have avoided the broad road of public service for the by-paths of personal profit.

The true relation between the public and those in high position has been misunderstood nowhere as in America. Although the phrase, "the servants of the public," is current freely enough,

3

it is of little force and effect. Former Mayor McClellan of New York, while in office, on being asked the name of his employer, by an itinerant statistician filling a blank for some now forgotten purpose, pointed to the city directory as a list of his employers. Yet true as this was, no citizen there listed, nor the mayor himself, would feel that their relationship as employer and employee was more than one theoretically so. Yet this mistaking of the substance for the shadow is one of the real causes of present conditions, as will be presently pointed out.

The feeling is that the public official has been elevated to a great dignity, where he must trouble himself—and does—but little as to the welfare of his employers.

The lack of virility in the attitude of the public towards its public servants causes the public to be poorly served, and while the individual may realize that his best interests are being neglected by the men he has elected and is paying to serve him, he yet takes no steps to improve matters.

He knows that wrong is being done; he is a victim and an accessory as well, yet his conscience is not aroused. The conscience of the public is asleep in fact, and while we feel things, as individuals, we do not feel things as part of an effective public sentiment.

Yet we are moral people. We uphold right and condemn wrong, but the voice of effective remonstrance has remained silent.

Only now, when the neglect of the public servants, whether governmental or corporation, has led to acute conditions, is the public rolling over in its sleep.

The whole country is in a condition, such as a business man's business would be, if he spent his working hours attending to something else.

To obtain from public servants the proper discharge of their duties, it is necessary to subject them to criticism. In the words of Bismarck, who said when in power:

"If the public would get what it wants, it must attack the administration."

To the almost passionate acceptance and following of this advice of Bismarck's, by the Germans, close observers ascribe much of Germany's present prestige as the leader of the progress of the world.

That a public official in Germany is a public servant to be

promptly criticized by the individual, a criticism, too, which those in authority act upon, is a well recognized fact. There the criticism of an official may cause him to quickly find himself merely a member of the general public again; whereas in America the complaint would reach a pigeon hole and the citizen be patronized as a crank, if not properly placed in an asylum.

The methods whereby the public may in this country attack the government in the meaning of Bismarck's phrase, are extremely complicated and ineffective. An opinion can only be had every second and fourth year, and at such times only between one of two groups of alternatives, so that in objecting to one set of officials known as a party and in turning them out, the set to go in while approved in the main issue cannot be prevented from carrying in with them many subsidiary evils which are not approved. A new four years of experiment must be gone through with, only to be duplicated again after another election. An administrative personnel of 412,000 officials must be changed, which only includes the federal governmental body, and the whole machinery of administration disorganized, while these amateurs are learning a new trade, the tools of which they must soon lay down again.

In solving the problem arising out of its own neglect, the public must find out first, the causes, and then apply the remedies. What the causes have been and what the remedies are to be, must deeply engage the attention of everyone who has either his own interests or those of his country at heart.

And in reaching conclusions, the experience of other countries will supply valuable lessons. The spread-eagleism of the past is disappearing; America is a country among countries, not a paradise among deserts, and the criticism of thoughtful foreigners on American conditions can only be welcome.

An Englishman, the Rev. Herbert W. Horwill, in the National Review of London, writes cogently:

"The necessity of making acquaintance with what is happening elsewhere in the world has been minimized for Americans, until lately, by the political isolation of the United States. That country has been spared, not only the entanglement of foreign alliances, but also the educating influence of direct contact with foreign problems. Its freedom from European complications, however helpful on the whole to the development of its internal resources, has certainly tended to circumscribe the ideas of its people. Farther, in the Old World, even if we are not able to go abroad, a constant appeal is made to the imagination by visible memorials of past centuries. We can travel in time, if not in space. We have before our eyes, persistent reminders that the civilization of the twentieth century is not the sudden creation of our own contemporaries, or of a generation immediately preceding, but has been slowly built up by the genius and toil of our forefathers.''

To consider how other countries are meeting their problems, and to adapt to the uses of America and to our conditions those of their expedients and policies which have proved most successful, and to learn from their failures lessons of value, is the duty of Americans to America.

Among the states which in modern times have shown the greatest energy and resourcefulness is Germany, and the methods of Germany in dealing with similar problems will be considered from time to time in greater detail, being of the first importance, since Germany has made greater advances than any other country in many respects, under, perhaps, the impetus of greater necessity, new nationality and a dominant patriotism.

German aims, policies and conditions are well summarized in an article, ''Monopoly and Progress,'' by Dr. Franz Erich Junge-Hermsdorff, a German consulting engineer and Doctor of Philosophy, who resided in the United States for a number of years and made a study of conditions here in the *Engineering Magazine* of March, 1911, of which he states in part:

''Nothing common to man is foreign to nations. The story of the prodigal son applies to families as well as to communities. Thus in every people there is a natural inclination to prodigality, but not every nation has a benevolent father ready to kill a fatted calf, if waste and destruction have depleted its natural inheritance. Germany is not a rich man's heiress. She must prepare her children for adversity, not for prosperity, must fit them to the lean years which are near, not for the fat years that are promised in the future. Thus and thus only will they be able to conquer the racking times which are approaching.

''Hence, to the prime rule of stragetic expediency dominating our national household is coupled the other no less important consideration of national economy, urging upon authorities the supreme duty of guarding the country's irreplaceable resources, material and other, which joined with the subtle factor of civic virtue are the pillars of every commonwealth. Having to support sixty-five million active people on a territory four-fifths the size of Texas, and being fully aware of our geographic limitations, of the precariousness of our central situation, of the scarcity of raw materials at our avail, of our dependence for certain supplies on foreign markets, and of the fact that in times of war they will be cut off by our adversaries—scientific administration and rational utilization of materials, emancipation from foreign support, the development of high grade industries and agriculture, and the exchange of gray matter for raw matter, are natural correctives of our limited opportunities and logical directives for the industrial and commercial policy of the Empire.

"Leaving aside the political argument and speaking more particularly of the attitude of the state, the present policy of Germany can be shortly defined as one of mutual partnership or co-operative nationalism; that state and its government attending to the more general and ideal, and the private individual to the more special and material ends of the national business. In spite of democracy pressing from without and of evolutionary philosophy pressing from within, there is a growing tendency on the part of the masses to rely on the state for support and inspiration, making the national government both co-active and co-responsible for their welfare. And, even among conservative statesmen, the leaning to-day is far more in the direction of state socialism than in the direction of democracy.

"This leaning on the paternal state is not wholly the result of modern tendencies. It is a result, in part, of the traditional policy of the Hohenzollern, radiating from Prussia ever since they took over the control of the affairs of that country. It was the proud boast of Frederick the Great that he was *le roi des gueux*. Of all the governments of the seventeenth century, the Prussian was the first to seek the welfare of the whole community. The "Landrecht" recognized the state as the protector of the poorer classes, and the supply of sustenance and work for those lacking means and opportunity of earning a livelihood as one of its duties. It was upon these clauses that Bismarck relied when, on May 7th, 1884, he declared to the Reichstag his recognition of the laborer's right to work. His idea of social reform, of the nationalization of railways, of state monopolies in brandy and tobacco (not realized), even of the return to protection, all spring from his profound conviction that "many measures which we have adopted to the great blessing of the country are socialistic, and the state will have to accustom itself to a little more socialism yet." (1882).

"In this age of monopoly when, under the sway of commercialism, the empire of business in all countries is encroaching upon national governments, anxious to seize their privileges without burdening itself with their responsibilities, the blessing of a paternal policy for the weal of the state is making itself especially felt. In reflecting upon American conditions, in this relation, it should be borne in mind—as distinguishing between our respective constitutional confederate systems—that in Germany every one of the twenty-six states is really a sovereign agency rendering public service, not merely a government or administrative district.

"In Germany private monopoly could never reach such gigantic proportions, because at the very outset of the industrial age a big slice of the national assets was withdrawn from private enterprise by the government, being reserved exclusively for public uses and operated on a strictly socialistic basis for the equitable good of all. The other major portion of the basic resource was, of course, left to exploitation and improvement by private initiative. In the course of time and under the influence of the economic revolutions in the neighboring European countries, especially England (Smith) and France (Colbert), the attitude of the state towards industry has, naturally, undergone various changes. But to-day the general tendency, under the pressure of the socialistic vote, is stronger than ever before for an expansion of national co-operation under the leadership of state or national government—representing a compromise, as it were, between the mercantilistic and the physiocratic doctrines, between the individualist and collectivist schemes—an attempt to infuse the cold reasoning of reckless commercialism and the utopian dreams of extreme socialism with the nobler motives of national expediency.

"While the authority of the state is invariably supreme, its functions are of the progressive variety, establishing the balance between all the productive and destructive forces of the land. The state not only partakes in every form of private industry, engaging in part of the three factors of production—nature, labor and capital,—but it extends its intervention in proportion to the growing needs of the commonwealth. Its functions of service are quite as marked as its functions of restraint, and, with the standard of German citizenship on the ascendant, there is, indeed, a tendency of diminishing restraint and of increasing service."

CHAPTER II

OUR POLITICAL SYSTEM

The "servants" of the public—Are they underpaid?—What is the matter with our state legislatures?—Laws—Their supply and demand— Poor quality of laws made by our legislators—When private interests pay the law-makers, who do they work for?—"Practical" men in office—A national canker—German administrative processes— Effectiveness of the bureaucracy—Why it succeeds—The constitution of the United States as a governmental system—How it automatically collects inferior congressman—Does it place a premium on demagogueism?—How the constitution keeps the greatest men out of the presidency—The Catholic, the Jew and the Atheist—Conventions as extraconstitutional growths—How the "slate" originates—The roots of graft—The origin of "pull"—Bosses and blackmailing laws—Every voter with a private interest opposed to public policy—Automatic opposition to good government—Log rolling—The constitution as an instrument for favoring self interest as opposed to the general welfare—Back yard patriotism—Confusion of differing state laws— Great waste of deciding the constitutionality of laws—National contempt for law.

THAT the public is poorly served by its servants; its officials, employees and managers of vast corporations charged with a public interest, is well understood.

The reason why is not so clear.

In the case of the great corporations, the fact that they are new, and their true relation to the public not yet understood, serves as an excuse, but for our public officials, they were grafting long before grafting was a word in its present meaning. They have, in fact, been serving their employers unfaithfully for generations.

Perhaps the principal reason why the public is so poorly served, is that it pays its servants starvation wages, compared with what the talent demanded can obtain for an equal service rendered to a private employer.

The greatest sources of governmental inefficiency are the legislatures of the several states. The salaries paid are eked out by graft and near graft, by laws favoring blackmailing schemes and laws favoring interests contrary to the public welfare.

If the salaries of the legislators of New York state, for example, were increased to $15,000 a year, instead of remaining at $1500, the state would be out of pocket immediately some $3,015,000, and this might seem an extravagance. But consider the effect of an annual salary of $15,000. It would attract a vastly better class of men to office. The present low grade ward politicians could not secure election, since brighter men would be after the prizes. Instead of incompetents, the legislature would be filled with competents; with men better able to reach proper decisions, and men able to see that the continuation in the lucrative offices, held, would depend on how well they could demonstrate to the public their fitness.

Considering the vast outlays authorized by legislators, the mere exercise of bad judgment in a single instance by a legislature would and does constantly cost the state more than the increased salaries of the legislators would amount to.

Without any question of graft or dishonesty, it is the part of wisdom to pay the highest possible price for legislative services, merely for the sake of efficiency, while morally, it is certainly better for the state to pay the price of legislation and get it, rather than to allow private interests to pay the price, as at present, and get it.

Aside, however, from the question of being poorly paid, there is a disconcerting lack of honesty among the servants of the public; a sort of a "take it while you can get it" attitude, as though an election to office were a license to plunder.

Why should this be so?

Why should the elected official be prone to graft and deals? In a country whose principal boasts are of liberty and patriotism, why such a general disregard of the rights of the public as a whole, why so many "practical" men in office?

So inured, however, are Americans to the dereliction of public officials, that to ask why a public official should not be honest, is likely to be regarded as a naïve stroke of humor. The contrary is so usual that it has become almost a matter of course.

But as a novel point of view, why not demand honesty of the elected official, and demand it seriously?

The effects of official dishonesty are widespread and enormously destructive, and while the importance of honest legislation cannot be over-estimated, the dishonest article continues in evidence. Why is it?

Some canker finally kills every nation. Is the canker that

will end American liberty, in early evidence now, in the bad faith of legislators? Can it be chopped out and a new growth stimulated, or is it characteristic of the whole tree? Such lack of patriotism in a free country is surprising to the foreigner. In Germany, for example, such conditions do not exist. That, at any rate, is not the German canker.

Office is held in Germany, mainly by the bureaucratic class.

They serve for a reasonable compensation, but render a high grade of service. Their motive is patriotism, the honor of serving their country. They would no more think of grafting than a private soldier in the army of Grant or Sherman would have thought of putting his hand in his general's pocket and taking his watch or money.

The success of this system of administration depends on the moral and intellectual qualities of the individuals composing the government. It stands and falls with decent officialism. If corruption and commercialism ever claim the bureaucracy, if public servants place gain above honor, the whole system will become rotten.

But against this possibility is the fact that honesty in the public service is held in high esteem by public sentiment, and this pronounced and appreciative endorsement of official integrity, as much perhaps as the quality of the personnel itself, calls forth and keeps uncontaminated the highest qualities in the official.

Although highly extolled, and rightly so, as the bulwark of liberty, the constitution of the United States is far from being a perfect political instrument. The system of requiring the residence in the congressional district of its representative in congress, has the effect of collecting at Washington biennially a large number of inexperienced and incompetent legislators, often persons of the smallest capacity, who look upon their term of office as a temporary adornment, and who have no thought of making law-making a seriously considered business, nor any capacity whatever for the making of laws.

The United States thus has its laws made largely by the tyros who happen to be in office. An experienced, capable and brilliant public man is likely to be retired at any moment through a change of political sentiment in his district, and thus there is no incentive to a systematic study of government on the part of those who govern.

The system has the effect of producing, and placing a high

premium upon men who have the ability to get elected, regardless of their ability to make laws. The careful and painstaking legislator, of judicial mind and broad views, whose services the country should have in the making of laws, gives place to the blatant demagogue who can influence a crowd; for the real law-maker and statesmen is not likely to be the man to arouse the passion and prejudice which go to decide the issue of an American election.

It is undoubtedly true that only accidentally does a really great man become president of the United States. Our presidents are more than likely to be neutral persons. Too often a president is the resultant of forces of which he is not one; a person crafty enough to float with the tide and conventional enough to be in harmony with the intensely conventional views of the electorate; that is to say, a man in whose armor the demagogues of the other side can find no opening.

No Catholic can become president of the United States, no Jew, no atheist, no Southerner and no philosopher however great; not because they could not be elected, but because they could not be nominated for office by any great party for fear of the demagogues of the other.

In the nominating of candidates for office, a system entirely extra-constitutional; a system that begins before the constitution begins and which the authors of that instrument never dreamed of, has evolved itself, greatly to the shame and discredit of republican institutions; and a horde of persons known as bosses has come into being; a boss for each city and each state, and these are the real rulers of the United States.

Candidates for smaller offices are selected by a method of two steps. The first is a convention of delegates who meet and are supposed, of their own free will, to select candidates. As a matter of fact, a selection of that kind seldom occurs. Usually the boss of the locality makes up what is called a "slate" or list of candidates loyal to him, and they are nominated by the convention without murmur, unless a second boss is aspiring to the power of the ruling boss, when a test of strength between the rival bosses comes before the convention, and the winning "slate" is carried through. With the exception of sporadic independent candidacies, the real contests over offices are confined to the struggles of the bosses.

From whence do the bosses who rule us derive their power? They are rarely elected officials, but they dictate the selection of every official. How do they manage to make themselves the rulers of America, to constitute themselves a nominating Trust? Again through a bad system, that of conventions.

The convention was originally a town meeting, which all might attend, and at which all citizens might vote. In such a meeting, a man of influence, one with many friends, would naturally carry many measures through the support of his friends and his own prestige. Such was the origin of the boss. He is a man of many friends. He makes a business of having as many friends as possible, and of looking out for his friends and having his friends look out for him.

It would thus appear that America is ruled by a class of men of a friendly disposition. So it is, but this friendship is not exercised towards the public, but on the contrary, directly in opposition to the public welfare.

Each of the great parties is thoroughly organized. Every district has its political club and its political workers, or minor politicians who mingle political activities with their ordinary business. Among the workers in each club is a leader, ostensibly elected by the club, but in reality the one among the club having the greatest ability in doing favors for others and in making them expect further favors. This local leader then busies himself in getting solid with greater leaders and other prominent politicians, so that when the time comes for a convention, through his real or supposed influence or pull, he is able to say which of the workers shall go as a delegate to represent that district. Such a delegate represents, consequently, not the voters of the district as he should, but the interests of his leader. Thus the convention is controlled by the main boss, acting through the lesser bosses, the main boss having evolved himself from a minor to a major position by his ability as a politician in making friends and gaining influence, by getting favors for his friends and then being able to deliver the votes of the delegates.

When a convention is held, the candidates are thus the puppets of the bosses, and the second step is then in order, the primary or initial or nominating election. At such a primary, which is where the constitution begins, the voters of a party are entitled to vote on the question of who shall become the candidates of the party at a later election. The primary is only of use in determining disputes between the "slates" of rival bosses who are unable to overcome each other at the convention.

A fundamental change, however, is gradually coming over

American politics, in that the direct primary is being established, the primary prior to which no candidates are indicated. The importance of the direct primary issue is not well understood by the voters generally, but it presages entirely new political conditions.

The candidates for the higher offices, president, governor and the like, are selected by party conventions, with delegates from all parts of the country or state, there being no primaries for the higher offices, the bosses controlling entirely.

There is as yet no boss for the whole United States of either party, since owing to the distinct organization of the states, the boss of one state gains no power in the other states, though supreme locally, yet there have been presidents who owed their nomination to the single favor of some other man.

A national convention is thus a struggle between groups of state bosses behind the curtain. The president in office usually has great weight and can do much to influence the result of the convention, but more often than not, the convention develops rivalries which can only be settled by the nomination of a dark horse, a candidate not at first considered and too often a man of minor abilities.

While this is a result that is deplorable it is not as much so as the situation in which the oppositions are so intense as to cause the rival candidate to continue in the field, organizing, when the occasion demands it, new parties, the result of which is simply to ensure each other's defeat and the putting in power of the candidate of another party who may represent only the desires of a minority of the electorate.

Spectacles of this kind discredit not only those who engage in them, but our methods of government, both in our own eyes and in the eyes of the world.

The most pernicious results of the boss system are seen, however, in its local manifestations. The local boss spends his time in looking after the interests of his district. If a criminal is released, he finds him work and gains a friend. If a man is arrested, the boss gets a bondsman for him and gains another friend. The little boss, through his pull with a more important boss, who selected the mayor who appointed the chief of police, succeeds in paralyzing the law which would reach a third man. A new friend is gained. A harsh law is slipped through the legislature. Business men cannot comply with its requirements. They evade it and contribute to the political organization, and the boss gains new friends perforce, and added power as well. The women of the street are blackmailed; saloons and gambling houses pay unofficial licenses to the organization and law after law goes on the statute books designed only to furnish means for added power and influence for the organization. Fat offices and commissions are created furnishing easy berths for friends of the boss, and these offices affect all classes of business, so that politics has a finger in every pie. This is politics in business and is called patronage, and since the holders of these fat offices and all their minor employees are kicked out if the other party comes into power, they devote most of their time to politics, that is to increasing the power of the organization in its manifold ramifications.

Contractors for vast public works or great private undertakings find it advisable to have in their firms certain politicians, as otherwise contracts would be lost. Financiers wishing public franchises supply funds to both the great parties, thus being sure of friendship of the right sort, irrespective of the whims of the voters and the fortunes of election day. This is business in politics.

Such conditions exist locally, in the states, and nationally, and the boss of each state has not alone the local patronage, but his share of the national patronage and graft, graft being the fat contracts and other perquisities both legal and illegal which have grown up.

A vast system thus exists, through which a large proportion of the voters are reached, directly or indirectly, through some form of contract of personal friendship or interest, and each voter votes for his own interest as an individual or the interest of a friend as against real public policy. The whole political organization of the country thus works automatically against good government and in favor of graft and dishonest administration, while the whole thing is entirely outside the constitution and opposed to liberty, progress and the true interests of all concerned.

The control of the legislatures in this manner, results in both national and state laws which are detrimental to the public welfare. The system rules through fear, favor and graft, and is most notoriously in evidence in the state legislatures where grab bills, in which valuable franchises are disposed of for a pittance; ripper bills, cutting the other party's office holders out of office and reducing the civil service list; and jokers, or hidden provision for ulterior purposes in various bills, are frequently in evidence.

City government is worse than state government, and the national government, in a different way, is worse than either, for owing to the intense light of publicity and its vaster machinery though it is not so dominated by bosses, it is subject to a certain financial overlordship, which will be described later.

In addition, there is in the national government a defect due to the constitutional organization of the government, which works out to the disadvantage of the country as a whole, to an enormous degree, dwarfing the vermin-like activities of the local politicians. It is known as log rolling and is worthy brother to the "pork barrel." It affects first of all tariff legislation, the most important of all legislation.

The tariff is not in reality an American institution. It does not represent the real feelings of Americans, but it is a resultant of various special interests.

The cotton manufacturer of New England wishes a tariff but the public does not; the farmer in the west wishes a tariff on wool, but the public wants cheaper clothing; the lumberman wants a tariff on lumber but the public wants cheaper houses; the iron manufacturer wants protection, the public cheaper nails; the planter in the south wants protected sugar, the public free sweets, and thus each section of the country has its own special interest for which it wants protection, while the public as a whole prefers free trade.

The sectional interests, when represented in congress, are forced to stand together. If the farmers' congressman threatens lower tariff on sugar, the planters' congressman demands cheaper clothing, and if the lumberman wants cheaper nails the iron manufacturer will ask for cheaper wood. Thus they stand in mutual fear and necessity of each other; and without graft, bosses, big business or any suspicion of any of them, the country is automatically forced into high tariff by the striving of each sectional interest for sectional advantages. The result is that the representatives in congress assembled get close together and each allows the other the desired advantage on condition of receiving his own advantage, and the rumble of the log rolling seems to disturb no one.

Likewise the "pork barrel."

Public buildings, particularly post office buildings, abound in the United States, all built by the national government. Small towns have great federal edifices, out of all proportion to their needs, while others have only a rented store. It all depends on the political complection of the district. If a congressman is elected, belonging to the dominant party, and the congressman is a man of ability, he "gets busy" for his constituency, and grabs all he can of the funds of the whole country to be expended in his own district, either in post offices or other public works, such as river and harbor improvements, canals and levees, which are always built by the national government.

He does not care about the rest of his country, if his own section fares well and he can return to the voters and say; "See, not what I have done for the country, but what I have done for you." This system of apportioning public improvements for selected localities out of the public funds; which is accomplished by coteries of influential congressmen grouping together in certain combinations for the benefit of their own localities, shutting out the opposition and the less influential congressmen of their own party, is termed cutting the "pork barrel." It is a vast abuse, and one of the greatest sources of waste and extravagance in America. It is a direct and inevitable outcome, however, of the American governmental organization as laid down in the constitution, and one of the things which the framers of that instrument, in their abounding wisdom, failed utterly to foresee.

In the formation of the republic, the framers of the constitution were compelled to take particular care to preserve the rights of the several states; which were at that time to a degree that can now hardly be determined, separate states or countries. The term United States has become the name of an entity, and not, as at first, the description of a union.

If we imagine, for a moment, the various countries of Europe forming the United States of Europe, it will be appreciated what difficulties the framers of a constitution for such a country would encounter.

The framers of the constitution of the United States of America had a task of but little less difficulty. Nevertheless, the United States as an entity and not as a coalition did not at first exist.

With the passage of time, the idea of the union as an entity, and not as a thing of discrete parts, became established, until now, the fact that the states were once sovereigns has entirely been lost sight of. The states are now merely political divisions and the American is a citizen of the United States, and has very little more patriotism for his particular state as such than he has for his back yard, and takes much less interest in it than he does in the baseball club representing his city.

The organizations of the state governments continue, however, with considerable vigor, though constantly being deprived of powers by the federal government through supreme court decisions.

Great confusion is caused by the fact that the governor, state senate and assembly, and the judiciary of the several states are duplicates in each state of the federal organization, while each state has its own constitution. The federal government has charge of certain matters, such as the coinage of money, the post office, collection of duties, the army and navy; while the states, in addition to their own internal affairs, regulate the conduct of their citizens in their personal affairs and are supreme in matters of divorce, punishment of crimes against persons and property and the maintenance of courts for certain classes of cases. A highly complex and cumbersome system of legal machinery thus exists and contradictions are innumerable. Thus an act which is a crime in one state is an innocent diversion in another, but as each state must give credence and effect to the laws of its neighbors, it happens that for example, a man in New York may have no legal right to re-marry through being the guilty party in a divorce action, yet he may re-marry in another state and return to New York, being protected by the credence New York must give to the laws of the other state.

Similarly, a man may be legally sane in one state and legally insane in another, he may have a legal residence in one state though actually living in another and escape taxes in both, and he may be legally dead in one state and alive in another. If a criminal escapes to another state, no power can return him to the state in which he committed the crime unless the governor of the state in which he has taken refuge wishes to have him returned. Not even the federal government can intervene, and the right of sanctuary in ancient times was no more complete or sacred. The states are thus supreme in certain legal matters, though having no place in the popular thought as separate countries.

All of this produces vexatious results, entails endless actions at law and permits the perpetrations of much injustice. The whole of England has fewer judges than the state of New York alone, and America is a paradise for lawyers. The individual who has committed a crime has so many loopholes of a legal nature to crawl through, that convictions are extremely difficult to obtain. The law's delays in civil cases are long and trying, and the English system is followed which adds further complications. Precedents are followed, including those of old English common law, and the attorney who can dig up the most precedents usually has the better of the argument in court, as judges prefer not to take positions contrary to those of earlier decisions.

This complex system of state and federal laws is highly wasteful, and the body economic must support the army of judges and lawyers who might otherwise be engaged in occupations better suited to the public welfare.

Another cause of much injustice and delay, amounting to a denial of justice, lies in the testing of new laws. Congress or a legislature passes a law, but it is not in reality effective until after the courts have decided its constitutionality, that is, whether or not it agrees with the constitution.

Whether or not a given measure will prove constitutional is not given much attention by legislators. The law is passed, whether good, bad or indifferent, and the courts must exercise all their profundity to ascertain what the law makers meant to say, and then decide whether they had the right to say it. And further, if the law is not in accord with public sentiment, judges construe it so narrowly that it loses its force. If a new law looks like a living thing and has the support of public sentiment, judges mete out punishment to the luckless offenders against the new statute, until finally someone, who has committed the new crime by an act which was not previously a crime, is encountered who is sufficiently wealthy and pugnacious to make a constitutional case of it and it then goes to the higher courts.

Often, however, no test case coming up in the natural order of events, an attorney or an association of some sort, by arrangement with the court, has an offender arrested for the express purpose of testing the constitutionality of the law; that is to say, of finding out whether the law-makers have really made a law or only another dead letter. In the case of the more important laws, repeated constitutional tests will be inaugurated, based on different provisions of the constitution and if the law does not square with all of them it is of no force or effect.

Thus, under the most favorable circumstances, it is several years after a law has been passed that it really becomes a law, if it does at all, and in many cases ten to twenty years elapse before the offenders cease to question a law's constitutionality. The number of laws declared unconstitutional, also, is very large, and thus endless confusion and uncertainty exist at all times in regard to many laws, with the legislatures constantly grinding out new ones to continue the farce. This ridiculous and clumsy system with its intolerable delays, entails enormous losses and clouds with uncertainty and discourages entirely, countless transactions.

It has a further effect of inculcating a contempt for law, so that the United States has more laws and fewer law abiding citizens than perhaps any country on earth. There is small fear of the law in the United States. With 44,000 new laws in 1910, no one can keep up with them, and the chances of a law breaker with a clever lawyer are very promising; much better in fact than for example in Canada, where laws are much less numerous and much more highly respected.

The effect of such a great number of laws is shown in the increasing extent of the law's delays.

Justice Howard of the Supreme Court of New York, states in a letter to Senator L. M. Black of Brooklyn, published Feb. 23, 1912:

"There are too many laws, too many courts, too many appeals, too many technicalities. Nobody knows the law, nobody can know the law. In these days a law library would fill a barn. The human mind cannot comprehend such a mass of stuff. And its bulk is increasing at an appalling rate. Judges, Governors and legislators are working at a feverish pace making law books. Thousands of thick volumes constitute the written law. A dozen volumes ought to contain all the laws of the State.

"Five Appellate Courts are in session at the same time in this State, rendering decisions and writing opinions, necessarily and in fact, in conflict with each other. One Legislature makes a law for the guidance of the people; the next Legislature repeals it. A Governor advocates the passage of a law and then in a few months urges its repeal. Under such conditions, who can know the law?

"The law should be firm and positive; it has come to be like quicksand, and slips faster than you can place your feet. This uncertainty of the law propagates litigation; it breeds lawsuits. Its havoc upon the tax-payers is frightful. In a large percentage of cases it costs the public more to foot the bills of the litigation than it would to pay the claim in dispute.

"An old maxim says: 'Every man is presumed to know the law.' But how absurd the saying is now. Nobody can know a mass so discordant. The citizens cannot know the law, the lawyers cannot comprehend the law, the judges cannot interpret the law. The Roman maxim might be modified so as to run: 'Ignorance of the law excuses no one—except the judges.' "

Respect for law in Germany is much greater than in the United States, and the law is greater than the individual. An example of this was seen recently in the arrest of the chauffeur of the Imperial Chancellor, Dr. von Behrmann Hollweg, while driving the Chancellor post-haste for an audience of the Kaiser. The chauffeur was fined five dollars. A similar fate befell the chauffeur of the Crown Prince while driving the latter, although the appearance of the Crown Prince as a witness in court, controverting the rate of speed alleged by the arresting officer, saved the fine.

We manage these things better in America, where the chauffeur of a city official or alderman may well feel aggrieved if he does not receive an apology from an officer who makes the blunder of interfering with his progress. The President, when he goes automobiling, on campaign and other tours, instead of attending to governmental affairs and serving the public at his post in Washington, is accustomed to make from 30 to 50 miles an hour, for which he is praised by the newspapers, who thus perhaps find justification for running their own delivery wagons and automobile trucks through the crowded streets at fire department speeds. If the President and other officials and near officials can make such speeds in contravention of law, certainly in a country where everybody is equal, a mere newspaper's wagon may do the same.

The economic effect of legal delays is that of vast waste, and its correction will be a slow and tedious work. All political influence is in favor of the law's delays, and the injured citizen rarely has even public sentiment on his side, being regarded as a kicker or a grouch and being listed in the police squeal book or squawk sheet, if he makes too insistent a stand for his common rights. Like the worms which riddle the piling of harbor bulkheads, our vast army of lawyers are undermining the whole social structure. They are a national pest and extravagance, and the country would be blessed if law schools were closed for a generation to let the course of nature eliminate the superfluity.

CHAPTER III

ADMINISTRATIVE WASTE

Economy not a national slogan—How indirect taxation fosters extravagance—Governmental inefficiency costs $1,000,000 a day—Where the
money goes—Squanderings of the post office—The pension office leak
in the pipe line of revenue—The citizen has no right to use the mails
—It is a privilege granted by the post master general—Growth of
official autocracy—Constant effort of officialism to increase its powers
—Inefficient business management of the post office—The real inwardness of the fraud order—Contrast with efficient governmental methods
—Technical advisers to German ambassadors—How Germany skims
the cream off the world's technical discoveries.

ECONOMY is not one of the American virtues; it is not a
ruling passion and the word inspires no answering heart throb.
In short, economy is not popular, and the economical are too
apt to be dubbed "tightwads." There being little economy in
the individual, little can be expected in public life, for the
public servant in America, as elsewhere, gives only what service is demanded.

No president desires to go down to posterity as an apostle
of economy. Even great financiers prefer to be known by large
dealings rather than by close acquirings. No congressman can
arouse the enthusiasm of his constituents at the following election by recounting his exploits in cheese paring. Economy is
not the watchword of the day, much less of the night.

Yet even the spendthrift has moments when the complacency
of the economical, founded on a snug surplus, may well be
envied. The United States is passing through such a period.
Loud protestations of economy are being made. The official
neighbor is blamed for expenditures, and while economy is of
no great value as a slogan, the accusation of extravagance made
by the demagogues of the other side is disagreeable campaign
shrapnel to dodge.

Administrative extravagance in the United States arises, however, not alone out of the natural sentiment of the public, but
out of other important considerations as well, among them be-

22

ing the short official tenure of office, the difficulty of placing responsibility for extravagance, lack of co-ordination between branches of the government, lack of incentives to economy, and the systems of indirect taxation which are such that the individual pays without knowing how many of the pennies of his dollar go to the government, and without knowing what they are spent for.

The extent of administrative waste is so vast that it can hardly be conceived. According to Senator Aldrich, not less than $300,000,000 could be saved yearly if the government were run on a business basis. Even if congress and the administration would work in harmony instead of constantly seeking political advantage, not less than $100,000,000 could be saved annually, or 10% of the government's total expenditures of $1,000,000,000. In an admirable article on the subject, "How a Business Man Would Run the Government," by A. W. Dunn in the *World's Work* for June, 1911, the following is given as an approximation of where the saving could be effected:

Consolidation of military posts and other army reforms..	$25,000,000
Consolidation of navy yards and general naval economy..	25,000,000
Purging pension rolls	40,000,000
Post Office economies and reforms, resulting in increased revenue	50,000,000
Public buildings	25,000,000
Rivers and harbors	25,000,000
Reforms in departmental bureaus	25,000,000
Congress	2,000,000
Cutting of courts, commissions, bureaus	3,000,000
Traveling expenses, junkets, etc	5,000,000
Inspection and special services	5,000,000
Miscellaneous	30,000,000
Total	$250,000,000

"The estimates are approximately on the basis of the cost of the government before the great era of extravagance began. It may be found that in several instances the estimates are too high, and in others too low, but the figures will serve as a good working basis.

"They do not touch upon the expenditures for interest or the payment of the public debt or for the building of the Panama Canal. In the eight years between 1902 and 1910, the expenses of the army increased $43,500,000; of the navy, $55,-750,000, of the pensions $22,000,000, and of the whole government, between $290,000,000 and $300,000,000. Such figures help to show approximately in what items savings can be accomplished and how large the savings might be.''

What does $300,000,000 a year mean?

For one thing, it means $16.50 for each household, or five time as much as the average governmental income taxation of the family head in Germany.

Each family in the United States thus contributes $16.50 a year, so that the government officials will not feel stinted.

The amount of waste annually would pay the schooling of fifty thousand young men in college or industrial training schools. This would be a larger number than the entire student body matriculated at a dozen of the largest universities of the country.

It would establish in every city of the United States having a population of 25,000 or over, every year, an additional million dollar factory, and leave seventy-five more such factories for still smaller towns, and give employment to many thousands of workers now in enforced idleness.

The two principal items in which great savings are possible are the pension and post office expenditures. The vast expenditures for pensions, increased in 1912 to $173,000,000 a year, are a burden which part of the public bears for the benefit of another part, and which has been carried so long that it has become a habit. Inherently, however, it is another evidence of the lack of respect which the citizen of a republic feels for the form of government which he so loudly extols. Everyone in America is willing to die for his country, if need be, but if he escapes a military funeral, he returns to private life with his sense of patriotism fully satisfied and ready to draw a pension on the flimsiest of pretexts. He respects his country's flag but the treasury is an entirely different matter. The vigor with which he fought the enemy in battle is now directed towards procuring a pension, and such is the success met with in this field, that in the case of the Spanish war in which the total number of casualties was but 9378 and the killed but 698, out of an enlistment of 312,000, there are now pensioners on the rolls more than the whole of Shafter's army, and in fifteen years there will be, at the present rate of increase, half as many pensioners as the entire enlistment.

The average pensioner who is drawing a pension that he is not truly entitled to, feels he has turned a rather clever trick on Uncle Sam. That his quarterly instalment is a species of pocket picking of the collective pocket of his neighbors, does not occur to him, or if it does he is not much troubled. There is in America little of the patriotism of honesty towards the government. It is a great grab bag and he that grabs most grabs best.

No one questions that the great majority of pensioners are justly on the rolls, that there are great numbers of veterans to whom the pension is the only stay and sole support. To these no one would deny the stipend. But under cover of their necessity, a great number of pensioners have gotten on the rolls; fake veterans, bounty jumpers, impersonators, camp followers, deserters, malingerers and bogus widows. The method of granting pensions by bills introduced by congressmen, has the effect of giving the congressman the greatest possible incentive to padding the pension rolls, since every pension obtained places the pensioner, if not the members of his family, under a debt of political gratitude. It is another phase of the political system which builds public buildings where they are not needed and improves rivers and harbors unnecessarily, another example of a public treasury which is without legislative guardians and in which all the keepers of the treasury have every incentive to squander and none to preserve.

During the discussion of the proposed pension appropriation for 1912, among the protests against the extension of pension waste was that of Representative Callaway, who said:

"I have a bill here introduced by the genial gentleman from Iowa (Mr. Pepper) for THOMAS BROWN. Gentlemen will find it on page 38. He is 64 years old now. He must have joined the army when he was only 15 years of age. I do not understand how he got in at that age. On looking at the laws I find that a person could not enlist until he was 17, but according to this statement, he got in when he was 15. He enlisted on the 10th of May, 1864, stayed in the service until the 24th of September, 1864—four months and fourteen days.

"He has drawn a pension of $12 a month from 1890 until now, and this bill proposes to increase his pension to $24. He was never in a battle. He never received any injury from the service whatever according to the statement and I take it that it is made as favorable to him as possible. He has already drawn from the government for that four months' service, $3,312, and if he lives after this bill is granted as long as an ordinary pensioner is expected to live, twenty years, which will make him 84—he will draw $5,760 more, or a total of $9,072 from the government for four months' summer service in the army when he never was in a battle, according to the statement and cannot trace any of his disabilities to service in the army.

"But that is not the worst part of it. I see from this report that he owns a one-third interest in a homestead worth $3,000. He is worth more, Mr. Speaker, than 75% of the voters in this country. Besides that, he has a yearly income of $180. We propose now to give this man a pension, in addition to the $12 he is already getting, of $12 more, making it $24 a month, Mr. Speaker, and saddle that on the voters of this country, the taxpayers of this land, the widows from one end of the Union to the other, who have to work for their living, and 90% of them are in a worse condition financially than he is."

The total cost of the Civil War is estimated at from 5,500 to 6,000 millions, but pensions approximating 4,000 millions have already been paid and it is estimated that before the last pensioner is removed by death, the pensions will have equaled the cost of the war.

While the burdens of the standing armies of Europe are a fruitful source of reproach, the cost to the United States of the standing armies of pensioners is much greater than the cost of four of the greatest pension armies of Europe, namely those of Austria-Hungary, France, Germany and Great Britain which total less than $100,000,000.

One of the causes of the great number of pensioners lies in the fact that most of the wars of the United States have been fought with soldiers and officers who at the outset were amateurs in the art of war. Including the Revolution, the number of regulars has been 549,115, compared with 3,686,175 volunteers, and excluding the Revolution, 317,344 regulars to 3,522,058 others. This accounts for the great losses from invalidism and an increase of pensions subsequently.

As the regular soldier is not the pension hunter that the militiaman afterwards becomes, and as the losses of the regulars are not so great, a safeguard against pension waste in the future lies to a certain extent in an adequately trained skeleton of regulars.

More, however, lies in a new system of granting pensions in which the just claimant may have justice done, and the fact that he is a voter has no bearing on the case. In short, pensions must be taken out of politics and politics out of pensions.

The post office department of the United States has powers more autocratic and inquisitorial than perhaps any department of the government, if not of any governmental department in any civilized country.

No citizen of the United States has any right to receive a letter, or have a letter delivered when mailed by him, except at the pleasure of the department. The courts have decided that the use of the mails is a privilege and not a right. Thus citizens who are taxed for the maintenance of the system are not entitled to use it. The officials of the department, if they decide that a business is being carried on in what they decide is a fraudulent manner, may issue at their discretion without review by the courts, what is termed a fraud order, and mail addressed to the person under fire is returned to his correspondents so marked. The individual is thus practically branded as a criminal without any trial, and is caused to suffer perhaps heavy losses without any means of defending himself. Many thousands of such fraud orders have been issued and they are constantly being used. No matter how urgent the business or how great the loss involved, the delivery of mail depends on the official pleasure of the post office department. They determine the character of the mail which they will allow the rest of their fellow citizens to receive.

They also have the power of refusing to transmit what they deem obscene matter. This may include medical publications, and in a recent instance, a sociological work on the subject of white slavery prepared by a committee of public spirited citizens, of whom John D. Rockefeller, Jr., was one, was so refused transmission.

The officials of the department also decide the fates of publications. The securing of the second class rate is a necessity to a publisher. It depends on the ruling of an official.

The post office department thus has to a great extent extra-legal powers. And where such powers exist, it is invariably the course of officials to seek to extend and enlarge them to the greatest degree. A government however wisely constituted, comes in time to be covered with growths of official usurpation, until the whole fabric falls to pieces. The change from honest, patriotic administration to one of official autocracy is gradual, but a sure indication of national decay. While the officials of the post

office department may be wise men, it is not within the wisdom
of any man to exercise justly such powers as they possess when
not subject to review. They occupy, however, a minor position
of culpability, compared with a public sentiment which permits
them to have such powers. Acquiescence in acts of official
usurpation distinguishes a subservient from a liberty loving
people.

A department thus, which possesses so much power, may be
depended upon to exercise it to the disadvantage of the public.
Bismarck when he recommended criticism of officials for the
sake of improvements, might well have recommended more criticism as a preservative for the service already being rendered.

The post office department has lately overreached itself in
an attempt to obtain, in an underhanded manner, legislation
which would have enabled it to make certain changes in postal
classifications, with the power of practically driving out of business large numbers of magazines; a form of periodical which,
unlike newspapers, being without political obligations, have
prospered greatly by a fearless criticism of governmental and
other usurpations.

In the course of the criticisms brought out, it has been proved
that while showing a great deal of activity in managing other
people's business, the post office department has not taken the
beam out of its own eye. It has been found that the post office
cannot tell the cost of transporting the different classes of mail;
that its system of keeping accounts is highly cumbersome and
old fashioned; that the method of paying transportation companies for carrying the mails is such that the government pays
excessively for the service, and that numerous wasteful methods
of business are in vogue.

At the same time the service rendered in the dispatch and
delivery of the mails is far inferior to that of the principal
European countries.

Every year there is a postal deficit where under proper
methods there should be a large actual profit, besides an enormous impetus to business.

It would appear to be more than a coincidence that the fraud
order law, which was passed largely at the instance of the
Chicago Board of Trade and certain eastern financial interests,
is chiefly directed at the suppression of financial undertakings
which come under question, and which compete directly for the
investors' money with the stock exchanges and boards of trades'

investment offerings. It would thus appear that if any undertaking desires capital, the course of wisdom would not be to tempt the post office department and its investigations, but to arrange for the flotation of the stock through some established brokerage channel. Thus the laws of a country may be made to work together for the good of those who love the lobby.

Even in minor matters, the post office department is able to exercise a remarkable intelligence. For example, if a special delivery letter is sent and the addressee is not found, the letter is carried back to the post office to be later delivered with the regular mail, instead of being left at the address when first taken there. In many cases the object of the sender is thus defeated. The utter stupidity of taking a letter to an address and then taking it away again can only be equaled by official regulations. Registered letters require excessively long additional time in transmission. The cashing of a money order is a process compared to which the opening of an account in a bank is a simple incident. And if a letter is refused by an addressee because of lack of postage, it goes to Washington instead of back to the sender. All these are examples of bad business methods which affect every user of the mails and create a vast amount of unnecessary inconvenience.

And it is cheaper, for instance, to send a package of a certain class the 6,000 miles from San Francisco to Germany than the 6 miles from Manhattan to Brooklyn.

What then is the matter with the post office department?

The answer is, inefficient business management. In no other department are the results of incompetency so pronounced. The distribution of pensions, though done in a cumbersome and costly manner, is still merely a governmental function in which incompetency, as in many other departments, escapes notice. But in the post office which is a business affecting other businesses, and in which comparisons can be made directly with other transporting organizations, the incompetency of its administration is at once in painful and profuse evidence.

And at the bottom of it again comes the question of politics. The business of transporting and delivering the mails is one that should receive the attention of men of long experience and training, but with each political change, a vast change is made in the post office. Postmasters all over the country are changed at wholesale, and inroads are made wherever possible in the civil service. The post office is the seat of the greatest federal patronage. The carrying of the mails is thus made an incident of politics and the prompt and efficient service which is liberally paid for and which would be a great boon to business and a vast convenience to everyone, is sacrificed to reward a horde of insignificant political workers with positions, in which the most noticeable thing they do is to display their incompetency.

The mismanagement and waste in the post office and in pensions have their counterparts, perhaps less pronounced, in practically every department of the government. The great honeycomb of politics in business and business in politics, runs through and through the government, with every incentive for its continued growth and nothing but sporadic, misdirected and ineffective flashes of the peculiar flash-in-the-pan American public sentiment, which burns hotly one day and is forgotten the next, to oppose it.

In contrast to the waste and inefficiency of our governmental system, is a recent movement made by Germany in the appointment of technological advisers to her ambassadors and ministers in foreign countries. This move is described in the United States Daily Consular & Trade Reports for Sept. 2, 1911:

"The assignment of commercial experts to various important German consulates has been found so advantageous in promoting German exports that it is now proposed to supplement them with special experts for answering technical questions.

"In many cases the commercial experts are not in the position to represent Germany industry so far as it relates to questions of a purely technical nature, and they do not possess the necessary professional knowledge to answer the detailed, exhaustive and at times right specific questions addressed to them. This task will be given to the technical advisers to be appointed. Their field of activity will lie in following the progress of the industrial development of a foreign country and reporting about all technical novelties."

"This," says the New York *Tribune,* "is characteristic of Germany, and of the superlative paternalism of her government. In no other land does the government pay so much attention to industrial and commercial education and to technical training in the arts and sciences. There is not a trade or department of industry of commerce for which the German government does not provide the most thorough training. There can be no doubt that to this circumstance are due in large measure the marvelous industrial and commercial growth of that country and its power to outstrip rivals which do not resort to such means of developing their efficiency. Now, having provided for domestic instruction, she proposes to learn all that there is to be learned abroad, discreetly beginning in those two countries which she recognizes to be her most formidable rivals and in which, because of their great efficiency and progress, there is presumably most to be learned.

"The new step is perfectly logical, in a double respect. It is as logical thus to seek national instruction abroad as it is to provide national instruction at home. If a government maintains industrial schools at home, it may properly send official students abroad. If, moreover, it sends diplomatic agents to observe the arts of war, it may fittingly send them to observe the arts of peace. It has long been the custom to appoint military and naval attaches to embassies. This new action of Germany's will be placing economics on the same plane of official recognition and cultivation as militarism. If it is quite natural that it should be taken by the government which has been paying most attention to industrial and commercial education, it is a significant circumstance that this noteworthy recognition of the arts of peace should be first given by that government which is supposed to be most of all devoted to and absorbed in the arts of war."

This supposition, it may be said in passing, is quite unfounded in fact, as a comparison of costs of armaments shows that the annual burden per capita is in Germany $5.30 as against $8.00 in Great Britain, $6.75 in France and $3.10 in the United States.

CHAPTER IV

WHAT IS CONSERVATION?

What conservation really means—Nature's reckoning—The forests of America—They cover one acre in four—The cost of locomotive sparks ——50,000,000 acres of forest fires every year—How two-thirds of the timber that leaves the forest is wasted—Methods of modern forestry —The army as a forest patrol—Success of rain-making cannons in Switzerland—Legislation that destroys forests—Decreasing mineral resources—When the last lump of coal is mined—Petroleum passing into history—The crime of phosphate rock exports—Chemistry, the science economical—The gilded romance of by-products—Untouched millions in American peat—The extravagance of the farmer—How his land goes to sea—How his opportunities take wings—How he might double his crops instead of his mortgages—An endless chain of disasters—Our unharnessed water power—Only one fiftieth of it utilized— A waste equal to 225,000,000 tons of coal a year—Undrained lowlands —Homes for 10,000,000 under water that might be reclaimed.

CONSERVATION, that dignified and easy-going old word, pursuing its pompous enough course through the vocabulary, must be rather astonished at the prominence that has been thrust upon it within the last few years. It is as though some respected old mutton-chops had suddenly been snatched from his small orbit of business and recreation, and placed at the head of Coxey's army. Conservation can hardly know itself in its new surroundings and prominence.

It is doubtful if many others know it, either. It does for a battle cry, a slogan of remonstrance, but what conservation really means, the complicated clash of interests back of it, and what it should mean, is as yet an unopened book to the American public.

To the average citizen, conservation means something about forests several thousand miles away. What conservation should mean is the proper use of the resources of the country, with a due proportion for to-day and enough for to-morrow's use left for posterity.

No country is so wasteful of its natural resources as America, nor so extravagant of human life and property. The vast losses through carelessness and neglect of proper precautions make a terrible annual total. The government might be left to waste as it will, if the waste of carelessness could be overcome.

Yes, administrative inefficiency is largely to blame for the wastes of carelessness, since with proper utilization of the facilities which the government has at hand, and a little additional expenditure of money and common sense, great savings could be effected.

According to reports of the Department of Agriculture,

"Our industries which subsist wholly or mainly on wood, pay the wages of more than 1,500,000 men and women.

"Forests not only grow timber, but they hold the soil and conserve the streams. They abate the wind and give protection from excessive heat and cold. Woodlands make for the fiber, health and happiness of the citizens and the nation.

"Our forests now cover 550,000,000 acres or about one-fourth of the United States. The original forests covered not less than 850,000,000 acres.

"We have 200,000,000 acres of mature forests, in which yearly growth is balanced by decay; 250,000,000 acres partly cut over or burned over, but restocking naturally with enough young growth to produce a merchantable crop, and 100,000,000 acres cut over and burned over, upon which young growth is lacking or too scanty to make merchantable timber.

"We take from the forests yearly, including waste in logging and in manufacture, 23,000,000 cubic feet of wood.

"Since 1870 forest fires have destroyed an average of 50 lives and $50,000,000 worth of timber. Not less than 50,000,000 acres of forests is burned over yearly. The young growth destroyed by fire is far more valuable than the merchantable timber burned.

"One-fourth of the standing timber is lost in logging. The boxing of long pine leaf for turpentine has destroyed one-fifth of the forests worked. The loss in the mill is from one to two-thirds of the timber sawed. The loss of the mill product in seasoning and fitting for use is from one-seventh to one-fourth.

"Of each 1,000 feet which stood in the forest, an average of only 320 feet of lumber is used.

"We take from our forests each year, not counting the loss by fire, three and one-half times their yearly growth. We take 40 feet per cubic acre for every 12 feet grown; we take 260 feet per capita, while Germany uses 37 and France 25 cubic feet.

"We tax our forests under the general property tax, a method abandoned long ago by every other great nation. Present tax laws prevent reforestation of cut-over land and the perpetuation of existing forests by use.

"Great damage is done to standing timber by injurious forest insects. Much of this damage can be prevented at small cost.

"To protect our farms from wind and to reforest land best suited for forest growth will require tree planting on a larger area than Pennsylvania, Ohio and West Virginia combined. Lands so far successfully planted make a total area smaller than Rhode Island; and year by year, through careless cutting and fires, we lower the capacity of existing forests to reproduce their like again, or else we totally destroy them.

"In spite of substitutes, we shall always need much wood. So far our use of it has steadily increased. The condition of the world's supply of timber makes us already dependent upon what we produce. We send out of our country one and a half times as much timber as we bring in. Except for finishing woods, relatively small in amount, we must grow our own supply or go without. Until we pay for our lumber what it costs to grow it, as well as what it costs to log and saw, the price must continue to rise."

In certain years, the losses from forest fires amount to $200,-000,000 in the standing timber alone, besides the other losses involved.

One of the greatest causes of forest fires is locomotive sparks. This is easily preventable, by requiring locomotives passing through forests to burn oil instead of coal. Until railroads are able to save a few dollars in fuel expenses by the adoption of oil burning locomotives, the forest fires will have to continue.

Proper forestation will save a large part of the loss at a very small expense. The most approved plan is to divide the forest into sections by cutting through longitudinal and laternal cross avenues of suitable width, from which the timber and underbrush is removed. Thus a fire in one section, in most cases dies out on reaching an avenue.

A suitable patrol with telephonic communication should be provided and in some sections under governmental supervision this is being done. It is a system which should be applied to all forests.

Although somewhat beneath the dignity of the regular army

in the United States, the fighting of forest fires is a field in which the army can be made of the greatest usefulness.

In Germany both officers and men equipped with picks, shovels and axes, are rushed to forest fires in quick order, running and walking in alternate stretches of four minutes until the locality is reached, when new avenues are cut, ditches dug and fires beaten out in the underbrush. Spectators, also are pressed into service, and the spectator who does not lend a hand when ordered to do so, is promptly arrested.

In the United States, the calling out of the militia has not as yet been done to fight forest fires, but it will certainly come about. The regular army is ordered to the scenes of great conflagrations in cities, and the militia as well. Their presence at forest fires is just as necessary and desirable, and will mean savings of magnitude great enough to make the army a source of profit rather than a burden. In the Northwest the use of the regulars in fighting fires has already been begun.

Germany's use of her army in forest fire prevention and fighting probably more than pays the whole bill.

Fire fighters in the forest, however, need some training and drill. During a fire in the Northwest in 1910, having no resources to fall back on, Congress was asked to appropriate $100,000 to purchase powder to be used in discharging cannons to make rain. The money was not forthcoming, however, and even if it had been, it would have been largely wasted, since they had no cannons especially adapted for the precipitation of rainfall.

In Switzerland, great skill is exercised in this direction, cannons of special design being used, which when discharged at a cloud, will produce a disturbance of air over a large area and cause the desired rainfall. When there is no cloud, however, no rain can be produced, and the ordinary cannon is of little or no use. The Swiss gunner is so skillful in the use of the rain-making cannons that he can direct a shower over a particular field, and thus prevent it falling in another where it would be wasted.

A little study of forest fire prevention, and fewer sham battles would be very desirable for the militia, as well as for the regulars, and the boards of strategy at Washington planning imaginary campaigns which can never take place might profitably devote some time to forest fire tactics.

We see the spectacle of railroads and mining companies planting forests for supplying ties and timbering, when at the same time the precautions taken to preserve the forests already standing are so totally inadequate. This is conservation at the spigot and waste at the bunghole.

For each 1,000,000 acres of forest in public ownership, over 4,000,000 are privately owned. The duty of the government towards its own forests would be more faithfully performed by the repeal of the present timber and stone act, in force for the last thirty years. Under it, timber worth $300,000,000 has been sold for about $30,000,000 and an annual yearly loss of $25,-000,000 of the actual value of the timber is being incurred.

Another example of destructive legislation is in the laws taxing forest land. Their effect is to prevent reforestation. What this amounts to is shown in the figures of re-growth of 12 cubic feet per acre, while in Germany the forests yield 48 feet annually per acre.

The waste of timber in careless cutting and handling can be greatly reduced. We now use but 320 cubic feet of lumber for every 1000 feet which stood in the forest.

Our extravagance of forests is shown by the fact that not counting the loss by fire, we take three and one-half times their yearly growth or 40 cubic feet per annum from our forests, which amounts to 260 cubic feet per capita, while Germany uses but 37 and France but 25 cubic feet per capita. In wasting our forests thus we are only increasing our fire bills for conflagrations, for the fire loss abroad is only one-tenth of our own loss per capita.

The waste in forests, while enormous, has in addition a certain sentimental interest, which attracts comparatively more attention to the subject than is given to waste of a more serious nature in other fields.

The tree in the forest is a living thing, with a certain individuality, and its wanton destruction excites the imagination, while the lump of ore out of the earth has no such appeal. Yet the annual waste in the treatment of the ore is five or six times that of forest fires.

According to the report of the National Conservation Commission, the mineral production of the United States for 1907 exceeded $2,000,000,000 and contributed 65% of the total freight traffic of the country. The waste in the extraction and treatment of mineral products during the same year was equivalent to more than $300,000,000. The report states:

"The production for 1907 included 395,000,000 tons of bituminous and 85,000,000 tons of anthracite coal; 166,000,000 barrels of petroleum; 52,000,000 tons of iron ore; 2,500,000 tons of phosphate rock and 869,000,000 pounds of copper. The values of other mineral products during the same year included clay products, $162,000,000; stone, $71,000,000; cement, $56,000,000; natural gas, $53,000,000; gold, $90,000,000; silver, $37,000,000; lead, $39,000,000; and zinc, $26,000,000.

"The available and easily accessible supplies of coal in the United States aggregate approximately 1,400,000,000 tons. At the present increasing rate of consumption, this supply will be so depleted as to approach exhaustion before the middle of the next century.

"The known supply of high grade iron ores in the United States approximates 4,788,150,000 tons, which at the present increasing rate of consumption, cannot be expected to last beyond the middle of the present century. In addition to this, there are assumed to be 75,116,070,000 tons of lower grade iron ores which are not available for use under existing conditions.

"The supply of stone, clay, cement, lime, sand and salt is ample, while the stock of the precious metals and of copper, lead, sulphur, asphalt, graphite, quicksilver, mica and the rare metals cannot be well estimated. But it is clearly exhaustible within one or two centuries unless unexpected deposits be found.

"The known supply of petroleum is estimated at 15,000,000,000 to 20,000,000,000 barrels, distributed through six separate fields, having an aggregate area of 8,900 square miles. The production is rapidly increasing, while the waste and losses through misuse are enormous. The supply cannot be expected to last beyond the middle of the present century.

"The known natural gas fields aggregate an area of 9,000 square miles distributed through 22 states. Of the total yield, from these fields during 1907, 400,000,000,000 cubic feet, valued at $62,000,000,000 were utilized while an equal quantity was allowed to escape into the air. The daily waste of natural gas, the most perfect known fuel, is over 1,000,000,000 cubic feet, or enough to supply every city in the United States of over 100,000 population.

"Phosphate rock, used for fertilizer, represents the slow accumulation of organized matter during the past ages. In most countries it is scrupulously preserved; in this country it is extensively exported, and largely for the reason that its production is increasing rapidly. The original supply cannot long withstand the increasing demand.''

The greater part of the enormous losses in the handling of minerals is due to failure to utilize the proper chemical processes known to the arts.

The report of the Twelfth Census discloses startling conditions and indicates what proper utilization of the chemical discoveries now known would mean:

''Probably no science has done so much as chemistry in revealing the hidden possibilities of the wastes and by-products in manufactures. This science has been the most fruitful agent in the conservation of the refuse of manufacturing operations into products of industrial value. Chemistry is the intelligence department of industry.

''The measure of a country's appreciation of the value of chemistry in its industrial development and the extent to which it utilizes this science in its industries, generally measure quite accurately to the industrial progress and prosperity of that country. In no other country in the world has the value of chemistry to industry been so thoroughly understood and appreciated as in Germany. And in no other country of similar size and endowment have such remarkable advances in industrial development been recorded; this, too, with steadily increasing economy in the utilization of natural resources.

''In 1907 over 40,000,000 tons of coke, valued at nearly $112,-000,000, were produced from about 62,000,000 tons of coal. Only 5,500,000 tons of this, or about less than 14%, was obtained in by-product ovens. About 54,500,000 tons of coal were coked in bee-hive ovens. This involved a waste of 148,-000,000,000 cubic feet of gas, worth $22,000,000; 540,000 tons of ammonium sulphate, worth a similar amount, and nearly 400,000,000 gallons of tar, worth $9,000,000.

''We are therefore wasting enough power to establish a great manufacturing center, enough ammonium sulphate to fertilize thousands of acres, enough creosote to preserve our lumber, and enough pitch and tar to roof our houses and briquette our slag and waste coal. Lignites have been found not only to give excellent yield of gas, but also tar, oils, paraffin and other valuable by-products. It has recently been claimed that one ton of dried peat can be made to yield 162 liters of pure alcohol and about 66 pounds of pure ammonium sulphate.

''In 1907, 4,000,000 tons of coal were consumed in the production of 34,000,000,000 cubic feet of coal gas for heating and illuminating, worth $36,000,000, in addition to over 100,000,-000,000 cubic feet of water and oil gas, worth $90,000,000; of all told worth $126,000,000.

"No accurate estimate can be made as to the total unnecessary losses in connection with the use of coal for different purposes, but lines of urgently needed investigation are indicated by the facts that the vast majority of power plants of the country convert less than 10% of the heat units in the coal into actual work, and that lighting plants convert less than 1% of the heat value of the coal into electric light. The large amount of gases from blast furnaces are being used to a small but an increasing extent in the development of gas-engine power. In the coking industry, including other by-products, the waste totals $55,000,000 a year.

"The first step in extending our fuel supply should be to lessen the waste in mining, handling, and transportation of coal. There are equally possible great savings in the use of coal, not only in the prevention of waste now recognized as such, but also in discovering means of avoiding the losses involved in the transportation of heat into mechanical energy, and this into electric energy and light.

"Water power will doubtless prove a valuable substitute for coal in the development of power and light in many parts of the country, and the use of the heat of the sun and of alcohol and other organic fuels as substitutes for coal is worthy of serious consideration and investigations.

"In European countries where fuel is expensive, 10,000,000 tons of peat are used annually for fuel purposes. A preliminary and incomplete examination of the peat beds of the country has developed the fact that they extend over an area of 11,000 square miles, the larger part of which is distributed through the New England states, New York, Minnesota, Wisconsin, New Jersey, Virginia, the Carolinas and Florida,—states which contain little or no coal. Extensive deposits are also found in a few coal producing states—Iowa, Illinois, Indiana, Ohio, North Dakota and South Dakota.

"This area indicates a possible production of 13,000 millions of tons of air dried peat fuel. At $3 per ton in the air dried form (which would be a reasonable price for fuel in the states having but little coal) this peat would have a fuel value of $39,-000,000,000. If all of it were used in by-product gas producers,

640,000,000 tons of ammonium sulphate could be manufactured as a by-product, and at current prices this would be worth an aggregate value of more than $36,000,000,000.

"Recent investigations have shown that much American peat when dried will be admirably adapted for use as a source of producer gas for charcoal, for certain grades of coke, for the production of various by-products, for illuminating gas, as a filler for fertilizers, in the manufacture of paper, and for packing material."

The vast losses which may thus be determined in forests, minerals and coal, have a counterpart in the loss to the country through inefficient agricultural methods.

The American farmer allows his land to go to waste, through erosion, he squanders his timber and impoverishes the fertility of his soil, and poverty staring him in the face, he takes refuge in the cities, or the Canadian northwest, when by proper methods, his land would be yielding him double its present crops with no greater labor than he spends now.

After the factory worker, no individual receives the sympathy accorded the mortgage burdened farmer, but the truth is that while he is a hardworking fellow he is a fool. A little more use of his head instead of his hands would save his hands and the prosperity of the country as well. The factory worker has the ignorant excuse that added work on his part would principally benefit his employer, but the farmer being his own employer has not even that excuse to offer, for every stroke he does is for his own benefit.

The average yield of wheat in the United States is less than 14 bushels per acre, in Germany it is 28 bushels and in England 32 bushels. We get 30 bushels of oats per acre, England nearly 45 and Germany more than 47. Our soils are fertile but our modes of farming neither conserve the soil nor secure full crop returns. Soil fertility need not be diminished, but may be increased. The large yields now obtained from farms in Europe, which have been cultivated for a thousand years, prove this conclusively. Proper management will double our average yield per acre. The United States can grow the farm products needed by a population more than three times as great as our country now contains, provided the waste land is utilized. The area of land for cultivation may almost be doubled.

In addition to land awaiting the plow, 75,000,000 acres of swamp land can be reclaimed, 40,000,000 acres of desert land irrigated, and millions of acres of brush and wooded land cleared. Our population will increase continuously, but as there is a definite limit to the increase of our cultivated acreage, we must greatly increase the yield per acre. The American farmer, more than anyone, must give ear to the call for efficiency.

The greatest unnecessary loss of our soil is preventable erosion. Second only to this is the waste, non-use and misuse of fertilizer derived from animals and men.

The losses to farm products due to injurious mammals is estimated at $130,000,000 annually; the loss through plant diseases reaches several hundred million dollars; and the loss through insects is reckoned at $659,000,000. The damage by birds is balanced by their beneficent work in destroying noxious insects. Losses due to the elements are large, but no estimate has been made of them.

Losses to live stock from these causes are diminishing because of protection and feeding during the winter. The annual losses from disease among the domestic animals are: horses 1.8%, cattle 2%, sheep 2.2% and swine 5.1%. Most of these farm losses are preventable.

A noticeable chain of losses is seen in considering the subject of conservation. The waste of forests is largely the cause of floods and freshets and soil erosion, the latter producing one of the great wastes of argiculture.

The wastes of forests and the selling of wood at the cost of getting it to market instead of the added price of its replacement, causes frame houses to be built in great numbers, and the fire loss on this account with the added cost of fire departments and water supplies in cities over the normal requirements is another link in the costly chain of inefficiency.

The floods, which would not be so considerable were the forests properly conserved, involve great losses and make more difficult the utilization of water powers, since the water comes at a single short season instead of being more generally distributed.

The forest tree is one of the best friends of mankind; and it deserves mankind's most grateful treatment.

The waste of our water powers is little understood. It may best be indicated by a quotation for the author's work, "Hydroelectric Developments & Engineering."

"Nearly every state in the Union has large water powers available. It has been estimated that the upper Mississippi and its tributaries have an available water power of about 2,000,000 horse power; that of the Southern Appalachin region, about 3,000,000 and that of the state of Washington alone, about 3,000,000 horse power.

"According to estimates made by the United States Geological Survey, there is a minimum of about 2,800,000 horsepower developed by the rivers in the Southern Appalachin Mountains. Mature consideration of the conditions leads to the estimate that at least 50% and probably much more of this indicated horsepower is available for economic development. If auxiliary power were provided, it would be profitable to develop up to 2.5 times this amount.

"Full development of storage facilities would increase the minimum from twenty to thirty times. Obviously an estimate of present value based on 50% of the minimum horsepower is sure to be extremely conservative. The rental of 1,400,000 horsepower at $20 per horsepower per year, would amount to an annual return of $28,000,000. This amount is equal to a gross income of 3% on a capital of about $933,000,000. Some of this power has already been developed, but a very small proportion —hardly enough to make any appreciable showing when the enormous resources of the region are taken into account.

"It has been estimated that in the United States more than 30,000,000 horsepower are available, and under certain assumptions as to storage reservoirs, this amount can be increased to 150,000,000 horsepower or possibly more.

"Using the smaller figure of 30,000,000 horsepower as an illustration; to develop an equal amount of energy in our most modern steam electric plants would require the burning of nearly 225,000,000 tons of coal per annum, and in the average steam engine plant, as now existing, more than 600,000,000 tons of coal, or 50% in excess of the total coal production of the country in 1906. At the average price of $3 per ton, it would require the consumption of coal costing $1,800,000,000 to produce an equivalent power in steam plants of the present general type.

"Of this immense power available, only a small percentage is developed, estimated to be about 3,000,000 horsepower."

The practical utility of streams for both navigation and power is measured by the effective low water stage. The volume carried when the streams rise above this stage is largely wasted and often does serious damage. The direct yearly damage by floods since 1900 has increased steadily from $45,000,000 to over $238,000,000. The indirect loss through depreciation of property is great while a large loss rises in impeded traffic through navigation and terminal transfers.

The freshets are attended by destructive soil erosion. The soil matter annually carried into lower rivers and harbors or into the sea is computed at 783,000,000 tons. Soil wash reduces by 10 or 20 per cent. the productivity of upland farms and increases channel cutting and bar building in the rivers. The annual loss to the farmers alone is fully $500,000,000 and large losses follow the fouling of the waters and the diminished navigability of the streams.

Through imperfect control of the running waters, lowlands are temporarily or permanently flooded. It is estimated that there are in the mainland of the United States about 75,000,000 acres of overflow and swamp lands requiring drainage; that by systematic operation these can be drained at moderate cost, and that then they would be worth two or three times the present value and cost of drainage, and would furnish homes for 10,-000,000 people.

CHAPTER V

CONSERVATION OF HUMAN LIFE

National criminal negligence—Division of responsibility and its terrible consequences—The death toll of transportation—The evil genius of the New York transportation interests—The demands of industry—8,531 killed and 102,075 injured—The frightful tragedies of the coal mines— The blight of white lead—Governmental inefficiency chargeable with the greater part of the loss—The white plague—Undermining the health of the worker—The death chambers of the poor—Factory sanitation— The proper protection of the worker is the duty of the state—The factory, the symbol of modern progress.

INEFFICIENCY, in addition to its direct losses, is chargeable with a vast account of poverty, misery and wrong. Criminal negligence is punishable by law, but the line between negligence and inefficiency, as little as the two may at first glance seem connected, is a narrow one, and the inefficiency of to-day has terrible results in the work of to-morrow.

Division of responsibility is the mother of inefficiency, and any degree of efficiency is likely to continue in force if the responsible man cannot be definitely located.

If this were not the case, there would be an instant reduction in the wholesale slaughter of human beings by the railroads and in the industries, and the vast amount of preventable injuries, poisoning and disease which levy their hourly toll all over the country.

In the daily battle of transporting itself about the city of New York, the population of the city is reduced by 350 killed and 2,700 injured every year. That is, of those who start out to ride on any given day, one will never return and seven will be brought back injured, the price of inefficient transportation.

The cost to the transportation companies amounts to about $2,500,000 in damages and $1,000,000 in legal expenses, while to the public the cost is vastly greater, since of the damages they receive, at least half is consumed in legal expenses, while the amount recovered amounts, in no case, to a very large proportion of the actual loss.

44

The inefficiency in preventing accidents and the inefficiency of the method of adjusting damages thus fastens itself on the public in the shape of heavy loss of life and limb; a loss which on the part of the companies amounts to 9% of their running expenses. The maintenance of a vaste horde of lawyers, who otherwise would be engaged in useful occupations, is another great drain. In Germany, there is only the recovery of pensions and seldom a lump sum, and the fees of the lawyers are properly regulated, so that there is not the tremendous prize offered to the encouragement of litigation which is hung up almost without exception by the American system of lump sum damages.

The history of the street railways of New York is one of the blackest chapters that was ever written in the pages of civic development. It is from the beginning a story of criminal bribery for franchises, stock market manipulation and stripping of investors, robbery of the companies by their officers through false bookkeeping, treacherous struggles between companies, outrageous treatment of passengers in transit and in case of damage suits, long delays, perjury, intimidation of witnesses and every form of trick and deceit that may be devised. Lawyers, even, who have honestly won cases, have had their witnesses bought over later and have been disbarred on charges of corruption of which they were never guilty. The evil genius which presides over the transportation interests of New York has had few parallels in any industry, and conditions to-day are all that might be expected of such a history.

The political activity of the rival financial interests in the New York transportation field, the desperate expedients of the two parties and the network of underground interests, make the subject, though veiled, one of the most menacing in American life to-day. Its ramifications are wide-spread and dangerous and it is like a cancer, attacking the political vitality of the state, for neither party escapes its influence and the voters have no means of expressing themselves on the subject, for however they vote, the taint will be found in the councils of the victors. This three cornered struggle between rival groups of capital and decent government is an outrage on the public and were our political system such that it could effectively reach the situation, unmistakeable retribution would follow.

America, however, is cursed with an antiquated and theoretical political system whereby no question can ever be decided on its own merits, as it can be in European governments through changes in ministries, and the public is thus left in helpless confusion, while unspeakable conditions continue. At every election, by devices of politicians, no matter what issue a party may be committed to, it always stands for other issues, and the total result is that the elected party does not know whether it was elected on one issue or another, and thus is free to proceed as interest and not as public welfare may dictate.

The situation in New York is duplicated in more or less magnitude all over the country, both in a political sense and in the inefficiency of operation.

Due to carelessness of employees, faulty methods of operation, poor equipment, disregard of proper safety appliances, carelessness of the public itself, negligence from beginning to end of all concerned and the final negligence of the public to place responsibility; the harvest of death, disaster and misery, the burdens of sickness and the sufferings of those bereft and injured continue.

In railroad transportation the situation is even more appalling. In 1910, 8,531 were killed and 102,075 injured, a total ranking with the great battles of history.

An important addition to the casualties is the great number killed while trespassing on railroads, which has amounted to 50,000 killed and 55,000 injured in the past eleven years. This includes not only tramps, but laborers, and their wives and children and others who use the tracks as thoroughfares in violation of the rights of the roads, a practice but little censured by the law. A more rigid enforcement of statutes on the subject, not so much in severity of punishment as in certainty of punishment, is highly desirable.

In mining, an exceptionally hazardous occuption, the losses have been as follows:

For the 20 year period ending 1908, an aggregate of 9,422,902 persons employed in coal mining were exposed to risk of death, an annual average of 471,145. Among this number there occurred, as far as officially reported, 29,293 fatal accidents or an average of 1,465 per annum, resulting in a death rate of 3.11 per 1,000. If the decade ending with 1906 is separately considered, it appears that the average fatality rate was 3.13 per 1,000, which compares with the corresponding rates for the principal coal mining countries of the world most unfavorably.

Comparison of Fatal-Accident Rates in Coal Mining Countries for the Period 1897 to 1906.

COUNTRY	Total number of employees at work one year	Fatal Accidents Number	Rate per 1000 employees
North America	5,179,343	16,273	3.13
Japan (1902-1906)	438,259	1,355	3.09
Russia, Finland (1901-1903)	330,147	805	2.44
Victoria	7,902	18	2.28
New South Wales	124,940	267	2.14
Prussia	4,389,174	9,327	2.13
France	1,629,177	2,944	1.81
New Zealand	27,268	37	1.36
Austria	1,186,510	1,599	1.35
United Kingdom	7,973,031	10,319	1.29
Queensland	11,714	14	1.20
Belgium	1,322,516	1,401	1.06
India (1808-1906)	790,070	676	86

It will be seen from this comparison that the risk of fatal accident in the coal mines of North America is decidedly more serious than in any part of any other coal field in the world. Considering the constant growth of the mining industry, on this continent, an increase measured by an enhanced output in the United States alone from 253,741,192 tons in 1899 to 415,842,698 tons in 1908 or 64%, the excess in the mining fatality is plainly a matter of most serious national concern.

The accident rate for the North American coal mines has gradually increased from an average of 2.66 per 1,000 during the first five years of the 20 year period to an average of 3.58 per 1,000 during the last.

The fluctuations in the rates from year to year are quite considerable. The maximum was attained in 1907 when the rate reached 4.15 per 1,000 against a minimum in 1897 of 2.32.

The true elements of risk of coal mining in North America are not, however, fully disclosed by the returns for the coal fields as a whole. More startling conditions exist, if particular areas are considered, for in these the hazards are much greater, so that if they were reduced to the general level the rate would fall quickly.

The *New York Times* of Sept. 17, 1911, states, in referring to the mining industry, including metal as well as coal mines:

"Thirty thousand miners killed in the United States in the last ten years.

"Seventy-five thousand miners injured, many of them maimed for life, in the same period.

"Eleven thousand widows made by the deaths of the miners.

"Thirty thousand children left fatherless.

"It is the story of the tragedy of the mines, but not the whole story. If the mines of the United States during the ten years had had the same standards of safety as in European countries; if the United States had killed two in every thousand employed, instead of three, four or five, 15,000 of the 30,000 of the American miners killed might be living to-day; 40,000 out of the 75,-000 injured might have escaped injury; 5,500 widows might not have been widows, and 15,000 orphan children might still have fathers."

In addition to the vast totals of accidents of a sanguinary nature, there is an enormous loss through poisoning and consequent loss and shortening of the lives of those engaged in certain occupations.

Among them is the lead industry, concerning which Paul P. Pierce in the *North American Review* of October, 1911, in an article entitled "Industrial Diseases" states:

"Lead poisoning was made the chief objective of the Illinois Commission on Occupational Diseases. They discovered in that state, twenty-eight industries in which this form of poisoning is a factor; but the great majority of cases were chargeable to five industries, viz: white-lead manufacturing, lead smelting and refining, making storage batteries, making dry colors and paints, and the painters' trade. The last was found to be numerically the most important lead trade in the state of Illinois, employing probably 30,000 men. Its workers acquire lead poisoning for the most part through chewing lead smeared tobacco, eating lead smeared food, breathing dry lead dust, mixing dry white or yellow lead with putty or paint, and especially sand papering coats of lead paint after they are dry. The hazard of this occupation might be greatly diminished, it is believed, by greater care on the part of the painters; by provision of wash rooms in which they may wash their hands, change their clothes and eat their lunches, as in Germany; by abolishing the use of white lead paint, as in France, or using it only for exterior work, and doing away with dry sand papering of lead paint, as in England. Indeed, it is contended that the lead trades in general are the more dangerous here than in England or in Germany.

Their evils, it is true, tend to lessen with the substitution of machinery for hand work with other alleviation of conditions; but the improvements in the care of the men do not keep pace with improvements in mechanical processes.

"In the absence of adequate statistics and research, the actual amount of sickness and death among the industrial population must be a matter of "scientific conjecture." With German sickness insurance as a basis Dr. F. K. Hoffman of the Prudential Life Insurance Company has attempted an estimate of the amount and cost of sickness among our industrial workers in 1910. Placing the number of persons gainfully employed at 33,500,000 and assuming the same sickness rate as is found in Germany, he finds that the number of cases of sickness among these workers last year must have been 13,400,000; the aggregate number of days of sickness 284,750,000; the loss of wages not less than $366,107,145; the medical cost 284,750,000; the loss through change of workers in industry on account of sickness, $122,035,715, making a total economic loss among the industrial classes of $772,892,860 for the year. Of this total, German experience indicates that no less than one-fourth is due to preventable causes, a needless loss of $193,223,215. In fact, it is thought that the sickness rate here is somewhat higher than in Germany, and consequently that the above estimates are too low. Moreover, these figures take no account of permanent invalidity, and excessive mortality involved in present industrial conditions; and Dr. Hoffman places the number of deaths among American wage-earners last year at 330,500 of which no less than one-fourth were clearly preventable. Nor do any of these figures take account of the handicap which industrial disease and premature death imposes upon the posterity of the worker."

All this tremendous waste is largely chargeable to governmental inefficiency. It should be the duty of those in office to forecast conditions of this kind of their own initiative. The office holder, theoretically the representative of the people, is too prone to remain inactive and do nothing that he is not compelled to do by reason of pressure of public opinion. He is by no means an initiator; indeed almost all reforms are brought about by the cowardice of the people's representatives.

Vigorous committees of active reformers initiate almost all laws, which are only passed when the legislator fears longer to disregard the public opinion which he thinks they represent. A system of government producing such legislators is primarily at fault and should be changed.

Counting it up in dollars and cents, the Department of Commerce and Labor shows the losses due to tuberculosis, a largely preventable disease, the principal steps in the prevention of which should be taken by the legislators of the various states.

"The average length of human life in different countries varies from less than twenty-five to more than fifty years. This span of life is increasing wherever sanitary science and preventing medicine is applied. It may be greatly extended.

"Our annual mortality from tuberculosis is about 150,000. Stopping three-fourths of the loss of life from this cause, and from typhoid and other prevalent and preventable diseases would increase our average length of life over fifteen years.

"There are constantly about 3,000,000 persons seriously ill in the United States, of whom 500,000 are consumptives. More than half of this illness is preventable.

"If we count the value of each life lost as only $1,700 and reckon the average earnings lost by illness at $700 per year for grown men, we find that the economic gain from mitigation of preventable diseases in the United States would exceed $1,500,-000,000 a year. In addition we would decrease suffering and increase happiness and contentment among the people. This gain, or the lengthening and strengthening of life which it measures, can be secured through medical investigation and practice, school and factory hygiene, restriction of labor by women and children, the education of the people, in both public and private hygiene, and through improving the efficiency of our health service, municipal, state and national."

On the subject of factory sanitation and labor protection, the Department of Commerce and Labor says further:

"The welfare of the laboring class has always been a subject of the greatest importance and most far reaching influence socially and politically. The miserable hygienic conditions existing in the working places of some industries, for example, are unjust to the working classes, and sometimes react with frightful results upon the public. The aspirations of the working classes to improve their condition in respect to sanitation is not only perfectly justifiable, but by all means should be encouraged. With the multiplication of factories, the improvement in the lot of the working man has become a vital question of the day. Statistics and clear thinking convince him of the dangers to which he is exposed by the conditions of his employment.

"Under the influence of long continued work under unsanitary conditions, the physiques of the workmen, and especially those employed in factories, often show more or less characteristic marks. The height is usually below the medium, the body, thin and weak, is poorly nourished and of sickly paleness. This condition is called lymphatic or anaemic. The spiritual and moral life may likewise become inactive and apathetic. Even the strongest factory workers under such conditions become more or less exhausted before they reach 55 or 60 years of age. Often they are completely wasted and utterly unfit for work at that age. Many of those who work in spinning mills, cloth-printing establishments, and in general plants where there is a high temperature and lack of pure air are cut off prematurely.

"Women suffer even more than men from the stress of such circumstances, and more readily degenerate. A woman's body is unable to withstand strains, fatigues and privations as well as a man's. This makes her condition all the worse because her wages are correspondingly smaller. The diseases which most frequently afflict the working class are a disturbance of the nutritive and blood-making processes. Weavers, spinners, and workmen employed in branches of industry, where work is done in close, poorly ventilated cold or hot rooms, are especially subject to these diseases.

"Among the diseases which the workmen of this class are subjected to most often are the so-called inanition, scrofula, rachitis, pulmonary consumption, dropsy, also rheumatic troubles, pleurisy, typhoid fever, gangrene, and the various skin diseases.

"Every epidemic, be it typhoid, smallpox, scarlet fever, dysentery, cholera, etc., draws its great army from this class. For every death that occurs among the richer and higher classes, there are many in the working class. It is the workman engaged in unhealthy factories first of all who fill the hospitals and their death chambers. Again it is more often the working woman who suffers from female troubles, and even cancer. The reasons for the high mortality and shortness of life among the working class can easily be perceived from the foregoing facts. These two evils are always proportionate to the danger and the unsanitary conditions existing in the industry.

"Loss of health and shortening of life are looked upon as

the severest of evils that can be inflicted upon the individual. The working classes themselves often call their condition white slavery, and their factories and workshops slaughter-houses.

"All the harmful influences which affect the workingman in his various callings must therefore be thoroughly studied and earnest effort made toward their amelioration or removal, not only that the interests and health of the weaker members of society may be protected, but also because the health of society in general is both directly and indirectly menaced by unsanitary conditions in any industry.

"When we go back to those causes to which the nations of the present day owe their advance in culture and social conditions, we find that one of the most important and essential causes of this most desirable advance lies in the deeper recognition of those natural conditions upon which depend the life and well-being of the individual and the prosperous development of society.

"The sciences alone would have added but little if any real elevation of the general conditions of well-being. Science, at times, had to descend from its lofty regions to meet the necessary demands of daily life. It had to make the laws and needs of human existence the object of its most comprehensive researches. It had to bring to light their relation to and connection with the external conditions of life. It is only by means of these that more rational rules of life can be formulated. It is in the manifold transgressions of these laws, in the unreasonable gratifications of certain needs, in the almost criminal ignorance and disregard of the injurious influences, that the causes and sources of many evils are to be found. Such evils are especially prevalent in the conditions which surround industrial establishments and their workers.

"To understand the evils which threaten the industrial classes and to search for their remedy, is one of the pressing needs of the day. To obtain the correct point of view for the solution of these important questions, an unprejudiced and searching investigation is first of all necessary.

"The attention of foreign countries has been for a long time directed to the economic traits which aim at the improvement and extension of the methods of production. Nothing is neglected which may protect and raise the interests of industry. But hitherto too little attention has been given to those unsanitary factory conditions which imperil the lives and health of

the worker. These conditions have risen largely as the result
of the increasing population in manufacturing towns and they
affect not only the workingman, but also the manufacturers of
the whole nation.

"The present concentration of population in large manufacturing cities is not in the interest of public hygienic and
economic principles in such a measure as might easily be assumed. The characteristic increase in the industries in American cities is nothing if not remarkable. The factory is the
symbol of the day, and steam and electricity are the rulers of
the present. Our age has learned to utilize the forces of nature
and thus has made gigantic strides forward. The more attention is paid to the improvement of the conditions of health of
the working class, the more surely will those favorable results
be obtained for which the American strives.

"The successful development of factory sanitation and the
protection of the workers in factories require:

"1. Systematic education in respect to the many dangers
which, in certain industries, threaten the workman and the
public.

"2. The institution of technical preventative measures based
upon a sound practical as well as theoretical foundation and
whose aim shall be to remove the causes of all existing evils
that injure the health.

"Public sentiment is more favorably inclined towards such
a problem than at any previous time. There is now in the industrial occupations little of that mediæval seclusion which
made the discovery of natural laws the closely kept secret of
the guild or school, and which always strongly opposed the
adoption of new discoveries. The great value of open inter-
communication and instruction, in so far as they concern factory sanitation, labor protection, and the preservation of life,
is recognized. The exertions and attainments of the individual under these conditions are thus of greater value to the
country at large. They smooth the way for those that aim at
similar results, and make their attainment more certain."

CHAPTER VI

BY-PRODUCTS OF INEFFICIENCY

National bungholes—Frightful wastes of carelessness—Cutting the throats of American forests—Train of evils of our forest policy—Terrible losses from conflagrations—How $500 a minute goes up in smoke—A thousand mile avenue of desolation—Insurance ten times as expensive in the United States as in Europe—Antiquated fire fighting methods of the United States—The fiery trail of the insect across the farm—The coddling moth and its hundreds of millions of annual damage—How the American farmer wastes $3,000,000 a day—The losses of transportation—Haphazard efforts of theatrical producers—The strangle hold of monopoly on the American drama—The gamble of the first night—"Giving the public what it wants"—Butchering foreign plays—Annual railroad waste—Inefficiency of railroads and industrial plants compared—Why the public is to blame.

As in many industries, the by-products assume a greater importance than the original, so in inefficiency, the indirect results aggregate totals comparable with the direct results. The failure to exercise ordinary precautions, the failure to take advantage of the best methods, the failure to adopt new ideas, and the failure to seize industrial opportunities are equivalent in costliness to direct losses from inefficiency.

In the failure to take ordinary precautions against fire, and in carelessness and faulty construction, losses amounting to three-quarters of a million dollars a day are incurred throughout the country.

The excessive and wasteful use of wood in buildings is largely responsible for fires, and wood is used because of its apparent cheapness. Ultimately wood is a high priced building material, since its true value, in the first place, as has been indicated, is much higher than the selling price. The sacrificial price of wood has thus resulted in the erection of a large number of buildings of an inflammable and quickly deteriorating nature.

If the wood were selling at its true value, and proper building laws were in force, both of which would be the case under efficient administration; the forests would be properly conserved and the great losses of fire largely prevented, and a double result of inefficiency cured.

The annual fire waste in the United States for the four years 1906 to 1909 was $1,257,716,955 or an average annual loss of over $251,000,000. This is a daily average loss of $689,160. It is true this period included the San Francisco and Baltimore fires. Extending the period to ten years the loss was $2,029,-734,345, giving an average annual loss of $202,793,434 or an average daily loss of over half a million dollars ($556,091).

The yearly losses, according to the records kept by the *New York Journal of Commerce* for the United States have been in the last fifteen years as follows:

1911	$234,337,250
1910	234,470,600
1909	203,649,200
1908	238,562,250
1907	215,671,250
1906	459,710,000
1905	175,193,800
1904	252,554,050
1903	156,195,700
1902	149,260,850
1901	164,347,450
1900	163,362,250
1899	136,773,200
1898	119,650,500
1897	110,319,650

It will be noticed that the losses, though varying greatly from year to year, have more than doubled during this period of time, a condition of the most disquieting nature. This waste is an absolute loss of the wealth of the country. The property destroyed by fire is beyond recovery. Insurance only shifts the distribution of the loss. An irrecoverable loss it still remains.

The cost of preventative measures, maintenance of fire departments, protective agencies and additional cost of water supply raises the annual total $225,000,000 more.

A notable fact in the analysis of fire losses is that 27% were due to exposure—that is, the fire extending beyond the building in which it originated. The extension of fire results from the use of inflammable materials in construction. It is even more noticeable that only $68,000,000 of the loss was on brick, concrete, stone and other slow burning constructions, while over

double that amount, or about $148,000,000 was on frame build-
ings. In the last thirty-three years, the total fire waste
amounted in value of property destroyed to more than $4,500,-
000,000.

It is a reasonable estimate that one-fifth of the city water
supply and distribution charges, three-fourths of the fire department charges, and over four-fifths of the fire losses, or a
total of nearly $400,000,000 per year, may be considered a pre-
ventable tax on the nation.

From reports of United States consuls it has been shown that
the loss in six European countries for a period of five years was
33 cents per capita. The loss in the United States for the five
years ending with 1907 was $3.02 per capita, nearly ten times
as much.

The result in thirty foreign cities gave a per capita loss of
61 cents as against $3.10 in the five years' average of 252 cities
in the United States.

Taking the number of fires to each 1,000 of population in the
same cities, the committee on statistics found it to be 4.05 in
the American cities, as against 0.86 for those of Europe, showing also that, in point of frequency, fires here are far in excess
of those abroad.

It is to be borne in mind that the direct fire loss is not the
only waste of resources. Owing to the greater frequency of
fires in the United States, and their greater destructiveness,
more expensive fire extinguishing facilities and apparatus must
be maintained here.

We may add that it has been stated that as many as 7,000
lives have been lost by fires in the United States in a single
year.

The excessive difference between the fire waste of European
countries and that of the United States is caused principally by:

First: The difference in the point of view and the responsibility of the inhabitants of Europe and those of the United
States.

Second: The difference in the construction of the buildings.

Third: The regulations governing hazards and hazardous materials and conditions, and in the enforcement of such regulations.

Mr. Powell Evans in ''Fire Waste'' in the Survey of July
1, 1911, states:

''The 1910 fire loss would pay the total interest bearing debt of the country in four years; or would build the Panama canal in less than two years. In other terms, it exceeds the combined cost of the United States Army and Navy and the interest on the National debt; or nearly equals the combined annual failures and pension payments in the United States; or exceeds the combined United States gold and silver production and Post Office receipts. These are all annual figures.

"It represents about 40% of either the total unused United States Government receipts or total expenditures, or the net earnings of American railways; it represents about 80% of either the United States Internal Revenue receipts or the United States Customs or the interest paid on the railways in the country. It exceeds the combined annual value of the wheat, hay, oats and rye crop, and it is twice that of the cotton crop. It costs about $30,000 for each hour in the year and $500 for each minute. It costs, moreover, more than 1,500 lives and 5,000 serious accidents annually.

"If all the buildings burned last year in the United States were placed together on both sides of the street, they would make an avenue of desolation reaching from Chicago to New York, and although one seriously injured person were rescued every thousand feet, at every three-quarters of a mile a man, woman or child would nevertheless be found burned to death.

"There are certain conditions in foreign countries that operate to affect a lower fire loss than would reasonably be possible here, viz: The larger use of non-combustible materials, due to the higher cost of wood; better building codes, in letter and practice; the lower height and smaller areas involved in city construction; and finally the intangible influence of older civilizations, which makes people more careful of small savings in all their affairs, and generally more cautious than we have yet become.

"Allowing duly for these fundamental differences between the countries compared, it is yet apparent that the differences in the fire loss in the United States over that of the principal western European countries is outrageously and criminally greater than it should be; and this condition must arise largely from the ignorance, the carelessness and the indifference of this country's inhabitants. Ignorance, carelessness and isolated self-interest, when they result in the tremendous sacrifices of life and property now habitually occurring among us from this one cause, become nothing less than criminal."

In the United States insurance costs on the average $3 per capita, while in Europe it is only thirty cents per capita. And everyone, although not insuring directly, pays his share, in one way or another, of insurance, through higher rents and higher prices of commodities manufactured and sold in insured buildings.

The application of the remedies for fire waste will be slow, but they are nevertheless forcing themselves upon the attention of a public as careless as the American public.

American Fire Departments need throughout, a complete overhauling. Antiquated methods and apparatus are proving a costly burden. The fancied superiority of the departments and the self-satisfaction displayed should be promptly exploded.

Often the system of fire alarm depends on a single center of distribution for a whole borough or city. It is as though the telephone system were centered at a given point, damage to which should put the whole out of commission. Surely there should always be a distributing system, so arranged with different centers that one or several might be eliminated and still leave means of communication between the remaining centers effective.

In outlying districts particularly, are fire alarm wires exposed and subject to damage and interruption. They are so frequently interrupted in fact, that in New York, for example, an average may be struck as to how many interruptions may be expected to occur during any given period.

Not only are fire alarm systems defective in this particular, but as indicated, the method of ringing alarms is such that there is much time wasted in starting to the fire. The alarms should appear instantly, as annunciators in hotel room signal systems. Often the horses are hitched and the engines ready to go before the alarm signal to tell them the location of the fire is completed.

Owing to the brave and capable personnel of the American Fire Departments the best possible results are produced with the equipment at hand, but it is in the administration that the departments fail. Although less subject to political interferences than the police departments, nevertheless interested motives appear and produce the customary inefficiency.

Abroad, the heads of departments are either trained engineers or administrators, and if not engineers, they are assisted by advisory engineers. The highest degree of technical training is thus brought to the service of the departments, for such men make the subject a life study.

The American public reading only the stories of heroism of the individual fireman, is not aware of the true conditions existing in the departments, and how behind the times the equipment and appliances are. Even when our reforms do come, they come in a most belated fashion. When we are beginning to adopt automobile fire engines, as at present, such engines are being discarded abroad in favor of electric engines. Many German cities, since 1905, have successfully adopted electrically propelled fire fighting apparatus and that is the universal tendency at present.

The United States Consular report of August 9, 1911, states:

"The city of Berlin has also adopted electricity as a motive power for their fire department, four stations being already fully equipped, horses and gasoline motors being dispensed with. Among the many advantages of the system was a saving of over half the cost where horses had been used, also a wonderful saving of time, it taking but 12 seconds from the time an alarm was sounded until the department was fully under way in the street. Safety and simplicity of operation were also fully demonstrated."

Perhaps the most striking illustration of the inefficiency of American fire departments was seen in the notable Equitable Life Insurance building fire in New York, 1912.

In the vaults of a bank in the building, several men were trapped, and the heavy gratings prevented their escape. Finally, after hours of work, the gratings were sawn through and all but one of the men escaped, but this one, an unfortunate watchman, died with his hands outstretched toward the street, his escape cut off by the heavy bars.

It might appear that all that human power could do was done to effect his escape, and perhaps it was, with the tools at hand, yet no man ever struck down in premeditated murder was a more miserable victim to human treachery than this man was to official neglect and incompetency.

Hours were wasted sawing iron bars, the most antiquated method of succor that could have been adopted. Had the department provided itself with a very simple device, in use for a number of years in scores of garages and repair shops in the city, the man could have been saved with little trouble. The device is known as the oxo-acetylene or hydro-oxygen torch, and it consists of a small but intense flame fed by the two gases, from portable tanks. It was used in the work on the Maine at Havana recently, and in the removal of the Quebec bridge wreck. The iron bars which imprisoned the Equitable victim could have been cut through in a few minutes by the flame, like so much cheese and the man's life saved.

Even had the department not had at hand such an apparatus, a telephone call to any one of a dozen establishments would have brought a suitable outfit, long before any sawing could have accomplished the desired result. Surely this man was murdered, and his hands stuck through the ice for days before his body could be reached and removed, were lifted in a mute, unconscious appeal for mercy and justice.

Yet even with this case before them, how many of the fire departments of American cities are provided with such apparatus for use in contingencies which are bound to arise.

During the progress of the fire, three men appeared on the cornice at the northwest corner of the building, directly above the vault in which the men were imprisoned by the iron bars. They were trapped by the flames and were in what soon proved to be a fatal extremity. What was done to rescue them? Surely the inefficient means employed convict the department of murderous negligence and on no less than three counts.

In the first place, a ladder was raised which by no possibility could have reached the men, being far too short. Certainly the length of the ladder was known in advance, while the height of the building was apparent. What possible purpose could be expected to be served by lifting the ladder is not obvious. Were the chiefs hysterical, or simply fools? They must have known in advance that there was no possible hope in lifting the ladder. Why then was valuable time lost in the operation?

Finding by experiment the fact that should have been realized in advance, the ladder was abandoned and efforts made to throw a life line from an adjoining taller building. Why, it may be asked, was the throwing of the life line delayed until after the abortive experiment of the ladder-lifting? Is a fireman unable to think of more than one expedient at a time? Nothing prevented the throwing of the life line earlier. It did not need to wait on the ladder.

Yet after the line was thrown and the men attempted to make use of it, it parted; according to the report being burned through by the flames below. The result was that two of the men fell to the street and were crushed, while the third dropped back into the hell of fire within the walls.

What was the occasion for the life line breaking or burning through? If it was burned through, it was not properly fireproofed, as such lines should invariably be. Perhaps it was only an ordinary piece of rope, picked up nearby. Or if it was fireproofed why should it break? Was it old and rotten?

For the third count, there was no life net in the street. Surely humanity can be shocked in no way as by the idea of men falling from such heights. No nets appear to have been spread and the men fell directly to the pavement.

Although falling into nets from a great height, while practiced with some success by acrobats, is likely to have serious consequences from the dislodgment of the internal organs from shock, surely the victims could not be worse off than in falling into the street. Properly constructed, life nets are not liable to give way, and the negligence of the department in not having such appliances ready or in not utilizing them if they were at hand is inexcusable.

Throughout the details of fire fighting, the systems are either out of date, or the latest modern devices have not been adopted. For example, the fireman's helmet, which is connected with an oxygen supply and water supply, is not in use. Clothed in a fireproof suit, breathing through the oxygen tube and with water pouring over him from such a helmet, a fireman can literally pass through flames, while smoke is no obstacle whatever.

A few such helmets in use in fire departments would be the means of saving a great number of lives every year, of those who, overcome by smoke, cannot be reached by firemen equipped as they are at present equipped. No amount of heroism can take the place of such an apparatus. Doubtless some of the apparatus may be expected to come into use in five or ten years.

The conservatism which prevents its immediate adoption is difficult to understand. In the principal piece of equipment, it is predicted that horse drawn engines will disappear in five years. They disappeared ten years ago in European cities. It may be that there are not enough "practical" men behind the new forms of apparatus.

The enormous damage from the use of too much water is another serious indictment of our fire fighting methods. Except in cases of conflagration or where buildings are gutted, the water damage is unnecessarily great, and often is greater than the damage from the fire itself. Not infrequently fatalities are due to drowning in flooded basements, rather than to suffocation.

The great consumption of water in American cities as compared with foreign cities may be seen from the following examples taken at random:

Pittsburg 220 gallons per day per capita; Buffalo, 310; Philadelphia, 205; Chicago, 225; Salt Lake City, 310; Paris, 65; London, 39; Liverpool, 38; Amsterdam, 37; Dresden, 26; and Berlin, 22. Even with these small amounts, the foreign cities have their streets and sidewalks flushed regularly. While only a small part of the American excess may be due to uses of fire departments, it is caused by reasons which produce inefficiency in the fire departments and throughout the whole municipal administrations.

It is the boast of American fire chiefs that they manage to flood buildings with certain enormous quantities of water. This is a boast of inefficiency. Abroad the fire chief reports how few gallons of water he was able to use in putting out a fire. There, apparatus is used which throws the water in thin sheets under high pressure and extinguishes the fire without flooding the lower floors, or in fact, in many cases even without wetting them, as it is evident that a small volume of water under high pressure will put out a fire more effectively than a mere flooding of the floor. Smaller hose is generally used, which makes it more available, while every modern device for fire fighting is also employed.

One of such devices which might be adopted with great benefit in many American cities is the endless bag fire escape, reaching from a window to the street, the lower end being held some distance away from the building. Thus a person sliding down inside the bag, shoots out at the bottom in a horizontal direction, instead of dropping vertically as down a rope.

The reason given for not adopting the small hose, high pressure system here is that it has been tried and not found practical. This may be the same practical that was encountered in the case of the fire engines.

The excessive and wasteful use of wood in buildings is largely responsible for fires, and wood is used because of its apparent cheapness. Ultimately, wood is a high priced building material, since its true value, in the first place, is much higher than its selling price, and its durability is so much less than other materials. The failure to renew forests and the sacrificial price at which wood is sold, representing only the cost of getting it to market and not the cost of reproducing the forest crop, has resulted in the erection of a large number of buildings of an inflammable and quickly deteriorating nature. If wood were selling at its true value and proper building laws were in force, both of which would be the case under efficient administrations, the forests would be conserved and the great loss of fire largely prevented.

The use of proper apparatus to extinguish fires would effect large savings, but it must not be lost sight of that the greatest saving would result from greater precautions on the part of the public, since the fire department is never responsible for causing a fire, leaving that entirely to the public.

The losses by fire principally occur in the cities, but though seldom considered by the public, the rural districts, by way of the compensations of Nature, seem to be subjected to a form of what, to see its results, appears to be a living fire. Swarms of noxious insects passing over a district will leave it almost as bare as would a forest fire, and undo in a few hours the labor of the farmer for months and years. Yet this form of destruction, too, is largely the result of carelessness and lack of the use of known preventatives.

The losses from insects in the rural districts amount to three or four times the total of city fires, and they are augmented by the depredations of mammalian pests.

The National Conservation Commission, 1909, states:

"Aside from careless or ignorant farming and such hostile climatic conditions as storms and droughts, the most serious enemies to crops are noxious insects and mammals.

"The chief insect enemies of the grains are the corn-root worm, the bollworm, the chinch bug, the Hessian fly, plant lice, grasshoppers, cutworms and army worms. The worst enemy of cotton is the boll weevil. Fruits are injured chiefly by the coddling moth and the San Jose scale. The Bureau of Entomology estimates that the annual damage by noxious insects is no less than $659,000,000. This total includes the cost of preventative measures which greatly reduce the annual aggregate loss.

"The average yearly loss to animal products from flies, ticks and other insects is estimated at $267,000,000. This does not include the enormous loss of human life and the cost of disease due to house flies, mosquitoes, fleas and other germ carrying insects—a loss much greater than that suffered by the live stock and their products.

"The Biological Survey estimates that the damage to live stock and crops by wolves, rats, mice, prairie dogs, foxes and other mammals averages over $100,000,000 yearly. This figure also includes the cost of preventative measures; without which the losses would be much greater. Birds are generally beneficent as destroyers of noxious insects and mammals.

"These figures are staggering in the aggregate, but they must be regarded as trustworthy and as representing an enormous scale of preventable loss."

According to the Bureau of Statistics of the Department of Agriculture, the average loss by disease during the past five years was:

"Among horses, 1.8%; among cattle, 2%; among sheep, 2.2% and among swine, 5.1%. The aggregate annual loss averaged $93,000,000.

"The most preventable disease among cattle and swine is tuberculosis; it is estimated that at least 1% of the beef cattle, 10% of dairy kine, and 2% of swine are affected. Sheep and cattle suffer seriously from scabbies, while hog cholera is prevalent among swine. Texas fever among cattle, transmitted by a tick, is a destructive disease, causing a direct animal loss estimated at $40,000,000. All these diseases are remediable and some or all may be eradicable.

"The total annual losses to the agriculture of the country including live stock, animal products, and grain in storage, from insects, mammals, and disease is estimated at $1,142,-000,000 or one-sixth of the total production.

With inefficiency of fire wastes and rural wastes, may be included the wastes of transportation, which has been so keenly discussed recently in the efforts of shippers to keep railroad rates within reason.

Yet in the discussion but little reference was made to the enormous freight hauls due to the location of manufacturing plants at great distances from the sources of their raw materials, a condition analogous to the allowing of emigrants to settle in one locality instead of distributing them to places where they might be needed.

The loss due to careless handling of freight is another, the total of which though large is difficult to ascertain. On a freight station platform, a boxed piano will be thrown on its side without the slightest care on the part of the handler. The piano company cannot object, as their goods would only be the more roughly handled thereafter, but several hundreds of dollars' worth of damage is done, and no responsible source can be reached.

Ordinary baggage is smashed without compunction, and no definite figures as to the loss can be computed. Instead of an objection which would have an effect in the discontinuance of such wanton destruction, the system merely furnishes point for witticisms in comic papers.

In the handling of eggs, however, it has been estimated that losses amounting to $40,000,000 a year are incurred through improper handling which extends back to the farmer himself.

The throwing around of eggs in this reckless manner on freight depot platforms is a particularly noticeable example of a double waste, since if the eggs so mistreated were reserved for similar uses in other places, theaters for example, the eggs, though still sacrificed, would induce no little improvement in histrionism and the drama generally, an improvement to which it is certainly entitled.

An improvement in the theater would reflect itself in an improved tone of the morals of the public. Thus it may be seen that the egg handlers are largely to blame for the uninspired condition of the theater, and consequently, any laxity of conduct which may be observed on the part of the public.

The theater, which holds the mirror up to nature, often a mirror of distorted glass in which Nature could hardly recognize herself, manages to have the holding done by a curious set of persons known as managers, who spend most of their time in "giving the public what it wants." A certain real want of the public, that of some convenient movable object, they seldom undertake to supply, preferring it scrambled.

Managers are strenuously engaged, along with some twenty-five thousand actors and other performers, in giving the public what it wants, or to be more accurate in giving the public what they figure out it wants. In this process they have unlimited access to all the dramatic ideas which have ever been used, or which are ever likely to be used, and in addition, a vast fund of plays from abroad, and yet statistics prove that only one play in five is a substantial success.

Managerial efficiency may thus be placed at about 20%, a

result which springs from the presence in the managerial field of a large number of individuals who have little or no knowledge of the drama as an art, but who are there for the purpose of making money. They gamble on new productions one after the other, selecting them with little rhyme and less reason, and the profits of the one success out of five attempts is sufficient to enable them to continue in the business. From the standpoint of social economy, the ratio of successes to failures proves that the present theatrical system is highly inefficient. No well-organized industry should show such poor results.

In the vaudeville field, an exceptionally absurd method is in vogue, that of trying out acts. The small manager or actor who would get his act into the vaudeville circuits of theaters, must rehearse and play it at his own expense for a time, until it is approved by the managements. All this waste of time and effort, for there are not less than ten try outs for every act that gets booking, could be avoided by the simple reading of the manuscript by the managers in advance. Yet they do not seem to understand that the expense which attaches to the numerous failures to get acts accepted, causes such loss and discouragement to the producers that the forces tending to supply them with new acts are vitiated, and the whole attractiveness of their programmes hurt permanently.

Separate trusts control the regular and vaudeville theaters to such an extent that the production of a piece depends on the will of one or two men. It is obvious with individual initiative choked off in this manner that the theater must lose its force and variety, and be permeated with a class of plays more or less in accord with the opinions of those who rule the destinies of the theaters. Variety is thus lost. That this condition exists is shown by the fact that the theater to-day is in a financial condition such as it never sunk to before. The theatrical managers who have shown independence are ruined or driven into other lines of business by the destructive methods of the trust, which largely consist in arranging the routes of the traveling companies of the blacklisted managers in such manner that great distances intervene between the stops on the route. Thus profits are eaten up by railroad fares.

Rebellion against this system is well nigh impossible since, owing to their control on the other hand of the privilege of booking the plays, should the manager of a theater leave the syndicate booking, he would get no plays to present in his

house. The syndicates thus stand between both the proprietors
of the theaters and of the plays, and use one with which to club
the other into submission. This iniquitous system has been in
vogue some fifteen years or more, but it is having a hard row
to hoe at present due to the fact that the public, having been
exploited by other trusts have no money with which to patronize the theatrical trusts' attractions, and instead are going to
the cheaper and inferior moving picture theaters and stock
companies located in the various cities permanently. It will
thus be seen that it takes a trust to scotch a trust.

One of the causes which produces managerial inefficiency is
that of "adapting" or "Americanizing" foreign plays. This
is carried on with so little regard for the integrity of thought
of the author that he is relegated to a most obscure position.
Even in the case of native authors, the smallest piece of furniture about the theater is usually the author. He is frequently
allowed no place at rehearsal, except the freedom of roaming
up and down the back aisle of the theater, while the stage manager and actors proceed to make the play into what the public
wants, according to their idea of it. The manager, risking his
money, feels that he has the right to mold the play according
to his own opinions. Too often, however, although the author
may show exuberances that should be checked, the manager is
similarly at fault with no power to check him, except the insulted intelligence of the audience which tells him in the end
unmistakably by the empty condition of the box office.

A great proportion of the plays from abroad fail in America,
yet this is after the managers have seen them played abroad,
know how the production should be made, and should know
how they ought to be received by American audiences. In
many cases, however, portions of the play, which the managers
decide the American audience "will not stand for" are eliminated, and then failure is wondered at.

A striking example of what a manager can do when he tries
his best, is seen in the production of "The Great Name,"
adapted from the German after having proved a great success.

Louis Sherwin, a critic on the *New York Globe*, writing in
the issue of Oct. 14, 1911, describes the process and its results:
"About the most remarkable recent instance of this is the
American production of 'The Great Name.' It is remarkable
because the changes made by the producer were more glaringly
unnecessary than usual. Here was not a case of an untried

piece of doubtful value. It was acted originally as the author intended it should be, and it pleased the public it was written for. The producer had every chance of seeing what effect it had when played before a theater full of people. It was— and is still to some extent—a comedy of real delicacy and sentimental charm. And yet all manner of vulgarisms were intruded in order to 'Americanize' it.

"Take the character of the music publisher, for example. In the original he is described as follows: 'A genial, well-dressed, well-groomed gentleman, without diamonds, shrewd, over-polite, and without accent except when under excitement.'

"In the American production this person becomes a vulgar and abounding old clothes merchant—one of the cheapest, most hackneyed figures of vaudeville and burlesque, the typical 'comic' Hebrew, brimming over with ten-twenty-thirty humor.

"As the German authors wrote it, the composer's mother must have been a charming old character, such a woman as you might imagine being the mother of a man half genius and half child, who was always very much in need of being mothered. This crops out all through the play; for whenever Hofer becomes excited, whenever he flies off in a tantrum, and is in danger of upsetting everything by his temper, it is his mother who calms him and smooths over all difficulties. It is she, moreover, who transacts all his business for him and sees that his home is quiet and comfortable. At the Lyric this part is acted by Lizzie Hudson Collier, who performs it in the stiffest manner imaginable, and makes of it the traditional grand dame —another hackneyed stage figure, quite out of place in a piece of this nature. Inasmuch as this actress has previously displayed much intelligence in other rôles, one is led to the conclusion that she employed such an incongruous method because she was told to.

"Furthermore, as the principal characters are musicians, the environment known as a 'musical atmosphere' is eminently necessary. But not in any one of the three acts do these personages move amid surroundings they would be likely to affect in real life.

"Now all these defects spring from the tendency of certain American managers to ignore the author. After all, the playwright has some rights other than to the payment of royalties. To be sure, they are the most important, but the writer is entitled to have some attempt made to convey his meaning to the public. Moreover, it is impossible to dismiss the conviction that in the long run it will pay to give some heed to the intentions of the man who wrote the play. In numerous other cases, the same policy has proved disastrous, and the 'practical theatrical men' have been so ruthlessly practical that they have lost money.''

Private management of theaters, while it gives full play to individual initiative, cannot greatly excel, it would appear, the results which would be achieved in municipal and governmental theaters.

Private management, though praised as a system, does not in reality have the great advantage over governmental management that is generally supposed, no matter what phase is considered.

Private management in its operation of the railroads, where it has had full sway, has proven wasteful and extravagant, and the much vaunted superiority of private management to government management is not clearly in evidence.

Mr. Harrington Emerson, eminent on Efficiency Engineering, says in the *Engineering Magazine* for October, 1911:

"Railroads spend for supplies $500,000,000 a year. The average efficiency in industrial plants is not above 60%. We can allow 70% for the railroads. The annual waste is $150,000,000.

"The railroad payroll is $1,000,000,000. The average industrial efficiency in personal service is about 60%. In the railroads we can allow 70%, and the annual waste is $300,000,000.

"The efficiency of fixed charges in industrial plants is rarely higher than 25%, unless they run twenty-four hours a day. Fixed charges cost railroads $800,000,000 a year; allowing an efficiency of three times that of industrial plants, or 75%, the annual waste is $200,000,000.

"SUMMARY

	Amount	Efficiency per cent.	Waste
Materials		100	
Supplies	$ 500,000,000	70	$150,000,000
Personal Service	1,000,000,000	70	300,000,000
Fixed charges	800,000,000	75	200,000,000

''As to each one of these aggregates, the reasons for and the extent of the losses can be ascertained item by item.

''Neither the comparative nor the actual amount of waste

is essential to the discussion; the problems, diagnosis and the cure are the same, whether 20% or 2% of the population is dying of the bubonic plague; the problems of diagnosis and remedy are the same whether the railroads are more wasteful or less wasteful than industrial plants, whether the annual preventable waste is $700,000,000 or $70,000,000.

"Railroad wastes are like hygienic wastes. The latter are due to a great variety of causes—inheritance, unhygienic location, avocations, ignorance, indifference, the pressure of other and more powerful incentives. Norway has reduced its death rate far below that of any civilized country, but first Norway realized the magnitude of the problem and put in a generation striving for its ideals.

"Railroad wastes are like agricultural wastes.

"Germany in twenty-five years has increased her output of staples per acre under cultivation between 30 and 40%. Germany to-day averages per acre 100% more than is realized in the United States. The German agricultural society has been busy for twenty-five years.

"When the whole country, governments, investors, executives, workers, patrons, committees, wake up to the fact that preventable railroad wastes aggregate more than two million dollars for every working day, that half of this loss could be rather easily eliminated, certainly as easy as the increase per acre and more easily than the lengthening of life in Norway; when it is realized that the cost of effecting loss elimination need not exceed 5% of the saving; when it is realized that the two million dollar a day gain will be inevitably distributed to those who do railroad work, to those who furnish money and to those who supply railroad traffic, then, and not before, will the great problem be taken up seriously."

CHAPTER VII

PRIVATE MONOPOLY

The goal of commerce—Origin of monopolies—The end of competition—
The great commercial triangle—The tyranny of the single seller—
Gigantic growth of American monopolies—The monopolistic parasite—
The point of saturation—The legal trick that made the trusts—The
two great camps of capitalism—Sympathetic control and its menace—
The total wealth of the United States—The aggrandizement of the
larger groups—Inevitable absorption of small business units—Diges-
tion of securities—Enormous capital controlled in New York—Con-
centration of wealth—Despotic possibilities of aggregations of wealth
—The dollar vs. the flag—The desperate problem of America to-day—
The money king of the future, now an infant in arms or a child at
play?

MONOPOLY is the effort of the individual, the group or the
government to profit at the expense of the public. The state
may at will create for itself various monopolies and monopolies
have often great beneficial effects.

The post office is a government monopoly, the power to issue
money and collect taxes are similarly government monopolies.
Some governments by engaging in commerce make sufficient
profits so that there is no taxation, thus dispensing with that
monopoly.

In previous times governmental monopolies were much more
frequently granted by the crown to individuals than utilized by
the governments themselves. At present, the principal monopolies granted to individuals by governments are those of patents
and copyrights.

Partial monopolies take the form of tariff in the interests of
certain classes of protected industries.

Competition is lauded as the desirable condition, and monopoly comes in for general condemnation, but in reality
monopoly and competition are different ends of the same stick,
for the whole effort of competition is to achieve monopoly.

There are three or more parties to a commercial transaction,
normally, the rival sellers and the buyer. The buyer encour-

ages competition in his own interest, but when out of the struggle, one seller emerges triumphant, the buyer is largely at his
mercy. The seller has reached the goal of monopoly, and the
buyer while applauding the process as long as it remains in the
stage of competition, is by no means enthusiastic over the outcome.

The United States, after a century and a third of competition, has reached the stage where competition has run its course.
The process is at an end, the single seller holds the field and
the buyer is vastly disturbed, in fact is being robbed right and
left by all sorts of single sellers of everything he needs to
buy.

Two courses must be pursued, either competition must be
restored and artificially fostered, or the buyer must take the
socialistic step of permitting the one seller to continue but of
regulating the price. All that competition can do is to regulate
the price so that however this is achieved, it would seem to be
the same in the end to the buyer, while as for monopoly, it is
evident that the price must be regulated in one way or another,
and governmental price regulation is rather sought by the monopoly, possibly because of the prospect of being able to regulate the government later on.

The price, while all important to the buyer, is not as important to monopoly as its continuance as the only seller.

At present the United States is in a turmoil. The customs
and usages of commerce for centuries have come to an end.
Monopoly has suddenly assumed gigantic proportions. The old
worm-eaten edifice of competition has been undermined, portions have collapsed, and a state of panic exists, with a thousand
leaders leading in a thousand different vortexes.

Groups are for rehabilitation of competition, others for regulation of monopoly, others for a policy of inertia and others
have each their own schemes to an endless number. The monopolies in control of the situation continue to grow in power
but fear the day of reckoning. Like swollen parasites, the
monopolies cover the body of the victim with but two results in
view: the exhaustion of the supply of blood or the point of
monopolistic saturation, the moment when the endurance of the
victim ceases and the parasite is shaken off at whatever cost.

America shows signs of shaking the monopolies off, but the
process is one that will be painful if not impossible.

The extent to which privately controlled combinations of capital have grown in America is a social phenomenon never before observed in the history of the world.

It has been largely if not wholly made possible by the commercial contrivance of the corporation, the association of individuals free from risk other than the amount of their investment in the corporation. It is safe to say that corporations if they had never been authorized by the laws of the various states to own stock in other corporations, could never have reached the importance they now assume. Even if the freedom from additional liability of stockholders had not been granted, the present conditions could not have arisen.

Especially rapid has been the growth of masses of capital since the former privilege was granted, a condition dating back less than a generation.

The states, by abolishing corporations, or by striking out the privilege of owning stock in other corporations or the freedom from individual liability of the stockholders, could, almost at a blow, stop further accumulations and initiate a policy which will work towards the reëstablishment of the old order of competition.

The inability of the states to revise the charters of corporations is also a bar to regulating conditions. It was originally assumed that the states could rescind powers granted corporations taking out charters, but a decision of the Supreme Court in the Dartmouth college case two or three generations ago, decided on a very narrow margin in the court, has caused more damage to the country than perhaps any other decision ever rendered by the court.

Will the states take action against corporations; will competition be restored or will monopoly be continued? It is for the public to decide.

The extent of the accumulation of capital in a few hands is seen by the following table, by John Moody, the noted financial statistician and writer in *McClure's Magazine*.

It represents the control of two groups of capitalists, and their followers: the Morgan group and the Standard Oil group. The percentages, where not otherwise indicated, are calculated from the figures of capitalization appearing in Poor's and Moody's Manuals.

PERCENTAGES OF INDUSTRIES AND RESOURCES CONTROLLED.

	Central Group	Alliances	Outside
Railroads	61	25	14
Express and Pullman	93½	..	6½
Anthracite Coal (supply owned)	88½	6½	5
Steel	82	5	13
Cement (output)	33⅛	..	66⅔
Petroleum (output handled)	67	18	15
Lead (output)	..	60	40
Copper (output)	..	60	40
Telephone	74	..	26

"This table gives a general idea of the control that these groups and their allies have gained in certain specified industries, while only a rough and only a partial statement. The control of these men has gone everywhere that it is possible to create a practical working monopoly of any kind. Steamship lines, cracker-baking, the manufacture of farm machinery; these and many other industries as widely varied have been combined into the so-called "trusts" controlled by them. And the list is always extending."

The vast amount of capital that is controlled in these industries is indicated by an estimate prepared by Mr. Moody:

"Outside of small, close business corporations, owned by individuals, the total corporate capitalization in par value in the United States at present is not over $43,000,000,000. The wealth of the United States, according to last reports, was in the neighborhood of $110,000,000,000, of which about 50% was represented by realty values, the balance being tangible property of thousands of different kinds. So that we see, after all, that the trend towards concentration in corporate control has now extended so far that approximately 80% of all the vital corporate capital of the country is under the domination or control of this powerful group of Wall Street interests which we have referred to. . . ."

From this it will be seen that probably $35,000,000,000 of capital is concentrated, if not in the direct physical control of men of this group, yet in such disposition as to be sympathetically under their dominance. Any movement which they initiate will be followed by the momentum of that much capital, and in opposition will only be found a much smaller amount of capital, in diversified control, acting at haphazard and in competition. The large bodies of capital being directed as units by men of greater experience and power, must inevitably swallow up the smaller units.

What proportion their control amounts to of the whole wealth of the country can be seen from the following table:

According to a Special Report of the Census Office, 1907, the Estimate of National Wealth is:

FORM OF WEALTH	1904	1900
Total	$107,104,192,410	$88,517,306,775
Real property and improvements taxed	55,510,228,057	46,324,839,234
Real property and improvements exempt	6,831,244,570	6,212,788,930
Live stock	4,073,791,736	3,306,473,278
Farm implements and machinery	844,989,863	749,775,970
Manufacturing machinery, tools and implements	3,297,754,180	2,541,046,639
Gold and silver coin and bullion......	1,998,603,303	1,677,379,825
Railroads and their equipment.......	11,244,752,000	9,035,732,000
Street railways, etc.		
Street railways	2,219,966,000	1,576,197,160
Telegraph systems	227,400,000	211,650,000
Telephone systems	585,840,000	400,324,000
Pullman and private cars..........	123,000,000	98,836,600
Shipping and canals	846,489,804	537,849,478
Privately owned waterworks........	275,000,000	267,752,468
Privately owned central electric light and power stations	562,851,105	402,618,653
All other:		
Agricultural products	1,899,379,652	1,455,069,323
Manufactured products	7,409,291,668	6,087,151,108
Imported merchandise	495,543,685	424,970,592
Mining products	408,066,787	326,851,517
Clothing and personal adornments..	2,500,000,000	2,000,000,000
Furniture, carriages and kindred property	5,750,000,000	4,880,000,000

The enormous degree of control exercised by the groups of Wall Street financiers, directly, and more particularly through sympathetic control, may be understood when the organization of Wall Street is considered.

In Wall Street are collected a large body of brokers who make it their business to be in touch with all the persons of means in the United States who have money to invest.

These brokers have the confidence of their cleints, and when capital is wanted for a new enterprise one of the great financiers underwrites the issue of stock; that is, he agrees to sell it at a certain price or over, or to buy all that he does not dispose of. He receives a certain percentage for thus guaranteeing the sale of the stock, called his underwriting fee.

He is merely a wholesaler of confidence, because he simply apportions out among the brokers certain amounts of the stock, which they agree to sell to their clients. They also receive a certain percentage. Thus they participate in the underwriting. They are the retailers of the stock, the great financier being the wholesaler of the whole amount.

The prestige of the financier and the confidence which the clients have in the brokers, results in the prompt sale of the stock with a large profit to all concerned; and the new body of capital put into the new enterprise, though the stock is owned by scattered holders, is yet sympathetically controlled by the financier, as the brokers will advise their clients to vote the stock as the financier wishes. This they invariably do, for the financier has retained a large block of the stock, as have the original promotors of the company, and the small holders feel that they will manage the company in its best interests on account of their holdings.

The capital, however, which has thus been withdrawn from all parts of the country, to form a new trust which operates in all parts of the country, but which is controlled in New York, buys out or destroys local concerns, which, if the trust had not been formed, would have continued to prosper and been strengthened by the local capital going directly into them instead of going to New York to be partially absorbed by the brokers in process. Monopoly thus takes the place of competition.

And the great financiers keep a close watch on the financial pulse of the public, new corporations being formed or the capital of old ones increased rapidly enough to keep absorbed as much as possible of the new wealth coming into existence throughout the country.

The central group of capitalists, too, have great power through the control of the savings and profits of the various companies they control, only a part of which goes out in dividends. What this amounts to is seen from the following table, taken from figures given in Poor's Manual and published in *McClure's Magazine.*

CASH HOLDINGS OF RAILROAD AND INDUSTRIES UNDER NEW YORK
CONTROL.

	Railroad	Large Industrials	Total
1880 ....$	11,281,626		$ 11,281,626
1890	51,872,152	$ 17,468,090	69,340,242
1900	160,561,811	46,536,909	207,098,720
1909-10	640,545,178	267,337,175	907,882,353

"The larger part of this money lies in the control of the men
whose great monopolies have grown to overshadow all the rest.
Together with it, they hold in absolute ownership individual
fortunes of their own, running from fifty to four hundred million dollars, and the alliance with the fortunes and resources
of the many lesser men—their associates and dependents.
This money power completes their control over the corporate
capital of the country—invested and uninvested. They own,
together or apart, a controlling stock interest in the dominating
industries of the country; they hold control, through these and
other means, of industry as a whole; and, finally, they hold
control of the capital which is yet to be spent for the use of
the great corporate enterprises of the United States."

While the stock of these corporations is distributed to a certain extent, it is only among the wealthy class of the population
of the United States. This is shown by the fact that the stock
for the most part, is in shares of $100 par value, while the
bonds are in units of $1,000. If the stock were widely dis-
tributed among the general public, there would be a class of
brokers dealing in small lots of stock from one to five, ten and
fifty shares. In the parlance of Wall Street, anything less
than 100 shares or $10,000 par value of stock, is called an "odd
lot." Certain brokers on the Stock Exchange make a specialty
of odd lot business, but the number of brokers who are specialists of this kind is very limited, an almost negligible proportion
of the whole membership, the great majority of brokers dealing
only in blocks of 100 shares, though they purchase for clients
odd lots when requested. Speculation on margin is almost
wholly in the 100 share lots and over, though there is a smaller
exchange which trails along after the big one, in which speculation in 10 share lots on margin is carried on to a limited extent.

What is called the general public, that is the small investor
who has $1,000 or less to invest, usually buys a mining stock
of $1 par value, in preference to the securities of the great cor-
porations.

A further proof of the concentration of wealth lies in the fact that a close estimate of the whole number of stockholders in the principal corporations is hardly more than 600,000, of which somewhat less than half hold railroad stock, while a large proportion, owning stock in several different corporations are counted more than once in such a summary.

According to the wealth statistics of the tenth census, 3% of the American people own 20% of the wealth, 9% own 51% of the wealth while 88% of the people own but 29% of the wealth.

In Germany, however, only 2% of the wealth is held by the wealthier classes while 54% is held by the middle and 44% by the lower classes.

What the concentration of wealth in the United States means is seen when the total national wealth of the two countries is compared. That of Germany is 45,000 millions of dollars and that of the United States, as shown, 107,000 millions of dollars.

The vast accumulation of wealth thus in a few hands takes on a new significance when its international effects are considered.

Dr. Franz Ehrich Junge-Hermsdorf, in the *Engineering Magazine*, has presented this phase of the question most admirably:

"If we admit that capital in its lesser accumulation has been and is conducive to national progress—progress which must include, besides the physical and intellectual, also the moral uplift of man—why does it become dangerous and tyrannical and harmful to the country when concentrated in a few irresponsible hands?

"There can be no doubt that capital and capitalism, based as it is on the institution of private property, has done an enormous lot of good to the commonwealth, as long as it concentrated its activities within the national borders, serving to multiply the values of the native soil. But when capital started to flow beyond the borders of its natural vessel—where it can be checked by competent authority, and where righteous governments can direct its course to the best ends of all—and when it started to combine with other streams of overflowing wealth from other countries, capital became a wild torrent of formidable force, an international power, whose movements are feverish and uncertain and can no longer be guided by established national authorities. Nor are they balanced by weight of international agreement, because there is no arbitrary power strong enough to enforce conciliatory measures, and none elevated enough to enjoy general recognition. International capital is its own arbiter, it is responsible to no one, and its supreme lex is to grow and multiply, ignoring sentimental considerations.

"Says William Howard Taft: 'A gigantic controversy between capital and labor will decide once for all how capital and labor shall share the joint profits which they create.' From our analysis of the situation, it will be more a fight between the legitimate power of national governments, representing the interests of the masses, and the arrogated power of international capital, representing the interests of the favored few.

"There is, indeed, a closer affinity of aims, a firmer alliance of action, traceable to-day, between the great industrial trusts of the different countries, preying jointly upon the world's markets, than there is co-operation existing between various social strata of one and the same country. The world is becoming an open shop, owned by the international association of manufacturers. National borders disappear, and with them all the loftiest motives for which they stood.

"But it is not only the subjugation of national ideals to international aims that is so much to be feared, but the fact that a small group of selfish men is able to swing, not only the factor of capital, but also the factor of government, setting up nation against nation, and hearthstone against hearthstone.

"Here is an illustration of this disastrous tendency as it exhibits itself in the commercial dealings of this very day. A small group of American capitalists, known under the name of the 'North Trust,' attempted in times of disorganization of the German market to buy up one of the fundamental resources of that country, making private contracts for the supply of 320,000 tons of potash per annum, on five years' option; thereby they could gain control of the American market, where about 360,000 tons are consumed annually, thus establishing a practical monopoly in restraint of trade.

"And this same trust is attempting, further, to engage and play the American government against the German government, because the latter has enacted a law (long ago planned and announced to the State department at Washington), which purports by the establishment of a national syndicate, to prevent over-production of potash and, for the benefit of the small producer, prohibits squandering irreplaceable resources, of which Germany has no plethora.

"It is a most reckless game of concentrated capital, and one which cannot be too severely rejected before the forum of publicity—this attempt to endanger and disturb the friendly relations between two great peoples for the sole benefit of establishing an artificial monopoly on some such commodity and reaping the excessive profits from its sale. But it is an instance which shows clearly that national communities must not let the control of capital slip from their hands, lest international complications of the gravest consequences arise, for which corporate capital will not and cannot be held responsible.

"It is the tragedy of our age, the way this artificial creature of capitalism, in its ubiquity, can forever escape the single justice which the natural individual must face. And it is the duty of every patriotic man, within the borders of his country, to see that the rule of capital is once for all subjected to the rule of government, viz: to the collective force of civic virtue evolved in centuries of nation building."

In what ways this is to be accomplished is the great problem of American life to-day, and it is likely to continue the dominant problem for many years. It has not arisen in a day. As John Moody and George Kibbe Turner in *McClure's Magazine* say:

"This central group is a perfectly natural evolution—the final product of thirty or forty years of unchecked movement towards monopoly. It has not been erected by any man's or men's arbitrary acts or theories. It has risen day after day and year after year upon the progressive bankruptcy of general industry under competition. The old economic axiom has been erased in the last twenty-five years; competition has not been the life of trade; it has been the death of industry in the United States. Monopoly has been built up on its ruins, and it is built to stay."

The United States is by no means alone in its struggle against American trusts. The Standard Oil Company, one of its most complete monopolies, has been gradually reaching out for the oil trade of Germany until a most acute situation has arisen.

Dr. Paul Schwartz, editor of *Petroleum*, the official organ of the German oil trade, who has for years carried on a crusade against the Standard and who has frequently been consulted by the German government as to the best ways and means of fighting the trusts says in an interview in the New York *Times* of Oct. 20, 1912:

"The cries of distress which for months have been sent up by our oil trade could no longer be ignored. It was not a question of the price of oil. There was no complaint from consumers on that score.

"The reason the government has been moved to take the drastic action of establishing a monopoly is that the Standard is throttling the life out of thousands of German citizens, who are deprived of the possibility of longer conducting an independent, self-respecting business in their own trade. They find themselves reduced to economic serfdom. Men who once had prosperous little oil businesses of their own have now the alternative of becoming drivers of the oil wagons owned by the Standard. They are asked to come down from the rank of business men to the level of peddlers.

"This is the state of affairs to which the Standard's highly organized campaign has reduced our oil trade. Their so-called can business has been developed to a point where they reach practically every individual consumer at his own threshold.

"By a system of speeding up the local representatives through its offers of premiums, the Standard has spread its nets so thoroughly that no competition can any longer stand against it.

"The Standard has taken the map of Germany and staked the entire empire out as its own particular claim. No hamlet is too small to merit the octopus's attention. The result has inevitably been the destruction of the small dealer.

"Although itself the classic land of organization, Germany is not accustomed to such methods in the pursuit of business. This sort of Americanization is offensive to our ethical susceptibilities, quite apart from the economic ruin it brings to thousands.

"Our people and government have for years been bombarded from all quarters for remedial measures. It had no longer any recourse but to proceed by the furthest-reaching means at its command to rid the country of a system, which was eating the heart of the economic body."

The future development of monopoly and accumulated capital is an ominous question. Not only in the mere power of capital lies the danger, but in its vast psychological effect, the sharp contrast between the citizen of small or average means, and the wealth of the rich, places a gulf between them, creating class distinctions and antagonisms which are fatal to the spirit of democracy.

The possibility will be present of a financial genius arising, a Napoleon of finance, and merging under a single control all this vast capital. Such a man would wield a power never before exercised. He could make or unmake legislators, judges, presidents; he could unite countries into new nations or disrupt political divisions, and if allied to his genius for money, he had genius for politics and ambitions for power, he might even become a dictator, the first sole ruler of the modern world. While such a possibility is remote, yet America has taken gigantic strides in the century and a third of its existence, and it is not beyond the probabilities that another century may bring such a problem up; that even now, the coming money king may be an infant in arms or a child at play.

Such a contingency would be impossible did the texture and composition of the American people remain of its present quality; but such a continuance is, however, gravely in hazard. The last decade or two has witnessed a serious impairment of American standards due to the hordes of a new immigration, and should this continue unchecked and unassimilated, a century would see America dominated by a people of characteristics so different from our own as to be unable or disinclined to preserve the bulwarks of liberty erected with such sacrifices by your ancestors. As will be pointed out in later chapters, in relative standing with other countries the United States is far from holding the position it held twenty years ago. It is constantly losing ground, the poor getting poorer, the rich getting richer, and the middle class disappearing, and unless the process is arrested, American institutions as we know them will pass into history.

CHAPTER VIII

GOVERNMENTAL SOCIALISM

The tyranny of the single seller—How inventions multiply the earth's population—Consolidated robbery—Rapacity of modern combinations—The logic of governmental price regulation—An embryonic function—What governments are really for—Public and private functions of governments—What governments cost and what they do for the money—The Interstate Commerce Commission—Its effective methods—Railroads no longer the pawns of business—Status of governmental price regulation—The hazardous step of governmental ownership—Governmental socialism as an economic necessity—Growing powers of public service commissions—Government by executive order—Qualitative regulation of food products—Success of experiments in governmental socialism—Where enlightened self-interest breaks down—Cicero on socialism—What socialism is—What it proposes to do—Elimination of the middleman or the cost of selling—How competition oppresses the worker.

In earlier times and under simpler conditions of life, competition was the only safeguard which the purchaser needed, but under the complex régime of modern life, the limitations of competition have been exceeded, and the purchaser has fallen a victim to the ravaging self-interest of the sole seller.

The new condition has been created by invention, not by any change in human nature. The activity of inventors, due to the establishment of patent offices and the recognition of their rights to their inventions for limited terms, has done more to revolutionize the world than any other single factor.

The invention of the harvesting machine made bread vastly cheaper, with the result that the population of the world increased far beyond what would have been possible with previous expensive methods of wheat harvesting.

Every invention which saves time has the effect, sooner or later, of increasing the population of the world, and in addition of increasing the comfort of its inhabitants. Once the majority of people went barefooted a greater part of the year. Now, through perfections of shoe making machinery, shoes have come to be so cheap that everyone wears them the whole year around.

The invention of the steam locomotive so reduced the cost of transportation that journeys thousands of miles may be taken where hundreds were traversed before.

But while invention has bestowed benefits, it has involved consequences. Where formerly several stage coach drivers were in competition over the same road, there is now one road of steel. The stage coach has become an impossibility and competition likewise an impossibility. In effect, the stage coach proprietors sold their coachs and built a railroad. One became the engineer, one the fireman, one the conductor, one the station agent, and collectively they carried more passengers than they could have done in competition.

They waxed so rich in fact, that they all became officers of the company and hired employees to do their former tasks. Where once there had been competition, the invention of the steam railway brought about monopoly, with all the factors working together against the purchaser of transportation, that had once been in competition.

The self interest of the proprietors of the railroad had nothing to check it. For generations they charged "all that the traffic would bear," and kept up a clamor about the benefits of private ownership and the sacred benefits of competition.

Only within recent years has the public realized, and acted on the realization, that where competition has been eliminated some other form of regulation must be supplied. The public must travel, must buy transportation and yet there is no divine right given to the proprietors to charge "all the traffic will bear."

It is impracticable and impossible for the individual to supply the regulation necessary. But the individual, in his collective capacity, a government, has just as much right to refuse to pay "all the traffic will bear" as the proprietors in their collective capacity as the company have to demand it.

Governmental regulation is thus the first and logical step after the boundaries of competition are passed. It is not necessary that the individuals as a government should purchase the railroad. Their whole desire is transportation at fair rates. Compared with governmental regulation, governmental ownership is a revolutionary step.

Beyond competition, however, a choice must be made, the rapacity of self interest must be checked, and it has been found that the choice of governmental regulation is thus in theory not only the best expedient, but that in practice it works out better than anything that has been attempted.

The regulation of price, however, is a governmental function that has never been employed to any great extent as yet. For some reason there appears to be considerable public sentiment in opposition to it. It is practically an unused power of the government, yet when exercised it affects the individual no more directly than various other governmental activities.

In classifying the activities and transactions of a nation, state or municipality, students of economics divide them into two different types; general functions and commercial functions, a classification adopted by the Federal census, which in a special report analyses the governmental functions in a most interesting manner, as follows:

"The general functions of nation, state and municipality are those which are, as a rule, performed for all citizens alike, without any attempt to measure the benefit conferred or the exact compensation therefor, the expenses being met by revenue obtained principally from compulsory contributions levied without regard to the benefit which the individual contributor may derive from any or all governmental activities.

"Most functions of this class are essential to the existence and development of government and to the performance of the governmental duty of protecting life and property and of maintaining a high standard of social efficiency.

"Chief among those activities are those of general government; the protection of life, health and property; the care of the defective, delinquent and dependent classes; the education of the young, and the performance of other duties of a similar nature; the purchase of land for government buildings, parks and streets; the erection, equipment and management of state capitols, country courthouses, city halls and other buildings for general governmental uses; the purchase or construction of electric light and gas works for the exclusive purpose of lighting the streets and governmental buildings, and of other structures and plants, such as printing offices, police and fire telephone systems and bridges; for furnishing free of charge any commodity or service required by the government in the common interest of all its citizens. In the same category are included the opening, grading, paving and curbing of streets, and the construction of drains and sewers, where such public improvements are made at public expense without conferring upon particular individuals measurable special benefits for which, in the opinion of the proper authorities, compensation should be exacted by the government. To the same general group belong the making and paying of loans and the payment of interest thereon, where such loans are made in connection with the other activities and transactions mentioned.

"The general functions of nations, states and municipalities may be classified in a great variety of ways, according to the point of view from which considered. The primary classification of general functions of municipalities which was adopted by the Bureau of the Census is based upon prior studies of the subject by Prof. Adolph Wagner, of Germany, set forth in his Finanzwissenschaft, and revised by Prof. Frederick R. Clow in the Quarterly Journal of Economics for July, 1896. The earlier treatment of the subject by American economists was ably discussed by Prof. L. S. Rowe of the University of Pennsylvania, before the conference of the National Municipal League in 1899.

"As a result of these studies and of conferences between accountants, economists and others connected with the National Municipal League, that organization arranged a tentative classification which was made the basis of the one later adopted by the Bureau of the Census.

"The commercial functions of a state, nation or municipality include those which create trade relations, industrial or semi-industrial, between the nation, state or municipality, and the general public, including other civil divisions. Among the transactions which arise from the exercise of such functions are those involving the loan of public money at interest, the use of public property for compensation, the sale of any commodity or article of commerce or the performance of any work or service for pay.

"All these transactions involve the performance of some service by the national, state or municipal government, or the granting of some favor by such government, for special compensation, whether the favor or service be primarily for this service or favor, or for the revenue to be secured; none of them is essential to the existence and development of the government, though they may contribute to its support."

The regulation of prices charged by monopolies is, strictly speaking, in neither of these classifications. While it is a service rendered by the government for the benefit of the public, it is not strictly a general function, as it is not necessary for the development of the government. It may be called, in short, governmental socialism, the stopping of what amounts to a conspiracy against the people constituting the government, by the government acting in their interest.

Being an innovation and the exercise of a power not hitherto called into use, it is natural that much opposition should be excited against it, even by those who will be most benefited.

In the activities which may be included under the term of governmental socialism, the United States has only recently taken part, though the field entered is one of the greatest, and the consequences the most far reaching of any activity of this sort which could be undertaken.

In the Interstate Commerce Commission, which regulates railroad freight and passenger rates and even the system of accounting of the railroads, in order that regulations may be uniformly applied, the United States has in successful operation one of the most extensive and practical of all the forms of governmental price regulation.

The vast savings to the public and the impartial adjustment of traffic and rates has made the Interstate Commerce Commission one of the most useful bodies ever created.

It has remained free from accusations of partiality and graft and enjoys the confidence of the public, the shippers and the railroads.

Indeed, it has been for the railroads a great benefactor, since it has relieved them of a great deal of grafting to which they were subject in the way of passes and other favors, which it had become customary to grant to persons of influence and large shippers. It has freed the railroads, too, of the necessity of allowing rebates to powerful shippers, and while advances in rates have been vetoed by the commission, the uniformity enforced has been to the advantage of the railroads as well as to the public.

Railroads, as railroads, and not as pawns of business, prefer to pay no rebates. Except in cases of competition, which are rare, the railroad is not the initiator of the rebate. It is usually forced to give the rebate by some powerful shipper, who has connections which enable him to dictate his own terms to the railroad. It enforces a condition of equity and justice which is beneficial to all concerned.

No suggestion is heard of abolishing the commission or even

of curtailing its powers, nor is it called a socialistic body, yet that is what it really is. Its decisions are respected and in important cases are awaited with all the interest which attaches to the decisions of the Supreme Court of the United States.

George W. Perkins, formerly a partner in the banking firm of J. Pierpont Morgan & Co., and the organizer of the Harvester Trust, a man who started with nothing and who is now many times a millionaire, an energetic, picturesque, breezy and cheerful, not to say irrepressible, millionaire is to-day a warm advocate of the idea of a court of commerce to regulate prices charged by trusts, similarly as the Interstate Commerce Commission adjusts railroad rates.

In the *World's Work* for June, 1911, Mr. Perkins says:

"Our business concerns have grown from the local firm and the state company to the great interstate corporations; and what we must have is Federal regulation and control of these great interstate business enterprises, and we must have laws that will punish the man who commits the crime, not the stockholder or the public which is being served. Federal regulation is feasible, and if we unite and work for it now, we may be able to secure it; whereas if we continue to fight against it much longer, the incoming tide may sweep the question along either to government ownership or socialism. The day has come when we need statesmanship in business and more business-like statesmanship.

"One important reason why business men have feared regulation of business by the government has been that such regulation would be performed by inexperienced men—those without business training, who would have no practical knowledge of the great problems involved.

"We now have at Washington a Supreme Court, to which is referred the final settlement of our legal questions. This court is composed, of course, of lawyers only, and it is the dream of every young man who enters the law that he may some day be called to the Supreme Court bench. If such a call comes, it matters not how lucrative his practice, he always drops it for the honor conferred. Why not have a similar goal for our business men? Why not have a court for business questions, on which no man could sit who had not had a business training, with an honorable record? This would surely come to be regarded by business men in the same way that the Supreme Court is regarded by lawyers. The supervision of business by such a body of men, who had reached such a court in such a way, would unquestionably be fair and equitable to business, fair and equitable to the public. Furthermore, it would not take out of business that invaluable asset, individual initiative. It would leave the everyday management of business untrammeled and allow men free swing to devise ways and means to improve, enlarge and develop our domestic and foreign commerce.''

What Mr. Perkins suggests as the alternative between socialism or governmental ownership, is a form of what we term governmental socialism.

Another important phase of this activity is seen in the Public Service Commissions of the various states, and in the sporadic laws of the various states, regulating the prices of transportation.

The New York State Public Service Commission (there being two, one for the state and the other for the city of New York) is a model for other states. Its functions are the regulations of rates of railroads, street car transportation, their service and improvements, bond and stock issues, and gas, electric and telephone matters. It has in addition to the power to regulate rates, very great powers in the supervision of the organization of public service corporations in the issuance of stocks and bonds, and has further remarkable powers in its right to specify the service to be rendered, such as the number of cars to be run, and various other details, which in effect make the state a superior superintendent of operation. Thus the state has by law every right and power, practically, that it would have under public ownership, aside from deriving profit from the enterprise. It prescribes the securities which may be issued, the prices to be charged, and the service to be rendered. No fuller powers could well be asked, although the commission as yet lacks the power to have its orders promptly carried out, and its findings are subjected to court review.

It is argued that the endowing of Public Service Commissions with such powers is an illegal delegation of the powers of the legislature, which the legislature has not the right to make. It is as though the legislature appointed another body to make laws and then adjourned. It is urged that this is government by executive order, rather than by law, but in spite of these objections, which are more theoretical than real, the operations of the public service commissions are entirely satisfactory to the public, with the exception that they are not as yet sufficiently drastic and severe; in short, the criticism is that the powers are not used, not that the powers exist.

Like the Interstate Commerce Commission, the Public Service Commissions are not likely to be dispensed with. It is a form of governmental socialism which has come to stay.

While the government has not as yet attempted the regulation of the rates of anything except public service corporations, it has undertaken what amounts to a price regulation in the pure food and drug laws. The thing regulated is the quality of the product, and while this, in a sense, is a form of protection of the public health, it is also indirectly an important price regulation, since in many commodities having a fixed price for a fixed unit, the improvement in quality demanded by the pure food law, is a cheapening of the price and an enforcement of uniformity in price.

In the provision of the "net contents of container," which, however, has not as yet been adopted, another price regulation, in force abroad, will be adopted, since the marking on the container of the net weight or amount of the contents will in effect reduce the price by guaranteeing a certain content, while usually the package, with the habitual honesty of the American manufacturer, contains something under the supposed content.

While this represents the most that has as yet been done in the United States in governmental socialism, it should be noted that it has been uniformly successful, that vast powers have been exercised for the benefit of the public and with even greater benefit to the corporations than the most "enlightened self-interest" that they were previously able to exhibit, and more particularly, that the result has been accomplished without graft and in an expeditious and effective manner.

Yet the commissioners have been but men, no different from other men. The system, however, is superior to other forms of governmental systems, since the great powers of the commission have caused the members to feel a sense of responsibility to the public, rather than the sense of responsibility to their own pockets so often manifested by aldermen. The intense scrutiny to which their acts are subjected, and the prestige of their positions have rendered this form of governmental activity one from which the best results have been achieved.

So efficient, indeed, has the commission form of government

been found, that it is being adopted by various cities throughout the United States and is proving one of the greatest political movements of the century. A further reference is made to it in a later chapter. Socialism is a mantle which is ascribed to a diversified throng of wearers. It does duty for a vast number of isms, and many arise to proclaim its meaning. To one man it means one thing, to another another, but for all, it is at once a protest and a panacea.

Cicero described what socialism really is, better perhaps than any modern expounder when he said:

"One thing ought to be aimed at by all men; that the interest of each individually, and of all collectively, should be the same; for if each should grasp at his individual interest, all human society will be dissolved."

Socialism should be a condition which answers Cicero's injunction.

Sir Thomas More also clearly described modern conditions, the only cure for which socialism claims to be.

Robert Blatchford in his famous book on socialism, "Merrie England," a book which has had an enormous sale and which merits the attention of every thoughtful reader, has prefaced his chapter on "Socialism" with the quotation from Cicero and with Sir Thomas More's prophecy, the latter of which is as follows:

"When I balance all these things in my thoughts, I grow more favorable to Plato, and do not wonder that he resolved not to make any laws for such as would not submit to a community of all things! for so wise a man could not but foresee that the setting all upon a level was the only way to make a nation happy, which cannot be obtained so long as there is property; for when every man draws to himself all that he can compass by one title or another, it must needs follow that how plentiful soever a nation may be, yet a few dividing the wealth of it among themselves, the rest must fall into indigence. So that there will be two sorts of people among them who deserve that their fortunes should be interchanged, the former useless but wicked and ravenous, and the latter, who by their constant industry serve the public more than themselves, sincere and modest men. From whence I am persuaded that till property is taken away there can be no equitable or just distribution of things, nor can the world be happily governed; for, so long as that is maintained, the greatest and the far best part of mankind will be still oppressed with a load of cares and anxieties.''

Mr. Blatchford continues in part, describing socialism:

"Before I tell you what socialism is, I must tell you what socialism is not. For half our time as champions of socialism is wasted in denials of false descriptions of socialism; and to a large extent, the anger, the ridicule, and the argument of the opponents of socialism are hurled against a socialism which has no existence except in their own heated minds.

"Socialism does not consist in violently seizing upon the property of the rich and sharing it among the poor.

"Socialists do not propose, by a single act of parliament, or by a sudden revolution, to put all men on an equality, and compel them to remain so. Socialism is not a wild dream of a happy land, where the apples will drop off the trees into our open mouths, and the fish come out of the rivers and fry themselves for dinner, and the looms turn out ready made suits of velvet with golden buttons without the trouble of coaling the engine. Neither is it a dream of a nation of stained glass angels, who never say damn, who always love their neighbors better than themselves, and who never need to work unless they wish to.

" No, socialism is none of these. It is a scientific scheme of national government, entirely wise, just and *practical*. And now let us see.

"For convenience sake, socialism is generally divided into two kinds. These are called—1. Practical Socialism. 2. Ideal Socialism.

"Really, they are only part of one whole; practical socialism being a kind of preliminary step toward ideal socialism, so that we might with more reason call them elementary and advanced socialism.

"I am an ideal socialist, and desire to have the whole socialistic programme carried out.

"Practical socialism is so simple that a child may understand it. It is a kind of national scheme of co-operation, managed by the state. Its programme consists, essentially, of one demand—that the land and other instruments of production shall be the common property of the people, and shall be used and managed by the people for the people.

"Make the land and all the instruments of production state property; put all farms, mines, mills, ships, railways and shops under state control, as you have already put the postal and telegraphic service under state control, and practical socialism is accomplished.

"The postal and telegraphic service is the standing proof of the capacity of the state to manage the public business with economy and success.

"That which has been done with the post offices may be done with mines, trams, railways and factories.

"The difference between socialism and the state of things now in existence will now be plain to you.

"At present the land—that is, England—does not belong to the people—to the English—but to a few rich men. The mines, mills, ships, shops, canals, railways, houses, docks, harbors and machinery do not belong to the people, but to a few rich men.

"Therefore the land, the factories the railways, ships, and machinery are not now used for the general good of the people, but are used to make wealth for the few rich men who own them.

"Socialists say that this arrangement is unjust and unwise, that it entails waste as well as misery, and that it would be better for all, even for the rich, that the land and other instruments of production should become the property of the state, just as the post office and the telegraphs have become the property of the state.

"Socialists demand that the state shall manage the railways and the mines and the mills, just as it now manages the post offices and the telegraphs.

"Socialists declare that if it is wicked and foolish and impossible for the state to manage the factories, mines, and railways, then it is wicked and foolish and impossible for the state to manage the telegraphs.

"Socialists declare that as the state carries the people's letters and telegrams more cheaply and more efficiently than they were carried by private enterprise, so it could grow corn and weave cloth and work the railway systems more cheaply and more efficiently than they are now worked by private enterprise.

"Socialists declare that as our government now makes food and clothing and arms and accouterments for the army and navy and police, so it could make them for the people.

"Socialists declare that as many corporations make gas, provide and manage the water-supply, look after the paving and lighting and cleansing of the streets, and often do a good deal of building and farming, so there is no reason why they should not get coal and spin yarn and make boots and bread for the people.

"Socialists point out that if all the industries of the nation were under state control, all the profit, which now goes into the hands of a few idle men, would go into the coffers of the state—which means that the people would enjoy the benefits of all the wealth they create.

"This, then, is the basis of socialism—that England should be owned by the English and managed for the benefit of the English, instead of being owned by a few rich idlers and mismanaged by them for the benefit of themselves.

"But socialism means more than the mere transference of the wealth of the nation to the nation.

"Socialism would not endure competition. Where it found two factories engaged in under-cutting each other at the price of long hours and low wages to the workers, it would step in and fuse the two concerns into one, save an immense sum in cost of working, and finally produce more goods and better goods at a lower figure than were produced before.

"But practical socialism would do more than that. It would educate the people. It would provide them cheap and pure food. It would extend and elevate the means of study and amusement. It would foster literature and science and art. It would encourage and reward genius and industry. It would abolish sweating and jerry work. It would demolish the slums and erect good and handsome dwellings. It would compel all men to do some kind of useful work. It would recreate and nourish the craftsman's pride in his craft. It would protect women and children. It would raise the standard of health and morality; and it would take the sting out of pauperism by paying pensions to honest workers no longer able to work.

"Why nationalize the land and instruments of production? To save waste, to save panics; to avert trade depressions, famines, strikes and congestion of industrial centers; and to prevent greedy and unscrupulous sharpers from enriching themselves at the cost of the national wealth, health and prosperity. In short, to replace anarchy and war by law and order. To keep the wolves out of the fold, to tend and fertilize the field of labor instead of allowing the wheat to be strangled by the tares, and to regulate wisely the distribution of seed corn of industry so that it might no longer be scattered broadcast—

some falling on rocks and some being eaten up by birds of the air.

"I will now give you one example of the difference between socialism and the existing system.

"Under existing conditions consider the state of the salt trade. The mines and manufacture owned and carried on by a number of firms, each of which competes against all the rest.

"Result: Most of the small firms ruined; most of the large firms on the verge of ruin. Salt boilers, the workmen, working twelve hours a day for three shillings and the public wasting more salt than they use.

"Put this trade under state control. They will cease to make salt to waste. They will establish a six hour day, and they will raise the wages of the men, to say two pounds a week.

"To pay these extra wages, they will abolish all the unnecessary middlemen and go-betweens. The whole industry will be placed under one management. A vast number of clerks, agents, travelers, canvassers and advertisers will be dispensed with, the salaries of the managers will be almost entirely saved, and the cost of distribution will be cut down fully seventy-five per cent.

"The same system would be pursued with other industries."

It is interesting to note that the process described by Mr. Blatchford as the ideal of socialism is exactly that pursued by American monopolies. It must therefore be a good system. In America, however, it is for the benefit of the trusts and not the public, which makes a difference.

CHAPTER IX

GOVERNMENTAL SOCIALISM IN GERMANY

What individualism has accomplished—Where it has failed—The long arm of the German state—How it guides the destinies of the citizen—Bismarck's great policy—The duty of the state to the citizen—The respect in which the German government is held by the public—The systematic organization of groups in all walks of life—The group or combination as a lever for individual rights—The post office as a bank of deposit—How money famines and panics are side tracked in Germany—Profits of nationalized railroads—The business of recurring functions—The German government as the biggest business man in Europe—How German states pay dividends to their citizens instead of collecting taxes—Right of the government to seize mines, lands, etc.—Theory of unequal taxation as a result of government in business—Holding down a job in Germany for life—Why "pull" does not pull—Politicians almost a curiosity—Respect shown for men of attainments—German trusts—How they benefit the country—How unfair competition is squelched—Real significance of trusts—The socialists only waiting for the capitalistic game to grow fat—Why the American president has more power than the German Kaiser—The German government really governs—The American government occasionally wakes up but seldom catches up—Cost of trust busting.

COMPARED with what has been done in the United States in governmental socialism, the extent to which it has developed in Germany is remarkable. This is due to the fact that the German takes an altogether different view of the relations of the state and the individual, to that held in England and the United States particularly and to a lesser extent by France and other countries.

Democracy and individualism are the key notes struck by the United States. Every opportunity and incentive is given for the development of the individual, even the family being a much weaker organization than that of France, for example, where the member of the family, as such, is subject to restriction of his individual privileges in favor of the family unit.

This insistence on the rights and privileges of the individual has made the United States avoid governmental socialism as far as possible.

In Germany, however, an entirely different view is taken. The state is regarded paternally, to an extent unimagined in America. The state is assumed to have certain duties toward the individual and the individual toward the state. The individual as an individual has a less important place in the organism. The welfare of the whole is the first thought, an attitude which is the outgrowth of Roman law and autocratic monarchical practices, while 'the individualistic ideas of the United States and England are derived from centuries of struggles for free political institutions, a rich heritage of liberty from which Germany, too, has derived no small benefit.

The German states early looked upon the protection of the weak from economic misery as one of the duties of the government.

The so-called Prussian common law, as modified by Frederick William II, promulgated July 1, 1794, condemned idleness, recognized the right of every subject to work, and defined the state to be the protector of the poor. The common law proclaimed:

I. It is the duty of the state to provide for the sustenance and support of those of its subjects who cannot obtain subsistence for themselves.

II. Work adapted to their strength and capacities shall be supplied to those who lack means and opportunity of earning a living for themselves, and those dependent upon them.

III. Those who, from laziness, love of idleness or other irregular proclivities, do not choose to employ the means offered them of earning a living shall be kept at useful work by compulsion and punishment, under proper control.

VI. The state is bound to take such measures as will prevent the destitution of its subjects, and check excessive extravagance.

XV. The police authority of every place must provide for all poor and destitute persons, whose subsistence cannot be insured in any other way.

The Stern-Hardenburg legislation of the early part of the nineteenth century supplemented this fundamental law, and was the basis of the doctrine of the right to work, one of the strong features of Bismarck's policy.

It has continued a characteristic German practice, and is carried out in various forms of insurance and pensions and other benefits to the less fortunate members of society.

In addition to the usual functions of internal government

common to most governments, as outlined in the previous chapter, the German government undertakes other functions. Prominent among them is the elimination of obstacles or restraints hampering individual, associated or other activity, and measures fostering commerce and trade, when the efforts of the individuals or associations cannot gain the desired effect; the operation of business enterprises when conducted unsatisfactorily by private owners, and legislation for the protection of the poor against the ills of sickness, accident, old age and extortion of the rich; and acts in regulation of competition and the regulations of powerful units or associations to the public as a whole.

In Germany, "Staatsnotrecht," or the right of the state in cases of necessity, is much more comprehensive than the corresponding "right of eminent domain" in Anglo-Saxon countries. It is applied not only to land but to business and other forms of private property. In considering the exercise of the powers of the state, the difference in the points of view of the German and the American are noticeable almost at the tone of the first syllable of the discussion. The German in speaking of the activities and powers of the government accords it a certain indefinable authority, while the American in speaking of the acts of the government, is without the same confidence and respect, there being no sense of conviction or finality. It is as though the act of the government were the act of a partisan and not a government, and by no means to pass unquestioned.

William C. Dreher in "The German Drift towards Socialism" in *The Atlantic Monthly*, July, 1911, states:

"It is astonishing to what an extent the Germans have gone in organizing life in all its activities. The individual is everywhere learning that his independent strivings are ineffective both for himself and for society; that as a unit he counts for little. The working people long ago learned that they could better their position only through organization; and as united labor became more self-assertive in presenting its demands, the great employers of labor, the manufacturers of the country, organized themselves for the purpose of protecting themselves from those demands. Now both employer and employee have surrendered their individual position, committing their rights to the organization, which acts in its collective capacity in the interests of its members; it fixes the wage-tariff and the length of the day's work, it settles strikes and lock outs by treaty with the opposing organization, and in a hundred ways it absorbs and discharges the functions of the individual in his own behalf. Combinations and syndicates of manufacturers facilitate the marketing of goods, make or dictate prices, assign allotments to each factory of the amount of goods that it may produce, in many cases handle all orders for goods and treat the individual manufacturer merely as their agent.

"The state, of course, takes hold of the individual's life much more broadly, and with more systematic purpose. The individual's health is cared for, his house is inspected, his children educated, he is insured against the worst vicissitudes of life, his savings are invested, his transportation of goods or persons is undertaken, his need to communicate with others by telegraph or telephone is met—all by the paternal state or city.

"A few years ago the post office established a banking department, designed more to facilitate payments than to take care of savings. It is a system of open accounts, on which moneys are paid in and out upon order slips—an admirable method for making collections. The system has already become very popular; in 1910, only the second year in existence, the department effected payments amounting to about $4,440,000,000. It is operated in connection with the Reichsbank, with which its balances are deposited. The Reichsbank itself, the great central note-issuing institution of the Empire, is a splendid example of what is done in Germany through efficient government administration.

"While its control is owned by private persons, its administration is wholly in the hands of the Imperial Government, and a large part of its profits, often more than half, falls to the treasury by law. With above 500 branches in all sections of the land, with an annual turnover of about $85,000,000,000, with a note circulation approximating $500,000,000 this great institution performs an incalculable service to the people.

"Its elastic note circulation, sometimes expanded by more than $125,000,000 in a single week, wholly prevents those money famines that have often proved disastrous to American business interests.

"Another semi-public interest is the Prussian Central Co-operative Bank whose function is to extend cheap banking facilities to the numerous co-operative societies that have sprung up in Prussia; its capital of $9,000,000 is supplied by the state, and its administration is under the supervision of the Finance Minister. The Seehandlung, which is the Prussian state bank, is the largest lender of money in the Berlin market. Nearly all the savings bank business is done by public institutions—only about eight per cent of the total deposits in savings banks being with private institutions.

"At the end of 1907 there were above 2,700 municipal and provincial savings banks, with 6,600 branches, and their deposits amounted to more than $3,000,000,000. At that time above twenty-eight persons in every one hundred Germans held an account in a savings bank. Such is the extent to which semi-socialistic banking has taken hold of the German people.

"The railway, as is well known, is almost wholly a state institution in Germany. The Prussian system, with its more than 400,000 laborers and officials, is the largest employer of labor in the world; and this vast business is administered with remarkable honesty and efficiency. Cases of embezzlement or other crime are extremely rare; relatively few persons are killed or maimed through accident; and the railways are kept quite aloof from politics.

"Freight rates, indeed, are considerably higher than the average American rates, but the bulk of the passenger traffic is carried at lower prices than in America. Bismarck's purpose to use the railway wholly in the interests of the people, as declared when he nationalized the roads, has not been fully carried out, since rates have been kept at a high enough figure to make them the largest source of revenue for the state, besides paying interest on the capital invested. On the other hand, shippers have the advantage of absolutely fair treatment; there is no discrimination among them, there are no rebates, secret or other. Another great advantage consists in having a single system to deal with, as well as simplified tariff schedules. Before the nationalization, there were 63 railways with 1,357 different tariffs."

There are certain forms of industry which seem peculiarly fitted for governmental control, among them being the railroad and post office. The reason for this may lie in the fact that they are vast machines which when once set in motion require little or no initiative on the part of the employees. They are forms of activity in which no concrete result is left; being rather a series of operations, carried out over and over again. Thus when a letter is delivered, no product is left, nothing has been created, the location of the letter has only been changed. A million letters through the same process require no further technical adaptation on the part of the employees. A vast organization, thus, which exists but to perform functions, when once erected continues of its own momentum, and is an entirely different problem from the conducting of a business, where new ideas must be constantly introduced, and the active competition of others met and overcome. If the letter carrier was constantly pursued by others, endeavoring to get the letters away and deliver them by another route, or if he met constant opposition to his progress, the delivery of the mail would be an entirely different operation, and more like business competition.

Yet the German governmental socialism has been carried to such a point, that the state can and does successfully conduct business of a competitive nature, involving great initiative and the constant adoption of new ideas. This is rendered possible in Germany by the fact that there the officials are willing to devote to the affairs of the state the same energy that they would devote to their private concerns.

The extent to which Germany as a state has gone into business may be grasped by considering the amount and the various sources of the profits of the businesses engaged in.

Elmer Roberts in "Monarchical Socialism in Germany" in *Scribner's Magazine*, January, 1910, states:

"The Imperial government and the governments of the German states took profits in 1908, from the various businesses conducted by them, of $277,385,095. Estimating the capital value at a 4% ratio, the value of the productive state owned properties is $6,933,627,375. Roundly, the governments operate dividend yielding works, lands, and means of communication worth $7,000,000,000, and the governments continue to follow a policy of fresh acquisitions. Taking the federated states together, 38% of all the financial requirements for governmental purposes were met last year out of profits of government-owned enterprises. Including the Imperial government, a new comer with relatively few possessions, one-quarter of all the expenses of the state and the imperial governments, on army, navy and all other purposes, were paid out of the net profits on governmental businesses. Among the undertakings are no tobacco, spirit or match monopolies.

"The miniature ducal monarchy of Schaumburg-Lippe, with a population of 44,992, and an area of 131 square miles, made $206,150 from property owned collectively, or 5% of the requirements of the state. The still smaller principality of Reuss, the elder, with 122 square miles, and a population of 70,603, makes a profit of $10,000, the smallest actually, and the smallest in proportion of any of the German states. The little neighbor of Reuss, Schwarzburg-Sonderhausen, draws 33% of the budget from farms and forests; Oldenburg, 22%; Mecklenburg-Strelitz, 49.14%. But it is the great states of the empire where state management of large properties shows the more important results. Bavaria pays 39% of all of the administrative costs from public-owned properties; Saxony, 31%; Wurtemberg, 38.7%; and Prussia, 47.36%.

" Prussia, which forms about five-eighths of the empire, has a constantly increasing revenue from state-owned enterprises, which yielded in 1908 net returns of about $176,000,000, or more than twice the state's income from taxes, which was $85,-452,000; the average income from its enterprises per capita was 18.1 marks, while the average per capita taken in taxation was 8.7 marks. In that year the state, owing to extensions in canals, railways and other public works, raised by loans what amounted to an average of 7.1 marks per capita.

"The state income from public properties amounted in 1908 to somewhat more than the total income from taxation and from borrowings. The railways were the largest source of income, and netted $149,755,000 or about 8% on the total invested by Prussia in its railway system since the state began to buy and build railways in 1848-49.

"Prussia derived from other sources, from its crown forests, the leased farms, the iron, coal, potash, salt and other mines, the porcelain factories, banking and a variety of less important industries, $26,900,000. The policy of Prussia, which dominates the empire, is strongly in the direction of increasing the participation of the government in industrial enterprises. The Prussian legislature, acting upon a recommendation of the emperor, in the speech from the throne, at the opening of the Diet in 1906, passed a bill extending widely an old act, giving the state the right to take over at a valuation any discovery of mineral riches on private lands.

"The theory of the Prussian cabinet and the crown is that it is for the interests of the people that the state should take part in industrial combinations that undertake to regulate the prices of articles, or the products in any industry. Public opinion supports this principle.

"A summary of the government owned properties and the income derived from them is subjoined:

	Values	Net Incomes
Farms	$ 198,122,725	$ 7,925,309
Forests	730,898,200	29,235,928
Mines	128,907,725	5,116,309
Railways	4,706,904,750	189,916,190
Telephones Telegraphs Express packages Mails	694,816,650	27,792,666
Other works	435,184,900	17,407,476

"Upon no department of industry do any of the state governments lose except on steamers. The grand duchy of Baden runs its internal navigation lines at a loss of $15,833. Saxony, Wurtemberg and Mecklenburg-Schwerin gain on their lines $7,163, so that on the whole of the state-owned steamer lines there is a loss of $8,670."

The question as to whether the government should or should not make any profit out of its enterprises is one which has been very practically decided in favor of profit. Theoretically the profit of a government enterprise is a form of indirect taxation. In the United States the taxation which business profits amount to, is laid on the public as an encouragement for individual initiative on the part of the business man and goes to the business man. The profits of a governmental business are a tax on that portion of the public which patronizes that part of the government's business. It is a discrimination against the customer in favor of those who do not purchase. On the other hand, if the enterprises were run without a profit or loss, the facilities of the state would be in a sense unduly extended to customers of the business, since they would be securing service at less than the commercial rate, and such a plan would be a discrimination in favor of the customer.

It is a question, however, whether this would not be the better plan, allowing the government to raise all the money needed by direct taxation.

Low prices to all would stimulate business greatly and allow the public to make profits in its individual business and have the use of all its capital to a later moment, thus being better able to pay the taxes when the time for their withdrawal came.

If instead of having to pay freight rates which show the government a profit, the business men had the advantage during the year of cost freight rates, the capital which he would thus retain in his own business could be turned over two or three times at a considerable profit, enabling him at the end of the year to pay the direct tax out of the profits of the turn overs. Thus the burden of taxation would be entirely lifted, merely by an administrative device, for it is highly important to the business man and to industry as a whole to have the benefit of as much capital and credit as they can employ to advantage.

The ease with which the government gets funds, through profits on its businesses, however, while an immediate drain on capital and an encouragement to official extravagance, is for practical purposes such an administrative convenience, that as a system it is likely to continue.

There is not, either, in Germany, the official extravagance shown by the servants of the public, as in the United States, for owing partially to the bureaucratic system and partly to an identification of the interests of the employee and employer, whether the employer be the government or an individual, better service is secured and temptation to extravagance is not given way to.

When a man gets a job in Germany, whether with the government or with a corporation or individual employer, he expects to hold it down for twenty-five years at least if not for his life time. He does not, as in the United States, expect to stay in the business just long enough to get a suit of clothes and start some other business on his own account. Expecting to stay with his employer, it is to his interest to contribute all he can to his employer's success. In the case of a governmental service, the employee enters it with the idea of making it his life career, and not, as in America, of making it a temporary but lucrative perquisite.

As every individual has his own ambition, and must express what his life means to him in some way, if as in Germany the ambition of the employee is in his employer's interest, or the state's interest, the service he gives will be the best that is in him.

This relationship between the employer and employee is one of the cornerstones of German progress. It gives a solidarity to an enterprise or a service that is wanting when the employees and employer are constantly warring and the employer watching the clock in the morning as closely as the employee watches it in the evening.

On their part, the government and the private employer, in taking on an employee, expect him to remain permanently. They realize that their interests are identical. In Germany the employee works for the employer and the employer works for the employee, the government for the public (its employer) and the public for the government, a system entirely different from the American plan of everybody for his own pocket and the devil take the hindmost.

In Germany, too, the greatest respect is shown for those in authority, a deference that seems to an American to reach the point of absurdity; but let the German official show the slightest dereliction of duty and the average citizen will report the matter promptly to the Polezei, Bürgermeister, Landrat or Governor as the case may require, successively if necessary, and something is done about it, a very different process from the American's bluff of taking a street car conductor's number as well as his back talk and going no further.

One of the adornments of the American street car which frightens the incoming German and arouses his indignation is the sign, "$500 fine or one year in prison for spitting on the floor." In Germany the penalty is three marks (75 cents) and the loss of half a day's time in paying it, but everybody who spits gets caught and is fined. When the German here, however, sees that the spitter spits at his own sweet will and nobody is ever imprisoned for it or fined, he gets a new insight into what may be called American humor, and finds that seemingly, the principal result of the sign is to provoke spitting. It is, in reality, however, but one of a vast number of American laws which are dead letters because the punishment does not fit the crime, that it is so vastly in excess of the requirements as to cover and serve rather as a hot house for the crime.

Another factor of great importance in the success of Germany's undertakings is the freedom from political influence observed in appointments. A striking example of this freedom is seen in the method of selecting governmental and city employees, all of whom must have a requisite degree of training. Cities advertise even for the most important of their officials, such as mayor, chamberlain, fire and police commissioners, etc. The larger cities have several burgomasters trained in different fields who serve under one head burgomaster, practically a commission form of government.

Die Stelle. des Ersten Bürgermeisters der Stadt Magdeburg ist infolge Ernennung des Herrn Oberbürgermeisters Dr. Lentze zum preußischen Finanzminister neu zu besetzen.

Das Gehalt ist vorbehaltlich der Genehmigung des Bezirks-Ausschusses auf 21 000 Mk. festgesetzt, wobei 3 000 Mk. für freie Dienstwohnung im Rathause mit einbegriffen sind. Diese Dienst-wohnung wird aber nur auf Widerruf nach einjähriger Kündigung gewährt, und werden, wenn von dieser Gebrauch gemacht werden sollte, 3 000 Mk. als Wohnungsentschädigung vergütet.

Neben dem Gehalte bezieht der Gewählte jährlich 4 000 Mk. Dienstaufwandsgelder, welche der Pensionsberechtigung nicht unter-liegen.

Die speziellen Wahl-Bedingungen werden den Bewerbern, welche ihre Meldung bis zum 1. September d Js. an den Unter-zeichneten einreichen wollen, auf Erfordern abschriftlich mitgeteilt.

Magdeburg, den 30. Juni. 1910.

Der Vorsitzende der Stadtverordneten-Versammlung.

Baensch.

The above is a reproduction of an advertisement of Magdeburg, a city of a quarter of a million population, for a mayor, which appeared with many similar advertisements in the German Municipal Weekly of July 23, 1910. Such an advertisement as this would give many local politicians in an American city a distinct shock. They would think there was an abundance of local talent to fill the position. German cities choose their mayors as well as other officials in this way, obtaining men who have made a reputation in other cities, just as American universities choose their presidents and professors. The following is a translation of the advertisement:

"The position of First Mayor of the City of Magdeburg, in consequence of the appointment of Mr. Head Mayor Dr. Lentze as Prussian Finance Minister, must be refilled.

"The salary is provisionally fixed by the council at 21,000 marks, included in which is an allowance of 3000 marks for free residence in the city hall. A year's notice of change of residence must be given, and subsequently the city will make an allowance of 3000 marks for residence purpose.

"The official selected will also receive an allowance of 4000 marks for incidental expenses, which however, will not be regarded as part of his salary when his pension allowance is determined. Copies of the specific requirements of the election which must be complied with by the candidates, whose application must reach the undersigned on or before the 1st of September of this year, are obtainable upon request."

Magdeburg, June 30th, 1910.
The Chairman of the City Council
BAENSCH.

The highest regard is shown in all German undertakings for technical experience and expert technical knowledge. In the United States an expert in any line is too apt to be regarded either as a book worm or a crank of some kind; while he may be supposed to have an ample fund of expert knowledge, he is too often assumed to be lacking in judgment, a quality more or less monopolized by the "business man," a term which variously embraces the banker, the promoter, the merchant and the administrator of commercial and manufacturing enterprises.

The "business man" in the United States occupies the center of the stage, which in Germany is held by the man of technical knowledge, the engineer and the chemist. From Emperor William down, the greatest interest is taken in the work of engineers, architects, chemists and other trained experts, and credit and other rewards are freely rendered them. The business man is much less heard of in Germany, and the "tired business man" who rules the theater in America in his insistence on pieces which demand little thought and supply much diversion, is entirely unknown.

The efficiency of German governmental undertakings as has been stated is greatly enhanced by the lack of politics in business, which is such a bane in America. In Germany there is little or none of the political activity, the clubs, organizations and wire pulling of the United States, and what little there is is usually done by the clergy, in the interest of returning certain members to the Reichstag. A ward heeling clergyman would be something of a novelty in America, but he would be much less harmful than a ward heeling bartender.

The few elective offices in Germany, too, compared with America, renders politics as a business one of small profit, and one which is not professionally followed as in America. Clergy-

men shaking the voters hands on election day is not a problem in
German life, while the small politician is one of the gravest of
America's problems.

Foreigners unacquainted with conditions in Germany and
whose German horizon is considerably limited by the large
looming of the Kaiser in the foreground, often talk of tyrannical domination, and one man power. These are idle expressions. The Kaiser has not the power of an American president.
Property and capital are more equitably distributed in Germany than in any other country and Germany is more of a
self ruled country than any other country, far more than England ruled by the classes and America ruled by the minority.

The governmental socialism of Germany, which is proving
such a distinguished success, is from the people by the people
and for the people; it is popular and has been instituted and
continued by them and is not an enforcement from rulers or an
aristocracy.

The treatment of the trust problem is vitally different in
Germany. Trusts such as we know them in America do not
exist in Germany, but trade combinations known by that name
or by the name of syndicates or cartels are very effective and
numerous.

Consul General Robert P. Skinner at Hamburg, describes in
the United States Daily Consular and Trade Reports, for Sept.
15, 1911, the operation of these trusts:

"There is no German law which either expressly authorizes
or forbids the creation of the so-called trusts so numerous in this
country. The law merely guarantees to the individual the
right to engage in trade, but does not withhold from him the
right to combine with any or all of his competitors. The theory
seems to be that in granting to trade and commerce the very
extensive privileges referred to by my correspondent, the general interests of the public at large are protected by the resulting prosperity of such interests, even though the immediate
effect may be to enhance the cost of the commodity controlled.

"In a recent discussion of the subject, Mr. Albert Ballin, the
general director of the Hamburg-American Line said: 'In
Germany syndicates are protected by several laws, and therefore
it may arise very easily that the American government would
require the dissolution of a syndicate, while the dissolution, according to German law, itself would become punishable.' The
majority of German business men and economists are not op-

posed to such syndicates, and the creation of monopolies, in which the state itself sometimes participates in combination with private producers, is lawful if the creators commit no injurious act, a limitation so difficult to define and comprehend that practically the only difficulties with which the ordinary cartels come in contact are the difficulties arising between the members themselves. The courts have frequently recognized the perfect right of producers to control their product in a monopolistic organization as a right somewhat akin to the right to make use of a highway, and only subject to correction of abuses of power.

"The profound difference between the German and the American conception of sound business conditions is best explained, perhaps, by the racial difference between the two peoples—the German with strong collectivist tendencies which manifest themselves in society, in government and in trade, and the American with a deeply rooted individualism which remains even when he engages in a collectivist enterprise. Thus it happens that the capitalistic classes of Germany, although opposing socialism in their public life, nevertheless drift in the direction indicated by their natural tendencies in their business life, and in so doing they have the tacit approval of the avowed socialistic classes, who perceive in the steady accumulation of the producing powers in a few hands a movement tending logically and inevitably toward the eventful realization of their dogma—that is, the state in supreme control.

"An extreme example of the German tendency may be found in the potash syndicate, of which so much has been heard. In this case the Prussian state itself was one of the producers, and when a certain situation was reached, the state interposed and required by law that the entire production of the country should be sold through a single selling agency, organized by law, which also established the terms of sale and the limitation of production. In this case it was argued that the monopolization of the industry was necessary to conserve the important mineral resources of the country. The commentators upon the claim of industrial organizers that some generally desirable end is to be attained point out, as has Gustav le Bon—that—'Socialism is much less dangerous in reality in its absolute form than when it takes on the aspects of simple projects of amelioration by regulating labor. Under its absolute form one sees the dangers and may control them. Under its altruistic form, one does not see them and it is accepted easily.'

"The German courts have repeatedly ruled, according to Richard Calwer, the socialistic writer, in his *Cartelle und Trusts*, that the syndicates do not violate the principles of trade liberty as they tend to protect the interests of the whole nation against the selfishness of individuals, and to protect the products of industry from the many disadvantages of price cutting.

"Under these rulings absolute or partial monopolization by many cartels has been brought about, the national output being reduced, with a consequent lifting of prices to a remunerative level. The danger point would be reached, from the point of view of the law, should a cartel of this character, on the possible refusal of one outside producer to accept its terms, undertake by unfair means to drive him into its fold or crush him if he refused its terms, and the difficulty of the prosecution would be to prove that any such results had been contemplated, even though its effect had been attained.

"The very form of commercial organization most common in Germany and America correspond to the temperamental qualities of the two peoples. In Germany the commercial trust or cartel is usually a federation in which each member retains its commercial identity while abandoning its freedom of action to the federation for a contractual period of three or five or ten years or perhaps longer, but expecting eventually to get it back, and then perhaps make another contract if the results of the first have been satisfactory. A German cartel is, as a rule, open to all those who submit to its provisions, and the control of the members is confined to the limits traced in the federal pact. In the typical American trust, instead of this association of units with influence usually rated according to productive capacity, we observe generally the permanent ownership of a large part of the enterprise by a small group of persons in which there is ordinarily some dominating personal element.

"The basic notion of the German organizer has been to control production definitely, leaving it to the resourcefulness of the individual producers in the cartel to make more or less profit out of the proportion of the production allotted to them; the basic notion of the American organizer has been, usually, to create a perfected and consolidated instrument, success following naturally as a result of its well-balanced and skillfully organized proportions. German cartel organizations has contemplated that all its constituent firms should remain in business; American commercial centralization usually has meant that the weaker or for any reason undesirable elements should go out of business, suggesting that the strong native individualism of our people rises to the surface even when an effort tending toward pure collectivism is attempted.

"The highest degree of syndication in Germany has been reached in the mining and iron industries. Although the number of cartels existing in these industries is not large, they are mainly well organized and very strong; for example, the Rhenish-Westphalian coal syndicate in Essen, the Stahlwerks-Verband, or steel syndicate in Dusseldorf.

"The Imperial German government issued statistics in 1905 showing that there were 385 cartels existing at that time in Germany, but these figures are said not to contain the Konditionskartelle (those, e. g. fixing terms of sale other than prices), and numerous other confederations, the existence of which was not then within the knowledge of the authorities. When these statistics were made up, it was understood that about 12,000 establishments were members of syndicates. The following recapitulation shows the variety of industries covered by commercial combinations in 1905.

Coal mining	19
Stones and earths	27
Brick industry	132
Earthenware industry	4
Glass industry	10
Metal trade	11
Iron industry	62
Machinery, electricity	2
Chemical industries	46
Textiles	31
Paper industry	6
Leather trade	6
Wool industry	15
Food products	7
Miscellaneous	7
Total	385

Consul Talbot J. Albert of Brunswick, reports in reference to the German potash syndicate:

"The potash syndicate furnishes an excellent example of what constitutes a German syndicate and what distinguishes it from an American trust. It is only by the study of a concrete example that the difference can be clearly understood.

"There are two most significant and material distinctions. The first is that the potash syndicate and most of the other syndicates have, as such, no capital or shares of stock which are dealt in on the stock exchange, as is the case with the American trust. The second distinction is that a syndicate is a combination for a limited period of time, usually five years, while the life of a trust is indefinite.

"The units composing the potash syndicate and most mining syndicates in Germany are companies of two kinds, namely those whose capital is divided into shares called 'kuxe' and those whose shares are of the ordinary joint-stock variety with limited liability. The shares of the joint stock companies are unassessable, but on the other hand ' kuxe ' are shares that are assessable at any time and are of unlimited liability. These 'kuxe' and shares of the individual concerns are dealt in on the exchanges of the large cities of Germany.

"Each company that is a member of a German syndicate has its representative on the board of management of the trust, and this board fixes the quota of production allowed each mine and generally administers the affairs of the entire combination under the constitution and by-laws (called statuten). The constitution and by-laws must be signed by each concern entering the syndicate and the provisions therein contained strictly observed under penalties enforceable in courts of law. The mutual obligations of the syndicate toward its constituent members and the duties of the members toward the syndicate are thus protected by law, making it a legal combination.

"The weak point in this form of organization is the dissension that often arises as to the quotas allowed the different members. Each company wants as large an allotment as it can get and there is disappointment if it is not received. For this reason, upon the expiration of the life of a syndicate, there is always uncertainty as to whether it will be renewed owing to the competition among the various constituent firms.

"The object of a syndicate is not monopoly but the prevention of competition. It is an agreement among producers of an article to prevent overproduction, so that the supply will conform to the demand and reasonable profits may be obtained. There is no outcry in Germany against syndicates; they are generally looked upon as organizations advantageous to well-regulated trade.

"The German potash syndicate, a combination of 76 companies, is now practically in complete control of the potash mining interests of Germany.

"As Germany is the only country in the world in which potash mines are being profitably worked, and as the mines are controlled by one combination and their production and sales of potash regulated by the special law recently passed by the Reichstag, the German potash syndicate may be fitly termed a legally reënforced trust. The unworked potash field in the Duchy of Brunswick, Province of Hanover, and elsewhere in Germany is immense, and the kali supply is inexhaustible, but under the law, no new mine or combination of mines can become successful competitors of the syndicate. As soon as the mine reaches the productive stage, it it taken into the syndicate.

"The propaganda conducted by the syndicate makes the demand for potash equal the supply. Special prices for manure salts are given by the syndicate to the German agriculturists and special railroad rates for transportation are granted by the government. The syndicate with its representatives in the United States and in other foreign countries will regulate the foreign prices for potash. This is an important matter for foreign agriculturists and for foreign consumers of chlorate of potash for the manufacture of powder and other explosives."

From the foregoing, it will be seen that Germany regulates the trusts to secure the best advantage to the public at large, while in America, the trusts after having been allowed to reach a high point of development, through the inefficiency of the government in not enforcing the law as it exists, must now be regulated or reorganized to the great disturbance of business and loss to the general public.

Developments have proved that the Sherman law has teeth, and that the courts will enforce it. The fact that it has not been enforced is due to the negligence of the administrations of Harrison, Cleveland and McKinley, and only with Roosevelt was a beginning made. While these presidents may be blamed, the public itself is most to blame, since it has only been its belated voice of protest that has finally caused action, a voice which should have been heard long ago.

In England trusts are very quickly killed by the public boycotting them. In America, the slight advantages temporarily offered by the trusts overshadows the certain subsequent higher prices, and the public patronize them until the small dealer is exterminated, later paying well for its folly when competition has disappeared.

The cost of breaking up or reorganizing the trusts is enormous, both in the direct expense of governmental legal actions and in costs to the trusts themselves, while it is incalculable in the disturbance to business.

The business of a self governing country is to govern itself. When it neglects the matter, it pays a frightful price. America is paying the price to-day, and the paying is by no means nearing an end. Its future depends upon the firmness with which it proceeds to discipline its law breaking citizens in high places.

The responsibility lies not alone with the native American but with the naturalized voter as well, and particularly with the German voter who has known better conditions in Germany. Naturalized voters would hold the balance of power should they act as a unit. According to the U. S. Census there are 6,646,817 foreign born white males of voting age in the United States of which number 3,034,117 are naturalized or 45.6%. Seventy per cent. of the 1,278,679 Germans are naturalized, the largest proportion, followed closely by the Irish, while only 26% of the 737,-150 Russians and 18% of the 712,827 Italians have become citizens.

Those who are not well informed are of the impression that Americans are largely of Anglo-Saxon stock but the figures disprove that belief. In the 90 years from 1820 to 1910 the immigration was as follows: Germans, 5,400,000; Irish, 4,800,000; Austro-Hungarian, 3,200,000; Italian, 3,100,000; English, Scotch and Welsh, 2,800,000; Russian, 2,400,000; Swedish, 1,100,000; French, 480,000 and other countries about 5,000,000, a grand total of 28,000,000. In 1820 the population was about 9,000,000, including a considerable Irish immigration. It is incontrovertible from these figures that the so-called Anglo-Saxon is but a small minority of the whole and that the effort to classify Americans as an Anglo-Saxon race is futile.

Germany in the last century has furnished us nearly 6,000,-000 immigrants, and it is obvious, if this element of the population acted as a unit and overcame its aversion to political activity, that much greater efficiency would result. Had the German ideals of public office been enforced rather than existing systems of patronage America would be a much better governed and more prosperous country to-day. It behooves the German element to rally to the standard of good government and overcome the disintegrating influences at work.

CHAPTER X

MUNICIPAL SOCIALISM

A great city-building epoch—How inventions have caused humanity to gravitate to cities—The reproach of city self government—German civic pride—Why home rule is denied to our cities—"Sacred" concerts in New York—Liberty and the size of spots on a comedian's vest—Lack of city patriotism—Debasing effects of private ownership of public franchises—The battlements of commerce—Masterpieces of architectural ugliness—Carnival of civic chaos—Rudiments of architectural taste in engineering works—Municipal Art Commission—The redeeming sky scrapers—Far-sightedness of the planning of German cities as wholes—American cities at the mercy of private landowners—Barbarous water fronts of American cities—German cities as great land owners and land lords—75 lessons which American cities may learn abroad.

THE city is the great factor in the life of the world to-day, particularly in America and in Germany. In a little more than a generation, a great transposition has taken place. The rural districts have been drained of their surplus of men, a surplus composed of its best blood and brain. The lure of the city, its greater possibilities and advantages have produced great changes which have taken place rapidly and which are continuing at the same if not at a more rapid rate.

What has brought about this wonderful change? There have always been cities since the earliest times. Cities of prehistoric epochs are constantly being unearthed, cities whose very names and existence were forgotten for ages, but never before has there been the growth of cities at the expense of the country that is now being witnessed, and the remarkable development of the building of cities, which makes the present an epoch in the history of the world comparable with the great city building epochs of the Romans in the age of the Antonines and the city building of the middle ages, produced by political considerations.

The underlying cause of the growth of cities in modern times is found in the numerous triumphs of invention during the last

115

fifty years. As has been pointed out, every labor saving invention reduces the stress between humanity and nature. Either more human beings may be fed and clothed and housed at the same outlay of human labor, or a given number may be made much more comfortable. The invention of cloth making machinery gives the working girl of to-day clothes which only nobility could afford in former ages, and the improvements in iron and steel and cement make houses far cheaper than formerly. Harvesting machinery and other improved farming implements enable greater crops to be raised with no more labor, making food cheaper. Summed up in their collective effects the enormous number of labor saving inventions have worked themselves out as a freeing from the bondage of the soil of a great proportion who previously found it to their advantage to remain on the farm to feed and clothe humanity. Before the days of improved farm machinery, a hundred farmers had to labor, for example, to supply the food of a hundred city dwellers, while the city dwellers supplied the farmers' needs in manufactured products. Now with improved farming machinery, fifty farmers, to assume a round figure, which may or may not be correct, can supply the wants of the same hundred city dwellers and in addition of the fifty farmers who have gone to town, while the city dwellers with their improved appliances can supply the fifty farmers left in the country and the fifty who have moved to town, with much better goods at less expenditure of labor than before. The comfort of all is thus greatly increased, and the less rigorous conditions enable the population to increase more readily.

The extent to which this process has been carried on may be best understood by consulting the statistics of city growth. Over 40% of the people of the United States live in cities. From 60 to 80% is the ratio in some of the eastern states. In our population of 90,000,000 there are 35,000,000 who would now be on farms instead of in cities if former conditions had continued.

In Germany a similar change has occurred as will be noticed from figures given later. The city is the thing of to-day, a great, cruel, criminal thing of poverty and disease, with vivid contrasts of wealth, like the glint of a diamond on a scrofulous hand, a place where human nature may find its own level, high or low, free of the restraints of the village and farm.

America's problem, the world's problem of to-day is the city, and it is the problem of problems, how humanity may best direct itself for its own good in its new found liberties, how the city may be prevented from doing the evil that is in it and made to render its advantages to humanity; in short, how the city may be made to make good.

The modern city, thus a new thing, has brought new problems and these must be dealt with in a new way. The city in America has proved a great disappointment, a reproach to republican institutions and a well-spring of pessimistic forebodings. But the city in America has not had a fair chance. Conditions have forced it to pursue its growth along the lines of least resistance, and strange growths have resulted, like the roots of an oak among flagstones and tombs, bursting the bonds of the past and embedding their fragments in the new growth.

What the possibilities of the American city are, may be seen from the development of cities in Germany, where the city has had every chance, where human nature and every social force works with the city and for its development, rather than in opposition. The city is the pride of modern Germany and made so by the same class of men, its leading business men, who work so tirelessly against the interests of the city in America.

The American city is poisoned at its well springs, principally by three causes, none of which operate to the disadvantage of the German city.

Perhaps the most important is the fact that American cities do not have home rule. Their affairs are regulated by legislators of the state in which the city is located. Their form of government is imposed on them by the state, their charters are granted and amended by the state and their officials often subject to removal by the governor of the state. The patronage of the cities, their best interests and everything that affects them are thus made the pawns of state politicians, and what the city might do to better itself, the politicians of the state usually block. This they can safely do, as they come, with the exception of the small delegation of the city itself, from other parts of the state whose votes usually hold them to no responsibility for what has been done to undermine the city's progress. In fact the rural voter is pleased, rather than otherwise, if his representative takes part in a scheme to disappoint the ambition of the city.

Many brilliant men of municipal renown, like Tom Johnson of Cleveland, Sam L. Jones and Brand Whitlock of Toledo and

Hazen S. Pingree of Detroit, with the best interests of their cities at heart, municipal patriots in fact, have worn out their lives in attempting to gain from rural legislators permission to do for the city what should be done.

It amounts to a most flagrant violation of the first principal of American independence, the right of self government. Besides producing bad results for all concerned, it has its ludicrous features as well.

The "rube" legislators of New York State, for example, prescribe the nature of the Sunday recreation which may be indulged in by the inhabitants of New York city. What this may degenerate into was well illustrated recently in a case over the violation of the law against Sunday theatrical performances; plays being prohibited while sacred concerts are permitted. The vaudeville managers are among the most saintly denizens of this mundane sphere, if we judge by the avidity they display for giving "sacred concerts" in their theaters on Sundays.

In order to show the public the wonders of providence, as an example to indolent humans, instances of the industry and learning of the lower animal kingdom are frequently made a part of such "sacred concerts" as, for example, tamed elephants and mice and "Daniel" in the Lion's Den with real lions.

Among the wonderfully designed rules, however, by which a theatrical performance is placed in the goat column and a sacred concert in the lamb brigade, is the prohibition of costume and changes of scenery and the use of a curtain. Thus in a "sacred concert" a single setting is used, the curtain remains up throughout the evening and the performers appear in their street attire.

On one historic occasion, a comedian appeared wearing a vest with prominent spots of purple. He was arrested on the charge of taking part in a theatrical performance, namely of appearing in costume. He denied the allegation and asserted that the spots on his vest were merely an evidence of his personal taste. He wore them on the street that way because he liked them large. The arresting officer declared they compared in size with fried eggs but the comedian considered them as representing plums. The controversy, thus, between the mighty opposites of church and the amusement world, of rural restraint and city liberty, resolved itself into a judicial interpretation of the size of spots on a vest; the magistrate deciding that in the particular case, though extreme, the comedian's taste was not illegal. Thus was justice vindicated.

In New York, however, the city has reached a point where its delegation in the legislature is almost as large as the rest of the state combined. When New York city gains the majority, it will be the first city in America to have home rule, and to control the state as well as itself. Provided political divisions do not vitiate this control, the city, responsible to itself alone should make considerable progress, which now lies beyond its legal powers.

American cities, too, have always lacked the political individuality of the European city. The American city is young. It has not existed for centuries, as have most of the large European cities, and there have never been times when an American city was a sovereign power, as has been the case with European cities in past ages. The American state has always been the smallest sovereign. Even this was more theoretical than real and existed only for a short time in the case of the original thirteen colonies a century and a third ago. The American thus has had no occasion to feel any patriotic interest in his city. No Philadelphian for example would ever conceive taking up any more deadly arms against New York or Pittsburg than a baseball bat.

In Germany, however, the remains of the former sovereignty of cities are still seen as in Hamburg, Lübeck and Bremen, where, as members of what was once the Hanseatic League, they have individually representation in the Reichstag as independent states with certain important exemptions and privileges.

The city in America is not thus the firm unit that it is abroad, and not the rallying point of patriotism. The average American feels more pride in Washington as a city than he does in his own town, and this lack of interest will always work more or less against the development of American cities.

Private ownership of public utilities, the great profits arising from franchises of various kinds, principally street railways, and the letting of great contracts of construction to private bidders, is the second cause that degrades city government in the United States.

The merchants and business men interest themselves in securing from the city these valuable rights, and a large body of the most aggressive men in any city, as well as outside capitalists, are generally interested either directly or indirectly in inducing the city to grant them the franchise, and in preventing competitors from getting the prize. In this endless struggle for franchises and valuable concessions, the officials of the city having power to make the grants are subjected to every species of influence, social, fraternal, political and financial, that can be devised. Fights over franchises thus debauch the city government, and distract attention from other necessities of the city.

In Germany, where the cities largely operate their own public utilities, no such condition exists, for the simple reason that no rich franchise prizes are at stake. Public operation of public utilities will undoubtedly prove for American cities, one of the greatest blessings that can ever come to them, if properly carried out.

And this form of municipal socialism will prove much more of a success than it has when the system of longer tenures of office is applied, and the commission form of government more generally adopted. The constant changes of administration and personnel disorganize the forces of municipally operated utilities, and thus play into the hands of capitalists, who desire to continue the present system, by furnishing bad examples of public operation.

A third cause of the lack of progress of American cities is found in the high regard accorded the rights of private property. The principle that a man's house is his castle is carried to such an extreme that the castle becomes a mountain of inconvience not to say of loss and damage to every one else.

In most American cities, a man may build any sort of house that pleases him, wherever he may own or lease the land. This unbridled liberty, or license, more properly speaking, has produced incongruous and heterogeneous cities principally distinguished as collections of buildings which are masterpieces of ugliness.

Although this system or lack of system has produced the great skyscrapers of New York and other large cities, evolving in an artistic sense an architecture distinctively American, it has had the effect of making American streets strings of unrelated structures in which all sense of beauty and proportion is lost.

It is a matter of wonder, passing through an American city, where the hordes of utterly unfit architects have come from that have filled the land with such frightful examples of their art. How the American can feel any interest in the purely utilitarian business buildings in which he transacts his affairs, or any attachment to the conglomeration of rooms he calls his home, is difficult to see. Indeed, it is surprising how he can find the place he calls home, for on many streets whole blocks of houses will either be duplicates of each other or in two series of duplicates, each alternate house being similar, like an endless sandwich with layers of bread and corned beef indefinitely.

America is only waking up, only commencing to exist architecturally. Some of the sky scrapers and some of the public and private buildings are good, but the taste of the public is not yet formed. An ugly house is simply a house. It gives no pain on account of being ugly, for the eye of the public is uneducated and as little troubled by bad architecture as the eye of the illiterate by bad spelling.

Mr. Ernest Flagg, designer of the Singer Building, and of many other notable structures, in an article "Are American Cities Going Mad Architecturally?" in the *New York Times* of August 6, 1911, describes conditions truthfully when he says:

"Our artistic sense is undeveloped. There is no great body of amateurs here, such as is found in more refined communities, who are capable of analyzing our productions and placing them at their true worth. It is only a question of time, however, when public taste will become more cultivated, and when that time does come, there will be a great tumbling of reputations which now stand high.

"Our architecture smacks too much of archaeology; it is not modern; we use modern methods of construction and antique methods of design. Why do not the people in the United States recognize that every great work of art which has had an underlying reputation was strictly modern when it was made? No copy, or adaptation, no matter how cleverly done, can endure the test of time and stand as a work of art.

"We are veritable barbarians in matters of taste, we ransack Europe for old fragments which though they may be charming in their original situation, become little better than so much rubbish when set up in the midst of inharmonious surroundings. We deck out our houses and gardens with these things in precisely the same way and with as little regard to propriety as savages when they array themselves with incongruous objects which they obtain from European traders.

"The savages which Henry Hudson, on his second visit, found wearing the hatchet heads he had sold them, as neck ornaments, present no more comical picture than our art amateur often does in his use of spoils from European churches and monasteries.

"One sees gardens attached to shingled cottages, decked out with marble seats, vases and fountains taken from Italian villas. Houses in our cities are fitted out with fragments from European palaces which are as much out of harmony with the surroundings as a steam engine would be in a mediæval church. Sometimes whole interiors have been taken from a European building and set up here. Rich men's houses are turned into museums, where there are as many styles as there are rooms, all warring with each other and with the exterior of the building.

"We have been having a very carnival of vulgarity, and an ostentatious display of wealth and bad taste by people who are regarded as leaders in refinement.

"In the midst of the chaos and confusion, with the public taste at as low an ebb as it probably ever reached among people who pretend to be civilized, with architecture for the most part in the hands of men who had little training in, or knowledge of, even the elementary principles of design, our new methods of building were ushered in and we were called upon to deal with a problem the proper solution of which called for a more technical and artistic skill than we possessed.

"The time is at hand when the absurdity and bad taste of our past methods will be fully understood and freely admitted. We shall cease to wonder that cultivated foreigners are not favorably impressed by our tall buildings, and will set ourselves to work to make them as perfect and reasonably artistic as they are ingenious and daring mechanically and constructively."

The lack of artistic feeling for architecture has its counterpart in not only other structures, such as bridges, docks and terminals, but also in various kinds of designs where the utilitarian purpose crowds out every other consideration. Engineers particularly design their works with little attention to the beautiful and in the most important feature of modern times, the rapidity with which the numerous discoveries in science are applied to commercial purposes, be it for a peaceful gigantic liner, or a powerful and destructive dreadnought, or for a stupendous bridge structure spanning the Hudson or Mississippi, or the housing of machinery for science and art for the utilization of natural resources of the Niagara, or the many other phenomenal power resources, all of which, with thousands of others are monuments to modern sciences; there is lacking in all the touch of artistry.

In order to have such engineering undertakings appeal to the public or layman, it is essential to give them consideration from the artistic standpoint, and this is doubly important when such structures are to be located in the vicinity of a considerable community. To secure such effects it is advisable that the engineer associate himself with an architect, as the engineer, though a good statistician and mathematician, rarely combines these qualities with architectural knowledge and particularly with artistic feeling.

As these structures form an important feature in modern practice, they should be of special interest to the architect as being work for which his particular training has made him efficient, and if he is to maintain the traditions of the past, it is necessary that he should take a like interest in the progress of modern times, which to the greatest extent is covered by engineering skill, although this does not seem perfectly clear to the mind of the layman.

While notable achievements are to the credit of the modern American architect, and while numerous individual buildings compare favorably with the best work of European architects, the failure of American city architecture as a whole lies importantly in the fact that each building is designed for itself alone, as if the eye of the spectator could see but one object at a time. No attention whatever is paid to adjoining buildings, indeed the architect seems to have taken a page from the writer of advertisements who endeavors to have contiguous advertisements as dissimilar as possible, thus attracting attention by the harsh, not to say painful, contrast between them. There are in New York and in other cities, numerous examples of buildings which have been designed with the idea of making them "stand out" by being as complete and abrupt a contrast as possible to the previously erected buildings.

The freedom accorded to private ownership has made such monstrosities possible.

The German city, on the other hand, has grown beautiful by denying the right of the individual to disfigure the landscape at his own sweet will, on the only condition that he pays the carpenter and the mason.

The city as a whole is planned, then its streets as wholes, and the buildings then are permitted to be built only in accordance with the general scheme which has been laid out.

Mr. Frederick C. Howe, an eminent authority on the subject, in "City Building in Germany" in *Scribner's Magazine* of May, 1910, states:

"I know of no cities in the modern world which compare with those which have arisen in Germany during the past twenty years. There are none in Great Britain, from which country official delegations are constantly crossing the North Sea to study the achievements of the German city. There are none in France, in which country the building of cities has made but little progress since the achievements of Baron Houssman made Paris the beautiful city that it is.

"Important as is the honesty and the efficiency of the German city, it is the bigness of vision, boldness of execution and far-sighted outlook on the future that are most amazing. Germany is building her cities as Bismarck perfected the army before Sadowa and Sedan; as the Empire is building its war ships and merchantmen; as she develops her waterways and educational systems. In city building as in other matters, all science is the hand maiden of politics. The engineer and the architect, the artist and the expert in hygiene are alike called upon to contribute to the city's making. The German cities are thinking of to-morrow as well as of to-day, and the generations to follow as well as the generation that is now upon the stage. Germany alone sees the city as the center of the civilization of the future, and Germany alone is building her cities so as to make them contribute to the happiness, health and well-being of the people. This seems to be the primary consideration. And it is unique in the modern world.

"Farsightedness characterizes Germany in all things. Alone among the nations of the earth, Germany is treating the new behemoth of civilization as a creature to be controlled, and made to serve rather than to impair or destroy humanity. In city building as in other things, Germany calls in her experts. If they do not already exist, she creates them. Town planning has become a science, just as much a science as the building of engines. And it is treated as such. A school has recently been opened in Berlin devoted to the subject. Exhibition of things municipal and congresses of various kinds are promoted. There has grown up a substantial literature on city building. There are experts like Stubben, Fisher, Gurlett and Baumeister, who go from city to city and consult with the local authorities on their projects. Nothing is haphazard. Nothing is left to chance. The get-rich-speculator and the jerry-builder are subordinated to the will of the community acting through its permanent and expert body of city officials.

"The German city is being built on a scale of generosity which halts at no expense. Its public school buildings rival in splendor the best modern buildings of our great universities. And the equipment is of the same order. I know of no public schools, even in New York or Boston, that seem as costly in their construction or more complete in every detail than those of half a dozen German cities. They contain assembly rooms and vestibules of the most artistic sort, while the gymnasiums and provisions for recreation are equal to those of the best schools in America. And when we consider the relative poverty of the German people and the burdens of taxation and armaments, the attitude of our own cities toward these matters seems positively parsimonious and niggardly.

"German cities recognize the controlling influence of the land on the life of the community, and they have become great landlords. The town of Breslau, with a population about the size of Cleveland, Ohio, owns twenty square miles of land, or 12,800 acres. But Berlin is the greatest landlord of all. That city owns 39,000 acres, mostly outside of the city, while Munich owns 13,000 acres, and Strassburg, 12,000 acres. German cities also possess great forests and they are constantly adding to their possessions.

"The motive of all this beauty, harmony, business enterprise and foresight is so obvious to the German that he cannot comprehend why it should be questioned. "Why does a merchant erect a fine store-room or build himself a mansion?" he asks. The German city thinks as an individual thinks about his business and his home. A finished city attracts people. It brings manufacturers and business. People choose a beautiful city as a place of residence. Visitors make pilgrimages to it. Well-educated children make better citizens, better artisans. The street railways, gas works, docks and other enterprises pay their way. They even make money. But more than this, they are a necessary part of the city, and of course they should be owned by it. If it be suggested that all this is socialistic, the German business man shrugs his shoulders and says, "It may be, but it is good business." It is much better than good business, it is good statesmanship."

At a meeting of the City Club, New York, December 4, 1911, the German Envoy, Count Von Bernstorff, tells how municipalities in Germany are governed and stated in part as follows:

"To be a Burgherr of a city in Germany, one must have a definite and tangible interest in the community. In the theory and practice of city government in Europe, a city has always been regarded as a corporation which had business to conduct and property to administer. According to this theory, a distinction is made between the civil and political rights, on one side, and on the other, what may be called municipal rights, the right to take active part in administering city property and determining city policy. As to the latter right, it is felt in Germany that the people exercising it should have some evident stake in the corporation whose affairs they are called upon to administer and control.

"The first thing that will strike a foreigner in German cities is the number and variety of the functions with which, for the benefit of the citizens, the public authority charges itself.

"In a modern German town, new streets are not the creation of private enterprise. The town council lays out the streets in accordance with the interests and needs of the whole population. There are no restrictions as to the width of them or of their construction. The council is in full control and can do as it pleases. In this way, open spaces are distributed all over the city. The council also decides what classes of buildings are to be erected. Some districts are devoted to factories, others to mixed quarters, where both dwelling houses and work shops may be erected, while the rest is set aside for a residential district.

"Most town councils not only supply water, gas, electric lighting and power, and make a good profit in relief of local expenditure, but also finance all the hospitals, treatment of phthisis, and all the schools, including colleges for advanced technical instruction. In most places the municipalities own and work the tramways with very low fares and very high profits; they maintain fire stations with the most advanced apparatus and they have abattoirs regulated by veterinary science for the slaughter of animals for human food. In such cities as Cologne, Frankfort and Manheim they manage enormous docks for the accommodation of fresh water navigation; they maintain for the recreation of the citizens museums, picture galleries, parks, playgrounds, baths, bands of music and even theaters.

"The city of Frankfort, for instance, and the institutions under its control, possess within its boundaries 12,800 acres of land, that is, more than half the entire area of the city. Outside, the municipality owns 3,800 acres of land, making a total of 16,600 acres. Of this, 8,500 acres are covered with wood, which will probably be used for building purposes. The largest part of the timber is produced by the municipal forest, or Stadtwald, purchased from the German emperors at the end of the fourteenth century.

"Now with reference to the provision of good and healthy dwellings for the working classes, there are in Frankfort, as in all large and ancient cities, a number of undesirable dwellings. But the area in which these dwellings exist is constantly decreasing, because the dwellings are being transformed into offices. A great many old houses have disappeared, owing to the laying out of new streets. These new streets, which cost many millions of marks, were made chiefly to secure better lines of communication, but at the same time they have improved the housing conditions. The building regulations also tend in this direction. At a very early period regulations existed which forbade the erection of unhealthy houses.

"Berlin, Cologne, Munich, Dresden and Frankfort are rich in landed estates, which form a large part of the city's assets. Leipsic is one of the cities which has devoted a portion of its real estate to the housing of the working classes. That municipality has leased for a hundred years at a low rent to a philanthropic building society, a large piece of communal land in the environs for the erection of cheap houses. The majority of the houses have to contain three and some of them more than four rooms. This society cannot transfer its leasehold rights to third parties without the consent of the municipality, and in the event of doing so, both the offending contract and the lease itself may be canceled.

"The municipality undertook the initial construction of all squares, roads and footpaths, and went further in undertaking to advance money on mortgages for building purposes should the building society's revenues prove inadequate, with the provision that the society must refund the loan by regular repayments in such a manner that on termination of the lease the mortgage will be redeemed.

"The following is the method of town planning followed by the municipality. First of all, a plan is made showing the general scheme of the proposed new streets. The public is invited to inspect the plan, and objections are received and considered by the body which has to sanction the plans, and which is known as the Bezirksausschuss.

"Only after the plan has been approved are buildings permitted to be erected. It is in the interests of the land owners that the street plans should be approved, and it rarely happens that sanction has to be refused to a plan on account of objections brought against it. Of course, the municipality could not exercise this power of town planning unless they had the power by expropriation. This power is given by law, and there is no need to go to Parliament for special powers in a case where expropriation is necessary. But as a matter of fact, it is rarely used.

"Within the last ten years, the city of Frankfort has expended more than $50,000,000 in the purchase of land. In German towns all works which have the character of a monopoly are to a great extent municipalized."

Municipal socialism, thus so far advanced in Germany, is one of the large subjects of modern progress. Its ramifications and advantages are both numerous and beneficial. A brief summary, including some seventy-five items, of the principal concrete lessons to be learned by America abroad, is given in the *New York World* of October 1, 1911:

STREETS; BILLBOARDS; PAVING; LAMP-POSTS; SEWAGE DISPOSITION.

1. In Berlin, Frankfort and many other German cities, street advertising is practically confined to corner pillars. There are no billboards erected on vacant lots to conceal refuse, shelter vagrants and lower values.

2. The German capitals require that news-stands and street-booths shall contribute to rather than mar the vista.

3. Paris has numerous isles of safety in the middle of its streets, with artistic lamp-posts. These light both sides of the street and reduce the number of lamps to two-thirds or one-half the number needed where the posts are at the curbs.

4. Belgium has a national society for the introduction of art in the streets. Particular attention is paid to street fixtures —lamp-posts, street-name signs, house numbers, tramway stations, public-comfort stations, letter-boxes, fire-alarms, etc.

5. Practically all German cities save Hamburg have strict regulations to prevent offensive illuminated signs.

6. The sewers of Paris are also pipe galleries, carrying telegraph and telephone wires, water pipes, pneumatic tubes for letters and pipes for compressed-air service.

7. Glasgow has iron bins with hinged lids sunk along the curbing and into these the street litter is brushed during the day.

8. Vienna uses covered ash-carts. Curtains attached to the frame are pushed aside while ashes are emptied, thus preventing the dust from littering the streets.

9. The German cities have ordinances which suppress most of the street and waterside noises common to New York—the flat car-wheel, the night-long shrieking of tugboats, the blatant automobile horn, the scissors-grinder's bell, the peanut-vendor's steam whistle, the cries of sidewalk merchants.

10. Traffic regulations have been so skillfully drawn and firmly enforced in London that traffic now practically regulates itself.

11. Cologne, Hanover and other German cities are well provided with waste-paper receptacles. They look more like vases than garbage-cans, and are made of iron strips fastened to lamp-posts or trolley or telegraph poles.

12. Paris is cleaned and scrubbed every day before it awakes. Between 4 and 6 A. M. all the streets and sidewalks are swept, and many of them washed and disinfected.

13. Paris fines householders who do not take in the emptied ash-can by 7 o'clock.

14. Glasgow sweeps its streets at night.

15. Berlin has done best what most other European cities have done well. At a cost of $30,000,000 it has constructed a sewage-farms system covering an area almost equal to its own. Barren heath land was acquired well beyond the corporation limits and is being reclaimed by wastes which are pumped to it from central stations. The farms return a considerable revenue.

MUNICIPAL THRIFT ABROAD; FUEL FROM STREET WASTE.

16. Stuttgart gets a revenue from its parks and other tree-covered areas. These are under control of a forestry bureau which obtains enough money from timber and firewood to maintain lawns and paths, pay salaries and turn over 50% of its gross receipts to the city.

17. Amsterdam converts street wastes into fuel briquettes. These are produced at $1.15 a ton and sold at $1.40, making a profit of over $20,000 a year. Heretofore this waste has been disposed of at an annual loss of $18,000.

18. When Frankfort lays out parks, boulevards or docks it condemns land in excess of its needs and pays for the whole enterprise by reselling the surplus and thus reaping the benefits of the new values. There is no "honest graft" from "insiders' tips" as to land to be benefited.

19. According to Frederic C. Howe in the *Scribner's* of 1910, "there are 1,500 smaller towns and villages in Germany which derive so much revenue from the lands which they own that they are free from all local taxes. Five hundred of these communities are not only free from all local taxes but are able to declare a dividend of from $25 to $100 a year to each citizen as his share of the surplus earnings of the common lands."

20. The cities of Continental Europe consider beauty a municipal asset with a tangible cash value in that it makes life more enjoyable, elevates the public taste and brings in tourists.

BEAUTY IN ELEVATED ROADS; CLOCKS IN STREET CARS.

21. In Dresden and other cities surface cars do not stop at every corner. Stopping-places are about 220 yards apart and are marked by a post and shield. This permits the making of much better time.

22. In Berlin and most other German cities if you jump on a street car in motion you are required to alight at the next stopping-place.

23. Berlin's elevated roads are so designed as not greatly to detract from the sightliness of streets. The posts and girders almost realize Russell Sage's dream of an "ornamental iron structure" and the most uncompromising parts are masked by trees.

24. Berlin has so deadened the noise of passing elevated trains by flooring the structure with masonry that in concert

halls underneath one can listen with enjoyment to orchestral music.

25. Bremen does not permit the street cars to carry passengers in their aisles and strictly limits the number on platforms.

26. Hildesheim and many other German cities have clocks in all street cars.

POLITICS AND ADMINISTRATION; POLICEMEN WHO ARE TRUSTED.

27. Such is the dignity of London's County Council, such is British public spirit, that Cabinet Ministers do not disdain to sit in it.

28. The police of Plauen inspect the moving-picture theaters twice a week and a majority of the school-teachers assist them.

29. When a policeman brings a prisoner before a London Magistrate, "the Judge treats him as an impartial, honest and fearless personification of the law of the land—practically consults him as to what he thinks should be done with the defendant in minor cases. . . . Here the policemen is the man on trial." The words are those of William McAdoo, former New York Police Commissioner, now head of the Board of City Magistrates.

30. London largely separates the detectives from the uniformed force. As Mr. McAdoo says: "They are not even known by name and cannot be located by the uniformed policeman, and their names are certainly not bandied about by crooks as common property."

31. "The honesty and good character of an ordinary London constable," says Mr. McAdoo, "is taken to be as sure as that of the Prime Minister."

32. Berlin and other German cities have bureaus of statistics which enable citizens to obtain an up-to-date view of local affairs.

33. The floating population of all British cities—"the lodging-house vote"—is practically disfranchised for municipal purposes by the slight property qualifications required.

34. Glasgow has made street-sweeping, street-sprinkling and garbage disposal part of its sanitary government and put them under one jurisdiction.

35. Paris has placed under one department the care of the parks and of the tree-shaded streets, the lighting of thoroughfares and the erection and supervision of booths and kiosks.

36. Berlin has drafted nearly 4,000 citizens for poor relief. These are divided into upward of 250 local committees and every member is sponsor for specified families, with authority to attend to their wants. No compensation is given to these committees. Refusal to serve may be punished by tax increases or the suspension of civil and political privileges.

37. Glasgow has women as domiciliary visitors, known as "lady inspectors," who make suggestions as to cleanliness and household reform to poor families.

38. After child-birth Swiss cities require a six weeks' cessation from work by women wage-earners.

39. Cologne has official visitors of the poor, one of whom calls on every wage-earning woman who has given birth to a child. If the mother needs to go out to work, the fact is reported and a grant of money is made on condition that she stay at home and nurse her infant.

40. The general death-rate of illegitimate infants is twice that of legitimate ones. Leipsic constitutes every illegitimate child a ward of the municipality and its condition is inspected. The death-rate of such infants is now even less than that of legitimate ones.

41. Paris has nearly a hundred *classes de garde* for small children whose parents are employed away from home. The children are kept until their parents have returned from work.

42. Charlottenburg has established a hospital school in a pine forest near the city for physically weak children under medical treatment. Tables and benches are set out under the fir trees and meals are served as well as lessons taught. "I marveled," said Sir John Gorst, "at the administrative ability which had at so small a cost provided such a great portion of health and happiness."

43. Glasgow maintains municipal wash-houses where for four cents an hour a woman may use a stall with fixed tubs for hot and cold water and appliances for steam boiling and drying.

44. Paris, like many other cities, has municipal pawnshops— the Mont de Piété—with three large auxiliaries and above a score of branches. These loan on an average $5 a year to every man, woman and child.

RAILWAY STATIONS WITH BEAUTIFUL SURROUNDINGS.

45. Paris has a belt railroad following the perimeter of the city. This connects the various railroad stations, and both freight and passenger traffic are facilitated.

46. The railway stations in German cities give upon plazas of grass and flowers surrounded by hotels and municipal buildings so designed as to produce a single architectural effect.

47. Berlin, Dresden and other German cities study the winds and refuse to let factories locate in outlying districts whence their smoke or odors might be blown into the city.

48. Düsseldorf has provided or regulated the designs for factories, office buildings and department stores, and these are ornamented with statues, frescoes and mosaics.

49. Paris and Brussels have improved advertising signs by offering prizes for the most artistic.

50. Germany has developed a school of commercial architecture headed by Alfred Messel. Wertheim's department store and the Rheingold restaurant in Berlin and the offices of the Allgemeine Zeitung in Munich are accounted in as good taste as the best public buildings.

BEAUTIFUL RIVER BANKS WITHIN EUROPEAN CITIES.

51. Instead of using their rivers to carry off sewage, instead of permitting unsightly commercial structures to occupy their shores, European cities have treated the rivers as assets of beauty and enjoyment. London has the Victoria Embankment upon the Thames—a downtown riverside park. Paris has lined the Seine with stone quays and faced it with public buildings and palaces. Cologne has occupied nearly all the Rhine river-front with stone embankments and tree-bordered avenues. Budapest has its river-front streets higher than the quays of the Danube and these are lined with fine public and private buildings. In the Brühl Terrace overlooking the Elbe, Dresden has "the Balcony of Europe." Berlin has built stone quays along the Spree and planted the banks with trees. It has made stone and cement walls for its canals.

52. The maritime cities of Europe insist that commerce shall make terms with beauty on their harbor-fronts. Hamburg and Bremen have handsome warehouses in a modified mediæval style The water-front of Antwerp and Stockholm is walled with cement and stone. The quays of Havre are recreation

centers and the buildings must conform to a general architectural plan.

53. Hamburg gets its drinking-water from the Elbe. In 1893, following the cholera outbreak of 1892, it installed the greatest filtration plant in the world, a system of subsidence basins and filters. Water which before entering these basins contained millions of cholera germs to the cubic inch emerged as clear as a mountain stream.

54. Stockholm, Paris, Liège and Budapest have bridges with architecturally imposing plaza approaches.

55. Dresden, Vienna and Amsterdam have introduced sculpture into their bridges with a monumental effect.

56. Instead of making its show island an asylum for paupers and criminals, Paris has on the Ile de la Cité its stateliest cathedral, its central Courts of Justice, a great hospital, the Tribunal of Commerce, the Prefecture of Police, &c.

GROUPED BUILDINGS; NEW STREETS; VINES AND FLOWERS; THE
CITY BEAUTIFUL.

57. European cities are discarding the checker-board street plan. Paris led the way in Napoleon III.'s time when Baron Haussmann, Prefect of the Seine, built great boulevards and avenues by the hundred, laid out diagonal avenues between important points and constructed engirdling boulevards. The sum of $240,000,000 was spent in this work, and last year it was decided to devote $175,000,000 more thereto.

58. London has done a similar but smaller work in King's-Way. The German cities are following neither the checker-board nor the radial avenue, ring-boulevard plan. Their new streets wind perceptibly so as to open fresh vistas and permit of collateral effects of parking and statuary.

59. Instead of locating their public buildings at random, the capitals of Europe arrange them with relation to each other and to some park, open space or boulevard, so that they contribute to one central effect. The finest is the Ring-strasse of Vienna, and other notable examples are Berlin's Unter den Linden and Lustgarten, Moscow's Kremlin, Dresden's Zwinger, the Louvre region of Paris and the Grande Place of Brussels.

60. In Dresden citizens have undertaken to induce every landlord and tenant to decorate yards, buildings and casements with plants, vines, shrubs and window-boxes. The authorities have co-operated by decorating municipal buildings, and at a

small expenditure the summer aspect of the city has been transformed.

61. The color sense has been indulged in all Russian cities. Building exteriors are of plaster to protect the brick from the frost, and every year these are repaired and repainted, and red, blue, buff, green, white and gilt diversified with mosaics are successfully employed.

62. Every important European city has regulations restricting the height of buildings, the width of balconies, the projection of cornices, the size of windows, and the character of lamps, signs, awnings, fences and doorways.

SCHOOLS OF TOWN-PLANNING; SAVING BEAUTIFUL FEATURES.

63. Ancient Athens and Rome set us an example of civic centers in the Acropolis and the Forum.

64. Frankfort purchased a number of mediæval buildings near the City Hall and restored them to the original style, that they should be in harmony with it.

65. Berlin has a school of town-planning.

66. Germany has experts like Stubben, Fischer, Gurlett, Henrici and Baumeister, who give advice on town-planning and travel from city to city. It is a new profession—"Städtebau."

67. Frankfort has built an exposition hall about the size of Madison Square Garden.

68. Munich has a group of exposition buildings comprising an auditorium, a theater, a hall for exhibits and a summer concert garden.

69. When a new street is opened in Brussels or Paris prizes running as high as $4,000 in Brussels and equal to one-half the street tax in Paris are offered by the authorities for the most artistic façades.

70. Vienna remits a percentage of taxes to landlords who will tear down an old building and put up a bigger and better one.

71. Copenhagen gives a prize every year to the architect who designs the most sightly building and best harmonizes it with older buildings about it.

72. Paris requires that all office and house fronts shall be periodically repaired or repainted, so that the street shall appear neat and fresh.

73. All wide Paris streets are in effect parks. They have

rows of shade trees. Many of them have a central park strip planted with trees, grass and flowers, and benches are placed here. Along chief streets are perhaps 100,000 trees, a large number for a city so compactly built.

74. In practically all European cities pavements are kept constantly in good repair.

75. All those European cities whose good government has something to teach America are managed not by politicians but by experts.

The civic pride of the citizens of American cities, so long practically non-existent, is now growing and the spirit of the movement is finding its greatest expression in the re-planning of cities.

During the last two decades, and principally within the last few years, some seventy-five cities have taken up the subject and have prepared more or less elaborate plans, while in numerous other cities the movement is taking form.

This means a greatly increased activity in building construction and the creation of a demand for a better class of buildings both architecturally and otherwise. It means a large amount also of alterations and remodeling, and it is from every point of view of the greatest importance to the public in general.

To be familiar with city planning is a duty which the city authorities, architects and engineers owe not only to themselves, but to the public, for even if they are not directly interested in the projects which may be put forward, the community looks to them for guidance in forming its opinions on the subject.

In many of the cities which have undertaken city planning, the plans evolved have been of the most elaborate and extensive character, and the draughtsmanship with which they have been prepared has made them beautiful objects of art. Unfortunately, however, in many cases, that is all they are, and their adoption in practice would be little short of a disaster to the city. They are attractive but impracticable, and dangerous in the extreme, not only to the cities which are tempted to adopt them, but to the whole city planning movement, since important failures are certain to react upon and tend to discourage other cities in their plans.

A city, considered in its essentials, is an apparatus of an

operative character and a means of operation for those who make use of its facilities. It is, in short, a depot and a distributing apparatus, and its principal functions are the housing of the public and the possessions of the public, their protection and distribution. The city is thus not only the static mechanism of buildings but the dynamic mechanism of a distributing machine, and it is therefore necessary to consider it, not only from the architectural point of view, but from the engineering point of view as well.

City planning, consequently, in which full consideration is not given to the engineering side, but in which only the architectural features are developed, are likely to be of doubtful value, if not worse than valueless, for if put into effect, new and unexpected difficulties would be encountered, which would more than overbalance their desirable features.

It is therefore of the first importance for those having a city planning project under way, to retain an experienced engineer, as only in this way can safe and thoroughly practicable results be obtained.

And the engineer selected must be a civic engineer, not merely an engineer with the customary training, but one who has the special training and experience necessary to consider all the varied features of the city as an operative mechanism and to take advantage of the most recent and advanced foreign practice.

The great part played by engineering in city planning is not fully appreciated, except by those who have had direct experience in such undertakings. Among the primary engineering features of city planning are water works, transportation systems, waterways and harbors, highway engineering, street lighting, sewage and refuse disposal, gas and electric supply, police and fire alarm systems, etc.

The laying out of the streets, squares and parks, and their embellishment by architectural or landscape treatment, though important, are only the beginning of city planning. The installation of the necessary utilities and their efficient operation and maintenance are of fundamental importance.

In the planning of a city, the architect and engineer should not plan or replan separate portions of it, but should plan it as a whole, with respect to the immediate requirements and to the requirements of the future as well, and the most careful attention should be paid to the probable direction of its growth, the presence of natural obstacles and of natural incentives to growth.

City planning is not only a question of architecture and engineering for it goes more deeply into the lives of the citizens, affecting them in numerous ways with a degree of importance that can only be realized by those who have made a study of the subject.

The effect, on its citizens, of the building of a city in accordance with the highest principles of the art of city planning will be one of a remarkable betterment in their social, ethical and physical condition. The superior appearance, beauty and harmony of the city will develop artistic taste and will result in increased civic pride and patriotism. This in turn affects the character of the individual favorably, improving moral conditions. The better hygienic system of the well planned city provides more light, purer air and more healthful and less expensive living quarters, affecting the whole lives of the citizens favorably.

The improved plan of the city, by providing safer and more direct means of transportation, prevents accidents and saves enormous amounts of time. The conveniently located parks, recreation places, public baths, gymnasiums and play grounds with ready access to woodlands and athletic fields, provides increased opportunity for physical development. The proper location of municipal markets affords cheap and wholesome supplies of food. These factors, with convenient location of schools, libraries, churches and other structures of a public nature, all unite to place the life of the citizen on a higher plane. A greater sense of responsibility is instilled while the comfort and enjoyment of the individual is added to, and an increase of population of a higher character effected.

The extent to which this improvement goes is far more than is realized by the average observer. In Germany, where city planning has reached its highest development, the results are most remarkable. This is shown by a comparison of six cities in Germany, selected at random, with six cities in the United States, which had in 1880 approximately the same population.

Cincinnati has grown 16.1%, 27.7% and 42.8% respectively in three decades, while Breslau's growth has been 22.8%, 54.9% and 87% during the same time. In the thirty years Buffalo has increased 173.4% and Cologne 254.6%; New Orleans, 56.9% and Dresden 147.1%; Louisville 80.9% and Hanover 146.2%; Providence 113.9% and Nuremberg 234.1% and Rochester 144.1% and Chemnitz 237.1%.

The German cities have increased almost twice as rapidly as the American cities, and while all this increase is not due to city planning, a very considerable portion of it can be so ascribed.

The arrangement of traffic, canalization, location of factories, the easy movement of products, the well nourished condition and the ambition of employees furnish a powerful impetus to industry. City planning justifies itself at every point, and America is waking up to it in a wonderful way.

While the movement in its present recrudescence is recent, the art of city planning is one of the greatest antiquity. The remains of the earliest communal abodes of man, of however primitive a nature, show a certain definite arrangement. With the development of races, villages became towns and towns became cities continually on a larger scale, and it is undoubtedly true that the higher the degree of civilization of a people, the greater will be the size of its cities. The civilization of the Romans was largely expressed in the city of Rome, and the glories of ancient peoples generally shown in their cities.

In the art of city planning, genius has occasionally arisen; among the early masters being Merian and Canaletto, the former developing the general plan of the city and the latter excelling in its interior arrangements. Sir Christopher Wren in 1666 after the great fire of London, had the genius to reconstruct the city on a plan that would have made it one of the most beautiful in the world, but he was ahead of his time and London was permitted to grow up into the disordered mass of streets and lanes that make it the greatest spot of confusion to-day on the face of the globe.

L'Enfant, however, who planned the city of Washington, admittedly the most beautiful city in America and one of the most beautiful in the world, enjoyed the double good fortune of having the support of the founders of the republic and an unencumbered site upon which to build, while most city planners have had to reorganize existing cities.

Equally fortunate was Baron Haussmann who rebuilt Paris. He was given a free hand and a plan was developed, in which conceptions of order, convenience, variety and grandeur were not allowed to be interfered with by any question of expense. Great avenues were cut through labyrinths of streets and foul and congested districts were replaced with parks and spacious squares. Hundreds of millions were spent and Paris is still spending gladly and with a lavish hand for extensions of his plan.

The early masters, however, did not impart their theory, leaving only their accomplished work as examples. Modern or practical city planning, therefore, is a new art, based upon principles, theories and practice only recently placed on a scientific basis. The modern masters are Reinhard Baumeister, the originator of the science of city planning, and Camillo Sitte, the definer of aesthetic principles, while Joseph Stübben is the greatest of practical city builders. Their work is available in theory, design and practice and will serve for future emulation as it has served modern Germany so well as the basis of her wonderful cities.

In the scope of practical city planning are included the broadest principles and the fullest details. The leading elements are the plan of the city as a whole, the segregation in suitable districts of the different classes of the population, and their proper housing in classes of structures suited to their requirements, the arrangement of such classes of structures in groups and district units and the placing of such groups and units in proper relation to the whole; the development of other classes of units, such as civic centers, parks, public squares, grounds, athletic and recreation fields and cemeteries and their location with reference to their uses and nature; the supplying of the units with the facilities and the public structures necessary for the business to be transacted in them; the location in civic centers of buildings suited thereto, both as to the uses and their architectural qualities; the arrangement of systems of transportation, the laying out of streams of traffic, location of railway stations and bridges and harbor facilities; the systematic location of schools, libraries, churches, hospitals, institutions, theaters and other semi-public structures; the general hygienic design of buildings and the system of city sanitation and waste disposal; the laying out of adjoining lands, woods and fields for purposes of recreation, the artistic regulation of structures and street plans and the laying out of surrounding territory, all in accordance with a settled plan, adapted to fulfill in the best possible way the purposes intended and to take care of the growth of the city and prevent its abnormal development.

The planning of a city, like the planning of anything else, should be carried out with a view to the use which is to be made of it, and to best adapt it to that use, and in addition to make it as pleasing from an artistic point of view as possible. There should first be strength in the design and if strength be economically manifested, the artistic enrichment of the design will be easily effected.

In city building, the strength of its design may be indicated by its plan. Its streets and avenues should be broadly and firmly laid out, advantage taken of its natural site and a sense of unity caused to pervade the whole as a result of its unity in structure. Its design should not be crowded, or its streets narrow and at haphazard, nor should they be throughout of such absolute uniformity as to destroy their individuality and make the city merely a monotonous aggregation of streets, as is so often the case in American cities.

A city should be planned and built with a breadth of view and boldness of execution; it should be built more for the future than for the present and its design should halt at no necessary elaboration nor consider expense.

What the city is for should always be considered and the most economical and effective methods of reaching its aims should be adopted, yet the fact that it is not merely utilitarian should not be lost sight of. A city should not only be a place of residence but an inspiration to its inhabitants and a worthy object of their civic pride.

CHAPTER XI

COMMISSION GOVERNMENT

Does popular government mean misgovernment?—A momentous revolution in municipal government—Its origin in a catastrophe—Its rapid spread—How the commission form of city government eliminates local politics—The death blow of graft—Automatic good government—Earlier examples of commission government—Washington a notable example—The autocracy of the whole—How concentration of responsibility produces efficient government—Actual workings of the commission plan—Similarity to continental systems of national administration—Efficacy of the political inventions of the initiative, referendum and recall—The direct primary—The passing of the boss—The efficient Interstate Commerce Commission and the inefficient post office—The absurdities of state legislatures—Irresponsibility of legislators—The remedy—Official usurpation under the American constitution—Pernicious and sensational activity of law officers—The law a tissue of loopholes—The constitution unable to cope with modern conditions—How it strangles the will of the people—Superior flexibility of European governments—Neutral types of our presidents—How minorities rule—The thick skinned office holder—Misrepresentative government—Congressional abuses—A drastic remedy—Who really rules the United States—How to do without a president and a congress.

POPULAR government has long labored under the criticism that the interest of the citizen in how he is governed is so slight that popular government means misgovernment. American cities have been particularly pointed out as examples of the failure of popular government, where, touching the citizen most intimately, it should be most successful.

A new order, however, is coming in. Municipal government is becoming a different thing, and the old reproach is being wiped out with a celerity that is astonishing. The average citizen is showing an interest in the way he is governed that amounts to a passion and the lengths to which the new form of government will be carried and the great services which it is rendering and will continue to render to the public, are difficult to appreciate.

It amounts, indeed, to a revolution, and is a striking illustration of the rapidity with which a desirable innovation, even in fundamental affairs, can be adopted, when it proves itself of real value.

This new form of government is known as the "commission plan" and in less than six years from its inception, has spread to over a hundred and thirty American cities, meeting with the greatest success. In twenty states it is optional with cities whether they adopt the plan or not, and at the rate of progress made and the satisfaction resulting from its adoption, it is safe to say that the commission form of government will become the exclusive method of city administration within a generation.

It is an illustration, also, of the vast difference between a good system, which automatically works out desirable results, and a poor system in which there are no incentives to efficiency and no checks on inefficiency.

The commission form of government had its origin in a catastrophe. It was an expedient, adopted in a great emergency, and produced, like so many inventions, by necessity. The Galveston flood left that city in a state of ruin, and the ordinary forms of government were inadequate. Martial law was declared and the necessity of the city continued so great that at the request of citizens the governor appointed a commission of five men to conduct the affairs of the city. Their powers were practically autocratic, and they were selected because of their reputation and abilities.

It was time when necessity could not wait on politics, but unrealized, the doom of the local politician was then and there sounded, for when the time came for the commissioners to retire, they were reëlected and that form of government became established permanently.

Its results were so good that neighboring cities, jealous of Galveston's splendid showing, also adopted the plan, and a distant city, Des Moines, Iowa, added desirable features and gave such publicity to the plan and identified the city so much with it, that it is often called the Des Moines plan and is largely supposed to have originated in that city.

In reality the plan of government by a small board with great powers, is one of the oldest and most effective of all forms of government. Nothing new has been added to the store of political wisdom by the device, but the applicability and practicability of such a form of government to the American city had been previously overlooked.

The commission form of government, in its most primitive form, is in evidence among miners as a miners' meeting, in which, being far removed from all laws, the miners resort to law of their own, which has all the effect and vastly more efficiency than ordinary law. Another example is seen in the vigilance committee of the frontier cities, which was practically what the Galveston commission amounted to. Emergency methods, the effective stroke which manifests itself in times of necessity, applied to ordinary affairs is what it resolves itself into.

Japan is practically ruled by a commission form of government, the council of Elder Statesmen forming the principal form of government. The ancient Greek and Roman cities at times were governed in much the same manner.

The city of Washington, long one of the best ruled cities, is a city government under a commission, in this case appointed by Congress. The city of New York, without realizing it, is being largely governed on the commission plan, the powers of the aldermen having been taken away, and the principal source of authority being in the Board of Estimate. Though lacking detail, the present New York plan is much better than the old system.

The originality of the present movement of commission government lies in the fact that the commission is elected by the people instead of being appointed by some other source of authority. It is in fact an elective bureaucracy, and is achieving the admirable results of the bureaucracy of Germany.

The rule of an autocrat, were the autocrat a perfect being, would be the most desirable form of government. In a democracy, the rule is, so far as the individual is concerned, an autocracy of all of his fellow citizens exercised through a system of officials. The citizen of a democracy, however, has, in feeling that he is a part of the autocracy ruling others of his fellow citizens, a saving grace as compared with the subject of a monarch, who is ruled by a power entirely outside of himself.

A democracy, being essentially an autocracy of the whole, should achieve its best results when the system of government is as nearly possible autocratic in operation, though democratic in selection of the ruling officials. The commission form of government most nearly approaches such a condition, and its great success as compared with the previous method is the marvel of politics to-day.

While the plan of a mayor and numerous elected officials is also a form of autocracy, it is one that has many broad avenues of imperfection, the principal of which is scattering of power and division of responsibility. It is a form of government, too, in which the control of the public over the officials is so vague and uncertain as to amount to no control whatever.

The number of officials elected is so great that the voters are unable to remember their names, much less to have any definite idea as to their fitness. After selection, the division of authority is so complicated that public business when it is transacted is accompanied with red tape and graft to an interminable degree.

The great number of officials, as for example, a large board of aldermen, causes each one to have but a small sense of responsibility. The vote of one alderman in a board of forty, however much against the public interest it may prove, is given with little compunction, as the grafting alderman, being surrounded by so many others, has little fear of being singled out for attack, and the voters have no effective means of rebuking his action. By the time election comes around again, they have forgotten just who voted wrong, and as he may have voted right on other propositions, the whole question becomes so mixed that the protest is lost sight of, so many factors enter into the election, that the wrath of the voters seldom reaches its proper object.

But with the commission form of government, the reduction in the number of candidates to five, enables the voters to find out who they are and to remember what they have found out, before election, and to exercise a control over the commissioners after election.

This is effected by the scrutiny to which their acts may be subjected, the meetings of the board being held in public during the day, instead of behind closed doors at night, and whoever cares may be present. The newspapers report the meetings and the conspicuous position of the commissioners and the certainty of censure and effective censure is such that, even when the members are professional politicians, as frequently happens, they are compelled to pursue the proper course.

upon the members the whole force of public opinion and making it certain that the responsibility for an act against the public interest will quickly be placed.

The citizen has thus a target for criticism, and when there are any complaints to be made, he knows to whom to make them and who will be held responsible if conditions are not improved.

Each of the five commissionerships carries sufficient power to make the candidate important to the voter. He informs himself about the candidate and casts his vote with intelligence. His vote becomes like a bullet, he can hit something with it, instead of as before, merely shooting in a general direction.

The commissioners in their meetings being, so to speak, in the spot light, are not without a certain self-consciousness. They are often playing a role, that of a public official performing his duty properly, and while the part rests uneasily on the shoulders of many who get into the commissionerships, it is the only role possible under the strenuous circumstances in which they are placed, for the meetings of small boards of highly responsible officials are usually accompanied by acerbity, not to say dissension. The characters of the five men, their inclinations, ambitions and prejudices are magnified as if by magic and the public gain a real view of their officials and know who the responsible men are that make or mar the city's progress.

The method of selecting the commissioners is such that politics is entirely eliminated. There are consequently no obligations of patronage to be met and the city's business is attended to by minor officials selected for their fitness, a great advantage at the outset.

The five commissioners are usually those of public affairs, corresponding to the mayor; finance; public safety; streets and public improvements; and parks and public property.

One of the main objects of this form of government is the treatment of the city as a whole, its improvement and development as a unit, rather than improvements in certain sections, due to the influence of the alderman of that section, as in the old order.

The cardinal principles of the commission system are the centering of responsibility without too great centering of power; the control of the public over the acts of its servants, and the unification of all the powers of the city, both legislative and executive in a single small board.

The details of the organization of the commissions and the method of selection of commissioners vary in different cities. In the Des Moines plan, the distinguishing features are the initiative, referendum and recall, and the non-partisan primary. The initiative is a provision whereby a petition being signed by a certain number of citizens and being presented to the board for action, goes before the public if the board fails to pass it. The referendum is similar in operation, that is where a certain number of citizens object to an ordinance, it must be rescinded or taken before the public at a general election. The recall provides for submission of the continuance in office of any commissioner, to the vote of the public on the demand of a certain number of citizens. It is the referendum applied to the commissioners personally. Both the recall and the referendum are similar in principal to the cabinet form of government in European countries, in which the cabinets, losing votes of confidence in parliaments, resign.

The non-partisan primary is a sort of eliminating preliminary election. No party emblems are allowed and the ten highest names become the candidates for commissionerships at the subsequent election. In the city of Grand Junction, Colo., the primary is superseded by the preferential ballot, in which the voter indicates his first, second and third choice, thus saving the expense of the primary election, which is entirely dispensed with.

It is obvious that this method of selecting the commissioners eliminates the political machine in local politics. A corporation seeking a franchise can be of no service to a candidate save by a house to house canvass of the voters previous to the primary, an expedient of doubtful value. The grip of the politician is broken, because the public is too numerous to be "delivered" and because, after election, the referendum and recall can so readily stop graft, jobs, jokers and deals.

Then, too, the candidate, owing no allegiance to an organization seeking a franchise, can be of no service to a candidate and is not obliged to make appointments at the behest of a boss, and added is the fact that there are no minor offices to be filled by election, which reduces the places to be filled, and without places there is little room for politics.

The effect of the commission form of government has been uniformly good. Indeed it is the custom now for cities having such a form of government to advertise that fact among their other advantages in attracting new population and manufacturers.

The following examples of the improvement effected by the commission form of government, taken at random, show the remarkable efficiency of the system.

In Keokuk, Iowa, the commission plan went into effect in 1909. At that time the city treasury was empty and there was a floating debt of 20% of the annual revenue of the city. After six months commission government, the city began operating on a cash basis and the bonded indebtedness decreased by $39,000. More than double the amount of street improvements made in the corresponding six months of the preceding year was made, while for less than one half of the results accomplished in the street department this year for $11,500, the city paid last year $14,000. It had been the custom to borrow from $25,000 to $30,000 to "carry the city over" from the beginning of the council year to tax paying time in August. On that amount the city would pay 5% interest. This year the commissioners did not borrow. Instead of paying interest they managed to keep a cash balance in the city depository on which the city realized interest.

In Kansas City, Kansas, the commission plan went into effect in 1910. When the new régime commenced, it was found that a deficit of $40,000 in the annual expenses was imminent. By energy in collecting licenses, dog taxes, taxes on street cars and telephone poles, $16,000 more was collected in the nine months than in the previous year. Cutting out superfluous city employees and economizing reduced the expenses sufficiently to enable the Commissioner of Finance to promise that the city would be free from debt in the first year.

In Berkeley, California, the commission plan went into effect in 1909. Interest in public affairs has been greatly increased. Daytime meetings of the council are well attended. Administrative matters are more widely discussed on the street than ever before. The idea of the old line political divisions which always dominated the city, seems entirely to have disappeared in municipal affairs. The city is overwhelmingly republican, but a socialist mayor was elected in 1911.

Of the results of the commission form of government, John J. Hamilton in his "Dethronement of the City Boss," says:

"Every city has its own story of deficits wiped out, floating debt taken up, bonds retired, business methods introduced, long standing nuisances abated, laws enforced, books better kept, streets kept cleaner, public works more honestly constructed, public buildings erected, additional parks and playgrounds acquired, economies enforced and taxes reduced—one, all or many. All report a revival of public spirit and improvement in business resulting from better civic conditions.

"There is no variation in the character of the reports; everywhere it is the leaks stopped, system taking the place of chaos, efficiency substituted for poor service, promptness for hopeless procrastination, lower for higher tax levies, or better values received for the public outlays. That which most commends the plan is the optimism which it brings back into our municipal politics."

The success of the commission form of government for cities stimulates interest in politics and proves that the public can attend to its own affairs when it can find a system that will enable it to do so in a practical manner.

The small board of commissioners has in other fields also proved its great value. The Interstate Commerce Commission of the United States is a highly effective body, which performs its duties without criticism, and which wields a vast power. Yet it is a body within the law, and acts consistently. in a legal manner. It is in contrast to the Post Office Department which also has vast powers, but of an autocratic, not to say extralegal nature. Though it comes in contact more intimately and more frequently with the public than any other department, the post office is as far removed from popular control as it might well be.

In it power is centered and responsibility to the public several steps removed. There is no method whereby the public can express its will in reference to the Post Office Department, or in fact in reference to any department of the government, and the power of the department head is, for practical purposes, unlimited. The violent contrast between the waste and inefficiency of the post office department, and the results of the administration of cities under the commission form of government, suggests the advisability of a change in the administration of the departments of the government.

In New York and other cities, the public service commissions and commissions of other natures, possessing large powers, use them in the interest of the public. The efficiency of these bodies is due to the same causes as the success of the commission form of government; that is, the small number of commissioners, the consequently conspicuous positions which they occupy, and the unification in them of more than one kind of power. In the commission form of city government, the commissioners have legislative and executive powers. In the Interstate Commerce and various public service commissions the powers are judicial, legislative and executive, that is, the commission hears evidence, makes orders which have the effect of laws, and then enforces them.

From the success of the commission form of city government, there would appear to be no good reason why a state government could not be conducted more successfully in the same manner. At present the system of legislatures and a governor, while not producing results as bad as the ordinary city government, is not much removed from it. There is the same division of responsibility and scattering of power, and legislators, being numerous and vastly inconspicuous, feel little concern over voting for improper measures.

The substitution of a state board of five governors, instead of one, with the abolition of the legislature, could not work much worse than the present system, and there is every reason to suppose that it would work vastly better. It would certainly eliminate the freak and ill considered legislation now so prevalent.

In the west, where conditions and traditions are less binding than in the east, the experiment is more likely to be tried. It should not be a long step for a state already filled with commission governed cities, to become a commission governed state.

In the framing of the constitution of the United States, the three powers of the government, the legislature, the executive and the judicial are distinctly set apart and the prerogative of each are carefully guarded, the assumption being that abuses would arise were any of these powers to be exercised conjointly by one set of officials. The framers of the constitution were near times of the oppression of monarchs and their principal care was to construct a form of government in which official encroachment would not destroy the liberties of the people.

Though they framed a document which has withstood the wrack of time for a century and a third, it has proven far from a perfect system of government; in fact, it is a system that is cumbersome, inelastic, unresponsive, indirect, tedious and subject to a great number of abuses. In fact, the American has less real liberty than the subject of a modern monarch, and official usurpation in enlightened countries flourishes nowhere as in America.

The citizen is liable to arrest and seizure at the whim of agents of the government, and from this he has no practicable redress. Arrests are vastly more numerous than necessary and are made in a spectacular fashion, and the whole energies of the departments devoted to securing convictions to save their faces.

The powers of the government in its inquisition into private affairs are quite unlimited, and a system of espionage exists in the post office department, whereby the mail of any person may be opened at will, not excepting the mail of the president himself. The powers of the government are not exceeded by those of any constitutional government.

In America a man may be imprisoned for intending to commit a crime (using the mails with intent to defraud), a case so extreme that other governments do not extradite fugitives for this crime. In addition, various societies are licensed to prosecute violators against certain laws, a system as pernicious as the informers of the Roman times.

The American thus suffers arrest and is brought to trial with its great expense, with greater frequency and less justification than in any other civilized country.

On the other hand real offenders plead technicalities and escape just punishment if they are well supplied with means, more readily than elsewhere, and the processes of the law are so expensive and long drawn out, that the citizen who appeals for justice finds it a long, expensive process.

Thus America is largely a lawless country, with less real liberty and more flags per inhabitant (as shown by the statistics of flag manufacturers) than any similar country.

The framers of the constitution took themselves with great seriousness. In fastening the constitution as it is upon the country, they took great pains to make its amendment exceedingly difficult. They seemed to assume that liberty lived and died with them, that they were bequeathing the blessings of freedom to future generations, who without their pains would otherwise be unable to obtain it. Indeed, they exercised, as is the way with statesmen, an over zealous regard for posterity.

Bismarck is credited with the cynical remark: "Let us leave a few reforms for the next generation to solve." Such was not the attitude of the framers of the American constitution. They were building for all time, in their own opinion.

It does not appear, either, that in endeavoring to provide the republic with a just constitution they took any special pains to do justice to those from whom the principal ideas came. A Philadelphia merchant, Pelatiah Webster, is credited with having been the chief source of the ideas embodied in the constitution, but no credit was accorded him by the framers of the document.

That the political wisdom of this merchant, however, based on the writings of theorists and the limited experience of other republics, was not adequate to the task, is shown, for example, by the process of electing a president by electors, a process which has no vitality whatever, and is followed only in form and not in effect. While nobody in the United States has ever voted for a president, but always for the figure heads known as electors, the electors have never exercised the real power that it was intended to confer on them, that of actually selecting the president. Instead, political parties nominate candidates for president, and electors are pledged to vote for such persons prior to election. Only in the case of the death of a candidate for president after election and before the meetings of the electors, would they exercise the powers which they possess according to the constitution.

The intention to have the vice president a man second in ability to the president failed to work itself out, the system really coming into force being such that only men of inferior ability will accept a vice presidential nomination. The result is that when a vice president is elevated to office, he is only a freak of politics. It was the idea of the framers that the man second in choice among the electors should be the vice president, that is, the defeated candidate for the presidency.

The irruption of political parties, however, automatically produced by the constitution without having been intended, caused such a plan to mean an entire change of policy in the government, and a defeat of the will of the majority on the death of a president by installing his opponent, and thus it was soon relegated to the alphabet of dead letters.

The system of government and the partisan methods of selection of presidents, do not result in the selection of the best men for the presidency, nor the men the public would prefer. The constitution is imperfect thus, in that it is not a means whereby the will of the people can be expressed; indeed it continually defeats and circumvents the will of the people, and offers no means whereby the will of the people can be expressed definitely on any given subject.

There is a well grounded suspicion that the framers of the constitution were influenced by motives which are now ascribed to the "interests." In those days men of wealth occupied high positions on that account alone. Washington was a man of great wealth, and the demarkation that now exists between capital and labor was not so sharply drawn. The constitution as it exists is an instrument under which the pursuit of wealth may be carried on to the greatest possible advantage, and it is reasonable to suppose that the Philadelphia merchant had such a consummation in view when he took a hand in the framing of the document.

The principal defect in the operation of the constitution is that exhibited in city governments under the same plan, the scattering of responsibility and the concentration of powers at points where they are not accessible to popular control.

The division of the legislative and judicial powers results in laws being passed by one body and passed upon by another knowing nothing about the intentions and desires of the legislators, and only able to enforce the law as it reads. This produces an enormous growth of technicalities and no end of injustice, because the law makers have made their law and gone and the judges have no option but to enforce it and no means of avoiding the absurdities that arise. If the law making and judicial powers were united in a single body, those responsible for its absurdities would come in contact with them in its enforcement and would then be compelled to eliminate them.

In most constitutional monarchies and in other republics, the cabinet expresses at all times the will of the people and is usually composed of the most eminent men, not the second raters that get into American cabinets. Should their views be out of accord with the majority, the cabinet falls and a representative cabinet replaces it. Such a cabinet is a living thing and a real power. The American cabinet, however, is only a collection of political obligations, without any political flexibility, expressing nothing and standing for nothing. To call them cabinet ministers, even, is ludicrous. Yet they have almost unlimited powers in their own departments, without any responsibility, save to the whim of the president.

In European countries, should the administration and the

cabinet feel that they are right, in the face of a hostile assembly the ruler or president may dissolve the assembly itself and go before the country for a new election. The public thus has a means of expressing itself on any topic of sufficient importance to warrant it, at any time and at the right time.

The American public has no such opportunity. Elections are held at fixed periods, irrespective of vital questions, and great disturbance of business has thus to be undergone periodically without any great questions being decided as such; the only thing being decided being the persons returned. What the issues of these periodical campaigns will be, can never be told in advance, and definite decisions on the policies of the country are formed with great difficulty, and usually not at all by the public, unless of the greatest importance.

The administration must go before the public on its record as a whole, and approval or disapproval of parts can only be approximately determined; indeed a president may be elected on the strength of his personality, irrespective of issues.

Thus the dominant party may continue a great number of small abuses in effect, which are quite beyond remedy by the public, since questions of greater policy overshadow them. Thus the ruling party carries many abuses, and is wrong and out of the spirit of the times on many questions, but owing to the prominence of its leading issues it continues in power.

A ruling party finally, however, becomes so overgrown with abuses that they sink the political ship, the minor abuses in the aggregate being more important than the main issue, and the new party cleans the political house. Self interest can thus manifest itself in political actions, up to about 49% of the party actions. This is the main cause of American misgovernment and governmental inefficiency.

The system of the selection of the candidates for president is such that the strongest men of the country, having by their strength aroused animosities and jealousies, are unable to secure the nomination, and compromise men are selected, chiefly distinguished for not being objectionable to any faction.

A sort of harmless type of person thus has the best chance of becoming an American president, and it is a fact that the presidents of the United States have been, during its history, by no means its leading men. This is a fault of the constitutional system which is held in such absurd veneration. Almost fanatical are those who hold the tenets of the separation of the legislative, judicial and executive functions, and that representation should be local in nature.

The result, however, of the separation of the powers, is a highly cumbersome and inefficient organization. The laws passed by congress are usually written by some one man in a committee, or a friend of his, and careful and mature deliberation of them by the whole congress is a physical impossibility. The government is thus a government by secret committee, and the laws are actually drafted by outside interests, those seeking favors and men with hobbies. It is stated that the Aldrich plan for new banking legislation was really drawn by a member of a prominent banking house in New York. In whose interest such a law would be it is easy to imagine. It is only another example of the old Philadelphia merchant plan of legislation.

After a law is passed, a long wait ensues before the courts, in reality the dominant branch of the government, through outliving the presidents by whom they are appointed, through their small personnel, and the great powers vested in them, decide whether the law is constitutional or not.

The power of the court is so great that it practically legislates any disputed point, but the long delay before the matter can be adjudicated, causes loss and stagnation at every turn.

Another of the great defects of the present system is that the country is ruled as a collection of parts, and not as a whole. As has been described, each congressman is for his own locality, and his own personal interests. The result is that the country is governed as a collection of units, the resultant of discordant forces, negatively so to speak, rather than as a whole, the resultant of general tendencies and for the general good, positively.

The effect of this congressional representation by districts is to repress the will of the people in that it makes the establishment of new political parties almost an impossibility, and practically denies representation to large minorities.

Unless a new political party is strong enough to muster a majority in a congressional district, it has no representation in congress whatever. If for example, there were 35% each of republicans and democrats in the United States, and 30% of a new party, the new party would have no representatives in Congress unless its members segregated themselves by moving into certain districts previously agreed upon.

But if, for example, there were 25% of republicans, 20% of democrats, 20% of socialists, 20% of prohibitionists and 15% of populists, generally distributed over the country as a whole. as is usually the case, fully three-quarters of the voters would be deprived of representation.

While this condition does not obtain at present, yet the large socialistic and prohibition parties which have cast a large vote throughout the country for years, have had practically no representation in congress, and have no prospect of effective representation unless they become dominant parties.

Certainly a system thus, under which it is impossible for a large proportion of the voters to have representation, is far from perfect. Even corporations do not treat their stockholders as badly, and the constitution might take a much needed lesson from the by-laws of the trusts, and establish cumulative voting. This would be accomplished by allowing the voters to vote at large for their congressmen, that is a resident of one district might cast his vote for a candidate in some other district. By agreement, the voters of a party over all the United States could concentrate their votes on candidates in certain districts, thus insuring a proportionate representation of minority parties in congress.

The effect of such a plan, allowing for example, prohibitionists in Indiana to vote for a congressional candidate in Georgia, and socialists in New York to concentrate on a socialistic candidate in Wisconsin, would have a profound effect. It would enable numerous new parties to spring up as if by magic, and the individual voter could vote on the subject which he deemed of the greatest importance, instead, to have his vote effective, of being compelled to vote either the republican or democratic tickets, standing for many things with which he has no sympathy along with the things he votes for.

It would make congress a true index of the will of the people and would break the grip of the politician so long held through the bi-partisan system now automatically produced by the method of selecting congressmen under the constitution.

The framers of the constitution did not contemplate the two party government which resulted from their document, in fact they had quite a different scheme in mind, but the system produced the two party method and there will never be a third party of any consequence as long as the present constitutional provisions of election by districts is continued.

The plan of voting thus for congressmen at large could be operated in the states separately, without applying to the whole country, and still produce great effects, since in the more populous states, the concentration of votes in certain districts would be sufficient to effect the election of respectable representations for the various new parties.

A further advantage of the cumulative plan would be the smashing of the "pork barrel." Congressmen elected at large would be under no obligation to the voters in their districts, and not expecting reëlection from them, would not attempt to curry favor by securing special appropriations. Being elected at large, there would be no occasion or even possibility of a system of patronage, as such representatives would serve the whole interest of the country, rather than those of certain districts. The country would thus be governed as a whole, or in the state mentioned, as a group of states, rather than as an aggregation of small parts, each striving for its own interest.

In Germany, although the rule of representation by districts is similar to ours, there are numerous parties in the Reichstag, due to the habits of the German people to segregate themselves in districts. Thus in a town, the Catholics will usually live in one section and the Protestants in another. Socialists are found congregated in industrial districts and thus each is proportionately represented. Unless Americans localize their abodes according to their political faiths, the present inequitable plan will continue to prevail.

In Germany a candidate may run in two different districts, thus being sure of election in one. If he carries both, he has the option of saying which one he will represent, and an after election is held in the other. In England elections are not held simultaneously, and a candidate for parliament defeated in one district may run in another later.

Thus the real leaders of the party are sure of reëlection, while in the United States the best and brightest men are continually being retired through narrow majorities in the districts in which they live.

The American plan, too, requiring the residence in the district represented, has the effect of producing a fever of political activity all over the country, and of stirring up political ambitions in all sorts of men, desirous of distinction but unqualified for legislative duties, who might better be left in obscurity in favor of the real leaders of thought and action who cannot be expected to scatter themselves in remote districts for the sake of political advancement, but who under a better system could remain in centers of civilization and progress, and still be of great value in the councils of the nation.

The very low grades of men generally found in the minor positions of American politics would thus be largely eliminated. Of particular value would be the dispensing with the thick skinned office holder, who makes a desperate fight for his office when he meets with criticism.

The American office holder as a rule, has no such sense of honor and propriety as is produced by other governmental systems in their office holders, who when questioned immediately tender their resignations. They thus demand almost unanimous support and receive it as long as they remain in office. Thus both the office and the official is respected. In America, the caliber of office holders is such that it is a popular saying that though some are fired and some die, none ever resign.

A further defect in the governmental system of the United States lies in the fact that the candidate receiving the largest number of votes in the electoral college for president, may not be the one receiving the largest number of votes of the voters, a direct defeat of the will of the people.

While congress has not developed the graft and corruption of legislatures and aldermanic bodies, it is because the congressman is actually, though not relatively, more conspicuous, and because the great size of the assembly makes the task of the briber much more difficult. In addition, congress is not a franchise granting body in the ordinary sense, though the influence of the protected manufacturers is so great as to amount practically to corruption.

Congress is notorious for log rolling. It is highly inefficient as an organization, and has created an official, the speaker, second in power, if not superior, to the President, an official hardly considered in the constitution.

Congress even comes in for criticism at the hands of satirists of the stage. Cliff Gordon is always sure of laughter and applause in vaudeville with the following estimate of the institution:

"People claim that our congress is to blame for the present condition of things. But look at Russia! The people over there are fighting to have a congress. Why not let them have ours? The Russian congress is called the Duma. It meets once a year in the morning and is dissolved at night. Then they meet the next year and get dissolved right away again. Lots of people laugh at Russia—but they know what to do with a congress. And now the congressmen speak of moving congress from Washington to Philadelphia. They want to get closer to the mint.''

Congress is notorious for many abuses, and its virtues may be as readily exercised by other bodies. Would it not be better, therefore, to abolish the present system and consolidate the executive, legislative and judicial powers instead of keeping them separate? Instead of one president, have a board of five presidents, with all power in their hands, chosen in a nonpartisan manner. Such a body would work as well nationally as the local boards do in cities, if constructed on the same principles. The expedient of the initiative, referendum and recall would supply the direct appeal to the public seen in the votes of confidence in European cabinets. The presidential board would have unlimited authority and would be individually responsible. Incidentally by continuing them in office until recalled, the curse of presidential elections would be done away with.

This may appear a revolutionary proposal, but it is not. The country is in reality ruled at present by a board of commissioners. The final power is in the Supreme Court, in effect a set of commissioners. They exercise legislative and judicial functions, but they are appointed by the president and the laws reach them in a circuitous and long delayed fashion. Why not elect them directly by the people, free from partisan influences, and take politics out of business and business out of politics for ever.

Eventually the country will come to some such plan in form as it is now in effect. The Constitution is defective, antiquated and unsuited to the purposes of liberty. It is bound to go.

CHAPTER XII

INDUSTRIAL HANDICAPS I

The passing glory of American inventors—Why American engineers are
straggling far behind in the world's progress—America from five to
twelve years behind the times in important industries—Empty boasts
of scientific progress—100 important inventions originated abroad—
Industrial supremacy of Germany—How achieved in the face of great
odds—How science helps industry—The German national testing offices
—All the facilities of the government at the command of the German
manufacturer—How the American manufacturer works in the dark—
The vicious American patent system—How it discourages inventions—
Better to abolish it entirely—How it pays the patent lawyer to advertise—Enormous losses of inventors and the public through patent
abuses—The farcical rules of the patent office—How the inventor fails
to get a square deal from the government—Millions for imitation, not a
cent for original research—Corporations as patent dogs in the manger—
Bottling up of valuable patents—The father of aviation in America—
Lilienthal's achievements—Stagnation in aviation due to "show-me"
spirit of business men—Patriotic support accorded Count Zeppelin in
Germany—Absurd position of the United States Government on aviation.

"Everybody is familiar with the claim that American inventors, engineers and manufacturers lead the world. A vast
amount of boasting has been done about American ingenuity
and originality and enterprise. If this claim were well-
founded, it would be indeed a matter for national pride; and
a quarter of a century or more ago, such a claim had a good
deal to justify it. There are a number of fields of inventions
and manufacture in which the pioneer work was done by Americans and in which the statistics of experts still testify to our
high standing.

"But when one views the whole field of engineering and industry and particularly the progress of the past twenty-five
years, it is rather humiliating to confess that instead of being
in the lead, the United States is lagging far in the rear," says
the *Engineering News* of May 25, 1911, in asking the question:
"Why is Europe in advance of America in Pioneer Inventions." It continues:

"Take for example, the advances made in iron and steel metallurgy during the past twenty-five years. Some original contributions have been made to the art by American inventors in that time, of course; but the great advances which have been made, have almost all originated abroad. We are to-day something like five years behind Germany in iron and steel metallurgy, and such innovations as are being introduced by our iron and steel manufacturers are most of them merely following the lead set by foreigners years ago.

"We do not believe that this is because American engineers are any less ingenious or original than those of Europe, though they may indeed be deficient in training and scientific education compared with those of Germany. We believe the main cause is the wholesale consolidation which has taken place in American industry. A huge organization is too clumsy to take up the development of an original idea. With the market closely controlled and certain profits by following standard methods, those who control our trusts do not want the bother of developing anything new.

"We instance metallurgy only by way of illustration. There are plenty of other fields of industry, where exactly the same condition exists. We are building the same machines and using the same methods as a dozen years ago, and the real advances in the art are being made by European inventors and manufacturers.

"Those 'effete nations of Europe' actually appear to take a certain pride in doing things that are worth while. Original work by engineers and designers is encouraged and rewarded. In some cases American manufacturers take up these foreign inventions after they have been developed on the other side of the water, and after four or five years the new improvement begins to be introduced here. In other cases, a dozen years or more elapse before any American has enterprise enough to introduce here what has been proved to be excellent on the other side of the ocean.

"It would be easy to cite fifty or a hundred important inventions of the past quarter century which have originated in Europe and have come into extended industrial use there and which we have either merely copied or in some cases almost ignored here.

"Take for example, the Diesel engine. Invented nearly a score of years ago, by one of the most eminent of German engineers, it is to-day so little used in the United States as to be practically unknown. In Europe, on the contrary, it is to-day attracting more attention than any other prime mover. Diesel oil engines are now being fitted to ocean vessels of large size. Ship and engine builders in England and on the continent are industriously at work in this field. Dr. Diesel, at the London meeting, declared that Diesel marine engines could produce a horse-power with one-fifth or one-sixth of the weight of fuel required for a steam engine. The enormous importance of such a reduction in the fuel supply, and the resultant increase in cargo capacity, is evident to anyone. From a naval point of view also, it is pointed out as among the possibilities of the near future that a battleship may yet be built for a European power, which will be able to sail around the world and home again without taking on fuel once.''

The views of the *Engineering News* are a confirmation of the facts as pointed out by Mr. L. B. Stillwell, past president of the American Institute of Electrical Engineers, who in an address at the dedication of a new hall of science at the Rensselaer Polytechnic Institute, Troy, N. Y., said in part:

''The voice of America in this age is one of exultation. If it be assumed that the daily press speaks for our people, it is not infrequently a voice of boasting. The press is not always discriminating in its estimate of the meaning of new steps and easily falls into the habit of exaggerating the value of a new thing and over-estimating its probable results. The man in the street believes that we easily lead the world in science and in its practical applications, but those better informed know that we have strong rivals; that while practice in America in mechanics and the electric arts compares favorably, as a whole, with that of any other country, the discovery of the facts upon which practice is based has been more often European than American. Even in the practical applications of physical science, it happens not infrequently that we follow and do not lead.

''The German Empire is a vast hive of industry, organized in a manner of which comparatively few Americans who have not investigated the subject have anything like an adequate conception. In an interesting and very valuable paper upon ''Engineering Education,'' read before the International Engineering Congress in St. Louis in 1904, Dr. Robert Fletcher, Director of the Thayer School of Civil Engineering, Dartmouth

College, said: "Realizing that even the most industrious people must have competent expert direction and that 'efficient direction of any industry to-day demands a large amount of technical knowledge which cannot be learned at the bench or in the shop,' the German government and the people, through trade associations, have established hundreds of schools of applied science for instruction in all the leading industries of the empire, and often many schools for the same industry.

"German foresight and system in the organization of educational facilities not less than the industry and the frugality of the German people have advanced Germany within fifty years from a position of comparative poverty and obscurity to a place in the foremost rank of powerful and progressive nations. As Dr. Fletcher well says: 'It is not her army of soldiers which other nations need to fear, but her armies of scientifically trained directors of industrial enterprises and of highly educated commercial agents.'

"While no other nation to-day provides as effectively as do the Germans for enlargement of the boundaries of science by original research nor for the systematic training of its people in the industrial and commercial use of scientific facts and methods, there is very much that is admirable, effective and worthy of our most careful consideration in the educational, industrial and commercial practice of some other of the great nations."

W. H. Dooley in an article "German and American Methods of Production" in the *Atlantic Monthly*, for May, 1911, says:

"The average American thinks that the success of Germany is due to low wages and long hours of work. This is not true, for, if labor is cheaper there, coal is dear, machinery dearer, and imported raw material pays a tax. The industrial supremacy of Germany is the effect of definite and deliberate political action. Thirty years ago the German statesmen realized that the nation was inferior to the American and English in natural resources and natural ingenuity; this inferiority forced upon their attention the value of thrift and of education. Thrift was multiplied by capital, and education multiplied by industrial efficiency.

"Few Americans realize the vast strides which the German industries have taken in the last few years. The great iron and steel manufactures of the Rhine district—of Dusseldorf, Essen, Duisburg and Oberhausen—have attained a remarkable

development, owing partly to the coal mines of the Rhineland
and Westphalia, to the great waterway of the Rhine and an excellent system of railroads, and partly to economic conditions
which it may be interesting to compare with our own, while the
rise of some of the great German shops reads like a romance.''

Henry S. Pritchett, President of the Massachusetts Institute
of Technology, describes Germany's great development in an
article ''How science helps industry in Germany,'' in the *Review of Reviews,* of February, 1906:

''In 1870, the manufactures, the inventions and the foreign
commerce of the separate German states were far below those
of England and of France. To-day United Germany stands
in the front rank of the nations of the world in industrial production, and she clearly leads all other nations in the applications of science to industry and to the arts. Her position is
all the more remarkable because this result has been achieved
in a country in which the agricultural and mineral resources
are not great, and in the face of the burdens due to long and
costly wars, to the maintenance of a great army, and to the
draining of a large part of its population through emigration.
No exploitation of the virgin resources of a new continent nor
millions of new citizens drawn from other lands have brought
Germany the unearned increment which the United States has
enjoyed during the same three and one-half decades.

''The reasons for this tremendous industrial development
are several, but they all spring more or less directly out
of the strong national spirit developed by the accomplishment of German utility. One of the important factors has
been the systematic development of scientific research and the
application of research to the practical industrial problems of
the nation.

''About a year ago I heard a famous chemist in Germany explain the present industrial supremacy of his country in words
something like these:

'' 'Forty years ago,' said he, 'the scientific men of the various
German states devoted their study almost wholly to theoretical
subjects. They were humorously described as given up to investigations of the dative case and similar impracticable problems. In a measure this was true. The investigation of that
day had a wholesome contempt for anything which promised
direct utilitarian results. But the development of the spirit
of research throughout the German universities trained a great

army of men to be expert investigators, and when a united
Germany arose to crown the labors of William I and of Bismarck, with it came a great national spirit in which the men
of science shared. They realized that to them were committed
the great industrial problems which must be solved in order to
make the nation strong; and scientific research, which up till
then had been mainly theoretical, was turned to the immediate
solution of the industrial problems of the nation. No longer
the dative case alone, but the development of the chemical,
electrical and mineral resources of the country formed the
avenues of scientific activity, and scientific research, which had
till then been looked upon as a theoretical accomplishment, became the greatest financial asset of the Fatherland.' There is
truth in this statement. The research habit, long cultivated
in German universities, had nourished a body of men trained
to research, men who had acquired the research habit and the
spirit of investigation. When, therefore, the problems of industrial development began to appeal strongly to the national
spirit, the country had a trained body of men to call upon who
threw themselves heartily and enthusiastically into these practical industrial problems.

"Perhaps the unique development of industrial research can
be appreciated in no better way than to recall the evolution of
the Royal Testing Office (*Das Koenigliche Materials-pruefungs-
amt*), which began thirty-five years ago in a modest shop adjoining the engineering school at Charlottenburg, and which
has within the last two years been transferred to a new and
magnificent series of buildings at Gross-Lichterfelde, just outside of Berlin.

"The meaning of this establishment, with its experts and
laboratories, may be better understood, perhaps, by briefly indicating some of the problems which were solved in it.

"A manufacturer who has a problem on his hands which he
finds difficult of solution, can at very modest expense bring this
to the research laboratory, where it will be not only attacked
by the experts of the establishment, but the experts of the firm
may also work side by side with those of the government on
the common problem. The advantage which is thus afforded
to the manufacturer can hardly be overestimated, for he finds
in the government establishment not only a corps of skilled
and enthusiastic experts, but he finds also all the literature of
the subject, brought together for their use and ready at hand

for convenient reference. The problem may be studied in the light of all that is known on the subject, and starting from the point of the world's knowledge rather than to go through the tedious plan of trying out methods already discarded elsewhere.

"It is worth our while to consider this idea for a moment; and the great difference between this spirit of dealing with the manufacturer and the inventor and that pursued in our institutions. Hardly a day passes at any scientific establishment in America, or at any great technical laboratory, that some inventor or some manufacturer does not come to its doors seeking expert aid in the solution of his technical problems.

"He is told, kindly but firmly, that the laboratories of the institution are not meant for his sort of problem and when he asks anxiously whither he may go for such expert aid and advice there is generally no source to which he may be sent except to employ the occasional expert with, at best, meager resources. I must confess to a great feeling of sympathy with such applicants, notwithstanding the fact that many of them are cranks, and many others do not know that the problems they pursue have already been solved or found insoluble.

"It is true enough that the college laboratories are in no condition to undertake many of these investigations, and yet this does not at all answer the fact that there should be some place well equipped whose business it should be to answer such inquiries, to sift the wheat from the chaff, to tell the ignorant seeker that his problem is already solved, and to point the man with a real problem to the way for a solution."

While the American government is thus inefficient and negligent in not providing facilities for research and testing, it is not in that department that it exhibits the greatest indifference towards real progress. It is in its treatment of inventors, the original sources of the industrial progress of the world, that our government exhibits a degree of hypocrisy, careless injustice and indifference to the interests of the public and the inventor alike, which is surpassed by no other country. It is by no means an exaggeration to say, as one of America's leading engineers and inventors of applied electricity, H. Ward Leonard, does, that American inventors would be better off if the whole patent system were abolished at a blow.

Writing in the *Electrical World*, May 16, 1908, Mr. Leonard says:

"The United States patent system purports to be a method of rewarding inventors, and thereby stimulating the production of inventions of value to the public.

"In reality the principal beneficiaries of the United States patent system are the patent lawyers and the large manufacturing corporations.

"There is no class of brainworkers in the world so dependent upon another class as are the United States inventors upon the United States patent lawyers.

"There is probably not an experienced inventor in the United States who would not prefer some one of the foreign patent systems to our patent system, unless he is really a representative of one of the large corporate interests. On the contrary practically all patent lawyers will tell you that the United States patent system is the best in the world. And so it is, for the patent lawyers. But it is probably the worst in the world for the inventor.

"As a class the American inventors are a most helpless class, and are growing more so every day. They do not come in contact with each other and have no representative organization. The quality of American patented inventions is depreciating steadily. This is the natural result of the fact that the inventor cannot get the reward which, as a patentee, he is entitled to. Most of the money he can earn has to be spent in lawyers' services and the enormous expenses of patent interferences and litigations, and meantime the large corporations continue to appropriate his new inventions as fast as he patents them. The non-technical and inexperienced judges usually fail to see the invention which the Patent Office saw, and hence decline to grant preliminary injunctions.

"The chief sufferer from all this is the American public, which in late years is surprised to find that to buy the latest and best inventions, it must indirectly pay tribute to foreign inventors, because the American inventors are being left so far behind.

"Where did the inventions found in the modern automobile come from? Europe.

"Where did the designs of our best battleships come from? Europe.

"Where did the inventions as to recent electric railway development come from? Europe.

"Where did the revolutionary inventions in high-efficiency incandescent and arc lamps come from? Europe.

"It is unnecessary to extend the list. Every observer knows that while twenty years ago we heard almost daily of important inventions of American inventors, nowadays we are obliged to talk of the inventors of the past generation in this country.

"What will be the outcome of this suppression of the constitutional rights of the American inventors? Probably the outcome will be the still further combinations of capital and new boards of patent control and further increase in the price to the public of every manufactured article.

"What is the relief for the public and for the inventor? The abolition of the so-called patent rights or else an intelligent revision of the laws by Congress in the interests of the public and of the inventors.

"The interests of the public and those of the inventor are in common. The interests of the large corporations and of the patent lawyers are certainly not usually in common with those of the public and the inventors.

"It is to the interest of the public and of the inventor, that the inventor should have for the life of his patent, the maximum protection at the minimum cost to him, because this enables the inventor to make new inventions, to the ultimate benefit of the public and of the inventor. The corporate monopolies rely upon capital and organization more than upon inventions, and it is to their interest that the unaided inventor should have the minimum protection and should have the maximum expense in trying to establish his rights. As to the patent lawyer, he is the chief beneficiary of the minimum protection and maximum expense system.

"Every real inventor would gladly pay to the government ten times the present patent fees, if the government would stop granting improper patents upon unpatentable devices, and, on the other hand, would carry out its agreement with him in good faith whenever he is really entitled to a patent.

"If the government cannot afford to guarantee at its present small fee, the exclusive right it purports to grant, and gets paid for, why does it not charge the inventor enough to do its work properly and guarantee its grants in good faith."

In another article, "Does the inventor get a square deal at the hands of the United States Government" in the same publication, Mr. Leonard points out the system of mulcting the inventor which is practiced by the government.

"The report of the Commissioner of Patents for the year ending Dec. 31, 1907, contains irrefutable evidence that the government is neglecting its obligations to inventors who pay to the Patent Office nearly $2,000,000 per annum in order to secure patent protection for their inventions.

"The Constitution of the United States says 'Congress shall have power . . . to promote the progress of science and the useful arts by securing for limited times to authors and inventors the exclusive rights to their respective writings and discoveries.'

"The greatest inventor of all the ages, if he were living to-day, might publish his most valuable discovery under the implied contract with the United States government that it would 'secure' to him by a United States patent the exclusive right for a limited time to his discovery, and, after receiving his United States patent, he would find that although he had performed his part of the contract fully and in good faith, he had not secured the exclusive right to his invention for 17 years as expected.

"He would find that no large corporate interest would respect his patent rights unless he was able and prepared to spend many of the 17 years and tens of thousands of dollars to establish the correctness of the judgment of the government in granting the patent to him, which was exactly what he had already paid the government to do. Under no conceivable practical circumstances would he be 'secured' by the government in having for 17 years the exclusive right to his discovery, which is what he was led to expect he would receive in return for disclosing his discovery, and paying all the necessary costs of the government investigation of his claim as against the original inventor, and all other costs of every kind incidental to the grant of the patent to him.

"The recent report of the Commissioner says . . . the surplus in the treasury to the credit of the Patent Office on Jan. 1, 1908, was $6,706,181.64. This surplus of the net receipts over all expenditures has been derived entirely from the fees paid by the inventors of the country, directly or indirectly.

"In speaking of the 'insufficient force of examiners and clerks,' the commissioner says:

"Their efforts under these conditions were at best spasmodic and simply resulted in thousands of actions being made which were nothing more than frivolous . . . A great many applications were passed to issue that were not ready for patent, with the result that the inventors and owners of meritorious inventions forfeited valuable rights by these careless, ill-considered and hasty actions on the part of the patent office . . . Complaints against the conduct of affairs in this office have been numerous, and many have been based on good and sufficient grounds.''

"It seems evident from these quotations and from facts familiar to all who have to do with patents, that inventors are not justly treated by the government as to the granting of patents. Every year, our patent system becomes more complicated, more expensive to the inventor of a valuable discovery, more untrustworthy, more unjust and more absurd. The rights and opinions of inventors themselves seem to be considered of no importance as compared with those of patent lawyers and large corporate interests, many of which exist solely upon the discoveries of unrewarded inventors.

"Our patent system seems to be based upon many absurd assumptions, among which may be enumerated the following:

"It is assumed that the half-paid men who act as examiners are invariably and absolutely trustworthy and are incapable of intentionally or unintentionally betraying the trust imposed in them when the inventor confidentially discloses his discoveries to the Patent Office, or of acting unfairly as between rival applicants. The Commissioner says in his report: 'The office has become merely a post-graduate school for the technical and legal education of young college men who enter the service. The General Electric Company has in its patent department, twelve or more men who were formerly examiners in this office, and other corporations have taken hundreds of them from the office.'

"No doubt, the examiners are as good as and no better than the average college graduate. As to whether such men are invariably and absolutely trustworthy, the records of the public press clearly show. One fact is evident—the 'corporations' find that it pays them to hire these Patent Office examiners by the 'hundreds' or they would not do so.''

Mr. Leonard continues his protest against the injustice of the patent system by showing how it places a premium upon forgery and perjury, when two inventors have applications pending for a patent on the same invention, usually the case when a true inventor is waiting for a patent and a rascal finds out the facts and files his application for the same invention and then proves by perjured testimony that he was the first to "invent" the thing. He also points out that many patents are issued to "inventors" of inventions which are already covered by the applications of previous true inventions not yet acted upon, and that many patents are issued covering devices that are public property, both abuses of the gravest sort. Speaking of the advertisements of patent lawyers, which are so noticeable a source of revenue to practically all publications, which keeps them silent on the injustice to inventors, he says:

"When one remembers that it evidently pays some patent lawyers to advertise in every publication in the land to 'patent your inventions' it is apparent that all but a small percentage of the patents which issue are merely a means of securing governmental aid in mulcting inexperienced men into applying for a detail patent upon a worthless modification of a well known device."

Referring to one of the worst features of the patent system, the absurd and involved multiplicity of claims attached to patents which are even to patent lawyers almost if not quite unintelligible, he says:

"The United States patent depends, not on the real invention which the inventor has made and published in good faith, but on the contrary, depends principally upon the refined use of peculiar phrases and punctuation points in a series of ridiculously spun-out claims necessitated by the United States patent system in order to prevent an infringer from hiding behind some semicolon or other equally absurd shield."

The system of claims, often upwards of a hundred in number attached to patents, is a noxious growth of verbiage which is chargeable to the hair splitting of judges. Many years ago, they decided that irrespective of the invention shown in the main body of the specification of the patent, where the real invention is described, if the claims appended did not exactly cover it in the most minute fashion, the whole invention was lost. The incalculable amount of damage that has been done to inventors and the people of the United States by this hair splitting decision it is impossible to estimate. To-day inventions are not decided on their merits, but exclusively on the adroitness and subtlety with which the patent lawyer has drawn the claims. This is one of the accursed farces which lawyers inflict upon the public which supports them.

The United States government, as we have seen, gets $2,-000,000 in profit per annum out of the inventors. The patent lawyers get at least $10,000,000 from the inventors for taking out these patents. The public gets the benefit of the discoveries. What do the individual inventors get for their discoveries?

It is probably true that the average United States inventor would be better off if there were no United States patents of the present kind. In that case, the inventor could use his money in marketing his discovery, and his manufacture would not be embarrassed by the many improperly granted patents to wealthy competitors, which patents he must to-day respect because of his inability to spend the necessary money in litigations. Of course, so long as the present patent system exists, an inventor cannot afford to not take out patents while his competitors are patenting every conceivable detail.

The patent system of the United States has thus become covered with barnacles of corporate self interest and growths of lawyers' technicalities. There comes a time in the history of every institution, as in the voyages of a ship, when progress seems to cease and former effectiveness is lost. At such a time, the vessel must go to the dry dock and be cleared of the foul accumulations of parasites. The United States patent system has reached such a stage. The sooner it is dry-docked for repairs the better off the whole country will be, for the American inventor needs only a fair chance to redeem himself. To-day he is engaged in other occupations, for invention has become too costly for inventors to engage in it.

The attitude of indifference to the great value of experimental work and of neglect in the development of inventions is illustrated by an occurrence which was reported in the newspapers at the time of the mobilization of the American troops on the Mexican frontier.

It was urged on President Taft, that the use of aeroplanes in the army be given greater attention, but the president was not in favor of the plan, being reported as opposed to having the United States spend much money for the purpose. He considered it wiser to let other countries do most of the preliminary work in discovering the uses of aeroplanes in war, there being plenty of time later to garner the harvest of good results, if any such should appear, which other countries discovered.

In other words, the president, with apologies to a famous slogan, meant: "Millions for imitation, not a cent for original research," or, let the foreigners experiment and perfect and we will buy a book. Thus the American aeroplane inventor is encouraged. And the attitude of the president is that of most manufacturing plants; to let others discover and then appropriate the results of their research.

The American inventor, in addition, has in the experimental workshop another system to contend with; that of being charged by the hour for experimental work; usually seventy cents an hour; and of seeing the work proceed at the most leisurely pace which the shop proprietors can devise. Thus in the development of inventions, the first cost is so excessive as to discourage a great number of improvements.

The United States patent system, while originally designed to afford the inventor the most complete protection possible, in doing so defeats its own objects in many cases. A patent if it is finally confirmed by the courts is absolute property. The inventor need not work it in order to hold it. As a consequence, many important patents are acquired from inventors by manufacturers and then not utilized at all. The invention may be one that would interfere with some machinery of the manufacturer already on the market, so that improvement is quietly laid away, the inventor loses possible royalties and the corporation acts the part of a dog in the manger, neither using the invention itself or allowing anyone else to do so.

Notable among the inventions of this character now bottled up, is the three phase system for electric railways, which stores up power while the car runs down hill to be utilized later. As this would have made it possible to make power plants much smaller for the same service, and would have introduced a new line covering equipment already on the market for the purpose, a big electrical concern purchased the rights and laid the thing away. Meanwhile it continues to sell to those needing power, larger and more costly equipment than would be necessary if the invention were in use. Such cynical employment of the features of the patent law intended for the benefit of inventors and the public may well cause its provisions to be questioned.

It is a well recognized fact in the electrical engineering circles that practically no progress has been made in electrical illumination for years. The recent improvements, the flaming arc and the metallic filament lamps which consume two-thirds less current for the same illumination, are German inventions. For the five patents on the latter, one prominent American concern paid $1,010,000 in addition to royalty. This is the white looking incandescent lamp, known as the tungsten lamp and also by the trade name of mazda.

Behind the trade name of "Mazda" is cloaked one of the most peculiar propagandas of invention and commerce. It is part of what may be termed the "Edison tradition."

The writer has discussed this subject in the technical press and the following is a quotation from an article of his in the *Electrical World* of November 16, 1912:

"A conspicuous example of the pervasive qualities of the 'Edison tradition' is seen in the name being given to the tungsten lamp, a German invention, as is well known to the engineering profession, but not as well known to the general public. For reasons that are not well known, the name tungsten, which is that of the principal element of the filament, has been more or less side-tracked, as far as it has been within the abilities of those interested to change a great public recognition of an important invention by attempting to dislodge a word that the public has universally adopted and which has become embedded in the language, and the arbitrary word 'Mazda' has been substituted as the first step away from tungsten, while the 'Edison-Mazda' is beginning to appear. No doubt finally both 'Mazda' and tungsten will be dropped and the 'Edison tradition' will be restored to its time-honored position in regard to lamps. The later tungsten lamp will probably become the new Edison lamp, while the present will be known as the old Edison lamp, and chiefly remembered as the one which became Edison at all, as the result of a court decision against a poor German inventor.

"In the immediate past the curtain has suddenly risen on a well-set rural scene, the 'Edison' farm. It has been discussed before engineering societies and in the public prints, and the latter report that Edison is equipping his country house with all kinds of electrical devices. Evidently electric farming in the United States is marked out for the 'Edison' label. Yet on page 489 of your issue of Sept. 16, 1905, some seven years ago, under the heading of 'Electricity in Agriculture,' M. E. W. Baker, of Barry, Ill., directed attention to the slow progress in the United States in the adaptation of electricity to agriculture, while in other countries, notably Germany, rapid advances have been made. Mr. Baker stated that from 1893 to 1901 he had searched the index of the *Electrical World and Engineer* for notices of electric plowing and found many references, but all to 'trials made in Germany,' and concluded: 'I think it high time that this odious German label should be removed in a branch of applied science where otherwise we Americans stand first.'

"Since that time (1905) I have endeavored in a modest way to arouse interest in electric farming in this country by means of articles in the technical and general press and in other ways, by reporting progress and results under practical working conditions abroad where electric farming is carried on to a large extent as it has been carried on for nearly twenty years. Nevertheless, the first electric plow has yet to turn a furrow in the United States, though hundreds of thousands of acres have been plowed by electricity abroad.

"If, however, any small efforts of mine have been the cause of attracting the attention of the 'Edison tradition' to electric farming—for a long while I was practically alone in calling attention to the subject—I shall feel honored in having made that contribution to an ever increasing convention. I shall gladly join the ranks of those whose ideas have gone to build up the marvelous figure of the inventive superman."

The progress Germany has made in street illumination largely due to their originality, may best be judged from a quotation from an article "German vs. American street lighting," by Mr. B. F. Pierce in "Public Service" for February, 1911:

"The preëminence of Germany in all that pertains to illumination is so generally acknowledged that ideas from German practice are, or at least should be, welcome to every progressive illuminating engineer. In street lighting, especially, Germany has far outstripped America; in fact, there is scarcely a single street in the United States to-day that could be called even fairly well lighted, according to German standards.

"Various explanations are offered as to the obvious inferiority of America in this respect, but few of them are at all satisfying. It is contended by some that the greater density of population in Germany permits a greater expenditure per mile for street-lighting purposes. This will hardly hold water, however, as many well-lighted German cities spend less per mile of street than American cities, which are undeniably poorly lighted. Another equally misleading explanation is in the low cost of carbons and labor in Germany, which permits high efficiency arc lamps to be run at a reasonable cost. This is not borne out, however, by a comparison of the cost per unit for operating such lamps abroad and at home.''

German superiority in this respect is due principally to her inventors, and to the efficient manner in which their inventions are utilized. In Germany an inventor is an inventor, not a joke, and a patent is a patent and not merely a license to bring a law suit.

The lax administration of the United States Patent Office in improperly granted patents, few of which get through the German patent office, causes a vast expense in litigation and wide spread discouragement of industry. In London an American patent is regarded as hardly better than a French patent, which the French government does not guarantee in the slightest respect. In France the inventor merely files his application and a patent is granted forthwith. Thus fifty inventors can get a patent on the same thing if they desire. But they work under no misapprehension about it. The system is similar to the method of the United States in granting copyrights, and works out much better in practice than our patent system, because with the American copyright and the French patent, the matter is up to the courts from the start, and whoever proves to be the first inventor is really protected, while in the American patent system, the first inventor is too often deprived by the legal machinery of all his rights through no fault of his own. In the French patent system and the American copyright system, the invention or the work is protected and somebody is decided to be the first inventor, somebody gets the protection, but in the American patent system, somebody generally gets cheated, the invention is fortunate if it is not lost entirely in the shuffle, and the one cheated is most apt to be the real inventor. This comes from the government pretending to do a thing which it does not do.

An illustration of the complicated processes of the patent system, as compared with Germany, is shown by the fact that in London the possessor of a German patent on any invention of

value can readily form a company and secure capital to promote
it, or he can sell an option to some promoter in twenty-four
hours, while the holder of an American patent in London finds
all doors closed against him unless it has been "adjudicated."
That is, until the courts uphold it after years of litigation, it
has no value.

Aviation furnishes a new commentary, if any were needed, on
the imperfection of the American patent system. The Wright
brothers have been granted certain patents, in fact they received
them before aviation was an established thing, and shortly after
the patent office outgrew the rule that aviation patents were
based on impossibilities and could not be granted at all unless
practical demonstrations were shown. It is claimed that the
patents to the Wrights were on features well known to earlier investigators. If this proves to be the case, and the Wrights'
patents are shown to have been improperly granted, a great injustice has been done those who are being sued for infringement.
The cost of litigation of this character which is always drawn
out to great and unnecessary lengths, with large expenses for
stenographic, witness and other court costs, is so much money
wasted out of the pockets of the public as a whole eventually,
and immediately, a heavy tax on the persons directly involved.

Of greater damage is the discouragement of aviation, owing
to the possibility of the Wrights' patents being upheld, which
checks and will continue to check for years, the proper development of the art. Not only will the infringers, if such they are
proven to be, be compelled to pay large sums to the Wrights,
but the latter are charging and receiving a license of $100 a
day for the use of their patents, none of which is ever likely to
be returned in any event. They are either in the right or in
the wrong, the victims of grave injustice or the perpetrators
of an outrageous imposition on the new industry; but the true
culprit is the patent system of the United States which permits
such doubt and uncertainty to exist and be continued, for no
useful purpose whatever, and accomplishing nothing but lining
the lawyers' pockets, while the industry is choked at its very
beginning.

The *Scientific American* of May 13, 1911, in giving a bi-
ographical sketch of Octave Chanute who is sometimes called the
"Father of Aviation" in America, states:

"On June 22nd, 1896, accompanied by Mr. W. A. Herring,
and two assistants, he went into camp among the sand dunes

on the southern shore of Lake Michigan, to study the art of navigating an aeroplane without artificial power. He and his assistants made some flights with a Lilienthal monoplane, but finding this unsafe and treacherous, they discarded it in favor of the multiplane wing glider designed by Chanute, which after many empirical modifications in the placement of the sustaining surfaces, assumed the form of the ordinary multiplane glider of the present day. This glider resembled the Lilienthal biplane in having the surfaces vertically superposed, the rider below them, and the rudder in the rear, but it was a five decker whose wings on either side, could swerve fore and aft, so as to bring the center of lift always over the center of gravity, in order to prevent excessive rearing.

"A full account of these experiments was published by Mr. Chanute in the Aeronautical Annual of 1897, and in a paper read by him before the Western Society of Engineers in the same year. This paper stated that the experiments were promising, and invited other investigators to improve upon them. Presently other persons in other countries did improve upon them, notably the Wright brothers and Montgomery in America, the Voisin brothers, Ferber and others in Europe.

"In March, 1900, one of Mr. Chanute's earliest disciples, Wilbur Wright, wrote inquiring of him as to the best materials to be used, construction of his machine, the most suitable place to experiment, etc., saying that he had notions of his own that he wanted to try and that he knew of no better way of spending his vacation. All that information was gladly furnished and the two men became fast friends.

"Mr. Chanute forwarded a quantity of aeronautic literature, visited the camp at Kitty Hawk, North Carolina, where Wilbur Wright and his brother, Orville, made their first glider experiments, and continued their steadfast mentor till they transformed the glider into a true dynamic aeroplane."

According to Lougheed's "Vehicles of the Air," Lilienthal is given a high place among the pioneers of aviation:

"Probably no other worker in the history of aeronautical science is entitled to a higher place than Otto Lilienthal whose early and thorough investigations have formed the groundwork for a large proportion of subsequent successful experiments. Lilienthal's investigations commenced in 1871; all told he performed over 2,000 glides, of a maximum length of 1,000 feet, and a maximum speed of 22 miles per hour. In 1896 he built a

2½ horse power motor, and it was in testing this power propelled biplane that he met his death by a fall from a height of 50 feet, on August 10, 1896.''

The Wright brothers made their first flight with a power propelled biplane at Kitty Hawk, Dec. 17, 1903.

It might here be of interest to quote further from Lougheed as to the originality of wing warping:

''This method of balancing, which is perhaps the most effective known, was patented in France by D'Esterno, was used by Le Bris, and was first patented in the United States by Mouillard (No. 582,757, filed Sept. 24, 1892, issued May 18, 1897, expiring May 18, 1914). Another early recognition of its merits appears in the *Scientific American* Supplement of June 4, 1881.''

Wing warping is used in modern machines, such as the Wrights, Bleriot, Montgomery and other machines.

The question would appear to be pertinent at this juncture as to what Mouillard is doing. Why with the Wrights suing on a combination of wing warping and steering, he does not open up on them on the wing warping device upon which their alleged improvement is based?

Although American aviators have achieved signal triumphs in aviation, the art has been almost wholly developed abroad. According to Augustus Post in *The World's Work*, July, 1911, the number of licensed aviators in the leading countries was:

France, 339; Germany, 43; England, 39; Italy, 27; Belgium, 24; United States, 18; and Austria, 18.

The interest in aviation abroad has no counterpart in America. The reason is not difficult to state. The grab-all tactics of the Wrights is one of the reasons. The other is the ''show-me'' spirit of American business men. Though it rarely occurs to the layman, aviation is a highly expensive matter, an aeroplane being worth from $3,000 to $10,000. It takes money to make the aviation mare go, and the American business man has not taken the enthusiastic interest in aviation and has not offered the numerous prizes that French men of business have devoted to aviation. The ''show-me'' spirit, the American business man's cynical tight-wadism has killed aviation in the bud.

The patriotic support and interest accorded Count Zeppelin has struck no answering chord in America. No American Zeppelin has been evolved. If he ever existed in embryo he has probably starved to death trying to get business men interested. After the destruction of a Zeppelin's airship, near the conclusion of its first long journey, a public subscription of 6,000,000 marks ($1,500,000) was made within two weeks. And with this money, he established the manufacture of airships on a commercial basis. Another public subscription, of $1,750,000, was made in 1912 for the national aviation fund. Public support of the airship in Germany also takes the form of traveling, and the Zeppelin ships, while they have had numerous accidents, have killed no one since the start of passenger service in 1908. The receipts from passenger traffic have amounted to $122,000 with one ship traveling over 15,000 miles between August 1, 1910, and January 31, 1911, carrying 5,000 passengers.

Governmental support of aviation, too, especially in Germany and France, is a great stimulus to the art, an aid almost wholly lacking in the United States. It is reported that the German government will shortly create the office of Minister of Aerial Navigation in connection with the Aviation Department, and that the first minister will be Count Zeppelin.

According to a recent report, as pointed out by Brigadier General James Allen, Chief Signal Officer, in his annual report (1911), the United States, although the first nation to recognize officially the aeroplane for military purposes, has been surpassed by Germany, France, Italy, Austro-Hungary, Russia, Great Britain, Belgium and Japan in aeronautical equipment.

The only aeronautical equipment which the United States government possesses besides three small captive balloons, is one Wright aeroplane and one small dirigible balloon.

"Germany and France continue to lead in the development of aeronautics, far eclipsing their competitors. According to figures recently published, the military powers have the following lighter than air machines or dirigibles.

"Germany, 14; France, 7; Italy, 3; Austro-Hungary, 3; Russia, 3; Great Britain, 2; Belgium, 2; Japan, 1, and the United States, 1.

"The figures given for heavier than air machines are:

"France, 36; Germany, 5; Great Britain, 4; Russia, 3; Italy, 2; Austro-Hungary, 2; Japan, 2; Belgium, 2; and the United States, 1."

It can be seen that the United States foots the list, being behind Belgium and Japan.

Considerable detail has been given to the subject of aviation, being a recent one much in popular interest, and showing in its various phases the patent mix-up, the lack of governmental initiative and the close fisted methods of American business men, a striking example of the attitude and methods of America in dealing with new propositions. The history of aviation is the history of every improvement in America; callous indifference by government and business men, hopeless struggles by inventors, and costly litigation of a most interminable character to fix the status of patents which should never have left the patent office. The thing is characteristic of America to-day, and one of the principal causes for the condition in which the country finds itself is outlined in aviation. Many other subjects could be taken up, in which our engineers realize that America is behind, as far behind the leaders of progress as she is in aviation. It is time for America to wake up. She has rested on her laurels long enough.

CHAPTER XIII

INDUSTRIAL HANDICAPS II

The grim destiny of the modern workman—The blight of standardization—The uniformity of the American—How standardization blocks progress—Unhealthy condition of American manufacturing industries—How the worn out human machine is scrapped—The passing of the old order—Fatuous efforts of labor unions to block progress—The new plan of common sense working, or so-called "scientific management"—How it may be utilized to cut the cost of living in two—False views of working men—Incalculable damage done by misguided restriction of output—What wage earners earn—An average of $9 a week—How the flood gates of prosperity might be opened—The deadly virus of "what's the use."—Regulation of employment in Germany—Daily schedule—The national efficiency movement.

THE relations between capital and labor in America, and their relations to the public, amount to a system of exploitation and spoliation at every turn which is undermining the foundations of prosperity and industry.

Employer and employee are at daggers' points and their interests become diametrically opposed. The organized laborer becomes a distinct species, so to speak, which like an insect out of the grub stage, is a full-sized fly never to grow larger, and never having been smaller. The union laborer has always been a laborer and he never expects to be anything else.

The old order in which a man had the possibility and incentive to become his own boss and an employer, has passed. With the growth of corporations, the consolidation of rival manufactories, the development of standardization and the cost of machinery, the number of individuals who may rise to positions of responsibility is restricted more and more. Only the most brilliant and resourceful can hope to gain a foothold sufficient to command the capital necessary to enter into competition with other masses of capital.

The workman is destined more and more to remain a workman, and as such, his former ambition to be a good workman in the hope of advancement has been abandoned. He is now out to get all he can right away and do as little work for it as possible. The capitalistic employer is out to get as much out of his men as he can as cheaply as he can. They are simply units of work. So many hours of labor, so many pounds of material, so many tons of coal and you have a given volume of manufactures. The question of personality, of individuality, is lost sight of. All idea of real co-operation is gone. The employer who has a large factory cannot know his men by name, or even their faces. They are numbers in the industrial game, and though sporadic efforts are made at improving the condition of the employees, it is always with the idea of getting more work out of them and is always met with ingratitude on the part of the employee.

This condition of affairs is typical of modern conditions, but in America it reaches its worst development. This is largely due to standardization, a thing that for the sake of cheapness, cheapens the workman and in addition reduces the customer to as dead a level of sameness as is possible.

Americans as individuals are largely standardized. They wear a standard hat, a standard coat and standard shoes. The same necktie rules from Maine to California and the umbrella in Chicago is a twin of the umbrella in New Orleans and likely out of the same factory. The standardization extends into the fiber of the individual and what he does and is and thinks, even. The hat, for example, has a standard season, the straw hat appearing promptly on June 15th by common consent, while on September 15th the faithful "Kelly" must be put aside in favor of the winter hat.

The European, who regards the American as a very practical person, is vastly mystified by the sudden abdication of the straw hat on this particular date. Although worn religiously through rain and wind which may come in the early part of the month, it must not be seen after the 15th no matter how warm the weather may turn. The foreigner is never able to fully explain it.

Styles, too, are standardized, and the fashion of women's clothing, though changing from year to year, is standard while it rules.

Standardization as it affects the public results in pronounced economies in the regular lines of merchandise. The vast number of articles of a single pattern turned out, whether hats, chairs or hardware, enables the cost of manufacture to be reduced to the lowest possible figure. The cheapness of the standard products causes their use by everyone, so that in any American home, much the same furniture will be found as in any other. The carpets, rugs and pictures will be the same or very nearly so. Thus a machine-made atmosphere, a lack of originality and personality and a lack of the opportunity for developing taste, envelops the American and still further makes of him a standardized unit, to live a standardized life and be buried in a standardized coffin by a standardized undertaker who furnishes a standardized funeral for $75. Many Americans are hurried to their graves by the great cost of articles which they may require outside the regular "lines." In a hardware store, for example, if an article is not "stocked" the customer is regarded in a very frigid manner. Does he think himself better than other people, or is he only cranky that the regular lines are not sufficient. Perhaps he can find it elsewhere but it is not likely. In any event he is informed that the store does not "carry" it, and that it must be made up "special" at sixty or seventy cents an hour for labor for an article that, if it were standard, would be turned out by the thousands per hour on an automatic machine.

The principal handicap of standardization, however, is the great difficulty of breaking away from the regular line. Improvements, thus, are not readily introduced and the antique lines continue to be forced on the public. One example is in the number of threads on a bolt. The standard threads are too coarse for most purposes, and not theoretically correct for modern materials. Yet no new standard has been able to force its way on the market to any extent, though a certain line of bolts for automobiles has appeared.

Another example in the line of machinery illustrates the strangle hold of standardization on industry. The *Electrical World* of April 6, 1911, in an editorial, "A Lesson in Economy," referring to German practice, especially to certain engines consuming an average of 8.5 to 9.5 pounds of steam per horse power per hour, which is near the record of steam consumption of seven pounds per horse power per hour, states:

"This ought to bring a blush to the cheeks of our countrymen who pride themselves on their progressiveness in engineering matters and in manufacture. We have been preaching superheated steam in season and out of season for some years past, and even now its use is only sporadic. When one looks at the record of the German units, his patriotic fervor for American enterprise receives something like a cold douche. When one considers that there are many thousands of these units in use, varying from less than 100 horse power up to 600 horse power, and on the average producing power on less than ten pounds of steam per horse power per hour, he can only wonder in a dazed sort of way how our engineers and manufacturers have allowed themselves to be outdone without a single recorded effort in self-defense.

"The usual excuse is made that these engines are difficult to operate, but if ignorant Chinamen, Malays, the bushmen of Africa and South American half-breeds can serve as combined engineer and fireman, as they do on units as large as 350 horse power, our own 'licensed' engineers should find no trouble in learning to do so. It is putting it mildly to say that machines of this class are capable of cutting the coal consumption and labor in two, as indeed the properly planned, superheated plant should do. They are doing the work which in this country is mostly done by high-speed, single-cylinder engines using at least 30 pounds of steam per indicated horse power, and requiring the services of two men instead of one. We hear rumbling in the distance, a deprecatory chorus about upkeep and repairs, but the fact is that the continental engineers have already had a good deal of experience with superheated steam and are not in the least afraid of it, while high superheating is here looked upon with the distrust that is born of ignorance. If anyone thinks that we are putting the case too strongly, let him the next time he wants a small generating unit try the experiment of asking bids on a superheated steam equipment with a guarantee of ten pounds of steam per brake horse power hour. It would be interesting to see the correspondence which would follow the proposition.

"The simple fact is that the American mania for so-called standardization has blinded us on this side of the water to what is really going on in the world. Yet the continental engineers who are working along that line lack neither skill nor experience and would not be willing to send equipment of this kind to the ends of the earth to be run by untrained men unless they were prepared to stand back of it. American manufacturers, we may be proud to say, can do as good work as any in the world, and American engineers are fully capable of holding up their end, but the latter cannot move until the former tell them to go ahead, and the former consistently dodge the introduction of unfamiliar apparatus until they are clubbed by commercial pressure into the path of progress. They move along the path of least resistance and unfortunately this is not upon an up grade. We understand fully the commercial forces that tend toward standardization of output, and we do not undervalue the convenience of this standardization, yet the time comes when a break has to be made, and when this time comes it is necessary to work quickly. In our judgment, the psychological moment in superheated steam work is near at hand. Suppose, for example, the not impossible case of the abolition of the tariff on such machinery as is here under consideration and the subsequent irruption of active German agencies. How, indeed, could competition be met if the tariff were even materially lowered? If our American manufacturers do not brace up and meet the situation they will wake up some fine morning to find their business imperiled.''

It is undoubtedly true, as the *Electrical World* states, that American manufacturers do not want to appreciate the advantages outside of standardization. The American manufacturer does not adapt himself to the needs of his customers, but bends them to his wares. This is accomplished by force of advertising and control of trade channels, but it is a policy that will not work abroad and the American manufacturer loses a vast amount of export trade in consequence. The Chinese, for example, it is said, prefer their tacks in blue boxes of a certain shape. This sounds like nonsense to an American manufacturer, and he sends out standard shaped boxes with red labels and wonders why they do not sell. And he is at a loss to understand why his exports of cutlery are small. It is because his few standard lines of knives cannot fill the requirements of the knives for the various trades and uses, and the German factory which turns out over seven thousand different kinds of knives gets the business.

The effects of standardization on workmen is one of the blackest tragedies of industrial life; the tragedy of turning men, first into machines, and then, their usefulness interrupted or ended, of setting them adrift, unfit and unfitted for any other kind of work.

In order to produce cheaply, large quantities must be manufactured, which involves frequent repetition of the same operations. As far as possible, these are performed by machines, but every machine, however automatic, needs some human attention, if it be no more than the throwing of a lever at certain intervals.

The man who throws the lever may do it for years. All he knows is to throw that lever, but he can do the task better than anyone else in the factory. Yet he can do nothing else, and when the time comes that that "line" is thrown out, the product no longer salable, and the machine has to be scrapped, the man, too, is scrapped—turned out to look for another job in his line of work, which no longer exists.

The monotony, the dearth of opportunity to learn anything and the lack of incentive to initiative created by automatic machinery enslaves the workman. He becomes merely a cog in the machine. His wages are small and his prospects smaller. He is apt to turn to socialism, but he turns in vain, for the public, the whole public demands the greatest value for the lowest price, as he does himself for the goods he needs for his own use, and standardization, the Moloch of industry, continues to demand its victims.

Modern conditions are relentless developing efficiency. Inefficiency, whether in men, machinery or methods is being eliminated. The man who can do one thing well is taking the place of the man who can do two things well, simply because, having learned one thing, he went to work at it and gained an advantage while the other was learning to do the second thing well.

And inefficient methods, like inefficient machines and men, are going into the scrap heap just as rapidly. The old order in which a workman after learning his trade became a foreman and then the owner of a shop, is obsolete. Such a system, while it insured a thorough understanding of all details by the head of the house, produced an establishment in which the head, after spending years learning the mechanical end, had then to learn the wholly different business of getting business. Such establishments have been superseded by those in which a competent workman who might not have had the initiative to start his own business, but who has sufficient ability and experience to be a foreman, is placed in that capacity, while the proprietor devotes himself entirely to securing orders, thus building up a large business before the master workman who becomes a proprietor has worked his way up.

The old method of apprenticeship is passing too. The apprentice, after several years, learned his trade and became a journeyman, capable of doing a large variety of things, knowing, in fact, all branches of his trade. He was taught by the foreman and gained his experience in the routine of the shop. He was admirably competent, but he is no longer in evidence. Modern methods do not require so much knowledge and such a variety of skill in any single workman. He may know how to do fifty things well, but fifty such workmen will accomplish no more than fifty others, each of whom can do but one thing well, while each of the latter will have learned his specialty in a few months or weeks, perhaps, instead of by years of apprenticeship.

The foreman, too, finds that his time can be more usefully employed than in teaching apprentices. He demands workmen already trained and wants to be interrupted by no pupils.

The labor unions, too, who of all men make the most systematic and successful efforts to stand in their own light, as well as the light of everyone else, restrict the number of apprentices, with an idea of producing a scarcity of skilled workmen. With a fatuity so complete as to be almost admirable, they often limit the number of apprentices in certain trades to one for each shop, irrespective of the number of men working in the shop. This prevents if it does not reduce the number of skilled workers in the particular trade. The wages of the remainder are accordingly enhanced and all seems well. But the increased wages attract the attention of young men, who find, however, that it is a very difficult trade to enter, and that the employers would take on more men if they could get them. The action of the increased wages being to stimulate the interest of those casting about for occupations, and there being a demand for instruction in that line, the trade school is produced. Here the workman, by specialized methods, can learn a trade in a few months that would take him years to learn as an apprentice, as he is taught systematically and does not pick up his knowledge at random while performing minor operations of manufacture and sweeping up the shop.

The trade school is thus a cheaper and a quicker system of instruction than the old method. It supplies the modern factory with workers who have learned their trades at small expense, and who can afford to work cheaply.

The action of the unions in having forced an increase in wages through restriction in the number of those engaged in a trade, causes the products to be more costly. For this the public pays. But capitalists, seeking opportunities for profit, and finding out that articles of that class are selling above the natural price are anxious to enter the business. Thé trade school graduates in that line cannot enter the union shops, and the new capitalists cannot get union men to man the new factories they build. The new capital and the new labor in the field are thus thrown together, and the new factories by producing the same articles at a lower cost undersell the union factories, and the unions being unwilling to make concessions, the old factories are ruined and the union men find themselves without employment. Their arbitrary efforts to defeat the natural laws of supply and demand are thus inevitably defeated. Labor unions have been most successful in the newspaper trades of typesetting and manufacture, for the reason that the price of the product must remain the same whatever the cost of labor, while the proprietor recoups himself in advertising charges, ultimately paid by the public, but into which so many considerations enter that the issue of the cost of labor can never be definitely met. But wherever competition can force a direct issue, the labor union is always defeated. Wherever a cost comparison can be definitely drawn, the labor union is lost. In railroading and similar occupations unions are successful. They have at all times less to fear from the competition of other men seeking work than they have of the public seeking cheaper products.

"Scientific management," a recent and high-sounding name given to the common-sense policy of shop efficiency, is also bitterly opposed by the labor unions. It amounts to a conservation of energy, and consists in reducing the number and difficulty of the bodily movements necessary to perform any given task.

Thus a bricklayer, by standing in a certain position, having his bricks placed on a platform at a selected level and adopting a certain sequence of movements, can lay three times as many bricks in a day as one who goes at his task in the usually inconvenient manner, and not be any more fatigued by his work if as much. A house built in such a manner is much less expensive than by the old methods, and were all houses so built, rents would be greatly reduced. Yet the bricklayer can only see the point that by producing three times as much work, he will be out of work three times as quickly, and he therefore adopts the opposite plan, restricting his output as much as possible. All other trades follow a similar policy, for except on piece work, it is almost the universal custom among workingmen.

If as a body they understood the advantages of efficiency, with the consequent cheapening of products, and doubled their output, an enormous effect would be produced.

If, for example, a million coats are made daily, and the makers increased their product to two million without any additional cost of labor, the cost of coats would be greatly cheapened. But if carried out, practically half the coat makers would be thrown out of work, a calamity more obvious than real, as they would be able to find work in other lines while the coats of all would be much cheaper, including their own. In fact, for each worker, the consequent cheapening of coats for the remainder of his life would be in itself more than compensation for the loss of his position.

The same process applied to all trades would throw half the workers out of employment sooner or later, depending on the time consumed in arriving at the new condition. But though half the workers were thrown out of work, the cost of living would be reduced to half its former figures, so that the condition of the whole would not be any worse while the necessity of women and boys under eighteen working would not exist. The whole family of the laborer could live on his earnings, instead of, as at present, having to work to make up the industrial deficiency caused by his ignorant attempt to get the best of his employer.

The labor unionist, however, will argue that if the worker doubles his output, it will throw half of his fellow workmen out of work and that the consequent over supply of labor will result in the unemployed half competing with the employed half, with the result that all are reëmployed, but each at half the former wages to turn out twice as much in products as before, not a pleasant prospect for the laboring man. Even admitting that such would be the case, the cost of production would by this process be reduced to one-fourth the present cost, for ultimately labor is the only item that enters into the cost of any article of commerce. The cost of living, being reduced thus to one-fourth its previous figure, the worker working for half his former salary would be twice as well off as at present, for his reduced salary would buy twice as much as it does now. He would be twice as well off for the simple reason that he would be doing twice as much work. The laborer cannot, considered as a body, divest himself of the fruits of his toil any more than he can permanently obtain a greater compensation than that to which he is entitled by natural laws, no matter what scheme or device he employs.

Consider on the other hand that the labor unionist were to be able to obtain double their present wages for doing half as much work. The cost of all products would be quadrupled immediately, but the wages of the worker being only doubled, he would be in a position only half as advantageous as at present. Some such process as this has taken place in the last generation throughout the world. The workingman has become filled with false ideas as to his rights and privileges and what his labor entitles him to, and with everyone else, he is to-day reaping the bitter harvest. Wealth is nothing but accumulated work and the more work that the individual can do, the richer will be the world. By the not very great addition to work of increasing its value a dollar a week, the wage earners of the country in twelve months would produce value equivalent to the entire fortunes of Morgan, Carnegie, Rockefeller and a half a dozen other of the richest men in the country, and give such an impetus to prosperity that hard times would be a thing of the past for years.

No worker working for himself ever restricts his output. But the worker imagines that in working for his employer he is working for someone else. Such is not the case. The public is composed of the public, not of strange gods or wealth devouring ogres, and work is always wealth. The worker's living expenses are certain, and more or less fixed. If he works twice as much he produces twice as much value. It goes somewhere. Into the pockets of capital, the laborer thinks, but this is not the case. As little popular sympathy as it arouses, competition among dollars for jobs is just as keen as among workers. Capital quickly flows into new and profitable enterprises and deserts old ones. If a moving picture theater makes money, a dozen others spring up to cut down the profits of the first. If a foundry or a factory in a certain line is very profitable, there is a rush to get into that business. Money is subject to the laws of supply and demand just as labor is. Everyone wants money, but few demand it so strongly as to pay 100% interest. In fact 6% is about the ordinary wages of money. The more money there is, the lower the rate of interest. Capital thus measures its own return by the amount of it in existence, the more capital the less return, just as labor is measured, the more laborers, the lower the wage.

The worker who is apparently making his employer richer by working twice as hard, is in reality working for himself, for although the employer may temporarily become richer as an individual, it gives him money which he must invest and throw into competition with money invested in other businesses or in his own. If he enlarges his plant, the worker is surer of employment. If some other manufacturer from some other field invades the field, the worker has a choice of employers, he is in fact competed for by the very wealth he has created in his own increased efforts. The enormous mass of fresh capital produced by a new point of view of the worker would in competing with existing capital reduce the cost of necessities. The wage earner would thus be deriving the benefit, since his wages though not increased would have an increased purchasing power.

Capital has certain limits of profit, just as labor has. Each takes its natural proportion in accordance with the relative amounts of each in existence. Thus the worker, by more effective efforts, when he increases the amount of money in other peoples' pockets, is improving his own condition by creating new purchasing power for his products, and is increasing his wages through reducing the relative returns to capital caused by his own efforts in bringing more capital into existence. He becomes vastly more valuable to himself, to his employer and to the world than in his previous condition.

Yet practically throughout the world, especially in English-speaking countries, the worker restricts his output. The new system of "scientific management" is violently opposed, yet it involves no more fatigue than present methods while producing much greater results. What it amounts to is a study of the bodily movements with a view to eliminating those which are superfluous or awkward, so that a worker at the end of a day has made no greater number of movements than ordinarily, and has expended no more strength, but his strength and his movements have been productive ones. Indeed, owing to the waste motions being eliminated, the amount of work done is often less. Even the housekeeper can introduce a little "scientific management" in the kitchen by the erection of a new shelf to save steps, by sweeping with a certain motion or by allowing the dishes to remain in hot water for a time before washing them. Scientific management is merely common sense applied to the daily task. The vast amount of wealth that dies still born in the factories of the world every day is almost incalculable. In the

United States there are 7,017,138 wage earners in factories, according to the 1908 governmental report, "Earnings of Wage-Earners."

The census of manufacturers of 1905 reported 216,262 establishments, of which 19,679 reported no wage earners in employment, leaving 196,583 to be investigated in connection with the report on weekly earnings. The returns from 72,880 of the establishments were so defective or unsatisfactory that they could not be used. Of the remaining 123,703, or 62.9% of the whole number having wage earners, the reports enabled the preparation of most interesting deductions.

The inquiry called for the segregation of wage earners according to groups of actual earnings, and not rates of pay; and therefore the distribution gives the actual numbers that earned the specified amounts during the week covered by the report. The terms "wages" and "earnings" are frequently used synonomously. Earnings and not rates of wages, either actual or other, are given in the report. The totals include piece workers, and cover all branches of employment in the manufacturing industries of the country, exclusive of the office force.

Of the 3,297,819 wage earners covered by the investigation, 2,619,053, or 79%, were men; 588,599, or 17.9%, were women; and 90,167, or 2.7%, were children.

The pay rolls of the 123,703 establishments for the week covered amounted to $33,185,791, and of this, men received $29,-240,287, or 88.1%; women, $3,633,481, or 11%; and children, $312,023 or nine-tenths of 1%.

As each establishment was requested to report the actual number employed during the week and the actual amount paid that number, it should be safe to use the above totals to compute the average earnings for the week. They give $10.06 as the average weekly earnings for all classes of wage earners during the selected week, and $11.16, $6.17 and $3.46 as the averages for men, women and children respectively.

The classification shows the concentration of men at the higher and of women and children at the lower weekly earnings. More than one-half (55.5%) of all the wage earners received $9 and over per week. Two-thirds (66.6%) of the men received $9 and over for the week, while only one-seventh (14.1%) of the women were paid at this rate. The children receiving $9 and over were so few that they are included in the general tabulations with those receiving $8 and over.

The greatest number of wage earners, namely, 464,875, make from $12 to $15 per week, while some 132,064 make less than $3 per week.

From a consideration of other tables given in this report, it is estimated that about 3,000,000 wage-earners are so employed that by the adoption of intensive work, they could greatly increase their output. The other wage earners are so employed that their output could either be but slightly increased or not at all. But the output of the 3,000,000 could readily be increased 50%, and at the average wage of all factory workers, approximating $9 a week, this would mean a saving of $2,340,000 a day or the vast total, figuring 300 working days in the year, of $702,000,000. That is, there is that much money wasted in misdirected efforts every year, by far a larger item than any that has been made in any computation in reference to the conservation of the country's resources.

The census of 1900 showed 29,287,070 persons, ten years of age and over, as engaged in gainful occupations, and assuming that the average weekly wage is $6, and omitting the 3,000,000 factory workers already referred to, the application of intensive work to the extent of only 10%, would mean an increase of sixty cents a week for 26,000,000 workers, or $2,704,000 a day.

In whatever employment the worker may be engaged, an increase of 10% efficiency may be obtained, and in most cases very easily obtained without any additional effort at all. In three hundred working days, the 10% increase would mean $811,200,000, which with the factory increase mentioned, makes a total of $1,513,200,000.

This vast sum that might be added to the wealth of the country annually, would be like quarts of blood transfused into the veins of an anæmic; where there is now financial lassitude, activity and vigor would result; where credits are restricted and capital wanting, there would be energy and prosperity. The attitude of antagonism, the fear that someone else will become too prosperous, jealousy of the success of others and particularly of those who are in the position of employers, brings misfortune for all.

The man who devotes himself to schemes for preventing others from making money, will never have the time to make much for himself.

Almost as bad as this grudging of effort in its costliness to humanity, is the time lost in strikes, the most direct expression of the differences between capital and labor.

The waste of grudging effort, or as is often the case, simply the inefficient or "what's-the-use" failure of the worker to put forth his best effort, lies in the feeling that no one else will do so. There is an utter lack of co-operation and concerted effort.

A group of laborers tugging at a timber will not move it unless there is a concerted effort. It is then moved with little trouble.

A method of introducing a concerted effort in intensive work needs to be devised. If all workers knew that on a certain day all other workers were going to put forth extra efforts, it would have the effect of contagious enthusiasm, and even the most indolent would be "on the job" on such a day. What the country needs thus, is a tuning up or period of forcing, a time during which prodigious efforts are to be made; after which the greater effort would become a habit, and the previous method, a remembrance as of the dreaded tasks of childhood.

Perhaps the only time the whole country has engaged in a concerted and prearranged effort, was the cessation of all activity for one minute at the time of the funeral of President McKinley, when all transportation and work was stopped. This had a great psychological effect.

A concerted effort of this kind to initiate a new attitude towards the day's work could not fail to have an enormous effect.

While such concerted action might prove an immediate expedient and a starting point, a more permanent change of the point of view is necessary. There must be systematic training. The right direction must be given and the sense of responsibility to humanity made a part of the technical training of all.

Each one should be taught to do his part for the sake of the rest of the world as well as for himself. The spirit of mutual helpfulness on the part of all concerned should take the place of animosity and jealousy.

One of the secrets of German success lies in the mutual helpfulness mutually exercised by the government, the employers and the employees.

Mr. W. H. Dooley in the *Atlantic Monthly*, May, 1911, describing "German and American Methods of Production," says:

"The German government recognizes the duty, and exercises

the right, of regulating industries in the interest of the employed; but in doing so, it is careful to keep in view the general industrial interests. The German laws are consequently in many respects much less stringent than ours, which seem to have been enacted under spasmodic influences without any guiding principle. This may be explained by the fact that the German government has been obliged to foster industries, and, in order to do this effectually, must strike in its legislation a happy medium between the claim of the employed for protection, and that of the community at large for the promotion of industrial enterprise.

"The most stringent regulations passed by the government are those affecting children and women, and it is in this respect that the state has clearly in view the interests of the community as represented by its workers. The total number of children under fourteen years employed for special reasons and exempt by law in the manufacturing industries in Germany is about 1630. These children are between thirteen and fourteen, and the hours of employment are restricted to six, with half an hour interval for meals. Between fourteen and sixteen they may work not more than ten hours but they must have an hour's pause at midday, and half an hour both in the forenoon and afternoon, unless their working day is not more than eight hours. No continuous period exceeds four hours. During the rest periods, any participation in work is forbidden, even remaining in the work room is allowed only when their own department of the work is brought to a complete standstill.

"When past eighteen, they cease to be youthful workers, and are under no special regulations except that all under twenty-one must be provided with a 'work-book,' or register, containing name, age, birthplace, nature of employment, date of engagement, discharge and other particulars. All boys under eighteen are obliged to attend a continuation school for nine or ten hours during the week where they receive instruction in the technical knowledge of their trade and religious instruction from their own clergyman. This time is taken out of the regular day-work without loss of pay. In a number of larger engineering and machine shops, the writer saw no youthful workers.

"Workmen may be fined to the extent of one-half of their earnings, except in the cases of acts against fellow workmen, of offenses against morality, or of those against regulations, maintenance of order and of security, when fines may be imposed

to the full extent of the earnings. All fines must be applied
to the benefit of the workers, and generally go to the sick fund,
but this does not affect the right of employees to obtain compensation for damages. All particulars of fines imposed must
be entered in a book, which is open to inspection by a government officer.

"Every industrial establishment must have a set of rules
hung up in an accessible place in each department, stating the
hours of work, with the regular interval for meals, the time and
manner of paying wages, the length of notice terminating employment, and the conditions under which notice is unnecessary;
also particulars of punishment, including fines, and the objects
to which they will be applied.

"Punishments which wound self-respect or offend morality
are inadmissible. These rules are equally binding on employer
and employed, but before they are issued, opportunity must be
given to adult workers to express their views, and the rules to
which objections are made must be submitted within three days
of issue to the factory inspector, who may order amendments if
they are not in accordance with the law or with special regulations. Punishments not provided for in the rules cannot be
imposed, nor can other grounds of dismissal be included in the
contract.

"It is a rare thing for a firm to have any difference with its
workmen. Indeed, I was definitely informed by one firm that
there had been only five cases of dispute in nine years, and these
did not come from the workmen as a whole, but were cases of
individual complaint. They have in Germany an institution
corresponding to the Conseil des Prud'hommes, in France, which
they call Gewerbe Gerichte, to which are brought all cases of
disputes of employees and employers. The average number of
cases tried by this bureau never exceeds five hundred a year.
The bureau consists of five or three people. The government
appoints a chairman who is a lawyer, and there are representatives of the employer and the employee also appointed by the
government. Sometimes two are selected instead of one. Their
decision is not final, as is that of the arbitration board in this
country. If a workman or employer does not accept this decision, it is binding for only two weeks. Then the workman
may leave, or the employer may discharge him. To give an
illustration: One of the workmen in an engineering firm thinks
he should receive four marks more a week in wages. He goes

to the firm and makes the demand. They refuse him. He appeals to the Gewerbe Gerichte. The Gewerbe Gerichte says, 'No, do not pay it.' The workman can leave at the end of two weeks' notice; or, if the decision is given in favor of the workman, the firm is obliged to pay him the increase for at least two weeks, and then they may give him a fortnight's notice to quit.''

It may be noted here that employers seldom discharge employees after appeals to the Gewerbe Gerichte. Indeed, they avoid as much as possible having employees appeal to it. To disregard its decisions in effect gives the firm a bad reputation, and to be before it is somewhat similar in damaging effect to the summoning of a lawyer before the Bar Association in New York.

Mr. Dooley continues:

''Notice of termination of employment is usually a fortnight, but it may be dispensed with on the part of an employer on the following grounds: false representation, theft, or other criminal acts; leaving work without permission, or refusing to fulfill the contract; carrying fire or lights about, contrary to orders; acts of violence or gross abuse directed against the employer, his representatives or family; willful damage; inducing member of an employer's family or his representatives, or fellow workmen, to behave in a manner contrary to law or morality; inability to continue work; or an alarming disease. Notice may be dispensed with by the workers on corresponding grounds; also for non-payment of wages in the prescribed manner; neglect to provide sufficient work for piece workers; or some danger to life and health in the employment which could not be inferred from the contract.

''The rate of wages is not included in these rules. The existence of such a code, legally binding on employers and employed, is a characteristically German method of doing business; it is in accordance with that respect for law and order which is such a marked feature of German life, and contributes materially, no doubt, to the smooth working of German industries. The rights and obligations of 'work-giver' and 'work-taker,' to use the excellent German terms, are publicly defined and guaranteed by law. This conduces to tranquillity, and makes attempts at individual bullying or vague talk about 'rights' palpably futile.''

The training thus given the German worker is such that he respects his work and is willing and anxious to do it thoroughly and for its own sake. This is the foundation of efficiency. When a task is well done, no one can profit by it as much as the man who does it; none can take from him the sense of pride and satisfaction which it creates, and though the employer profits apparently more in a financial way, in the end natural forces work themselves out in such a way that each receives the compensation to which he is entitled under the circumstances. The channels of industry may be fouled and obstructed at certain places and at certain times, but the level of recompense for the worker and the employer is justly reached in time.

A national society has recently been organized in the United States, composed principally of four groups: men of affairs, members of university faculties, specialists in accounting and efficiency engineers, the purpose of which is to promote efficiency. The names of the organizers are among the most prominent in the country in their respective groups. The movement for the formation of such a national society seems to have come at the moment of maximum effect. Nothing ever attempted in this direction (and there have been several attempts during the past ten or fifteen years) took such instant and unmistakable hold on the enthusiasm of those whose co-operation was invited.

The *Engineering Magazine* writes:

"Probably the catholicity of view and interpretation that mark the new society has much to do with its evident power to enlist support. It has very clear ideals to advance, but no special system to exploit. It recognizes the financier, the commercial manager, the accountant, the educator, the engineer, as co-ordinated powers, each potent in his own field, to originate and direct effort toward conservatism, toward reduction of the preventable waste of money, time, energy, of physical and human resources, that now burdens our struggle toward greater prosperity. It accepts any conscientious discipleship and works contributing to this purpose, and places all emphasis on principles of faith and none on points of ritual.

"Better concepts of efficiency are indeed sorely needed everywhere. Attention has been focused upon inefficiency in railroad operation and thence reflected upon inefficiency in manufacturing, although in every probability efficiency is far higher in either of these fields than in departments that hold themselves much above commerce and transportation—the law for example.

"Consider the McNamara trial as an object lesson. The

prospective jury held in jail, and the panel generally shadowed and investigated by detectives; counsel taking days to examine one talesman, announcement made that each side will take thirty minutes to sum up, not the case, but the question of a single juror's acceptability, and all ending in nothing; six weeks estimated to be necessary to filling the jury box alone.

"Louis Carroll, collaborating with Gilbert and Sullivan, could have imagined nothing more frantic.

"When the larger fraction of our legislature is drawn from professions in which the great fundamental efficiency principle of common sense can be grotesquely ignored, it is not surprising that much of our legislation should lack this and other principles of efficiency; should uphold mistaken ideals, fail to enforce discipline and violate the fair deal. And when the car of justice takes to the mire, the wheels of industry also are clogged. Perhaps the attempt to enforce the Sherman law may prove its *reductio ad absurdum;* but the present spectacle is disturbing. The attempt to remedy specific wrongs by general legislation leads to results wholly unforeseen and chaotic. We fulminate against forms of organization because they permit wrongs to be done, and let actual wrongdoing go unredressed and unpunished. Everywhere we grapple with forms and miss the substance. Surely some great organized movement for efficient common sense is fully due!

"In marked contrast to the confusion wrought by the lawyer-politician in attempting to regulate industrial affairs, there are beginning to appear, here and there, clean-cut exhibitions of wholesome ideals and efficient performance in political office where the influence of the engineer and the experienced industrial manager has had opportunity to make itself felt.

"Visitors to the Budget show in New York city (not generally thought of as having a model city government) are strongly impressed with the extent to which the standards and purposes of conscientious and economical performances are being upheld by many of the men in the engineering departments; and the administration of the affairs of a large city is increasingly a matter for engineers to control. From Chicago comes a note that the Civil Service Commission has ordered examinations for positions of 'expert on system and organization' and 'examiner of efficiency' and that to secure technical men of the highest grade to fill the positions, local residence has been waived. The methods appearing in some of the work done under the state government of Wisconsin are described by a competent engineering critic as inspiring. And in Federal affairs, a new concept of the relations between government and industry is thus impressively voiced by Congressman William C. Redfield:

" 'If the American makers of goods would practice the modern idea of scientific management, or greatest possible efficiency, no tariff wall would be needed to protect them from competition. This principle we may safely lay down; manufacturers must go to the limit of self-help before they can ask the public to tax itself to keep them. No tariff can righteously cover costs arising from mistakes in management, errors in location, bad equipment, faulty methods or neglect to adopt the most modern system of cost keeping and supervision.' This represents the best genius of constructive political effort.

"When such leaven is working in municipal, state and national governments, it gives courage and hope for the ultimate leavening of the whole mass."

"Scientific management" is a fine phrase of recent origin and quite unknown in Germany where the results so accomplished are merely regarded as the results of common sense practice and are not considered worthy of being so brass banded. Motion study, a phase of the same subject, is likewise a matter of course in Germany and the author recalls that during his extended shop practice in the early 90's with a concern employing some 14,000 men, he was taught what is now discovered to be motion study, by a superintendent who had been practicing it for forty years.

Quite as innocently the author had occasion, in this country, some years since (1904) to recommend certain changes in the operation of plants, effecting in one instance a saving of $50,000 and in another a saving of over $200,000 a year, without realizing that proceedings of such kind would come to be known as "scientific management," and not only so known but regarded as a newly made discovery, and trade marked with the names of so called originators.

Many other methods now in vogue in Germany are doubtless similarly destined to "discovery" here.

CHAPTER XIV

H,OW TO SUPPLANT THE TRUSTS

A NEW METHOD OF REVIVING SMALL INDUSTRIES.

How the trusts have ground out the small manufacturer—The cumbersome but crushing system of the trust—How it may be opposed by aggregations of individuals—A new field for bankers in establishing communal manufacturing plants—Solving the problem of working capital—Advantages in extending and obtaining credit—Cheapening the cost of supplies—Furnishing the sinews of competition—Convenience to the public—Advantages in purchase of coal and raw material—Special facilities and testing apparatus—Quick and efficient service rendered to the public by communal manufacturers—Stimulating effect on workmen—Better facilities for odd jobs—Saving in transportation charges and delays in local deliveries—Communal bookkeeping—Incentive of the banking interest—Certainty of financial success—Cumulative effect of advertising—Elimination of the middleman—Example of automobile manufacturing on a communal system—Superiority of product over that of a trust owned plant—Impossibilities of the trusts withstanding the competition of communal groups—Great value of good will to the communal manufacturer—Beginnings of the system—How small cities could establish such a system—Moderate investments required—Importance of competent engineering—Great advantage to the city seeking to promote its growth—Psychological effect on workmen—The yeast in the industrial loaf—The small manufacturer as a necessity in the scheme of industrial organization—The true selling price of every article—The greatest of industrial forces.

In the battles of modern industry, the small competitor is constantly being vanquished by the larger rival. The latter has the superior resources and the small manufacturers gradually disappear, unable to compete in efficiency with the larger ones, and a condition finally results in which the activities of an industry are carried on by a few large manufacturers and a number of isolated, struggling repair shops.

The large factory, however, works under certain disadvantages. Its organization is necessarily cumbersome and much red tape is involved. It cannot serve its customers as expeditiously and it confines itself to certain lines of goods and makes no attempt to supply goods for which there is only a limited demand.

It suffers all the evils of standardization, which are referred to in the previous chapter, and it is usually rigid in operation and slow to adopt new ideas.

The small factory serves the customer in much better ways than the large one. His patronage is more necessary to its existence and it is far more adaptable to his wants.

Yet in spite of its many admirable features, the small factory, lacking specialization, capital and equipment, cannot compete in cheapness with the larger units, and is constantly being driven out of existence.

A system whereby the small factory may be able to get into the field again is being attempted in Germany on a small scale, here and there, while the same principle is being applied in New York to a limited extent in warehousing and factory buildings. It has already attracted considerable attention and if developed along the right lines may very quickly become a Daniel in the industrial battle, slaying the Goliath of the trusts, and a means of quickening again industrial activity through the revival of competition in effective form.

It is a system especially inviting and adaptable to small cities desiring to increase their prosperity. They will be the most likely backers for it, and will find in it a highly effective weapon.

The system is in principle a communism of facilities on the part of the small manufacturers, preserving competition in the market. By a lumping together of themselves as manufacturers into producing groups, while maintaining their identity as individuals in their relations to the public, they can compete successfully with the larger concerns and utilize in addition the great force of individual initiative.

Under ordinary circumstances, the plan needs to be started by a capitalist, banker or financier, whose purpose would be to obtain a secure investment for large sums of money in what may be considered a highly equipped real estate development, rather than as an investment in a manufacturing concern.

A suitable district should be selected, having accessibility to supplies of labor, convenience of transportation for workmen and customers, and, of the greatest importance, proper railroad and water terminals. At such a location, an enormous factory building or series of buildings should be constructed, designed especially to accommodate the industries intended to be quartered there. The buildings should be subdivided to suit the needs of the individual manufacturers, each taking the space and facilities best suited to his work.

The purpose of the banking interests is best accomplished by the organization of an operating company, in which the tenant manufacturers have a share and a vote, and the duty of which is to co-operate with the manufacturers in the administration of the plant, to unify them as a purchasing unit, and to act toward them as a supplier of working capital, the greatest need of the small manufacturer.

If several hundred small manufacturers are thus grouped together, the system of communism thus indicated would administer their affairs in a highly economical and efficient manner.

Among the advantages, the following are the principal:

The unlimited capital and credit back of the group would enable the individuals to secure the equipment necessary to manufacture their products on long term payments, thus giving them the means of adding to their manufacturing capacity as rapidly as their business expanded, and not limiting their capacity, as it is at present with small manufacturers, to the amount of new equipment that can be purchased either outright or on ruinously high installment rates, out of profits as realized. Equipment would include machinery, machine tools, dies, lathes, furnaces and all kinds of labor saving machinery and devices.

The operating company would supply the necessary working capital at fair rates of interest, advancing working capital on the basis of orders in hand as security. Working capital is one of the great needs of the small manufacturer. On the receipt of the order, he needs money to buy materials to be made up. During manufacture he needs money to pay his workmen, and after completion of the goods he must meet freight and delivery charges and wait for from thirty to ninety days to be paid by his customer, who in turn is waiting for the ultimate consumer to take the goods off the shelves.

The small manufacturer's hands are too often tied by lack of working capital to tide him through the manufacturing period. Under such a plan as this, feeling secure in his supply of working capital, he is able to make closer prices, promise earlier deliveries and prompt deliveries, and offer discounts and credits which enable him to meet the competition of the larger factories on their own ground.

The operating company would have a credit department for advising the individual manufacturers as to the reliability of their customers, and this undertaken for the hundreds of manufacturers would result in a much more economical system of ascertaining credit than could be put in force by the manufacturers acting individually.

In the collection of accounts also, the group would be able to exercise a considerable power, since the credit of a merchant being bad with one manufacturer, it would consequently be bad with all, and a merchant thus purchasing various different kinds of products from the several manufacturers of the group, would be compelled to keep his credit good with the group to obtain the superior advantages which they would have to offer him.

In the purchase of supplies, the group buying for all its members would be able to command the lowest market prices, and obtain the longest credits, where credits were desired, while the individuals would be free to purchase what they chose in the name of the group, enabling them to exercise their own individual abilities in purchasing, backed by the responsibility which would accrue to them as members of the group.

It will be seen that in its fundamental financial features, the group would be of the greatest possible service to its manufacturers, and would place them on a basis whereby they could compete with any factory or trust, however great or powerful.

In its internal relations, the group would not be less effective. It would have a staff of well trained business men, engineers and master mechanics, who would be competent to advise the individual manufacturers as to the best methods and machinery to be employed in their respective industries. The small manufacturer would thus be afforded the same technical advantages now enjoyed alone by the greater units.

This would result in the best possible arrangement of machinery and facilities for handling, manufacturing and delivering the product, and would ensure efficiency in operation and production, while the business men as administrators would be of assistance in arranging credits and promoting the business of the various concerns.

A plant thus fitted for numerous small manufacturers, would have for them many advantages over isolated locations, and they would accordingly remove to it. It would also be particularly convenient for the public, who would not have to go from place to place in search of the articles they desired. The manufacturers so grouped would thus have a considerable advantage over manufacturers whose locations were scattered throughout the rest of the city in being more accessible.

The buildings being planned for the purposes intended, better light and air would be obtained than in isolated plants, with a consequently greater and superior output on the part of the workmen. The janitor service would be effected with the greatest economy and waste materials utilized to the fullest extent.

Through the purchase of coal for a single central station, supplying light, heat and power to the whole plant, great economies would be put in force. The isolated manufacturer buying light, heat and power as he does, must pay a profit to each of the supplying concerns, while the grouped manufacturers would receive their light, heat and power at cost. In this particular, at present, the isolated small manufacturer suffers a great hardship, since the electrical and steam concerns supply his larger rival at an extremely low cost, to prevent them from installing their own plants. This not only gives the large manufacturer an enormous advantage, amounting in many cases to as much as his rent, but it also kills at the outset the manufacture of electrical machinery for isolated power plants.

The purchase of raw materials in quantities by the group and distribution to the units at the wholesale price, would also prove a great economy.

Tool rooms in common would be provided, saving each shop the heavy cost of capital tied up in tools seldom used. Machine tools and machinery of such a nature as to be but seldom used by any of the individuals, but occasionally very necessary, would be provided in a central shop for the use of all, at an equitable hourly charge, saving the units the investment in such tools which is ordinarily required.

In this shop could also be included testing machines for testing materials, a class of machinery very seldom found in manufacturing plants, and not at all in small shops where most needed.

If somewhat enlarged, such a department could take in outside work, as there are but a very limited number of such plants throughout the country, and they are mostly connected with technical colleges, which do not take commercial work, needing their facilities for their own researches.

Occasional work of great accuracy could thus be undertaken by shops which would ordinarily be unable to attempt it.

A portion of the plant would be taken up by fully equipped

shops to be rented to the manufacturers ready for operation for limited periods in cases where the manufacturers did not wish to purchase machinery outright or on the installment plan, and such shops could be utilized by inventors perfecting their inventions, to the great benefit of all industries.

In the matter of repairs, both in the equipment of the shop itself and in outside work, the facilities of the group would enable the best service to be rendered at the least expense and delay. The public would find among a number of small manufacturers thus, means of having odd jobs done more quickly and satisfactorily than in the case of large manufacturers. Their varying wants could be much more readily served and new business developed more rapidly than under present conditions.

For the workman, the conditions would be highly stimulating and beneficial. Work in a small shop is always of greater variety and of a nature requiring greater initiative on the part of the workman than in a large shop. In the latter the workman is ordinarily confined to one particular operation. For the apprentice, the small shop is much more desirable, as he learns his trade more quickly and thoroughly than in a large shop.

The plant would have a labor bureau, enabling the workman laid off in one shop to be shifted to another, and thus being assured of practically permanent positions with working conditions of the best, workmen could be had at lower wages than in isolated plants, or at a given wage, a more efficient class of men could be obtained.

Such a plant would contain reading rooms with trade journals and technical books; recitation rooms and lunch rooms, giving workmen means of relaxation and enabling them to return to work with fresh energy.

In cases of accidents which would be less frequent, owing to precautions enforced by the group, medical attendance would be at hand, and every aid given the worker, while the units of the group would be better protected through insurance systems against the financial cost of accidents.

The business routine of the plant would be performed by the group, and bookkeeping and the details of routing and shipping attended to by a few clerks for all. A manufacturer finishing a product could turn it over to the department of shipping, without having to bother with looking up the best freight rates and tariffs. The plant enjoying the best obtainable shipping facilities and being practically a terminal freight station itself, could forward its products with the least trouble and expense.

Loading would be on cars, right at the doors of the manufacturers. The group would also have a delivery system of its own for local deliveries, serving in addition to its terminal facilities. A most important saving would thus be effected, for the expense and trouble which is experienced by small business men in making deliveries when they do not maintain a delivery service of their own, amounts to nothing less than a species of extortion, and is not only a drain on profits, but a source of continual annoyance and friction to all concerned.

The shipping being attended to by the group, its system of bookkeeping could readily be extended to include the operations of the individual manufacturers with the public. Thus the employment of individual bookkeepers by each would be avoided, and an important saving of clerical help accomplished.

The knowledge which the group would thus have of the operations of the individuals, would serve to protect both, and as the purpose of the group would be to promote the welfare of the group units, no inimical action would arise out of such an arrangement. It would be somewhat similar to the accounts which a bank keeps for its customers.

Indeed the whole relation of the group to the individuals would be rather in the nature of the relations of a bank to business men. The group would be essentially the banking or moneyed interest, rather than an association of the individuals in the form of a trade syndicate. The banking interest would supply the capital, build the plant, provide the means of obtaining the equipment, and such additional service as bookkeeping, expert advice, credit arrangements, shipping, and the like, as supplemental features. It would be, in a way, a hotel for industries in which the units instead of only getting a bare room as in the case of isolated plants at present, would get the space and equipment and such services as have been indicated, just as the hotel guest receives much more when he rents a room in a hotel than he would in renting an unfurnished room.

Among the beneficial activities of the group would be a department of information and publicity, preparing reports of progress and results of work for the benefit of the units; compiling tables of market prices, and keeping in touch with technical developments and referring them to the units most interested in such matters.

In advertising, the products of all the manufacturers would be advertised together as being manufactured in such a group. This would add a trade mark value of importance to the products of each manufacturer, besides effecting a saving in the rates and placing of the advertisements. Instances of communal advertising of this general character are seen in the cases of the manufacturers of a certain town who club together and make the name of the town a general trade mark for goods of a certain character. The name Grand Rapids is thus identified with furniture and Oneida with underwear. Communal advertising has a very marked effect and is a highly valuable form of trade mark.

A communal group of manufacturers could accomplish great results in the lines in which several kinds of products are manufactured by specialists but not sold to the public direct, being combined by a final manufacturer into the product which the public purchases, such as the manufacture of pianos and automobiles.

The purchaser of an automobile, for example, gets a motor made by one factory, a magneto made by another, horns, lamps, wheels, shock absorbers, radiator, ball bearings, hood, body, frame, pumps, etc., each manufactured by a specialist and assembled by the manufacturer owner of the trade mark name under which the car is finally sold. Even the largest of the manufacturers of automobiles secure portions of the mechanism or equipment of their cars from other manufacturers. They thus add these trade mark values to their own. The condition has been created, partially by patents but more by the concentration of effort in perfecting the separate devices.

In a communal group of manufacturers in which all the parts of the automobile were manufactured by members of the group. and the car sold as assembled by the group, the highest degree of efficiency would be achieved. As compared with a large factory making practically the whole machine, the communal system would amount to separate factories for making the parts, which would correspond to the separate departments of a large plant. The individual shop owners, having so much more at stake than the department foremen of the large plant, and being backed by equal capital and having equal facilities, would turn out a better car at a lower price. They need not devote their whole output to the car, but could sell the surplus to other manufacturers, and they would have every incentive to supply their own car with the best and cheapest of material, as in the division of profits of sale, they would participate in the proportion that the cost of their product bore to the cost of the car.

No trust could withstand competition of this sort, for the initiative of a group of active individuals would be opposed on equal terms to the inert mass of the large corporation, responding sluggishly to conditions and being poorly or inefficiently served by its employees from top to bottom.

The communal group would be at a great advantage over outside assemblying manufacturers working in isolated plants and drawing their parts from other isolated manufacturers, in the saving of freight costs and other charges, as well as by being able to build up more quickly the trade mark and good will value which would from the sympathy of the public and the excellence of the communal car, so much more readily be commanded by the group. In the purchase of supplies, the group would cut out the cost of the midlemen, and in the establishment of sales agencies, reduce the cost of selling. In the saving in overhead charges, such as fire insurance, depreciation, interest and sinking fund, office expenses, etc., the communal system with one plant, would possess great advantages over the charges of a number of separate plants.

An illustration of the efficiency of the communal principle is seen in some of the large department stores in the principal cities of the country. In such stores, certain counters are rented by individuals who own the goods on the shelves and conduct the business, just as if the aisles were streets and their own counters separate stores. The store as a whole has the advantage of individual initiative at the various counters. Such stores are of the most successful sort.

The principles of communal manufacturing are, as mentioned, being carried out to a certain extent in New York in the form of factory and storage buildings, the Bush Terminals. These buildings offer exceptional facilities in light, heat, power, convenient construction and location at terminals, thus saving drayage charges, while insurance is lessened and many other advantages obtained.

It has even been proposed that New York city should take over the Bush Terminal buildings, thus following the example of German cities in their ownership of improved real estate. This would be a form of municipal activity of a new sort for

American cities, but one that should in all probability, if followed, prove of great advantage.

In the smaller cities particularly, great results could be accomplished by the promotion of communal enterprises. The city furnishing the capital and site, could induce manufacturers to locate there, owing to the superior advantages thus to be enjoyed. At present, cities often offer free sites and freedom from taxation for a certain period to induce manufacturers to locate their factories with them. The offer of communal facilities and the use of capital on fair terms, if it were a system adopted by cities generally throughout the country, would produce most remarkable effects, as numerous new manufactories fostered in this manner by municipalities would be able to compete with and eventually break up the trusts. Such a plan could be put in operation in a commission governed city with little trouble and in such a city an efficient administration of it could be expected.

It is obvious that legal measures will never effect much change in the industrial situation as it exists. The trusts must be beaten on their own ground, as manufacturing mechanisms. In the communal plan, the much vaunted superiority of the business methods of the trust could be met and overcome by the superior initiative and efficiency and adaptability of the communal manufacturers.

Nor does the plan necessarily involve a large investment to institute. While the larger the number of factories together, the better the results obtained, a communal group of even a dozen or twenty manufacturers, requiring no great financial backing, would suffice for a start in many places. Such groups could be instituted in buildings already existing, but if new buildings were erected, they should be designed to permit enlargements on a well organized scheme. Here, as elsewhere in the system, the services of a competent engineer would be of the first importance. In the whole design, erection and operation of such a system, the competent engineer would occupy an indispensable place. Indeed the success of the whole undertaking would depend largely on the work of the engineer and the ability shown in properly planning and organizing the proposition.

It may be asked what incentive a banker would have in advancing large sums of money for such a purpose, when with the same capital he could establish a large plant under his sole control and direction? Certainly the return would be greater for the large plant to the banker than for the communal enterprise, where the profits would be intended to go to the individual manufacturers, since they would have the use of capital at regular rates of interest. It is not, however, invariably, the object of the banker to secure the greatest profit out of invested capital. Indeed, it is a well known law of finance that the greater the profit, the greater the risk, while the lower the profit, the greater the security. The banker, putting money into a communal enterprise, would, owing to the number of individuals, have much greater security than by trusting all his eggs in the one basket of the large plant, with its responsibilities of management. While it is known that sooner or later 95% of all men in business go into bankruptcy, it does not follow that 95% of communal enterprises would fail, indeed there is no reason why any should fail, for while the individual units might succumb from time to time, all the manufacturers could not, in the nature of things, fail simultaneously, so that the communal group, while its units would change from time to time, would persist indefinitely as a group.

The banker would thus be hazarding his capital not against one business, but against many, and in numbers there is financial security. The financing of such an enterprise need not require any great body of active capital, that is, capital at hazard and subject to loss. After the purchase of the land, if indeed it were not donated by the city, it could be mortgaged for enough to supply funds for the buildings, and they in turn mortgaged for enough to get money for equipment. The equipment, being placed with the manufacturers, who would in turn give mortgages, the whole enterprise could probably be organized on an equity of one-fourth, that is three-quarters of the money would be borrowed, only one-fourth being subject to loss. The establishment by a city of such an enterprise would not be a very serious drain on its finances, and the credit of the city would ensure its success.

It is a plan which would be particularly suitable for a small city, where the cost of power is usually high to the individual, and supplies and other costs, except rent, greater than in a larger city. One active and public spirited citizen in each city could stir the matter up and put it through, and a hundred such organizations in a hundred of the cities of the country could bring about enormous changes in the whole organization of society, since the changes the communal system would bring about would not only be economic but psychological. One of the chief causes of industrial discontent now is that the large plants have crushed the smaller ones and in doing so have taken away from the workman his last hope of rising in the world to a position of economic independence. The best that he can expect to become is the foreman of a room or the superintendent of a department. While under former conditions, the proportion of men who could rise to the position of employers was small, as indeed it must remain under any condition, the fact that such opportunities existed, placed upon the workman himself the burden of proving that he was competent. Now, however, with such opportunities closed, even the most incompetent can claim that but for existing conditions, he might rise and no one can gainsay his assertion. The burden of proving his own competency has thus been lifted off the workman's shoulders, and his discontent increases, while the industrial combinations are charged with the failure of each and every one of their employees to reach a commanding position. The number of those whose rise is checked by the trust is necessarily small, but the yeast is taken out of the industrial loaf, and a sodden and discontented mass remains.

In any state of society, the interest of the public is the superior interest. The fact that trusts have managed to drive out the smaller manufacturer does not prove their superiority as an industrial expedient; that is, that they can serve the public best. When they are under proper control, they may supply a given product at a lower selling price to the consumer than can the small manufacturer, but the selling price is not the only index of the cost to society of an article. Every article has a natural or normal cost. Time and labor are consumed to produce it, which should be properly measured by the selling price to the actual consumer, but when this selling price is too low, the cost of the article is made up at the other end of the line in the blighting effect on the lives of the workers. This affects society as a whole so that ultimately the entire body of purchasers pays the full ultimate cost of every article, no matter how low its immediate cost may be placed to the consumer, by the oppression of workmen and shaving of prices. When part of the cost comes out of the lives of the workmen, their purchasing power is reduced accordingly for other articles. When part of the natural cost comes out of the manufacturer's pocket through the exigencies of competition, he finally goes broke and throws a number of workmen out of employment, the natural cost being made up in the waste inflicted on them. The proper method of reducing the selling cost is by efficient methods of manufacture and improved machinery, and not by crushing out any class of society.

The small manufacturer is an economic necessity. A system which removes such a class from the social organization is at fault; it is a stairway from which the intermediate steps have been removed, a stairway upon which progress is possible only for giants.

The restoration of the small manufacturer must be accomplished. It is a duty which society owes to itself to free itself from the fetich that competition is the cure for every ill, and to see to it that the small manufacturer is again given his deserved opportunity. Society is paying the price in high costs of living for permitting the small manufacturer to be crushed, and self-preservation demands his reinstatement in the social scheme.

The system of communal manufacturing here outlined should gradually prove itself an effective means whereby society will again utilize the force which should be the greatest of all industrial forces, the initiative of the newly risen manufacturer, an initiative which is now crushed by aggregations of capital, which smother competition on one hand and oppress the consumer on the other.

CHAPTER XV

BUSINESS IS BUSINESS

What "Business is business" really means—A grueling contest—Business in politics—Its twin evil of politics in business—Blackmailing laws and exploitation of business men—Results of unbridled competition——Genesis of the trusts—Destructive effects of the "show-me" spirit—Characteristics of the American business man—Capital and the patentee—Business men and the banks—Why 95% of business men ultimately fail—How our 23,000 banks strangle business—Menace of our antiquated banking methods—The over-lordship of the capitalist—Remarkable advantages of German banking system—Wild-cat promoting in the United States—Dangerous powers of the post office—What the post office can do to your mail—Spectacular arrests—Political motive back of police raids—Formation of public opinion—Editors with axes to grind—How Edison in Germany turned a newspaper grindstone—What Edison learned abroad—German architecture—Consumption of alcohol—What a German thinks water is for—Eight suffragettes at a soda fountain—Effective method of German government in dealing with newspaper correspondents—How Edison's eyes were opened in German cities—36 lessons that he learned in Germany.

AMERICAN business men, while energetic and resourceful, are suspicious, largely unscrupulous and given to the use of questionable methods, too readily excused by the phrase, "business is business." The "business" that is "business" is usually some kind of knavery or double dealing that "gets by" because "nothing succeeds like success."

There is prevalent much of the spirit which is reflected by the slogan "do other people before they do you," and this with graft, "rake-offs" and the "show-me" spirit and cut throat competition, makes business life a grueling contest, which in the final sum total, amounts to everybody sacrificing everything that a few may succeed.

The evil of politics in business is only the other side of the mask of business in politics. The municipal plums tempt the business man, and in his greed he does not scruple to take any and every advantage and exert every expedient and bribe to gain the prize. The politician, when the business man has over-reached himself, in turn takes advantage, and by exposing and

215

harassing him, turns the business man's shortcomings to his own political profit.

This process is worked out in numberless ways, and obtains from one end of the scale to the other. The policeman accepts a bribe and allows the saloon keeper to keep open during forbidden hours. The law was passed for the purpose of enabling the policeman, and those "higher up," to take advantage of the saloon keeper's greed. If the saloon keeper was honest and shut up and refused to give the bribe, if he controlled his greed, both he and the policeman would be out of pocket; but blackmailing laws would not exist, and in all probability a fair closing law would be worked out, in keeping with the real public sentiment of the community. It is very easy to get such blackmailing laws passed in American legislatures, on account of the professional reformer. The moral intimidation that he exercises, a strange contrast to the ulterior aims of the boss, fits like a hand in a glove to the latter's purpose, and they produce the whitened sepulcher of American laws, the reformer polishing the exterior and the boss's evil designs well concealed within.

At the other extreme, presidents make political capital out of large combinations of capital, which would not have come into existence if earlier presidents had executed the laws. The usual course of legislation is, when an abuse arises, to pass a drastic law, which settles the matter for the time being. Violators are blackmailed, either directly or indirectly through campaign contributions, and everything is under cover, until finally the stench becomes so great that public opinion demands action. The politicians then loosen the full fury of the law on the heads of the violators, gaining great political capital thereby, until the sympathy of the public is aroused, and a reaction comes, in which the final condition is very similar to that existing before the whole farce began.

This alternate blackmailing and exploitation of business men by politicians and the bribery in one form or another of politicians by business men, causes continual turmoil, which hampers development and never promises to end, beginning in a new quarter when it dies down in an old one.

Competition in America is a cut-throat thing which ruins business men by hundreds of thousands, to the ultimate disadvantage of the consumer. While competition is held up as a panacea for trusts, it is in reality the cause of trusts. Business men in seeking to escape destruction from unbridled competition, as well as to procure greater gains, were drawn into combinations which in turn crushed the more independent business men or forced them to join the combinations, sacrificing their own business identity. Had competition been properly regulated and unfair methods prevented by law, trusts could not have arisen. In Germany, for example, a competitor is not allowed to cut prices simply for the sake of killing a rival. No such industrial wars are allowed, as the public realizes that this is the seed of monopoly. Consequently the trusts, as we know them, do not sprout so readily, and all the turmoil and the shouting are nipped in the bud. The fetich of free competition has cost the American public dearly, for free competition includes unfair competition, and leads directly to monopoly.

One of the means whereby unfair competition is prevented in Germany is the law against false representation.

Consular-General A. W. Thackara, at Berlin, states in the U. S. Consular Reports:

"The laws of Germany are very strict regarding false representations in advertising, such as putting extravagant values on goods that are undoubtedly misrepresented. Article 4 of the law which applies to such cases is as follows:

" 'Whoever, with intent to call forth the appearance of an especially advantageous offer, shall in public announcements or communications intended for a larger circle of persons, as touching business relations, especially as touching the character, origin, manner of production, or the fixing of the price of goods, the possession of marks of distinction, the motive or purpose of sale or the abundance of supplies, shall knowingly make false representations tending to mislead, is liable to imprisonment up to one year and to a money penalty up to five thousand marks or to one of these punishments.'

"When a person is found guilty, a fine up to 5,000 marks ($1,190) is imposed for the first offense; for the second offense, a fine up to 5,000 marks or imprisonment up to one year; and the third offense, invariably, the guilty party is sent to prison for a term not exceeding one year.

"In addition, a person convicted of false advertisement is obliged to insert an advertisement in a certain number of newspapers stating that he has been convicted of unfair competition. Usually he is required by the Judge to insert the advertisement in at least twenty-five papers, and sometimes in as many as a

hundred. The Judge usually dictates the text of the advertisement and specifies the papers in which it shall be inserted.''

The extent to which false representation goes in the United
States is shown by the prosecution of the government officials
during the fiscal year 1911, in which 522 individuals were indicted on charges of using the mail in furtherance of schemes
to defraud. During the same period, 196 persons were tried,
of which 184 were convicted, 12 acquitted and 177 awaiting
trial, while 72 are awaiting Grand Jury action, and 28 were
arrested but not indicted. The number who got away and are
being traced is 46.

The schemes in which there were convictions generally fell
under the following groups:

Promoting and sale of worthless mining or other stocks.

Inducing betting on fake horse-races and athletic contests.

Fake land schemes.

Commission merchant swindles.

Selling worthless goods through misrepresentations.

Obtaining commissions on fraudulent orders.

Work-at-home schemes.

Failure to furnish goods schemes.

Fake correspondence schools.

Sale of cheap books and divining rods for locating minerals.

Phoney guarantees of stocks and bonds.

Forged bills of lading in cotton deals.

Brokerage swindles.

Obtaining money by impersonating others.

Selling state rights and establishing fictitious agencies.

Selling unfair gambling devices.

''No fund'' check schemes.

Matrimonial schemes.

Selling canceled postage stamps and Mexican money.

Turf tipster schemes.

Selling cigar outfits.

Defrauding employers by means of forged leases and keeping
money received from cash customers.

Defrauding insurance companies for alleged injuries.

Obtaining expense money on promises to sell stock.

Requesting fees for fake positions.

Selling the rights to a patent many times over in the same
state.

Securing advance payments on goods not delivered.

Obtaining payments from relatives of deceased persons for goods supposed to have been ordered before death.

Obtaining money from alleged heirs to estates.

Obtaining money to assist in securing fake inheritances.

Sales of fake receipts.

Green goods swindles.

Obtaining subscriptions for charitable institutions.

Fake employment bureaus.

Selling interest in non-existing moving picture theaters.

Selling diplomas and requiring little or no study before granting them.

Offering to instruct persons in the science of mind concentration.

Fake trance mediums.

Forged checks and blackmail schemes.

The cost in time and money to the government in the investigation and prosecution of these cases has been so great and the corresponding loss to other important features of the postal service demanding attention is so apparent that Chief Inspector Sharp recommends that the Department of Justice take over the investigation of "get-rich-quick" cases.

The attitude of mutual distrust and suspicion which the employer and employee exhibit, is also seen in the relations of business men to each other and between business men and the public.

The American even takes a great pride in his suspicious disposition, which is glorified in the expression, "I'm from Missouri, you must show me," a phrase which sprang instantly into wide currency after having been used by a western lawyer who was prosecuting a trust in an eastern court. The vast popularity of the expression, which is excessively vulgar and commonplace in itself, reflects a characteristic feeling of Americans. In many respects, the American is gullible, and consequently a great number of fakes of various kinds are perpetrated. Having been repeatedly "stung," he is constantly on the lookout for further trouble. To announce that he must be shown is therefore done with a certain pride, a warning that he is not to be stung again. But with the usual extravagance of the Americans, the "show-me" spirit is overdone, and it becomes a destructive cynicism.

The American business man is not to-day a constructive pioneer. He waits until he sees a thing fully demonstrated with other people's money before he is willing to invest. He is always looking for a sure thing and wants 51% of it. If a new proposition comes along in the shape of drawings, by which it should be readily understood and passed upon by his engineers, he waits to see the thing in concrete shape first. The American inventor thus has a hard row to hoe, and finds capital an almost impossible thing to obtain, while business men are much more interested in seeing how they can infringe the patent than in acquiring a legitimate interest in it. They always desire exclusive control, not only of the invention, but everything else the inventor may invent in the future, for which their most frequently offered terms are a small salary per week until the inventor is fired. If a valuable invention comes along that threatens a standard article, it is most likely to be acquired and bottled up, serving no useful purpose whatever but to prevent the manufacturer's antiquated article from being driven off the market.

Capital goes slowly and grudgingly into new ventures, and the result is that a multitude of new things which prove so profitable abroad, do not come into existence at all in America, and foreign improvements are adopted only after they have been used for years.

Yet the moment a good thing is developed by someone else there is a rush to grab it, and all kinds of imitations appear on the market and the business is apt to be ruined for everyone. Too often, however, when exclusive control is obtained of an article, the greed of the proprietors exhibits itself in the form of charging extortionate prices, when with better business men in control, the article would have a vastly larger sale at a fair price. The tendency to "charge all the traffic will bear" is thus, in every line of business, a disastrous characteristic. The lack of initiative in new propositions, while at the same time enormous sums are spent in advertising trade marks, holds development back. The creation of a trade mark is a strange process in America. The press and dead walls are suddenly flooded with some combination of letters supposed to be a word, almost always idiotic in the extreme, though sometimes stupid, infantile or in bad taste, and this monstrous thing is jammed up in every conceivable space until the backers of the idea either go broke or make a fortune by the sale of the hideously named article. Thus is the English language enriched from day to day.

The attitude of banks towards new ventures and toward their
regular customers is in America to-day totally out of line with
the proper functions of banking.

Mr. Joel Shoemaker in "The Brutality of Business" in the
Trend for October, 1911, says:

"Ninety-five per cent of the business men in the United
States become financial failures while living, or die in debt.
The chief asset left to the wives and children is some form of
life insurance, the policy not becoming a part of the estate.
Such statements come from experts in their field of research,
and may be considered as about correct. For when we go into
the details of commercial life, and read the daily tragedies written on the faces of the oppressed, the only wonder is that the
ninety and nine human sheep go over the precipice to death,
and leave one able to stand alone and look down upon the
wrecks.

"The banking system is the foundation of what we designate
as our business plan of action. It covers the city and country
and marks the pathway to financial success or commercial destruction. As we have always been taught to judge a tree by
its fruits, and the returns from our banks show almost complete failure, the natural conclusion must be that the system is
responsible for financial distress, commercial loss and general
devastation of the country, periods of poverty, and money
scarcity in the history of the past have established precedents
for indicting the banking system as one of the worst enemies
to individual and community success, known to the civilized
world.

"We have in this country about 23,000 banks, representing
a combined capitalization of $1,900,000,000 shown on paper
through the articles of incorporation, or on the stock books of
the various banks. The deposits of these financial institutions
aggregate approximately seventeen thousand millions, or more
than eight times the capital stock of the corporations holding
the funds in trust for the depositors. The figures are borrowed
from one of the best informed financiers of Boston, and must
be taken seriously. They give an insight into the secret
chambers of modern finance and show why so many men fail in
business.

"There are 7,200 national banks, having the monopoly of
issuing notes, to be covered by government bonds. Those banks
have outstanding at present something like $700,000,000 of that

bond secured circulating paper. Such notes are comparatively safe, although as one banker says, 'It is probably the most unscientific and inelastic note circulation in existence.'' But the depositors have no guarantee of even safe handling of their funds, unless they live in the advanced localities where wise men of the day have enacted laws requiring guarantee of deposits.

''Money is not personal property to be hidden away in deposit boxes, buried in tin cans, or locked in legally authorized bank safes. It is the property of the people, a circulating medium, and its use is an absolute necessity in the daily business transactions of the masses. Every dollar in excess of legal reserve fund designated for banks, diverted from its legitimate channels of trade, and stopped on its mission of a debt payer, assists in clogging the wheels of commerce and producing panics. The reserve being 25% of deposits, every sum stored away above that amount, constitutes a robbery of the people, in taking from the masses the use of that which belongs to them and which brings food and clothing.

''The common people must stand for the losses in the business world. The farmers suffer because of not getting reasonable prices for their products; the workingman loses in decreased wages, being out of employment, and risking the possibility of ever getting pay for his work, and the whole consuming public —the masses—foot the bills. As a grocer said, when asked to sign a protest against exorbitant freight rates: 'It is nothing to the merchant what the freight bills amount to, the consumers must pay the bills.' So, in this fluctuating market the consumers are the ultimate losers in all that goes to make up for deficiencies caused by poor management, ignorant manipulation and false standards of financial tokens, in the business world.

''Why are such conditions permitted to continue in the commercial centers of our country? The answer is plain enough. It is in the interests of capitalism. A stable financial system would prevent extortion in interests, commission on loans, selling of human slaves into capitalistic bondage, and establish a sound money basis that would insure peace and prosperity. Such conditions are desired neither by the politicians or capitalists. Both live on strife and uncertainties. Trouble among the people is capital for such leaders, because it brings money, votes and power to their hands and forces the masses to humiliating acts of beggary.''

Banking and currency form a subject, not only of the greatest importance to the public, but a subject which is difficult to understand, and which should be settled by disinterested experts. Yet lawmakers see possibilities of political capital in it, and attack it with ignorant recklessness, while as for the experts, most of those who really understand finance are more or less tinged with capitalism and hence cannot view the subject in the proper light.

Our present system is particularly well adapted to promote the interests of trusts as opposed to the small business man.

The thing works itself out, briefly, in the following manner: Large corporations are formed and those backing them are ready at all times through the instrumentality of the Stock Exchange to repurchase the stock at varying prices. In fact, by buying and selling among themselves, they keep up, often, when necessary, a fictitious appearance of interest. Thus any owner of the stock may sell at any time, there always being a market.

Money which is deposited in banks is loaned by the bankers who accept stocks of such companies as collateral security. Thus the owner of such stock may either sell it or borrow money on it at any time, since the banks, knowing that there is always a market for it, may, if the loan is not paid at maturity, get their money back by the sale of the collateral. Thus the stocks and bonds of trusts are convertible into money at short notice.

Organizers of trusts often borrow money on their own holdings to form other trusts, and thus one by one the industries of the country fall under the control of financial interests, the latter using the very bank balance that the manufacturer has in the bank to form the corporation which destroys his business.

There are two kinds of loans based on corporation securities: call loans, which the banks may require payment on at any moment, and time loans running from thirty days to a year or more. The rate of interest on call loans is readjusted every day and most of them are loans which banks have made to brokers.

At seasons of the year when money is plentiful, the business man deposits it in his bank, which redeposits it in a New York bank, where instead of remaining idle, it can be loaned out from day to day at a certain rate of interest, but at the same time it is always available.

The speculator, in the office of the broker, sees from the rate of interest that money is plentiful. He therefore puts up, say $10,000 cash of his own, orders his broker to buy $100,000 worth of stock in trust, and the stock is handed to the bank in exchange for a loan, the speculator thus raising the necessary money to pay for the $100,000 stock he has bought, $10,000 being his own money and $90,000 borrowed, eventually from the deposits of banks all over the country.

Thus whenever money is plentiful, the speculators buying for a rise, make the stock scarcer, as all want to do the same thing and only a certain amount of the stock is in the market at any one time. With numerous buyers, the stock goes up, and a boom in the Stock Exchange is on, which presently attracts the attention of the public. They buy at high prices. They withdraw money from deposit for this purpose. The speculators sell at a profit. He acquires his profit, he has removed that much money from the pockets of others without giving anything in exchange except the risk he went to. The money that might still be free to go into business has passed, partly to the profit of the speculator and partly to the organizer of the trust in exchange for its stock. No actual values have been lost, but a transfer of ownership has taken place from the small man to the greater. The readiness of the public to buy the stocks of the trusts has created a terrible business depression. The wealth of the country has passed to the control of a few persons, through their ability to operate the device known as the stock exchange and through our currency and banking system, since the stocks of the trusts formed have been sold at prices far in excess of their actual value by means of this device. The public have bought stock worth much less than they paid for it, and have impoverished the sources of supply of money so that the small business man has been snuffed out, in two ways: One simply by the weight of capital that the trusts have thrown in the scale against his business and the other through the banking system.

Thus if a business man has in hand orders for $10,000 worth of goods and has only $5,000 in hand with which to buy the goods before he can resell them, he cannot transact that piece of business unless he can raise $5,000. With proper banking facilities, he should be able to go to a bank, borrow the money at a fair rate of interest on his notes secured by his $5,000 assets in hand, which need not pass to the possession of the bank. He could thus complete his transaction, pay off his obligations and prosper. But can a merchant go to a bank and arrange to get credit for ten times as much as the capital he has in hand, as the speculator can at the stock exchange. Certainly not. He is indeed fortunate if he can get even a small part of the money after signing a bond that would make Shylock blush. The bank will only loan him on the best security, which is proper, but it will often refuse him on any security. The cash is in New York working for the speculators, and the business man's business languishes while the speculator prospers.

Then hard times come. The speculator has killed the goose that lays the golden eggs. The business man, being unable to carry on his transactions for want of available capital, cannot make reasonable profits. The trusts crush him out and absorb the money he might do business with. Money becomes scarce and the result is immediately felt in New York. Banks do not have so much money. They are not anxious to take call loans. The call loan rate rises. Speculators cannot make so much money. They watch the call loan rate as the weather man does the barometer. It shows coming storms.

Then the speculators begin to sell. The men behind the trusts buy only what they must to keep the market from breaking and a panic ensuing. Prices decline a few points a day, but this liberates money, and the business man finds his bank more reasonable, but if speculation has been too great and too many people have borrowed money to buy stocks, the banks refuse further call loans, from want of cash themselves or for the ulterior purpose of furthering a reduction in the price of stocks, so that they can repurchase at lower level; and a great rush for cash ensues. There is too much credit outstanding, too many have borrowed money. One may ask how could it be borrowed if it did not exist. Very simply, because a ten dollar bill can be borrowed and loaned through a chain of a dozen friends in a day, but if in such a chain of friends, the bill comes back to the first man and he holds it and demands repayment from the man he has loaned it to, and no other ten dollars can be found, or nobody else willing to lend any of them a ten spot, all the friends will be in a hole. And if the bills are $100,000 instead of $10, the matter is not so simple, although the principle is the same.

In conditions of a panic, when the speculators have borrowed too much all around, and everybody is withdrawing money from banks for fear they will fail, from being unable to get back their money from speculators, all the money is practically locked up at once, and perfectly sound concerns all over the country whose assets are greater than their liabilities go into bankruptcy because they cannot collect what is owing them to pay what is demanded, even though the latter be less. Thus out of the activities of the speculators playing with the public's money real panics grow which ruin thousands of banks and business firms and throw millions out of employment. Their purchasing power lost, the business of remaining firms is greatly reduced and many of them fail. A period of stagnation results in which a large part of the workers are out of work and only such expenses are incurred as are absolutely necessary to keep body and soul together. In time the surplus on hand is devoured or worn out, and new purchasing power appears, which reemploys men, restores their purchasing value. This serves to reemploy other men and gradually the row of blocks which fell over in the panic, draws itself into an erect position again, ready to tempt the speculator to further excesses.

What the country needs is a banking system which will place the business man in the position of advantage, rather than the speculator. The Stock Exchange, which is the greatest menace to American liberty that has ever appeared, should be curtailed or entirely abolished. Very effective measures can be easily taken. For example, a bank is not allowed to lend more than 10% of its capital to any individual. Laws should be passed forbidding it to lend more than 10% of its capital on stocks and bonds as collateral. The convertibility of one share of stock into another is one of the cornerstones of Wall Street. That is you buy 100 shares of stock. Certificate No. 1561 is the same as No. 52. Either may be delivered to you. Or you may borrow Certificate No. 52, sell it, and at a lower price repurchase, say No. 1561, or any other number, and use it to repay the loan of stock, thus making a profit. This is the process known as short selling. It is one of the pillars of Wall Street, and the instrumentality whereby markets are broken. While it works automatically to prevent over-inflation, it is a highly dangerous remedy. It would probably be impossible to destroy the convertibility of stocks, but real estate is not convertible, and true speculation cannot exist without such convertibility, and does not exist without it. Speculation in commodities depends on convertibility also, as one bushel of wheat is the same as another.

Short selling, however, while at times a serious evil, is a powerful brake against a runaway market, and prevents the reckless inflation of stocks to enormously high levels and the consequent panics such as occurred in the times of the South Sea bubble. Short selling is merely a weapon, a dangerous one, but capable of being used to the advantage of the public as well as against the public. The amateur speculator, the lamb who so quickly loses his little fortune in speculation, seldom tackles the short side, almost always buying in hope of a rise, a process really more dangerous than that of selling in hope of a decline.

The great twin evils of Wall Street, however, are its use of bank funds for speculation and the system of "wash sales."

A "wash sale" occurs when a speculator not necessarily a broker, but usually a promoter or in some way interested in a company's stock, gives one broker an order to buy the stock and another broker an order to sell an equal amount of the same stock at a price which he fixes. The brokers meet on the stock exchange and carry the deal through without either knowing who the other is acting for, as they very jealously guard their customers' secrets.

Several such "wash sales" during a day give an appearance of activity to the market, at prices either rising or falling as suits the purpose of the speculator working the wires. The ability thus to fix prices fictitiously is used to fleece the public, and is in reality nothing short of a crime. Stock Exchange brokers are in effect only a private club of auctioneers, bidding and knocking down stocks to each other for their clients, the speculators. There is a law in New York against conducting a fake auction and small fry auctioneers are going to jail all the time for violating it. A large part of the transactions of the stock exchange are fake sales made to influence the public. If brokers were licensed as other auctioneers are, and were compelled on closing a sale to disclose their principals' names, such fake transactions as wash sales would be automatically disclosed and would have to cease. A very stringent rule requires the brokers to know who their customers are. A supplementary statute forbidding speculators to carry accounts in false names with brokers would effect the complete remedying of this gigantic swindle.

The stock exchange, in fact, aspires to a monopoly of gambling and swindling in the United States. The community of interest which it represents has promoted legislation against lotteries, race tracks and swindling by mail and is now the only form of open gambling not forbidden by law.

The slight skim of legitimate transactions is the cloak of respectability which the organization throws over its huge body of gambling and most terrific outcries are made when it is accused of gambling. Nevertheless its major purpose is gambling and the crafty system which has been built up for exploiting the public with the public's own money obtained through banks can never be thoroughly broken up until the stock exchange is abolished, and prosperity can never return while the leeches of finance continue to drain the life blood of commerce into their own creations.

Wall Street is a great Frankenstein of finance, a monster whose claws are deep into the body of public enterprise, too deep it would seem to be torn out, but torn out they must if worse conditions are not to come. The world existed for centuries without Wall Street and only in the last generation has this great parasite grown to such threatening proportions. Wall Street is unnecessary, criminal and insatiable. It should be destroyed at whatever cost, if not for our own benefit, then for that of future generations.

While a very few simple laws with teeth in them would suffice to destroy the financial incubus, if enforced by resolute executives, the moneyed powers have so thoroughly identified themselves with the government by secret avenues and political obligations that they are in fact the government's government.

The units of the public are widely separated, an army of Lilliputians, and each one is in awe of the financial giant. A paralyzing sympathetic influence is thus wielded and each Lilliputian fears to bestir himself for fear of attracting unfavorable notice and all remain in slavery.

Such spectacles come to be witnessed as a president of the United States sanctioning monopolistic combinations and another doing all in his power to block the progress of a congressional investigating committee.

Such presidents are mere lackeys of Wall Street and their names deserve to be smudged out of history with the thumb of public disapproval.

Although servitor after servitor of the financial powers, discredited in the public offices to which they were elected under false pretenses, has gone down in defeat and disgrace, their successors again and again prove of the same stripe. The quickly shifting sands of politics breeds traitors to the public interest who though having constituted the government one day are seen to emerge the next day as presidents of banks and financial companies and salaried employees of the trusts, while a new gang infests the seats of power. The government is thus intangible and irresponsible. The crimes of one set of officials cannot be visited either effectively on their heads or on the heads of their successors. There is nothing definite that can be called the government. It is only a badly working impersonal mechanism, now in control of one set of engineers and now another, all interested in running it for their own ends and not for the benefit of the public.

The evils that confront us are deeply rooted in an ineffective system, and to effect a cure measures must be taken which will go to the bottom of things. It is not time to temporize or delay; it is a fight that must be fought, and the sooner we know who is to survive, the financial powers or the public, the better off we will be.

The first thing the business man must have is at least an equal chance with the speculators. He should, in fact, have the advantage on his side that the speculator now enjoys, instead of the advantage being on the speculator's side. One of the prime requisites is to give his assets convertibility, and convertibility must be given to his obligations. That is to say, we should institute a new system of banking whereby the business man's notes which he gives to the bank, could be rediscounted by the bank, that is, passed on to some other bank in some other part of the country where money was more plentiful. If the notes of business men were in denominations of $100, $500, $1,000 and $10,000, and on being given were stamped by the bank in a manner which pledged not only the resources of that bank to their repayment, as well as the resources of the merchant himself, and in addition the resources of every other bank in the United States, such notes would become convertible and could be sent to financial centers and become objects of barter and sale in the place of the present corporation securities. Under present circumstances the government only issues currency to the value of its bullion and national banks are allowed to issue currency to the value of certain government bonds which they hold. Thus the amount of money in existence is rigidly fixed and cannot be increased or decreased in volume without the greatest difficulty. In times of a panic this bit of money, which is vastly less in value than the possessions of the citizens of the country, but the only medium of exchange, is instantly locked up by everybody who has any of it, and ruin results for all, through inability to get hold of a few tokens of value, although all have no end of valuables worth money, if they could be exchanged for the tokens, the supply of which, through a faulty legislative and banking system, is reduced to a minimum which cannot be readily expanded. Bankers, too, are loath to expand their currency issues, as when money is free again, they are paying 3% and 4% for the use of government bonds to make currency which they can only lend at 2% on call loans in New York.

What the country needs is convertibility of business men's obligations or notes, and an asset currency, that is to say, that when a man goes to the bank and pledges his house on his note and the bank pledges its resources and all the banks of the country through some central institution, pledge their resources for its repayment, the banks should be permitted to issue actual currency in the form of bank notes against say 25% of that value. An unlimited supply of the tokens of value would thus be available whenever wanted, and no panic could ever arise because panics are caused by the locking up of tokens of money, and with such tokens producible readily, there would be no lack of them to meet every obligation that might fall due.

The foundation of our money now is the credit of the United States Government. An asset currency would give it as a foundation the credit of all the owners of property in the country, which is better than the government, because the government is only the ability to tax that property, and the property itself is certainly more valuable than the ability to tax it.

A currency based on lumps of stored gold is a currency based on the value of that metal. A currency based on stored iron would be just as solid as a gold currency. Gold is simply used because its supply is somewhat uniform and its rarity makes a small amount of it valuable. A bank can store gold, but to store an equal value of iron would require larger quarters. Gold in itself, aside from its value as money, is intrinsically less valuable than iron. A currency founded on iron, or on lead, or on silver, if universally followed would be as useful as a gold currency. Any currency, however, founded on one material, like gold, is full of hardships, because when gold is discovered in great quantities, as in the last ten years, its value decreases, because it is more plentiful. Imagine gold suddenly becoming as plentiful as iron, and the dream of the miner is to discover the mother source of gold, in which case it would be as plentiful. It would lose its value immediately. Dollars would not buy what pennies buy now. To-day prices are seemingly higher than formerly, partially due to more gold being found. While the dollar remains a dollar, the man with twenty pounds of iron, for instance, will not sell it for less than a dollar, whereas formerly he would sell twenty-five pounds of iron for a dollar in gold.

The only scientific currency is one based not on one metal or material alone, but one based on all materials and metals. To give business men's notes convertibility, and instead of circulating them and selling them like so many bushels of wheat, to have a portion of them, or all, deposited at one point and used as the basis for currency, would be to make the standard of value, on which that currency was based, a standard including all forms of value. This would be a true currency, and being backed by the business assets of all the banks with the credit of the government behind that, would make an ideal currency, one perfectly elastic and suited to the needs of business. Panics could not then arise. A governmental tax on money in circulation higher than the tax on property would drive currency out of existence when it was not needed, without preventing its coming into existence again when more currency was needed to conduct the actual transactions of business life. It would be a system far more stable than the present one, in which every bit of commercial paper is always under suspicion, is not convertible and represents a source of friction between the bank and the borrower at all times with possibilities of a panic at any moment. There is no confidence in our present system by those who know anything about it, because they know that it is based on the inflated values of stock exchange securities. Thus if all depositors want their money at once they cannot get it. They should be able to but they cannot because the credit of the country depends on the ability and willingness of the managers of corporations to repurchase stocks in their companies. Their inability or disinclination to do this will at any time plunge the country into a panic.

All our business men are thus at the mercy of Wall Street, but with an asset currency which could be readily expanded, everybody could have his money at any time he wanted it. The fact that it was taxed by the government in the form of taxation on the notes on which it rested, would cause the makers of the notes to redeem them as rapidly as consistent with conditions and not to issue them unless required to do so, and this would automatically draw the actual currency back into the banks and to physical destruction as bits of paper, keeping values at all times out of the form of currency and in the form of property and other assets, except such proportion as might actually be required for daily transactions.

With the possibility of the banks loaning to local depositors, the small business man would have at his command the same degree of credit which is now monopolized by the trusts. Business would revive amazingly and every bit of capital in the country could be used in developments, instead of being tied up as it largely is at present.

The organization of banks, however, is carried out in a thoroughgoing spirit of monopoly which will not be upset without great difficulty. They are a kind of impudent band of leeches grown fat by manipulation and skimming of interest and other devices and they are an incubus on the prosperity of the country instead of the help that they should be.

Particularly dangerous are the consolidated banks which acquire great power through their enormous holdings. Their disintegration or unscrambling is a duty which the public owes to itself to perform without delay.

As an example of how great a profit the banks may make out of a very small item of their operation, may be cited the collection charge on checks passing from city to city. It was brought out in the 1912 hearings of the Congressional Committee investigating the money trust that the banks of New York derive a revenue of some $50,000,000 a year out of the charges made for collecting checks, practically the sum they pay out in dividends. Although in any individual case the amount of the collection is small, yet in the aggregate the absorption of this much value from the channels of commerce is a serious and indefensible drain.

Banks are given to small pluckings not much noticed by those plucked, but profitable in the aggregate. The charging of $2.00 a month for "carrying the account" of small depositors, one who maintains a balance of less than $200, is one of the profitable little side grafts of banking. In fact the whole subject of banking is one of many ramifications far beyond the scope of this volume. The sudden rise to positions of financial importance of many young men in the banking world is an evidence of the fine art of blackmail which thrives nowhere as in the world of finance, where slight deviations from the legal path on the part of high officials provide the foothold. With such men in such positions of power it is little to be wondered at that the banking system is one in which the position of the public is not dissimilar to that of a picked chicken.

The ability of the public which it should have, to use its money in any direction, free of the domination of Wall Street, would enable the establishment in this country of banks similar to those in Germany for promotion purposes.

The conduct of the treasury department of the United States has been contrary to the interest of the public and in favor of Wall Street. The national banking system is partially to blame for this, as banks are the avenues whereby the government reaches the public; and banks are not under governmental control.

While the citizen can lend the government money, by the purchase of government bonds, the government cannot directly lend the citizen money, and there are times when governmental lending is essential to the welfare of the country. In the panic of 1907 in order to prevent a great collapse of banks in New York, the government deposited many millions of its reserves in New York banks. This was unknown to the public, but the money, through the avenues of great financial houses, was placed at the disposal of the members of the stock exchange at an enormously usurious rate and the day was saved and a noted financier was given credit for saving the country. Under proper banking laws in which the government might lend direct to borrowers instead of having to put its money into banks and having no control of the use to which it is then put, save the privilege of withdrawing it, such an outrageous farce would be impossible and the financiers instead of wearing halos of glory and reaping huge harvests of interest, would be left to the last, in case of such necessity, like rats on a sinking ship, and the real business men of the country saved first.

The banker and broker are essentially middlemen of monetary dealings, but they are in such a position of advantage that they reap a large percent of the fruit of the labors of others without sowing themselves. They are monopolists of the avenues of distribution of money and credit and the government must place its money with them if the public is to gain any advantage. It has no other means of placing its surplus funds at the disposition of the public.

The government could retain its funds in its vaults and that has recently been done to a greater extent than usual, but such a course while it hurts the broker, hurts the business man more. It is as if the cook refused to deliver the dinner to the waiter to prevent him from stealing the tid-bits en route to the patron. Although the waiter broker is inconvenienced, the patron suffers a greater degree of starvation.

The accumulation thus of a great "dead mass of currency" in the government's vaults is nothing short of an economic crime.

A surprising negligence, too, is shown by the government in its relations with the banks which are depositors of the government funds, for such institutions do not have to pay the government interest, nor do they have to maintain a high reserve.

What actually happens when a bank receives a great government deposit is that the loan clerk of the bank telephones the loan clerk of a brokerage house that they have such a sum to lend, at a rate of interest which is fixed by the bank. The transaction is immediately concluded for the next day, such transaction being regularly carried out on one business day for deliveries the next day; the broker gets his check and the bank accepts as collateral the stocks of the big corporation or trusts as security. Sometimes the bank and the broker deal through an intermediary known as a loan broker, who does the telephoning, or who chases from broker's office to broker's office making the arrangements for a very small rake-off or the loaning may be done on the floor of the stock exchange itself, especially if it is late in the day. Such loans are usually for $100,000 each, though often for $250,000, and are made with a degree of convenience and celerity unmatched in ordinary business life. The government's money, as well as any other money on deposit in banks, thus slides as if on greased rails directly into Wall Street where the speculators who congregate to buy and sell in the brokers' offices may with the utmost facility borrow it again from the brokers to buy stocks with, in the corporations that crush the business man, who if he desires to borrow $5,000 or $10,000 even, must go to great trouble if not humiliation to get it, though he himself may borrow it from a broker's office to buy stocks with, with the greatest of ease.

The government has lost, it is estimated by officials, $100,000,000 in the last 25 years in interest on money placed in depository banks, if interest be only figured at 2%, a low but fair rate since the funds are withdrawable on demand. The banks, however, have under very rare circumstances ever loaned any money at less than 2%, and as they loan a large part of their money on time loans at higher rates and occasionally on demand or call loans, on which the money must be returned on one day's notice, at from 3 to 4% ordinarily and from that up to 20, 40, 60 and 75% and higher occasionally, with very little risk of the government withdrawing its funds suddenly, the banks have thus profited not less than $250,000,000 during the 25 years, or some ten millions a year on this one small, unnoticed item, a sum which would match the philanthropies of even a Carnegie, a Rockefeller or a Morgan if devoted to the public's good instead of to the banks.

Thomas A. Edison in an interview, after his recent return from Europe, in the *New York Times*, copyrighted by the Publisher's Press, and written by Edward Marshall, points out the advantage of this feature of German banking.

"One great advantage which the manufacturers of Germany have over us and over every other country, is to be found in her great promoting banks. In the United States, a man who wishes to get something new on the market, must get hold, in one way or another, of a promoter of his enterprise, and our promoters are notoriously irresponsible. There, inventions are brought out by promoting banks.

"For instance, the Deutscher Bank, which in the first place is one of the largest banks in the world, has a corps of engineers and auditors ready to investigate every phase of any proposed invention. If the invention which is taken to them proves, after the most careful investigation, likely to be useful and profitable, the money is forthcoming. The financial and technical investigation is rigid to the last degree, but if the idea stands the test, the capital is ready.

"The same plan can be followed by a manufacturer who wishes to extend his business. If he can prove that he can do so profitably, he can get the money for the purpose from the bank at a reasonable interest and very promptly. It saves time and keeps him from the clutch of that particular breed of sharks, who in this country would be likely to make a prey of him.

"The bank, then, will watch the progress of the invention or of the manufactory, will place its stock on the Exchange, and, when it reaches a certain point of prosperity, will take its money back, charging only a fair profit for its use, and leaving the in-

ventor or manufacturer with his invention or his factory ready
to go ahead with it alone.

"This is an enormous encouragement to the inventive faculty
of Germany, and I predict that it will soon put the German
nation in advance of us in the origination and development of
new mechanical ideas.''

Promotion in America, as Mr. Edison indicates, is certainly
carried on in an irresponsible manner.

The promoter usually demands an extortionate proportion of
the capital secured, and in many instances the promoter exists
solely by getting advances in fees from those looking for capital,
without ever securing the desired money for the enterprise.
Many companies are floated by promoters, knowing that they
can never succeed and the promoter thus fleeces the public and
the original owner of the project.

The government has lately found a means of stripping the
notoriously fraudulent promoters of their powers, and in many
cases of their liberties, through a law which prescribes penalties
for using the mails to defraud, but the post office department, to
effect these results has been given dangerous powers, which are
subject to abuse, and in addition to having the potentiality of
evils worse than are cured, places those prosecuted in the light
of martyrs. Animus is ascribed, and the use of the mail has
been declared by the highest courts a privilege withdrawable
by the department and not a right of the citizen. A means of
reaching fakirs without such tremendous executive power should
be found, as the agents of the department carry out the law in
the most sensational manner possible, bringing it further into
disrespect by sudden raids upon suspected parties.

A spectacular arrest, with struggling prisoners, a gaping
crowd, axes, patrol wagons, broken doors and furniture and
other stagey accompaniments, is one of the specialties of American administration of justice. In Russia, an officer who cannot effect an arrest without a disturbance is discharged. It is
there usually only necessary to let the accused know that he is
wanted. He has respect enough for the law to come when he
is invited. In America the culprit has so little respect for the
law as to often engage in a physical struggle with the arresting
officer. This is a picture of legal inefficiency and explains much
of America's lawlessness. Having no respect, and properly so,
for most of the legislatures, the culprit feels that his liberties
are being invaded, which they often are, as is proved by the

highly numerous collection of laws decided unconstitutional, after citizens have been arrested and tried under them.

The underlying cause of spectacular arrests is political. Flourishes of this kind are supposed to impress the public with the thoroughness of the party in power. The administration of the police is a matter of politics and the head of the department, who very seldom has any previous experience in police work, feels the necessity of showing the public what it is getting for the money it is paying. Usually the gamblers, pool room men and resort keepers are made the victims, since no one will feel disposed to defend them. The police thus gain a little cheap advertising, and a certain amount of public opinion is formed, at least as affects those who do not see further than the ends of their noses. As there are many of this sort, whatever is sensational and spectacular, has a certain effect.

Ulterior motives so often are back of enforcements of the law as to render it still less worthy of respect. Certain busybodies make their living by getting up societies to enforce certain laws. Rich people contribute to such societies and in order to secure further contributions, the professional salaried reformer must show a certain degree of activity. Rescue homes for women, societies for preventing various cruelties and vices flourish, with consequent frequent miscarriages of justice, and the postal laws are often found a very useful medium for the reformer's activity. A characteristic incident of this kind was seen in the case of Oscar Krueger, for whom President Taft issued a pardon on Jan. 19, 1912, as told in the news dispatches as follows:

"President Taft granted to-night a pardon to Oscar Krueger, a New York plasterer, who has been serving a term of eighteen months in the Atlanta Penitentiary on the charge of sending improper matter through the mails. The pardon followed recommendation of District Attorney Wise of New York of the Department of Justice, on the theory that Krueger was wrongfully convicted last February, as investigation having convinced the Department of Justice that the accused did not write the offensive letters.

"The Department's version of the case is that a respectable young woman in New York advertised for a place and received a letter in response, which was considered improper. Anthony Comstock got possession of the letter and inserted a decoy advertisement, arranging for an appointment. The young woman went to the place, found no one there, but looking around saw a man in the neighborhood, and asked him whether his name was 'Ed,' the password for the meeting.

"Krueger was the man whom she met, but denied that his name was 'Ed,' explaining afterward that he said it was for a joke. He denied that he had written any letter. The Department of Justice compared Krueger's handwriting with that of the letter and was satisfied that he had not written the missive."

The formation of "public opinion" is achieved in many devious ways in the United States, and very largely by those who have some sort of ax to grind, generally unknown to the public.

Some newspapers grind their axes not only in the editorial columns, but most dangerously in the news columns and chiefly among the expedients are the concocted interview and the misleading headline. A striking yet artistic example of newspaper ax grinding was accomplished by the *New York World*, when Thomas A. Edison was made to do duty for its German ax, and a sorry figure the venerable inventor was made to show.

On leaving Hamburg, where he had received many courtesies, an interview was cabled to the *World* by its own special correspondent traveling with Edison, which included the following:

"There is something wrong with the German æsthetic lobe. They feed their brains too much on beer, and the result is beer architecture. The only dignified buildings I have seen are copies of the Greek and Roman. In architecture as in all else, the Germans lack proper initiative; they are good adapters, that's all.

"Another thing that handicaps German progress is their over-economy. They grudge spending money, and if a new machine comes out, the German will not buy it until he has used up the old one.

"Where American intelligence comes in, is in the willingness to spend money when necessary. There is no short-sighted penny-saving among our business men.

"One hears great talk about the high standard of business in Germany, yet at luncheon the other day with German financiers they admitted there is no comparison between English business standards and their own.

"The Englishman's is the highest standard of integrity in the world," Edison is made to say that he was told. "Our German aristocrats are entering largely into business now to get rich quick, and they don't care how it is done. Their methods have affected business ideals generally.

"It is my own opinion that the English are the highest type physically and mentally over here," the great inventor went on. "I do not believe in the talked-of industrial world-dominance of Germany.

"We have nothing to learn from her and she has much to learn from us."

This was published in the morning edition of Sept. 29, 1911, and in the afternoon, the *New York Globe* answered it as follows, not being, as it would appear from the opening sentence, too well convinced of its contemporary's accuracy.

"Did Mr. Edison really say, as the *World* makes him say, that "in architecture, as in all else, the Germans lack proper initiative; they are good adapters, that's all?" Somehow this does not sound like an exact likeness of the Germans. Translate Mr. Edison's general statement into particular statements, and the result looks rather queer.

"In music the Germans lack proper initiative. They are merely good adapters. Richard Wagner was a good adapter; that's all. The same thing is true of Richard Strauss. In statecraft and war, Germans lack proper initiative. Examples, Bismarck and Moltke. In philosophy they are nothing but good adapters. See the works of Immanuel Kant, *passim*. Goethe lacked proper initiative in dramatic poetry, lyric poetry, natural science, criticism and *lebensweisheit*.

"Even if we confine ourselves to our own day and to the single province of poetry, Mr. Edison's assertion is just as wide of the mark. We suppose most Germans would say their most eminent living poets were Richard Dehmel and Stefan George. It is conceivable that Mr. Edison may hear nothing but the echoes which undoubtedly make up part of George's talent, that he may be deaf to the equally undoubted originality, but can Mr. Edison or anyone else seriously maintain that Dehmel is a mere adapter without initiative?"

On October 1st, the *World* published a letter from its special correspondent traveling with Edison, dated Dresden, Sept. 20th, in which Edison is reported as having said:

"Germany leads with its industrial chemistry; there's no people that can touch it in that important branch. The German brain seems perfectly fitted for success in such experiments;

they leave all other countries behind in their magnificent initiative in that line.''

While Edison found that the æsthetic lobe of the German brain is too much fed on beer, with the terrible result of beer architecture, it is evident that they have magnificent initiative in chemistry, whether on account of beer or in spite of it does not appear.

The question of beer drinking, for which Germany is so famous, needs a little consideration on its own account. Beer drinking in Germany is carried on in such an open manner that it forces itself upon the attention of visitors. But the quantity of beer consumed in the United States in 1910 was 1,851 million gallons against 1,704 million gallons in Germany, making 20.09 gallons per capita in the United States against 26.47 per capita in Germany. In the United States, however, there are nine dry states, 882 dry counties and 6,994 dry towns against none in Germany, and as it is more convenient to drink distilled spirits in the so-called dry states, counties and towns, the remaining states of the Union easily lead in beer consumption per capita as compared with Germany. American beer, in addition, contains twice as much alcohol as German beer as consumed in Germany, therefore the American consumption of alcohol in beer is twice as much as German consumption. The German can thus drink two glasses of beer to the American's one with no more inconvenience. He thus seems to be a large beer drinker but in reality consumes only half as much of the intoxicating principle as the American does.

The distilled spirits consumption of the United States in 1910 was 134.6 million gallons, which is more than ten millions more than the German consumption. Further, American whiskey is 50% stronger than German whiskey, as newly arriving Germans quickly find out, to the amusement of bar tenders and waiters who first serve them, and to their own eye opening surprise.

And a large proportion of American whiskey is not the real thing, but a doctored composition of nobody knows what. If German architecture is beer architecture, American architecture should be rot gut architecture.

On Mr. Edison's arrival in New York, having shed his special correspondent with other impedimenta of his journey, he denied to the assembled reporters many of the statements that had been attributed to him. The *World* of October 8th, however, in order to save its face, headed its interviews: "Edison Stands by What He Said About Germans." In the article the following appeared:

"I gave the reporter who was with me all the time, a lot of 'dope.'"

And the *World* in passing the "dope" along, stated further:

"I had no means of knowing what the report did say until I saw this interview. I said that what the Germans themselves acknowledged was that the integrity of their commercial classes was not as high as that of the English.

"They admitted it themselves.

"I had to take their own word for it. I had no means of knowing the standard of integrity of the German business classes. I will say personally that I believe the Germans entirely honest, the most honest in the world. I have had them in my laboratories all my life.

"I think Germany is the most advanced nation in Europe. She has a million factories and is building more and more all the time, and growing more and more prosperous.

"When a German sells $100 worth of goods, they weigh about 30 pounds; when a Frenchman sells $100 worth, they weigh 400 pounds, and when an Englishman sells $100 worth of goods, they weigh half a ton."

As to the integrity of German business men and the statements made to him by the Germans themselves; although not so reputed in America, the German is in reality a very polite person. In Spain, the visitor has but to praise an object to be informed that it is his, while in Germany if the visitor deprecates any condition of his own country, the German will declare something similar in Germany to be much worse, whether it is or not. The statement that German business honor is inferior to English was probably made to comfort Edison on American trusts.

In an interview in the *New York Times* of October 22, 1911, Mr. Edison, speaking of the German appetite says:

"At German restaurants, the general tendency toward overeating is a painful sight to witness, really. Americans, as a rule, I have observed, eat about twice as much as they need; Germans eat twice as much as Americans, which is four times as much as they need. The prosperity of the German nation is in spite of the most extraordinary overeating. And a people who take into their systems every day, 75% more food than is necessary to give the proper strength and weight must necessarily suffer from it.

"I made an interesting but necessarily crude calculation in Germany. If Germany ate as much as she ought to, she could export food products instead of importing them at the rate of $2,000,000,000 annually. She pays, therefore, far more than $2,000,000,000 every year for the food which she consumes in plain excess of her needs.

"This, in an era of prosperity along most scientific and commercial lines, is a startling contradiction, an astonishing instance of extravagance and foolishness in the midst of careful economies and common sense.

"She eats far too much, but she drinks with a more reckless absurdity than she eats. Her tremendous consumption of beer, wine and high alcoholic ciders, is appalling. It hurts her people mentally and physically and hurts the nation economically."

As to the overeating, it is quite possible that Germans in public eat more than in private, as is the case in America. In New York, for example, there are numerous popular restaurants which are patronized by a transient class. New Yorkers entertain their visitors, and on particular occasions go out to eat at these restaurants. Although they are always filled, the patronage is not the same crowd night after night. One such meal will upset the average digestion for a week. With the Germans the same is true, so that the eating that is seen in public restaurants is by no means an index of the actual amount of food consumed under normal circumstances. However, it is customary with all Germans to eat five times a day. Even manufacturing concerns during working hours are compelled by law to allow employees three periods for eating which are in addition to their meals before and after working hours.

As the consumption in America of malt and alcoholic liquors is greater than in Germany, and as the alcoholic liquors are 50% stronger in America, Mr. Edison's admonitions are more applicable to America than to Germany. Only in wine consumption, mostly taken with meals, is Germany in excess of America. The German cannot understand a three dollar dinner with water on the side. Water, although filtered in Germany and without river ice, is believed to be best suited for ablutions.

In America drinking is not carried on as frankly as in Germany and is only witnessed by those who go into the bars to drink themselves, although the parade of "souses" is more noticeable in America. If eight persons enter a bar room, as a rule good fellowship requires a treat all around, which means sixty-four glasses all told. Even if the later ones are only beer in whiskey or champagne glasses, for the benefit of those who can no longer lift the heavier receptacles and the saloon owner, there is still an appreciable quantity consumed. In America when the suffragettes come fully into their own, and eight visit a soda fountain, 64 ice cream sodas will then be customarily served.

It would appear that the *World* succeeded more or less in embroiling Germany and Edison, and placing the latter in a very ridiculous light. The criticisms which he was credited with did not injure Germany, as they were obviously ill-considered, but the interviews had the effect of making Edison belittle himself.

Emperor William makes every effort to receive distinguished American visitors, and the failure of Edison, the most noted inventor in the world, to meet him, may have been due to these newspaper inventions.

Mr. Edison may have came in contact with a phase of the system described by Mr. Charles Edward Russell in "Germanizing the World," in the *Cosmopolitan Magazine* of January, 1906:

"A hostile or critical correspondent finds in Germany the avenues of information gently but firmly closed against him. So quietly is this done that the unfortunate man is slow to believe that he is really boycotted, and so effectively that he can get nothing he wants."

In order to show the real opinion which Mr. Edison formed on his visit, and to do justice to him, the following extracts from interviews with him in the *New York Times* of October 22nd, and 29th, 1911, from which we quote by courtesy of the Publishers' Press, show at once the facts in the case and the many things that Americans can learn abroad.

"The Germans have wheat which seems to show a higher gluten content than our own. We should investigate this carefully.

"I looked into the matter superficially and discovered that the fact is well known to the experts, so well known that some of the best American hotels import this wheat to have their flour ground from it. Its gluten content is so high that people fed on bread made from this wheat do not actually need meats.

"They are careful in investigation of such matters over there, and we should be, but are not. We don't seem to care. It is a pity.

"They gave us 'balanced bread' as a matter of course. We do not get it in America. Over here we take out all the phosphorus and certain other things and unbalance it.

"It no longer remains a really normal human food, and I believe that to be a bad thing for us. Beri-beri, one of the disease curses of the Asias, is due to eating rice unbalanced by the removal of the shell.

"This has been sufficiently demonstrated, so that the demonstration of the cause has pointed out the way to certain cure. To sufferers from beri-beri, they give water in which rice shells have been boiled, which amounts to an essence of the very properties the lack of which has caused the trouble. The sufferers get well.

"There is undoubtedly good cause for a great national food reform movement in the United States. I don't know that the white bread that we eat is bad for us, but I do not believe that it is as good for us as German bread is for the Germans. I believe that nature knows better than we do, and that we'd better not unbalance our grain rations.

"I saw," says Mr. Edison, speaking of housing in Berlin, "what made me ashamed for my own United States, I am afraid. The workingmen of New York City are not housed as are these Berliners. What a contrast to the dreadful tenements which disgrace and deface New York's crowded districts.

"The buildings which these workingmen went home to could not properly be spoken of as 'tenements'—a term which in this country has fallen into disrepute. They may better be referred to as apartment houses, beautifully constructed, perfectly supplied with air and light, safe against fire and made up of large and conveniently arranged rooms.

"Each story has its large iron balconies, and the balconies are generally jammed with flowers. In this country, flowers or anything else upon the balconies are violations of the law, for they might obstruct their use as fire escapes.

"In the German city, not only are they not forbidden, but are, I am informed, actually compulsory, because of the belief that beauty helps to make life pleasant, and that the pleasant life is likely to be the useful one. And the flowers upon them do not peril human life by obstructing them when they are needed for escapes from fire, for the very simple reason they are not needed for escape from fire. These German buildings do not burn. They are well built of good materials and really fire proof.

"I did not go inside to see the rooms, but was informed that the littlest apartment in them has four rooms, and that most of them are five room flats, and that they are provided very adequately with all the conveniencies of modern city life. It was a beautiful sight to see, in Berlin, block after block of these fine, model, workingmen's apartment houses.

"The rentals are extremely moderate, proportioned to the incomes of the men.

"They are doing great things in Berlin to make the people happy—making an incredibly fine city of the German capital. I went through many factories in Berlin, and its environs, and after I had finished my long visit to one of them, I stood outside to watch the workmen as they left it at the end of the working day. I wanted to see how they looked and acted, and then, I wanted to follow some of them and see how they were housed— what sort of homes they had.

"The Germans are the world's most persistent people. When they start a thing, they usually get it, and they have started now to capture our mechanical prestige. It will take hard work and intelligent work in the United States to prevent them from outstripping us.

"I went into the packing rooms of several large German factories, and there found indications that their foreign trade is larger than their domestic trade, which is enormous. They are wonderfully energetic and intelligent. They organize with singular ability and extraordinary patience. They have started a solemn, unsensational, but ruthless, and never slacking campaign for the world's trade, fighting us where we oppose them, fighting England where she has business which they covet, pushing ahead everywhere.

"It behooves us to take thought of this, and watch them closely. There is much which we might learn with profit in their methods.

"I was informed in Germany that German capital has established banks in all parts of the world for the purpose of assisting German merchants resident abroad, so that she not only exports goods, but makes the profit from their sale abroad and furnishes the necessary banking facilities, also highly profitable, through which the business is concluded.

"I became interested with another thing—I believe I see the

true inwardness of the Emperor's naval policy. No one wants war less than he, no one would do more to keep out of war. But he considers a large navy a good investment. The German navy is a commercial proposition. The money spent upon it is a mere premium paid on the insurance which it offers to German capital invested in remote spots of the world; it protects German merchants wherever they may be, and assures them of what T. R. is fond of calling a square deal.''

Mr. Edison summarizes the difference which he observed between this country and Germany in the following list of items, many of which are of the greatest importance. Interviews of this kind are much more illuminating and useful than misrepresentations hot off the cable.

"German industries are pushing ahead faster than ours, and a new financial scheme threatens our prestige, even in the production of new inventions.

"German factory construction, factory management and protection of workingmen is far in advance of ours.

"European land is not nearly so good as ours, but the average crop per acre on it is three times as large.

"Our people are wasteful and unscientific all along the line.

"We neglect our opportunities with startling carelessness.

"An enormous roadside crop of apples is grown in Germany on land which would be wasted in this country.

"The immense advantage of intensive farming, not realized in the United States.

"Our farmers diffuse their time and energy on crude cultivation of large areas.

"Good European building laws, absolutely enforced, are far superior to ours.

"Fire horrors like those peculiar to America are impossible in Germany.

"German building depreciation is only a small percentage of ours.

"Germany is not behind us in general manufacturing and far in advance in chemical industries.

"The Continental European farmer is infinitely more effective than the American farmer, because he is more careful and less wasteful.

"A great movement to increase rural efficiency is in progress in Austria, and America needs something of the same sort.

"The German peasant understands many of the great requisites of success far better than the American farmer does.

"From a soil so bad that we would scorn it, the foreign agriculturist produces marvelous crops.

"Berlin is full of energy; Berliners even in their walking gait show signs of their great progress.

"Berlin night life is as brisk as their day life; it is brisker, even, than New York's.

"Night life is much maligned; it means progress and efficiency; and stupidity and night life do not go together.

"Too much sleep may be a national curse.

"One added hour of night life will do wonders with a nation.

"Berlin is truly wonderful and has a street finer than any in this country.

"They are doing more in Germany to make the people happy than we are in America.

"The homes of Berlin workingmen make one ashamed of the United States; the dreadful tenements which disgrace and deface American cities, threatening health and happiness, are supplanted there by magnificent apartment houses.

"Law means law in Germany; in the United States it does not; and this is particularly true of building laws to prevent loss of life by fire.

"Management of public officers is better in Germany than in the United States, fewer laws and these more competent than ours.

"Germany has taken her city governments out of politics.

"Graft as we know it here does not exist in Germany.

"In the chemical industries, Germany far surpasses us.

"Germany controls trusts admirably, but she encourages, not discourages them.

"And Germany is very prosperous while we are grumbling at hard times.

"Emperor William not a war lord really, but a potentate of commerce.

"He'll never go to war if he can help it; his army and navy are business investments.

"William is a marvel among monarchs, a sporadic case of great ability in an ocean of incompetence.

"We are careless, even in our wheat selection; Germany is not.

"No similar journey in the United States could have been made for the same money."

CHAPTER XVI

STIMULATING PROGRESS

Foreign criticism as an unintended stimulus of progress—Germany's well planned policy—Expansion of the German merchant marine—Germanizing the world—Self criticism one of the secrets of German success—Absorbing the wealth of the world's knowledge—What England pays for self satisfaction—Blunders of English statesmen in relation with Germany—Origin of the phrase, "Made in Germany"—A blundering naval demonstration—Futility of the new English patent law—Recent German industrial colonies in England—The stimulus of criticism and the dangers of flattery—Vast influence of the press—How directed to useful purposes—Remarkable control of the press in Germany—How all things work together for the benefit of German policy.

In the world rivalry of the great powers, the tremendous advances made in the last generation, particularly in Germany, are disconcerting to other powers, and to some a source of the greatest distrust and irritation.

Yet no little of the stimulus which Germany has received has been unconsciously applied by envious rivals in the form of criticisms intended to harass and destroy her commerce.

Internally the conscious criticism, that with which Germany regards her own efforts, has been the informing motive of her well planned policy.

Of the workings of the German system, Mr. Charles Edward Russell under "Germanizing the World," in the *Cosmopolitan* of January, 1906, writes:

"In well considered, definitely planned, undeviating, relentless but peaceful aggression, the rest of the world seems asleep in comparison with the German government. No man can mention an instance in the last thirty-five years in which they have been worsted.

"They are persistent, tireless, indefatigable, always at it, pushing German goods here, German ships there and German influence everywhere. In politics and diplomacy, or in trade and commerce, they work with the same inspiration to the same end. We have seen them here at our doors steadily elbowing the British from the North Atlantic carrying trade, steam and sail.

Look over the lists any day and see the number of German steamers that enter the port of New York now and think back to the days when the German flag was a rare sight in our harbors. Is it not amazing?

"And what they have done in a small way here, they have done in a great way around the globe. Look at the map of one of their steamship lines. They send ships to every maritime country. They go into Southampton and take the cream of the Eastern trade from under the very faces of the British. They go into India and Australia and crowd the British out of their own markets. England itself they flood with goods, they force themselves into the English colonies; they have steamship lines to Montreal and Melbourne, they drive into Calcutta and Bombay; they have huge settlements in South America, they get the fat concessions in Turkey and Argentina. And at the head of all this is the German government urging, encouraging, advising, pushing. Not many years ago we used to draw a greater part of our immigration from Germany. Very few Germans immigrate now. They have too much to do at home. You can hardly find a considerable German town that cannot show a new factory or an old one enlarged. The prosperity of the country seems boundless and has a novel kind of patriotic inspiration; for it is not alone to make money but to spread Germanism that the merchants strive and dare. Every enterprise that carries German influence abroad can count upon the government's intelligent support.

"Trade may follow the flag or the flag may follow trade, I do not know which; but one thing is sure enough: German influence follows German commerce. The clever German government sees to that. First comes a German steamship carrying German goods, then a German branch sets up; then other German houses come in, then there is a German consul in that part and in ten years the place is saturated with Teutonism. It has been so all about South America, the East, the South Seas and elsewhere. It will be more and more so from this time on."

Such is the German policy. It is the policy which has made Germany what it is to-day, envied by many short sighted nations. The tremendous advantages which Germany possesses over other nations is in almost all cases the reason why Germany is attacked by other nations. Even for the only fairly well informed observer, it is rather amazing to see part of the daily press expressing their views, or rather making statements regarding Germany and everything pertaining to Germany, which in nine cases out of ten are self-contradictory. Their efforts no doubt succeed in forming a certain phase of public opinion, especially as regards those unfamiliar with what is going on abroad, or those who flatly refuse to make themselves acquainted with conditions.

Some papers imagine that they have an ax to grind, and they proceed to do it at the expense of their readers, and to some degree of the nations at large. Would it not be a great benefit to the public instead, to be kept informed of progress in other countries, and have the fact kept in mind that there are things which can be learned from other nations?

Germany openly and frankly acknowledges that she learns many lessons from America. Exchange professors are one striking example. The Germans are proud of their methods. They send their young men the world over to study foreign methods, languages and customs. They then adopt such as are practical and combine them with their own thorough practice and theories. Is it any wonder that to-day they lead the world?

Germany, forty years ago, a poor second rate country, stands now as an example for the world; Japan, ten years ago likewise poor and less than a second rate country, has achieved the most remarkable historical progress of our generation. These startling advances have been principally due to the ability to recognize their own inferiority compared with other nations, and then achieve the superior position. The costly price of inefficiency which England paid and is paying and will pay for a long time to come, is due to the self-satisfaction she exhibits, the belief that she cannot learn from other nations, and this is the principal reason she is standing still if not retrograding.

In her relations to Germany, the statesmen of England are continually making blunders. Among numerous examples, a notable one is the phrase "Made in Germany" which has become famous the world over. This phrase had its origin in an English regulation, compelling articles of German manufacture sold in England to be so labeled. What was intended as a means of discrimination, soon became a trade mark of great value, just as the queues of the Chinese, a Manchu ordinance, became a Chinese badge of honor, defeating the intentions of the discriminators.

Ordinarily, the German is inclined to be easy going, to let well enough alone, but he does not like to be rubbed too much the wrong way. England some years ago made a great and overawing naval demonstration in the North Sea, with the idea of frightening the Germans. The result was that the German government seized the opportunity to invite the public to the North Sea coast, providing excursion rates, and the impression intended by England was duly registered, with the contrary result, however, that vast naval expenditures were authorized shortly thereafter, the English thus playing directly into the hands of the German administrators. King Edward thus proved to be the greatest promoter the German navy ever had.

A recent example of the futile efforts of the English ministers to curb German development is found in the new English patent law, which compels patented articles to be manufactured in England. It was argued that this would keep millions of pounds in England, and it was aimed at the German manufacturer, and also against the United States.

The result has been disappointing, many patents lapsing, other companies withdrawing, while in the case of the more important inventions, especially the German chemical patents, the result has been the employment, not of additional English labor, especially of the lower class, but the importation of trained German labor, since the English were not skilled and could not readily be trained. Thus numerous German colonies have been established in England and the patent laws have proven abortive, while at the same time putting in England a large number of men who have served in the German army, adding further to the great English bugaboo of a German invasion, one of the most curious examples of national hysteria that has ever been exhibited, and which has a fresh outbreak every time an imaginary Zeppelin is sighted.

The idea of a German invasion of England would probably never have occurred to a single German, not even the "terrible" German waiters or the sellers of frankfurters in the London streets, so feared as German spies, had it not been suggested in England, and the constant reiteration of the subject is the only thing that might, at some future time, tempt Germany to make the absurd attempt.

The growth of German colonies in England as a result of the patent law, has gone forward so quietly that the English ministry is not yet awake to it. What sort of an explosion will occur when this "peril" is fully recognized may readily be imagined.

English newspapers, realizing the blunders that have been made, and impotent in the face of German progress, have adopted a policy of continual attacks. Like the anti-German press everywhere, their efforts only redound to the injury of those making them. The "knocker" generally hurts no one as much as his own country. "Every knock is a boost."

Flattery would be a far more dangerous weapon, for if it is wished to destroy the ambition of a nation or of an individual, flattery will nine times out of ten succeed, inducing the fatal self-satisfaction of the belief that the ambition is already realized, potentially if not actually. The benefit of national criticism is too little understood. To criticise another country is to put it on its guard, call forth a defense, or if none be possible, the way is pointed out for an improvement which would not otherwise have been seen.

The tremendous influence which is in the hands of the press for the betterment or otherwise of a country is too little understood by the general public. The assumed superiority of American inventors, with other causes, has resulted in placing America in a second rate position in invention, and her inventors are in a most deplorable position.

The press of England and Germany are particularly flexible instruments for the expression of inspired opinions, thus exerting enormous influence.

Charles Edward Russell in the *Cosmopolitan* of January, 1906, on "Germanizing the World," says:

"Intelligent observers have often marveled at the way the English press is controlled to further the ends of England's international interests no matter which party may be in power. For example, the government having concluded that it is for the best interests of England to frighten Germany by affecting a partiality for France, the entire press, Liberal, Conservative, Radical and Socialistic, breaks out into elaborate eulogies of France and the French, those that on such an occasion as the Dreyfus trial, for instance, had exhibited the most violent hatred for anything French, being now the most elequent and fervent in chanting praises. But the German government can beat such an achievement and not half try.

"The British press, it must be admitted, is not skillful about these things. Too often the praise sounds forced, the welcome has a false ring. The German government can influence the German press to say things in a way that carries conviction.

"Moreover, the British government can, as a rule, influence only the newspapers in Great Britain; the German plan is to influence the papers of the world so far as German affairs and interests are concerned. This seems at first thought merely a grotesque fancy, in reality it is not fantastic nor even difficult. The center of German news is Berlin. The news that is sent out from Berlin flows through certain well-defined and recognized channels. Five or six news bureaus supply the bulk of the correspondence for all the newspapers of the world.

"The news despatch, wisely conducted, is therefore the strongest weapon of the modern government, and in its use of this weapon, the German government has shown all others to be children. The English have the mere rudiments of the art; the French and we know naught of the matter. It is not merely in international politics that the German government finds in its press its greatest instrument; in the limitless field of German influence and German commerce the press plays a mighty part for Germany.

"In Berlin is the best, the most complete, and the best managed press reading and clipping bureau in the world, run by and for the German government. There is not anywhere around the world a conspicuous publication affecting in any way the interests of Germany, that does not find its way to this bureau. The great newspapers of all languages are watched incessantly and every correspondent in Berlin is rated according to his disposition towards the German plan. A simple but tremendous force is brought to bear to discourage hostility and what the government regards as misrepresentation.

"The value to his newspaper of any correspondent lies in his facile access to the sources of news. A hostile or critical correspondent finds the avenues of information gently but firmly closed against him. So quietly is this done that the unfortunate man is slow to believe that he is really boycotted, and so effectively that he can get nothing that he wants. He is, in fact, marooned, he might as well be on a desert island. But for the astute correspondents that never offend and never tell what they should keep quiet, life in Berlin is made easy and the path straight.

"Sometimes a newspaper, say in London, prints an objectionable letter or telegram from Berlin and obtains it from other sources than its regular correspondent. In such a case apparently disinterested inquiries are made. The correspondent clears himself, and all is well, for the system is conducted with perfect fairness.   Once or twice a careless or youthful correspondent has undertaken to deny the authorship of his own work and woe has been his portion for his indiscretion.   In Germany, the government operates the telegraph; it can easily discover who sent any particular message in which it may take an interest.

"The system is ingenious, elaborate, ably conducted and most useful.   It amounts to a censorship without the name or appearance of that odious institution, and in another way it is far better than any censorship could be, because it is inspirational and creative, and it is positive, not merely negative, it avoids the unpleasant and spreads the agreeable.

"For instance, the German government prefers that little be printed about the German navy and that that little shall not be commendatory.   Persistently it has fostered the notion that the German navy is a poor thing lagging at the heels of other navies. As a matter of fact, man for man and ship for ship, it is one of the very best navies afloat, but the world in general does not suspect the fact and the German government is satisfied with the world's ignorance.   The German newspapers say so little about the navy of Germany, about the new ships and the preparations and the maneuvers, that when there is some demonstration, like that at Kiel last summer, the unprepared spectator learns with a shock that here is a sea power surely to be reckoned with.''

Other countries pluming themselves over the construction of 14" naval guns are disturbed to find Germany in the possession of 15-inch guns, on several ships, though the fact had not been allowed to become public in Germany.

Germany in the dissemination of news has recently gone to the extent of reducing cable rates, so that cables go direct from Germany to the United States instead of going via London. This has the effect of preventing any possible discoloration of the news while passing through English hands, which has, it is claimed, so frequently occurred.

Such a discoloration is peculiarly an English expedient, the depreciation of a rival seeming to satisfy the public of its own inferiority.   British stupidity is summarized in an interesting manner by Mariano Herggelet, a German writer resident in England for fifteen years, in a recent volume in which he sums up the Englishman's doctrine as follows:

1. Don't think, reflect, or bother your head about anything.

2. Don't make any unnecessary exertion.

3. Don't get excited about your mistakes, neglect, or failure to do things. They don't matter.

4. Don't learn any foreign languages; there are always plenty of foreigners about to do what may be needed in this line.

5. Don't change anything until it is too late.

6. Don't learn anything from other nations.

7. Don't take any preventive measures—just calmly let calamity approach.

8. Don't have any exaggerated sense of duty; there are other people for that.

9. Be sure to forget everything promptly; a long memory simply disturbs the peace of the soul.

10. Keep no promises, except when they concern pleasure or sport.

11. Never be thorough—do only what is absolutely necessary.

12. Don't begin anything too soon. "Mañana!" To-morrow is another day.

13. Remember that unconcern and indifference will carry you gently and pleasantly through life.

14. Remember that superficiality and comfort save trouble and beautify existence.

15. Dream, idle happily, lull yourself with delicious thoughts of riches and sport, sleep long, eat much, work lightly and little, spend a quarter of an hour daily inveighing against your exasperating political opponents, pay your taxes, be satisfied, believe implicitly in the natural superiority of the British Nation, and act pleasantly toward everybody, so far as externals are concerned.

There can be no doubt of the accuracy of this estimate of English characteristics, as it is attested by numerous other observers. Traits such as these are in fact more or less evident in all Anglo-Saxon races of modern times. It might not be unprofitable for them to seek example for improvement from the German descendants of the original parent stock which boasts a history of fifteen centuries before the branching off of the Anglo-Saxon branch. Many of the traits which have proved so disastrous to the English people are jeopardizing American institutions and are the basis of our present inability to cope with conditions which have arisen. They are the primary cause of the unequal distribution of wealth which is the most serious condition in this country to-day, where 3% of the people own 20% of the wealth, and 9% of the people own 51% of the wealth, and 88% but 29% of the wealth, while in Germany only 2% of the wealth is held by the rich, 54% being held by the middle classes and 44% by the lower classes.

Wealth in Germany is more uniformly distributed than in any other country, due largely to the efficient administrative system, while prosperity is very rapidly increasing. The average savings deposited in savings banks per capita of the whole population, in 1910 was in round numbers as follows: Germany $64, United States $46, France $28 and Great Britain $24, while the number of depositors was 21, 9, 14 and 13 millions respectively. From this it will be seen that nine million depositors in the United States saved a little more than did twenty-one millions in Germany, and that only one person in nine saves in the United States to one in three in Germany. This shows still further an unequal distribution of wealth in the United States.

A few laws or hurried emergency measures will not be sufficient to cause any considerable redistribution of wealth in this country. The condition is one which goes vitally into the habits and characteristics of the people and a fundamental realignment will be necessary to effect the cure.

CHAPTER XVII

UNDEVELOPED RESOURCES

The magical triumphs of modern chemistry and engineering—Coining the air—Romance of air nitrate—How it supplements dwindling resources —Soil fertility and its meaning to mankind—Norwegian air nitrate factories—Cyanamid as produced in Canada—Great natural wealth of the United States in water powers—Waste of 200,000,000 horse power annually—Costly ignorance of American engineers on hydroelectric subjects—The decline of American waterways—Ruthless methods of railways—Bright future of waterways, due to recent legislation—How cheap water transportation has enabled the United States to command the world's iron markets—Neglect of waterways and England's decay—Fatal self-satisfaction of English iron masters—Marvelous developments of German waterways—Why the tonnage of the Rhine is 100 times that of the Mississippi—Berlin the center of a web of canals—The extravagance of the "pork barrel" in Congress—Decline of the port of St. Louis—Receipts of modern canals—Electric towing —Lack of progress in manufacturing electrical implements—Co-operation of farmer and engineer—How it will double the farmer's earnings —Details of electric farm machinery—Lower cost of electricity on the farm—Multiplicity of uses of the electric motor—Electric plowing superseding the most ancient of labors—Profits of farm by products— Harvesting by electric light.

OF the great triumphs of modern chemistry and engineering, the reduction of the nitrogen of the air to a commercial product is one of the most notable that has ever been achieved. It is far reaching in effect and appeals to the imagination as few discoveries have ever done.

To get a tangible and salable substance, and one of the highest value to mankind, out of the impalpable air is a result that few would have dared predict a generation ago.

The great value of the discovery of the production of air nitrate is realized but little by the general public; but it may be understood when the fact is known that the natural supply of nitrate, which is known most commonly in the form of saltpeter, is near the point of exhaustion. Nitric acid is one of the fundamentals in the arts and nitrate is the principal fertilizer of the world, while saltpeter is an indispensable element of explosives. Besides these, there are a great number of important uses of nitrate, such as in the form of ammonia, etc., and a synthetic source of supply is therefore of enormous importance.

If before the discovery of air nitrate, the world's supply had been exhausted or cornered by some aggressive nation, the rest of the world, without explosives, would have been at its mercy, and an incalculable impoverishment of the earth's soil through the cutting off of the supply of nitrates would have resulted.

One of the greatest problems of the present time is to increase the fertility of the soil. The growing crops are constantly extracting from the soil three chemical substances,—nitrogen, potassium and phosphoric acid,—and it is necessary that they should be replaced in a form available for plant life.

The nitrate which has previously been used to improve the soil has come entirely from manures worked into the soil, supplemented of late years, owing to the insufficient supply and cost of manures, by deposits of nitrate of soda taken from South America, and sulphate of ammonia recovered as a by-product when coal gas is made.

The output of Chili saltpeter, or nitrate of soda, is at the rate of 1,500,000 tons per annum, and it has doubled in the last fifteen years, while 500,000 tons of sulphate of ammonia are produced annually. Owing to its high cost and scarcity, the demand is very much less than would be the case for a cheaper fertilizer.

The production of nitrates from the air, which, unlike water, is a mechanical mixture of various gases and not a chemical unity, will assist in keeping the composition of the air in a balanced condition, as most of the huge chemical processes of nature involve oxygen. The production of air nitrate assures inexhaustible supplies of a highly necessary substance since the air contains about 80% of nitrogen; and in addition it affords a means of utilizing water power, which under ordinary conditions, being of great volume at some seasons of the year and very much less at other periods, can only be partially utilized.

The energy thus running to waste amounts to an enormous total, and the production of air nitrate affords a means of transforming the waste energy of rainfall into soil fertility.

The Department of Commerce and Labor in its report on the manufacture of air nitrate fertilizers says:

"The original inventor of the electro-chemical process for manufacturing nitrate fertilizers and other chemical productions from the air was Prof. Birkeland, a Norwegian by birth. After Prof. Birkeland had made his discovery, some nine or ten years ago, he associated himself with Mr. S. Eyde, an experienced civil engineer.

"By experimenting on a small scale, it was ascertained that their electro-chemical process for the production of nitrate fertilizers from the atmosphere was likely to prove a success. Their process and subsequently their improvements and new inventions have been patented in the majority of European countries as well as in the United States. They organized a stock company entitled Aktieselskabet de Norske Kvälstofkompani, with a capital of $134,000 with which their first plant was built at Notodden, in Telemarken, some 70 miles from Christiania.

"Regarding the method by which the Birkeland-Eyde lime saltpeter or calcium nitrate is produced, it should in the first place be noted that it is a new way of utilizing electricity, although it is a succession of the experiments which the English physiologist, Cavendish, made in the eighteenth century, by which he produced combinations between the nitrogen and the oxygen of the atmosphere by letting electrical discharges pass through the air during the presence of a decomposition of alkali, and whereby he succeeded in producing small qualities of nitric acid. The Birkeland-Eyde method is in principle the carrying out on a larger scale of the same process as Cavendish started on a smaller one, with this difference, however, that Birkeland and Eyde have introduced new auxiliaries, which in themselves constitute highly original discoveries."

The process, briefly stated, is to pass air through an enormous electrical flame, of about 75 inches in width, which heats the air to 3,000 degrees Celsius, and the gases are then cooled and passed over lime in water, resulting in calcium nitrate which is sold in granular form like salt.

The company later consolidated with the Badische Anilin und Sodafabrick, a German concern, which had added improvements, and there are now several branch companies, with a total capital of over $16,000,000 all paid up, while the annual production will soon reach 80,000 tons.

Two German chemists, Adolph Frank and Nikodemus Caro, of the technical staff of the Simens-Halske Co., a great electrical firm, have discovered an entirely different process of extracting nitrate from the air. They combine coke and lime at 3,000 degrees Centigrade, resulting in a substance that has a great affinity for nitrogen, and draws it directly from the air. This is known as the cyanamid process and is a strong competitor of the Birkeland-Eyde process. Cyanamid is equally if not more valuable as a fertilizer and is easier to handle in its commercial form, being less liable to liquefy and cake.

Twelve companies will manufacture it in Europe, six of which are already in operation, while a plant has been erected on the Canadian side of Niagara Falls. The foreign plants have a capacity of 167,000 tons annually. Plants are in course of erection in Japan, Mexico and other countries.

Cyanamid sells at $55 to $60 a ton at present. Tests by 37 various governmental stations in Europe show its superior value as compared with Chili saltpeter as a fertilizer.

The United States has $70,000,000 invested in fertilizer factories of various kinds. Chilian saltpeter to the value of $75,-000,000 annually at two and one half times its former price is exported by Chili, $15,000,000 of which comes to the United States, and yet while, with almost criminal carelessness, we disregard our own resources and allow phosphate rock to be exported in large quantities, our imports of fertilizers of various kinds are $17,000,000 in excess of our exports annually. The whole of this amount could be saved by the erection of hydro-electric plants to utilize our vast wasted water power and to manufacture air nitrates.

The opportunity of the United States in this respect is unusual, since we have an enormous amount of water power going to waste, a condition not found in Europe, where a large part of the available power has already been utilized, while the total is vastly smaller than in the United States.

Norway has five and one half times the available water power of Germany and has 3,409 horse power available per 1,000 inhabitants, while Great Britain and Germany have only 23.1 and 24.5 per 1,000 inhabitants and but 3.06 and 2.6 horse power per square kilometer respectively (1 sq. kilometer equals 0.386 sq. miles). Switzerland, Sweden and Italy are next in order, Switzerland having 36.6 horse power per sq. kilometer, the largest of any, but practically all utilized. The following table, taken from the author's article, ''Hydro-electric Engineering Practice'' in the *Engineering Magazine,* shows the available horse power of the several countries:

Great Britain	963,000 H.P.
Germany	1,425,900 H.P.
Switzerland	1,500,000 H.P.
Italy	5,500,000 H.P.
France	5,857,000 H.P.
Austria Hungary	6,460,000 H.P.
Sweden	6,750,000 H.P.
Norway	7,500,000 H.P.
Total	35,965,900 H.P.

The United States has a total of 30,000,000 horse power in water power running to waste. If properly utilized by means of storage, economically constructed and properly designed plants following the latest European practice, this would amount to from 150,000,000 to 200,000,000 horse power. A steam horse power per year costs $20 so that a waste of power of $4,000,000,-000 is occurring annually.

Air nitrate cannot be economically produced by means of steam power as a lower cost per annual horse power is required than can be obtained with coal.

The utilization of water power in the United States has been greatly retarded by two main causes. The first is the fact that hydro-electric engineering is comparatively little understood in the United States, and a great number of plants have been erected by incompetent and inexperienced engineers so that they cannot even compete with steam power plants.

Not only are the plants usually badly designed, but the machinery is inferior. So little understood is this branch of work that the first book in the English language on the subject of the design of water wheels and turbines has only recently been announced for publication, and it is a translation of a German book not of the first class. The most successful manufacturers of turbines and water wheels in the United States employ German engineers and first copy foreign machinery, and then have the audacity to claim that the originals are imitations of their manufactures. A policy of bluff of this kind has some effect in a commercial way, but the forces of nature cannot be bluffed into accomplishing efficient results with inefficient machinery.

Progress in engineering depends on the interchange of ideas between the engineers of various countries the world over, and the American engineer in this respect has not kept up to date. The latest European practice is known to but few, and the practicability of building water power plants on an economical scale, which will be able to compete with steam and also to furnish power cheaply enough to justify the manufacture of air nitrate commercially here as it is abroad on such a large scale, is not therefore known to the capitalist, who does not accordingly invest. The progress of the whole country is thus held back by the ignorance and incompetency of its engineers, vast agricultural benefits lost and stagnation inflicted where there might be prosperity, all on account of engineering inefficiency.

Our American engineers either build too strong or too weak. They dislike the complicated calculations necessary to ascertain the proper size of members and constructions. It is not a question of ability to make the calculations, but they are simply not thorough and do not do it. The result is that there is a vast waste in all kinds of engineering projects. The cost of bridges, skyscrapers and other works is greatly more than it should be through use of too much steel and other materials, and machinery of all kinds, though compact in appearance, is inefficient in operation.

This tendency when applied to water power plants eliminates them entirely, and thus a vast industry is still born through engineering incompetency. Bankers will not advance money for new projects and the incompetent engineer himself not only keeps capital idle, but being idle himself, discourages by his example brighter men from seeking to enter the profession.

Engineering incompetence exhibits itself in lack of experience largely and in the building of constructions in a haphazard manner. Either too great a margin of safety is allowed on the one hand or else too much risk is taken on the other, as may be seen in the failure of the Austin dam and the Quebec bridge.

The second cause which retards the development of water power in the United States is the uncertain attitude of the government.

The government scented a water power site trust, which if it does exist should have been nipped in the bud in the first place, and has accordingly withdrawn many of the concessions and has the whole situation bottled up. The fear that capital will make too much is in this case, as in many others in the United States, the cause of much of the stagnation existing.

The inability of the government and private capital to reach a working arrangement retards the water power developments, and in the meantime horse power to the value of $10,000,000 a day goes to waste.

The United States, on the other hand, is standing at a new era in the development of its water transportation. The use of the great waterways, the Mississippi, the Missouri, the Ohio and their tributaries and water transportation on the great lakes and through the many important canals is about to be restored.

If public opinion secures the enforcement of the recent amendment to the Court of Commerce Act introduced by Senator Burton of Ohio, the millions that have been spent in waterways and their improvement will begin to bear fruit.

The practical extinction of water transportation in the United States, as in England, has been due to the fact that railroads were allowed unbridled and destructive competition. Railroads, at a loss to themselves, have cut rates to a point where the water transportation companies, unless powerfully organized, have been driven out of business. Then with competition gone, the railroads raised freight back to the original point or higher. The waterways, fearing a repetition of the same treatment, have not ventured to reenter the field again.

This process reduced river traffic at St. Louis from 2,130,525 tons in 1880 to 374,093 in 1909. A corresponding section of the Rhine carries 40,000,000 tons annually. The Mississippi is thus a graveyard of waters, her commerce assassinated by the railroads.

This condition, however, should be changed by Senator Burton's amendment, which in effect provides that if a railroad reduces rates in competition with a waterway, it cannot again increase them after the waterway succumbs. This will give the waterways an opportunity to compete on equal terms. A similar law fundamentally applied to all business would save a vast proportion of the business failures of the United States and go a long way towards solving the trust problem.

The heretofore ruthless domination of the railroads has resulted in a dog in the manger situation, the railroads having but 60% of the capacity necessary to handle the traffic of the country, even at their extortionate rates. Car famines and congestion of traffic with no prospect of relief in either facilities or rates is the situation that will be relieved by the operation of the new law if it proves successful.

How important cheap water transportation is may be seen from the condition of the iron business. In Germany water transportation under governmental encouragement and in the United States under conditions of ownership in which the self-interest of the railroads did not throttle it, has been the factor of most importance in the realignment of the iron producing nations.

The Department of Commerce and Labor in its Bulletin of January, 1909, states in part:

"The German iron and steel industry is the growth of the last quarter of a century. Within that period Germany has distanced Great Britain and has become second only to the United States in raw iron production. In 1885, the production of Great Britain was 7,534,000 metric tons, the United States, 4,109,000 and Germany 3,687,000. By the end of 1907 the relative positions of the three countries which together produced 81% of the world's raw iron was: United States, 26,194,000; Germany, 13,046,000 and Great Britain, 10,083,000 metric tons.

"In the conversion of raw iron, that is in making steel, the change has been even more momentous. In 1900, when Germany passed Great Britain, the figures of steel production were: United States, 10,382,000; Germany, 6,646,000, and Great Britain, 5,131,000 metric tons. In 1907, the steel production of the three countries, comprising approximately 80% of the world's total, stood: United States, 23,733,000; Germany, 12,064,000 and Great Britain, 6,627,000 metric tons."

These figures are an explanation of the larger part of the disaffection existing in England. The loss of dominance in such a vast industry in less than a generation is a staggering blow to British self-satisfaction. Its possibility, while foreseen by German and American engineers, was brushed aside as an impossibility by British experts.

The preliminary report of the Inland Waterways Commission, 1908, states:

"More than twenty years ago, a British student of commercial conditions visited the United States to investigate the outlook of the iron and steel industry in this country. On his return home, he gave assurances to British iron manufacturers that they need have no serious fears of the competition of the United States, because in America the great iron ore deposits were too far distant from coal. He was positive it would never be possible to bring the ore to the coal or the coal to the ore at such rates as would enable production of iron and steel cheap enough to compete with England.

"How completely erroneous was this conclusion need not be suggested now, because everybody is familiar with the marvelous facilities for bringing the Lake Superior ores to the Pittsburg iron district, and with the success of the American iron and steel industry in competing with all the world, despite the initial disadvantages they had to overcome. Witnesses before the British Royal Commission repeatedly declared that the process of bringing the Lake Superior ores to the docks on the upper lake, first by rail, then by Lakes Superior, Huron and Erie to ports convenient to the coal districts and finally by rail to the seats of the iron industry is the greatest achievement in transportation the world has ever seen.

"So much for the British ironmakers' error in underrating the possibilities of internal transportation in the United States. As to Germany, their error was hardly less striking. In the beginnings of the development of the great German iron trade, English iron interests declined to take German competition seriously, because the government ore deposits were considered utterly inadequate for the development of a really great industry, and it was presumed that the transportation of great quantities of ore to the seats of the German industries would be so expensive as to make it utterly unprofitable. Yet, in fact, the Germans have developed an iron industry which is now a matter of concern to every competing country, and which is based, like that of the United States, on a system of extremely cheap water transportation. While there is a large and increasing production of iron ore in Luxemburg, which is utilized in the German iron industry, and while Germany itself produces a large and growing annual tonnage of ore, and brings still other amounts from Austria-Hungary, it is nevertheless true that the major part of the iron ore reduced in Germany comes from the Scandinavian peninsula and from Spain. To the canals and canalized rivers of the empire is due the credit for making it possible to thus bring foreign ores to the German industrial regions. Exceedingly low rates are made and the tonnage handled by rivers and canals is tremendous.

"Thus it appears that both in Germany and the United States the development of the utmost possibilities of cheap inland water communication is entitled to recognition for having made possible the upbuilding of the industries which a generation ago seemed economically impossible. With their great supplies of coal and ore located very close together, and with ocean transportation at their door, British manufacturers seemed sure of a domination in the world's iron trade that could only be ended by exhaustion of their supplies of coal or iron. A very different situation has been brought about largely by the utilization of internal water transportation in the United States and Germany. This one object lesson has deeply impressed the British community, and in no small measure has been responsible for the present agitation of the waterways question.

"Great Britain is the one exception among the industrial countries of Europe to the rule of encouraging both rail and water transportation. British railroad policy has aimed at the suppression of waterway competition, and has pretty thoroughly succeeded. To-day the British business community finds itself paying higher transportation tolls than continental countries, and because of this fact is at a great and increasing disadvantage in competitive markets.

"So serious has this situation come to be considered by British traders that Parliament has taken cognizance of the demand for rehabilitation of waterways, and a careful inquiry into the entire subject of water and rail transportation is now being carried on by the board of trade.

"It seems interesting and significant that Great Britain and the United States are the only industrial countries of the first class in which water transportation has so long been neglected, and it is a suggestive fact that in both these countries a powerful opinion has lately developed in favor of following the lead of continental nations, emancipating the waterways from railroad domination and vigorously developing them as an independent factor in transportation."

No country has developed its waterways to the extent that Germany has and the results achieved are astonishing.

Hubert Bruce Fuller in an article, "European Waterways," in the *Review of Reviews,* for May, 1911, describes the German system:

"The great aim of Prince Bismarck was a compact and permanent German Empire. He believed that nothing would so much contribute to this end as the improvement of transportation facilities and their control by the central government. After the Franco-German war, Bismarck set himself to the task of modernizing and extending the German waterways system. The essential dogma of the German commercial creed is that the waterways must be maintained by the state if they cannot maintain themselves.

"The German canal system is based upon the practical utilization of the great rivers, their improvement and connection by a scientific and practical system of canals.

"The Rhine, the most important and the largest German river, flows through Holland at its mouth, but it is developed and maintained as a great artery of German commerce. East of the Rhine in order are the Weser, the Elbe, the Oder and the Vistula, all of which have been improved by the German government and now carry an enormous and constantly increasing tonnage.

"Owing to the supreme importance of the Rhine, the German government early saw the desirability, both from a commercial and military point of view, of securing a connection within German territory by which boats could reach the Rhine from a North Sea German port. The solution was the Dortmund-Ems canal, connecting with the Rhine near the Dutch border and extending northwestwardly to the North Sea at Emden.

"The German Rhine is commercially the most important stream in the world. It furnishes a most illuminating contrast to the decadent Mississippi. The United States has expended more money in the twenty years ending in 1907 on the most important stretch of the Mississippi, 206 miles between St. Louis and Cairo, than the German central government has expended in the improvement of the Rhine from Strasburg to the frontier of Holland, a distance of 355 miles. Yet the amount of tonnage handled on this portion of the Mississippi was 374,093 tons in the year of 1908, while that on the Rhine in the same year was between 40,000,000 and 45,000,000 tons, an amount from eighty to one hundred times as much.

"The Elbe carries 20,000,000 tons of freight a year. The Oder River at its upper end at Breslau and Kosel even in these shallow reaches, carries 3,500,000 tons of freight a year. This river, though small, carries more traffic each year than the entire Mississippi. The reason is that the German people use sane methods, modern barges and towboats and efficient terminal handling apparatus.

"The city of Berlin is to-day the center and market place of a labyrinth of canals and canalized water courses. The Spree and Havel, with their network of canals reaching from the Elbe and Oder, have made possible the prosperity of modern Berlin. These rivers and tributary and connecting canals are at all times crowded with boats bringing the coal and briquettes of Silesia, timber, stone, bricks, lime, fruit and other heavy freight from the interior, and give Berlin direct water communication with

Hamburg and Stettin. Modern Berlin with its 2,000,000 inhabitants and its vast industries, would never have been possible except for the combination of natural and artificial watercourses which have given easy and cheap transportation for fuel, building and other raw materials. The Maerkischen, Wasserstrassen, or marsh canals, which lead from the Oder and the Elbe to Berlin, are none of them more than six feet deep. Yet they carry 13,000,000 tons of frieght each year.''

The inefficiency of the congressional system of government is nowhere so glaringly evident as in our treatment of the canal and water systems. The ''pork barrel'' is here most openly in evidence. The improvement of waterways for the purpose of circulating money in the locality of the favored congressman has resulted in a vast system of improvements, pursued without reference to any organized plan, and to practically no useful end.

Millions have been thrown into the work of improving waterways while the railroads were all the while killing water transportation, so that the more highly improved the waterways became, the less traffic they carried.

The lack of reason shown in our river improvements is obvious at many points. For example, the Green River has a channel of 6 to 8 feet while the Ohio into which it flows has at certain seasons but four feet. The lesser is thus made deeper than the greater.

Mr. Hubert Bruce Fuller in ''The Crime of the Pork Barrel,'' in the *World's Work*, of August, 1910, says:

''A good illustration is the condition of traffic on the Tennessee River near Chattanooga, where the Muscle Shoals canal has been built at a cost of $3,191,726. More than $1,100,000 has been expended for repairs and maintenance since completion. In the year 1908, $53,443 was expended for this purpose. The amount of freight of all classes carried through this canal in 1908 was 12,539 tons. It fluctuates from year to year, but that is a fair average. Thus, simply based upon the amount expended for maintenance and repairs for the year 1908—the last for which figures are available—the cost to the people of the United States was $4.26 for every ton of freight carried. And if we compute interest at 3% on the original cost of improvements, a further sum of $7.65 per ton must be added, making a total of $11.91 for every ton of freight passing through this canal.

''It cost $38,218.50 to maintain a lock and dam in the Wabash River at Grand Rapids, Illinois and Indiana, in 1908. The total traffic through this lock for the same year was 5,121 tons of which more than 4,440 tons were lumber and timber. Lumber and timber do not require canalization for their transportation, since they can best be carried by rafts floated or poled down stream. A balance then of 680 tons, remains of corn, shells and miscellaneous freight. The mere cost of maintaining this lock, therefore, was approximately $7.46 per ton for all classes, including lumber in its various forms, and $56 for every ton of freight carried through it excluding lumber.

"The Mississippi River, famed in history and tradition, is a notable object-lesson for the student of American waterways. On the entire river between St. Paul and New Orleans, the government has expended more than $90,000,000. In 1880 fourteen times as much river freight was received and shipped at St. Louis as in 1909, when it amounted to but 374,093 tons.

RIVER BUSINESS, PORT OF ST. LOUIS

YEAR	Total boats arrived	Total tons of freight rec'd	Total tons freight shipped	Grand total tons
1880	4,692	1,092,175	1,038,350	2,130,525
1881	3,951	1,208,430	884,025	2,092,455
1890	3,201	663,730	617,985	1,281,715
1891	2,900	592,140	512,930	1,105,070
1900	2,217	512,010	245,580	757,590
1909	....	....	....	374,093

"The United States has spent more on this stretch of 205 miles of the Mississippi than the central government of Germany has expended for the improvement of the Rhine from Strasburg to the frontier of Holland, a distance of 355 miles. Yet on this section of the Rhine the total tonnage in 1908 was approximately 40,000,000 tons as against less than 375,000 tons on the Mississippi as has been pointed out. The United States has spent more on the Mississippi River than any other government has spent on any other stream in the world. And we could take the 40,-000,000 tons of traffic of the Rhine and handle it with better advantage on the Mississippi with room for untold millions more. The simple fact remains that the Mississippi to-day possesses the channel, but it is not used."

As an illustration of what may be expected in American waterway transportation under the new law, examples may be taken of German traffic.

The Duisburg-Ruhrort district had a tonnage of 2,935,000 in

1875. In 1905 this had increased to 19,462,000. Berlin and Charlottenburg increased from 3,239,000 to 10,114,000 and Hamburg from 799,000 to 7,853,000 during the same period.

The total length of all navigable waters in Germany is 10,000 kilometers (6,000 miles) while there are 54,000 kilometers (32,-400 miles) of railroads. The railroad receipts are $500,000,000 a year, and the expenses $350,000,000, leaving a net profit of $150,000,000 (for year 1909). The railroads haul 45,000,000,000 ton-kilometers per year while the waterways haul 15,000,000,000 ton-kilometers. The waterways, less than one-fifth the length of the railways, thus handle 25% of the total traffic. (Governmental report, 1905.)

The average charges on the railroads are one and one-tenth cents per ton-mile, while on waterways the average is but four-tenths of a cent per ton-mile.

The above railroad receipts include passenger as well as freight receipts as the German government controls the railroads. The passenger charges per mile are as follows: First class, 2.8 cents, second class 1.76 cents, third class 1.2 cents and fourth class .8 cents.

If the United States is to achieve the proper results the waterways must be conducted on modern principles. The old towpath, the mule and the barefoot boy, made famous in Garfield's case, must no longer be in evidence. Instead, canals must take advantage of electrical development. The latest practice in Europe is to drive them as trolley cars, with a wire overhead and the barge motor driven, or where this is too expensive, or produces too much wash, a small trolley engine of special design runs alongside, either on tracks or on a roadway, and taking power from central stations along the lines, draws the barges at a speed which makes the canal a real rival of the railroad.

The engineering features of electric haulage for canals are highly developed in Germany, but it is an almost unknown industry in this country.

The development of canals in such a manner will produce an effect in manufacturing similar to the creation of suburbs by trolleys. If the German policy is followed, that of decentralization of industries, manufacturing plants now congested in large cities will be widely distributed. The rapid development of canals in Germany produced at first considerable speculation in land alongside, but the government now condemns a kilometer (.06 of a mile) on each side of the canal, and then sells the land in such a way as to encourage its plan of the decentralization of industries.

This plan should also be adopted in the United States, and a beginning has been attempted in New York state, where a recent amendment of the constitution proposed that the city, in opening new streets could condemn additional strips on either side the re-sale of which would repay in most cases the cost of the improvements. This amendment, however, was defeated.

To obtain the best results, our waterways must have a broad administrative policy, free from politics and be constructed by engineers of the highest skill. Such waterways will repay richly all that may be invested in them. The increased facilities will benefit no one as much as the farmer whose products are bulky and being in staple form largely, do not require rapid transportation. The example of the use of electrical power on canals will be of great value to agriculture for here also electricity can be used to the greatest advantage. The tendency of the average producer is to ignore new machinery. This is particularly true of the farmer, the slowest of all to adopt new machinery, except the fire departments, which show the most stubborn and costly neglect of new devices. The farmer, though his manual labor is of the hardest, adopts new machinery with the greatest reluctance, and when he does he allows his machinery often to stand unprotected in the open field through the winter for use the next season. His failure to take advantage of his mechanical opportunities is costly alike to himself and to the whole country.

The electric plow, long successfully in use abroad, effecting the greatest savings, has not yet scratched the earth in the United States and has been completely ignored by our manufacturers who do not desire to take up new devices which cannot readily be standardized. The general use of electricity on farms and in rural industries is also entirely neglected.

But the use of electricity on our farms is sure to be greatly increased with the progress of intensive cultivation, which is becoming an acute national need; and the farmer and the rural industries in general should take advantage of the engineering profession, to utilize our national resources through the medium of electricity, for the benefit and welfare of our country as a whole. The present decade will be notable for our farmers for its scientific agricultural developments with the aid of electricity.

No sharp line of demarkation exists between farm and urban power needs and electrical power should benefit the farmer as

well as the city man. As a class, the farmer is a large user
of power, but the sources from which he draws it are at present
inefficient and uneconomical, compared with industrial standards
in other lines. Of the 29,000,000 persons engaged in gainful
occupations, reported by the United States 1900 census, about
10,000,000 devote their energies to the farm. About 89% of the
horses and mules in this country are also at work on the farm.
The farmer uses more implements and a greater variety of mechanical devices than any other class, and it is important that
he should co-operate with the engineer in order to take advantage of our national resources, to replace the much sought for
and the much needed manual labor, to cut down considerably the
number of draft animals, to make the farm produce more, and to
make rural life more congenial and agreeable.

Better methods of agriculture are of such vast importance to
everyone, farmer and consumer alike, that the following résumé
of the present state of electricity on the farm taken from a series
of articles by the author, under the title, "Domestic and Rural
Applications of Electricity," in the *Electrical Review and Western Electrician,* should prove in the nature of a revelation to the
layman.

"There is no mechanical power which can supplant as conveniently and cheaply, manual and animal labor on the farm
or country estate, as electricity. Electricity is far superior
for supplying energy to steam or any internal combustion
engine. In fact, there is no other agent which can supply
all three necessities, light, heat and power from the same
source. Due to this fact, working hours on the farm and
other rural industries can be regulated, similar to city or
other commercial industries, and life in rural communities
can be made equally if not more attractive, than that found
in the cities, where the struggle for existence is incessant, and the
living accommodations, or what corresponds to home life, falls far
short of the pleasant and healthful occupations of the country,
and the agreeable surroundings found in the rural communities.

"Our giant industries are of recent origin and started in a
humble way, and now surpass and are far superior to any branch
of agrarian pursuits. This condition is readily accounted for;
the services of the trained engineer were used to advantage in
building up our great manufacturing plants, while the farming,
though the oldest of industries, has been neglected even to the
point of becoming an abandoned industry."

Up to the present time, especially in America, the aid of the technical man is seldom sought in solving many of the problems which arise in rural industries. Probably there is no better authoritative statement on the value of technically trained men as an aid to modern farming, than that made by Col. Roosevelt on Aug. 23, 1910, at Ithaca, N. Y.

"One reason why the great business men of to-day—the great industrial leaders—have gone ahead while the farmer has tended to sag behind the others, is that they are far more willing, indeed eager, to profit by expert and technical knowledge, that can only come as a result of the highest education. From railways to factories no great industrial concern can nowadays be carried on, save by the aid of a swarm of men who have received a high technical education in electricity, in chemistry, in engineering, in one or more of a score of special subjects. The big business man, the big railway man, does not ask college trained experts to tell him how to run his business, but he does ask numbers of them to give him expert advice and aid on some one point indispensable to his business. He finds this man usually in some graduate of a technical school or college, in which he has been trained for his life work.

"In just the same way, the farmers should benefit by the advice of the technical men who have been trained in phases of the very work the farmer does. I am not now speaking of the man who has had an ordinary general training, whether in school or college. While there should undoubtedly be such a training or foundation (the extent differing according to the kind of work each boy intends to do as a man), it is nevertheless true that our educational system should more and more be turned in the direction of educating men toward, and not away from, the farm and the shop.

"During the last half century, we have begun to develop a system of agricultural education, at once practical and scientific, and we must go on developing it. But, after developing it, it must be used. The rich man who spends a fortune upon a fancy farm, with entire indifference to cost, does not do much good to farming, but on the other hand, just as little is done by the working farmer who stolidly refuses to profit by the knowledge of the day, who treats any effort at improvement as absurd on its face, and refuses to countenance what he regards as newfangled ideas and contrivances and jeers at all book farming."

The ex-president voices a sentiment that the farmer should

heed, both for his own benefit as well as for the benefit of humanity at large, who on account of his lack of progress must pay more for their food and thus have their condition in life rendered more miserable.

Continuing from the author's article:

"There are thousands of steam and internal combustion engines in use on our farms to-day principally for replacing draft animals and of course a proportionate number of farm hands; they are used with machinery, such as plows and threshers and especially pumps. However, for operating small machinery, such as required in dairies as cow milkers, cream separators, butter kneaders, etc., an internal combustion engine could not be as advantageously used as an electric motor, for the reason that the smallest commercial internal combustion engine is about two horse power, while the electric motor may be chosen in capacities of one-tenth horse power and upwards to suit the machine to be operated, and again, no fuel is necessarily carried along, the only requirement being to turn a switch to start the motor.

"In fact the practice has proven that all farm machinery can advantageously be operated by electric motors. The usually operated machines on the farms are, plows, rollers, reapers, threshers, corn grinders, corn shellers and shredders, fodder cutters, wood saws, horse and sheep clippers, unloading and hoisting hay and other farm products. Another great labor saving in the use of electricity is in serving washing machinery; carpet cleaners, sewing machines, fans; further, heating appliances for cooking purposes and heating irons, all of which could hardly be served with any agent other than electricity. Aside from this, what is mostly needed is light, and the electric light is the only light. As electric energy has to be supplied to the motors either from an outside source or from its own central plant, it is but natural that electricity be applied as far as possible for light and heat as well as for power.

"An up-to-date farmer should possess his own electric generating station which may be operated by water, steam, gas, gasoline, oil or windmill power.

"In many instances where a stream runs through the property or the neighborhood of same, cheap power may be derived from this natural source, as regards the first cost and operating expenses.

"Generating current by steam power, the cost per killowatt hour is comparatively high, yet by proper engineering skill, one horsepower may be obtained as low as one cent per hour. Practically the same results may be obtained with a gas producer plant, in which case, instead of burning the coal in a steam boiler, using the steam for driving the engine, the coal is slowly burned in a producer, generating gas for operating the gas engine.

"Gasoline, oil and alcohol engines work on the same principle as the gas engine, all of which are of the internal combustion type. Great strides have been made in the last decade in this type of engine, and to-day it operates with reliability and economy and requires but little attention.

"Another source of energy for generation of electric current for farm and country residences is the windmill. The early Dutch windmills were built with sweeps from 50 to 100 feet in diameter; our modern American windmills have sweeps from 12 to 18 feet, and generate more power than the early Dutch mills, with less attention, etc.

"All the prime movers can be connected to electric generators by belt, gearing or couplings, and the control of same by modern engineering skill can be accomplished automatically so that little attention is required.

"As the greatest amount of energy is used in the day time, while the load for illumination is small and principally comes in the evening, it would therefore be an impracticable proposition to run the prime movers at that time. The use of a storage battery is consequently of the greatest service, supplying energy at any time of the day or night. In connection with the storage battery and with the new development of the low voltage Tungsten lamps, the cost and size as well as the maintenance expense may be considerably reduced by proper engineering.

"The main feature, and in which the great advantage of an electrically operated farm lies, is, that the farmer himself has at all times under his direct control the entire supply of electric energy being used, which may be obtained from some public service corporation at from 5 to 10 cents per kilowatt hour, or better still, the energy may be supplied from his own private generating plant at cost varying from 1 cent per kilowatt hour and upward.

"A policy much adopted abroad is to install a rural central station for the purpose of supplying a number of farms, rural industries, country residence and estates with electric current. By establishing a rural central station, either steam, water, gasoline, oil or gas, a great saving in the production of electric energy may be secured. To-day we find in Germany as many as 100 to

150 consumers being supplied with electric energy from one of the numerous rural central stations.

"Many of the German farmers have connected with their farms, rural industries whereby they utilize their by-products and herein lies the secret of success of many well-to-do farmers. For instance, in the last mentioned central station system, there are connected four grist mills, with five motors, having a total capacity of 105 horse power; one tile works with a 40 horse power motor; one saw mill with a 20 horse power motor, four wheel-wrights have motors amounting to 16 horse power; and in connection with same, using motors of varying capacities, are other industries, such as cabinet making, distilling, blacksmithing, bottling works, etc. There are also connected with the system some 20 consumers for light only, having a total of 343 incandescent lamps and 5 arc lamps, one railway and freight station with 120 incandescent lamps; one club house with 72 lamps and 6 arc lights, and further two towns are supplied, having a total of 1,692 lamps.

"From the above facts and figures, it is obvious that electricity can give a new stimulus to agriculture and farming, and at the same time opening up a new way by which the rural population can be induced to remain on the farm instead of flocking to the cities, and being forced to take an entirely new branch of service in order to earn a living.

"A very decided feature is that a few motors properly selected can operate all of the machines on the farm, instead of having a steam or gasoline prime mover attached to each machine. It is just in this feature that lies a great advantage of electrically operated farm machinery. Take, for instance, a motor placed on a low four wheeled truck, and brought to the threshing machine and connected by means of a belt; the motor is connected to the electric supply mains by a flexible cable plugged into a suitable outlet. By throwing a switch, the motor starts and operates continuously without attention. After the threshing is completed, the motor may then be connected to the baling machine, which packs the straw into bales, and if necessary the motor can be used for loading the bales onto wagons by operating a hoist. At other times, the same motor drives the water pump, wood saw, etc.

"It is readily seen that the electric motor can operate without the attention necessary for steam or gasoline prime movers, which have to be supplied with water, coal and gasoline as the case may be. With all other prime movers, when placed in the barn or hay mow, or beside the stack in the field, the fire risks are a thousand fold greater than with an electric motor in the same place, in fact an enclosed electric motor can be placed anywhere on the farm without fire risk or fear of an explosion.

"The motors used on dairy appliances and for the various household operations are of such small size and weight, that they are easily carried around by one or two persons, and applied to one machine or another wherever needed; thus many farms can get along with one large and one small motor. As the various farm machines operate at different speeds, the motors are supplied with suitable regulating devices, so that the desired speeds may be obtained.

"The great advantage of cold storage is not properly recognized to-day by farmers. By means of electrically operated cold storage systems, butter, milk, eggs and other perishable goods may be saved from spoiling. In many cases, especially with fruit, a farmer is forced to let his fruit lie on the ground and rot, because the price offered does not pay, him the expense of picking, packing and shipping his goods to the commission merchant. A cold storage system would enable him to pick his fruit in the proper season when the market price is low, and store it until he receives his own price.

"Ice machines for refrigerating plants, in this case, are preferably electrically operated, and the motor applied to the equipment will start and stop automatically, and will keep the temperature in the cold storage room within a few degrees, up and down, of the desired temperature.

"For irrigation purposes, electric pumps are of great service, whether on large or small scale. As these pumps operate only in certain seasons of the year, and certain hours of the day, public service corporations have recognized of late that the pumps for irrigation purposes assist in giving a good load factor on the station and consequently offer energy for this purpose at exceptionally low rates. The motor-driven pumps may be stationary or portable.

"Large sums are yearly spent for irrigation purposes and waterways regulation and drainage systems, and seemingly in almost all cases, without due consideration, of utilization of the energy of the water for generating electric current which might be advantageously used for farming or rural industries. Good examples on a large scale of such combination systems will be found in Switzerland and particularly in Germany, where all kinds of advantages are taken of natural resources, and proper husbanding of same for the benefit of the public in general.

"Electric plowing has been carried on in Germany for some 15 years, and particularly in the last few years, great strides have been made. Of the several systems employed, the one and two motor systems are most extensively used. Both systems are carried out in the same way, that is, a cable on a drum pulls the plow across the field.

"Electric plowing has great advantages over the gasoline or steam engine plow system; for instance in the latter case, a great amount of coal and water must be brought to the field by numerous teams and drivers which must be held in readiness. Electric plowing can be carried on in practically every kind of weather, for instance, steam operated plows may freeze in cold weather, whereas the electric plow is not affected by the cold, and the latter can also be used in soft or loamy soil where horses cannot work and in hilly ground.

"As far as the cost of electric plowing is concerned, experience shows that it can be done cheaper per acre than horse or steam plowing. The field of electric plowing of to-day is found principally in Germany. It is an established fact that American agricultural machinery in its wide practical application is in most respects far superior to that of any foreign make, and should the domestic manufacturers devote themselves with the same skill to electric plowing, it would be a question of only a short time when our farmers would recognize the advantages of the system.

"The practical application of electric plowing is not confined to farms of large acreage, it can be carried on to good advantage on farms of small size, and a number of farmers may have but one plow in common, to do the work of the different farms, or the plow may be rented out.

"The idea of utilizing farm refuse for by-products must not be discarded without close study and consideration; it must be borne in mind that our modern industries make use of all possible substances for by-products. In thousands of cases, it has turned out that the by-product has proved more valuable than the original and practice has always shown that this applies proportionately to rural industries and the farm as well as to manufactures.

"Many of the by-products of the farm which now are allowed to go to waste, could be turned to good account by the use of electrically operated apparatus, especially designed to turn by-products into marketable goods.

"Nearly all fruit is rich in sugar, varying in contents from 10 to 5%; of the common fruits, the grape yields the largest percentage of sugar. The normal wine-grape contains from 16% to 30% with an average of 20%. The two most important plants for yielding sugar are the sugar cane and the sugar beet. For instance, the Louisiana sugar cane contains 19% to 40% of sugar while sugar beets contain from 12% to 18% of sugar. Sorghum contains, in the staff at the time the seed is matured and the starch hardened, from 9% to 15% of sugar, according to the report of the United States Department of Agriculture.

"In packing fruit for the market, such as apples, grapes, etc., only sound fruit is selected; that which is in any way bruised or in the first stages of decay is thrown out. Instead of allowing this refuse to go to waste, it can, by the use of electrically operated presses, or stills, be turned into cider or grape juice. The pumice which remains can be used as a fertilizer for the soil. The amount of electric energy needed to operate the machinery necessary for such purposes is much less than five horse power. One of the portable outfits used for various purposes can take care of these outfits during the time that it is in operation.

"Farm products from which starch may be obtained as a by-product are the potato and cassava; the American potato contains 15% to 20% of starch, which in turn may be converted into alcohol. In many instances, potatoes are accidentally frozen by exposure to severe frosts, or are sometimes frozen in storage. In Europe, potatoes in such condition have still some value, yielding a considerable percentage of alcohol of high strength. This practice of converting frozen potatoes into alcohol is a common practice in Germany.

"In recent German reports, in bringing out facts on electrically operated farms, it is shown that since the government has taken an active interest in the matter, a number of plants have been installed for drying the leaves of the potato and the beet, to be used as food for cattle, because they are so high in protein or fat producing elements. Germany used to buy $8,000,000 worth of cattle food from foreign countries. The records show that there are yearly 24,000,000 tons of green leaves for drying, giving about 6,000,000 tons of preserved good food stuff, of a value of nearly $12,000,000."

"In 1901, when the potato crop of Germany was 53,682,010

short tons, efforts were made to discover practical and economical methods for preserving the potatoes, so that the surplus could be preserved and used for supplying subsequent demands, without the loss due to storing potatoes in silos or bins. When put into bins for storage, their value shrinks 10%, which would mean a total loss of $25,000,000. At present there are 436 plants established in Germany for drying potatoes, with an estimated production annually of 110,230 to 165,345 short tons, or 3,674,000 to 5,511,500 bushels.

"The process of preserving potatoes is washing, drying, peeling and cutting and again drying, and the product is finally placed on the market in the form of potato flakes. The prices vary from $1\frac{1}{2}$ to $1\frac{3}{4}$ cents per pound.

"A large part of the German potato yield is converted into the so-called potato flour, and sold at retail in the groceries throughout Europe for cooking purposes. There is also a flour produced by grinding and bolting dried potatoes, but this, however, is a comparatively new product.

"There are many vegetables and plants grown on the farm which can be converted into one form of by-product or another, especially for the manufacture of alcohol. There is over 20% of starch in the South Carolina sweet potato and as high as 2,600 pounds of starch per acre have been produced.

"The average yield of sweet potatoes per acre is, of course, much less than in the above cited South Carolina case, where heavy fertilization was employed. On plots to which fertilizer was not added, the yield was about 8,000 pounds of sweet potatoes per acre, yielding in round numbers about 1,900 pounds of starch. The quantity of sugar in the 8,000 pounds is about 350 pounds, which makes about 1,250 pounds of fermentable matter. This can be turned into industrial alcohol yielding about 160 gallons of 95% proof.

"The need for an efficient lighting system is well recognized as being of equal importance for the country as well as for the city. It will assist in fixing hours of labor as they are in the city, which is necessary to satisfy the just demands of the farm hands, as well as others living in the country. In consequence of better light, greater efficiency and cleanliness are secured all around, fire risks are diminished and insurance rates are reduced. Electric lamps require no matches and burn without flame and consuming no oxygen do not vitiate the air of the room. Electric lighting is of particularly great service in stables and barns, where the use of lanterns has caused numerous fires and destroyed millions of dollars worth of property. Electric lights are turned on and off by a suitable switch located at any convenient point and are unaffected by any change in weather conditions.

"Another great advantage in using electric illumination is that similar to the street, the yard and field may be lighted and controlled from the residence. This feature is especially convenient when in the fall of the year, harvesting is necessarily carried on after dusk, in order to ward off any changes due to weather conditions. In such cases, the field under the harvesters can be illuminated to advantage and work continued long after nightfall.

"Electricity is a ready servant for cooking or heating. No heat is wasted as in a coal or wood stove; all heat is concentrated in the one piece of apparatus being used. The cost of operating a small electric range is in almost all cases cheaper than burning wood or coal. In many instances, electric current can be bought for 5 cents per kilowatt hour, and as the average price of gas throughout the country is $1.50 per thousand cubic feet, the cost of electric cooking is the same as that done by a gas range, provided there is no heat wasted on a gas range, which is hardly avoidable. This is not taking into account that when one has his own generating set, current can be generated for 1 or 2 cents per kilowatt hour. Further it must be borne in mind that electric cooking means perfect cleanliness. There is no soot or smoke and as far as convenience is concerned, all that is necessary is to turn a switch.

"In country residences, where during certain hours of the day little cooking is carried on, such as making coffee, boiling eggs, preparing toast or supplying heat to chafing dishes, all is done in a few minutes, right before your eyes on the dining table itself.

"The heating of flatirons by means of electricity has proven one of the greatest boons to the household. The electric flatiron is so constructed that the current is supplied to the iron during use, and it maintains its working temperature, does not overheat and accidentally scorch the work, and is kept ready for work at a minimum cost. As no stove is necessary, there is no constant change of irons, also no intense radiation of heat into the room to make the operation more tiresome, and in the summer particularly trying.

"Other electric heating appliances for household convenience are electrically operated facial and scalp massage apparatus, foot warmers, heating pads and bed warmers, radiators, etc. Many of them are conveniently applied to country hospitals and sick rooms; among the appliances especially made for hospital use are sterilizers, X-ray apparatus, cauterizers, electric blankets, ozonizers, etc.

"These by no means comprise the entire list of necessary and convenient appliances which can be found to-day. New devices are appearing every day, so that at the present time there is hardly a household or farm where electric energy through the skill of the engineer could not supplant many of the most laborious operations.

"At the present time, fully 90% of all skilled labor comes under the supervision of the engineer, who has taken advantage of the various kinds of natural resources, and has built up the great industries which we have to-day. Our nearly seven million farmers in the United States should in a similar way take advantage of the engineer, who is especially capable in the art of development and husbanding of the natural resources through the medium of electric energy, for our agrarian industries, upon which not only financial standing is dependent, but the general welfare of the country as a whole."

The technical man in Germany has done wonders for agriculture. By the development of fertilizers Germany averages 31½ bushels of wheat per acre to 13 in America, rye 29 to 16, oats 51 to 25, and potatoes 158 to 83. If American farmers should increase their yields to the German averages, it would mean a gross output of products which could not be raised under present methods on a country twice as large as ours.

Yet Germany was formerly but little if any in advance of America, and these yields are made on soils in use for centuries before America was discovered. The scientific selection of seed and use of fertilizer has told the story. Two thousand, six hundred and fifty pounds of potash salts and manure are used per acre in Germany on cultivated lands while but 311 pounds are used in the United States. The German farmer practically uses his land as mechanism for transforming fertilizer into products, while the American scrapes and scratches along trying to get products out of his land without feeding any raw material whatever into it.

CHAPTER XVIII

THE PROBLEM OF IMMIGRATION

The fundamental change in recent immigration—Floating immigration and its financial effects—America as an apple orchard—The responsibility of the American of to-day to the American of the future—The Iberic and Slavonic menace—Lowering the level of American prosperity—The sullen negro—Orientalism—The flood of yellow blood at our western gates—Governmental inefficiency in congested immigration—American emigration, a new phenomena—The movement to the Canadian northwest—The ebb and flood of immigration.

THE most vital and important problem of the United States is and has long been immigration. To what extent it should be checked, if at all, the question of the varying races and the ultimate effect on the standard of living and character of the nation which will result from unregulated immigration need long consideration.

Immigration in principle needs no discussion. Without immigration, America would still be a wilderness tracked by a few savages. But if the whole world crowded here, we should have all the problems that they have and others in addition. There is thus a happy medium to be achieved.

In the first two or three centuries, immigration was not immigration in the present sense, but pioneering, and the early settlers came to make their homes in the wilderness. During the middle of the last century, the immigrants still came largely as settlers, in the spirit of pioneering, but towards the latter part of the century and at the present time, immigration has taken on a new character and while a considerable portion of it is comprised of intending settlers, it contains a large proportion of what may be termed floating labor, a current of workmen drawn by higher wages; to return to their own countries with the surplus they have obtained when conditions render their employment here less lucrative.

Another feature of immigration at the present time which is of grave concern is the fact that the bulk of it is of Iberic and Slavonic character, an entirely different blood from the Teu-

283

tonic, Celtic and Anglo-Saxon which constituted the principal part of the immigration up to a generation ago, and which blended readily with the native population.

This vast influx, a million a year, of races of a different character, and almost without exception of examples of such races drawn from the lowest orders, if it continues, will transform the race. The American of the third century of the republic will be a different person from the American of the first and second centuries of the republic; in fact he will be a new amalgam, not before produced in the melting pot of the world, for not alone will he be of mixed blood, but the effect of the climate, soil and latitude of North America, will produce a race never before known.

It is within the power of the American people of to-day to decide the complection of this future race which will be their inheritors, and whether the Iberic and Slavonic elements are to influence it in the proportion indicated by the present vast flood of immigration.

Whether this proportion will continue is doubtful. It would appear that the United States, so full of possibilities, has actually drained Western Europe of the available supply of immigrants. A condition of equilibrium exists between the demands of America and the demands of the home countries. England sends us few immigrants and fewer of them take out naturalization papers. The immigration from Germany is less than a tenth of what it was formerly, while Ireland has few to send.

In a reasonable length of time the southern and eastern European countries may also be drained and immigration may cease as compared with its present volume.

What this signifies is pointed out by Henry P. Fairchild of Yale University, in a communication to the *New York Times,* October 14, 1911:

"If it is true that from now on the stream of immigration to this country is to be a diminishing one, irrespective of any increased stringency in the matter of selection and admission, it can mean only one thing—that the United States no longer enjoys such a position of economic, social and political superiority to the other nations of the world as to make it worth while for foreigners to take the trouble to come here. Gen. Francis A. Walker long ago said that immigration of the lowest class 'will not be permanently stopped so long as any difference of economic level exists between our population and that of the most degraded communities abroad.' Modern authorities agree that the volume of immigration responds directly to the conditions of economic prosperity in this country.

"At the beginning of its National life, the United States enjoyed such natural advantages as made it worth while for the citizens of the most advanced of the older nations to try their lot in the new world. Many of these advantages are already gone, and as stated in your article, the better class of immigrants are now seeking other lands. Argentina gets the North Italians while the South Italians come to us. Canada, while encouraging and soliciting immigration from Northern and Western Europe, discriminates frankly and effectively against natives of the southern and eastern portions of that continent. In our own case, the so-called 'new' immigration vastly outnumbers the 'old.' And there are still plenty to come. Barring any further legal restrictions, they will continue to come from ever lower and lower sources until conditions in the United States so closely resemble those in the most unfortunate foreign countries that it is no longer worth while to make the effort."

One of the most ominous problems of America to-day, but one which from long familiarity has made itself to a large extent an unrealized problem, is the result of a form of immigration in the past. It is the problem of the negro, who was compelled to enter. Those who do not understand the negro problem, wonder at the violence it arouses.

If left to solve itself, the negro problem would be settled by a gradual absorption of the race into the white race, and the result would be a contamination of the whites, until America would be a negroid country, its racial purity forever lost. The most vigorous restrictions are therefore necessary to prevent intermarriage of blacks and whites. Similarly the first view of the Chinese problem is that their cheap labor would develop the country. Nevertheless the hordes of Chinese that would be attracted would form a condition far worse than the negroes, who are not too numerous to be controlled. The infusion of Chinese blood that would result through the peculiar attraction of white women for the Chinese, would in a few generations produce a mongolianized caucasian, a mysterious, possibly defective and certainly inferior race, which would in time be totally submerged by the increasing influx of Chinese, until America would become a Chinese country with the Mongolians slightly caucasianized.

To a lesser degree the immigration of all races having oriental characteristics is charged with a similar danger.

Against such a possibility, the policy of the United States has been definitely settled. Chinese exclusion is a policy more immutable than most of the provisions of the constitution itself.

That the United States needs immigrants of the proper character, however, is beyond question. There are only 38 persons per square mile in the country as against 359 in Great Britain, 290 in Germany and 629 in Belgium, and while the latter countries have more than they should have, that is a population which is so numerous that they could not gain a livelihood from that portion of the earth's surface on which they reside did they not draw supplies from elsewhere, the sparse population of the United States makes it certain that for many years we shall have a place for all the desirable immigrants that may wish to come.

The real problem of immigration at the present time is one that has been created by governmental inefficiency, that is the lack of proper means of distribution of the immigration. With an appalling lack of foresight, the government has allowed the immigrants, particularly during the last ten or twenty years, to accumulate in the big cities along the eastern seaboard. These cities are made cosmopolitan in character and thus differ from the normal American cities. Conditions of over crowding arise and other evils of congestion of population, while the demand for labor in other places remains unsatisfied.

Governmental inefficiency extends also to the manner in which the immigrant is treated during the process of distribution. The alien arriving in the land of freedom too often finds that freedom means for practical purposes, a license to private bankers, notaries public, lawyers, collection agents, insurance companies, real estate agents, employment agents, benevolent societies and naturalization clubs, to cheat and rob him. The first annual report of the Bureau of Industries and Immigration of the New York State Department of Labor, states that: in the matter of transportation the combination of steamship agents, emigrant hotels, runners, porters, expressmen and cabmen throughout the country, operating chiefly through New York

City, forms one of the most stupendous systems for fleecing the aliens, from the time he leaves his home country until he reaches his destination in America, and vice versa.

The report says:

"In labor camps aliens are discriminated against in regard to housing, sanitation, food supplies, and employment methods, being denied the ordinary decencies of life; aliens are checked and tagged, amounts ordered by the padroni are deducted from their wages without their knowledge or express sanction, and exploitations occur in hospital charges and the purchase of supplies.

"The private banking laws are affording only a small measure of protection owing to evasions of the law, and no protection whatsoever outside of cities of the first class; frauds in the sale of homes to aliens by means of the solving of puzzles or by means of excursions arranged to interest aliens in 'show' pieces of property, or by other means, are widespread and the settlement of affairs in the old country, when an alien wishes to settle here, is in the hands of a most unscrupulous class of lawyers, notaries public, collection agents, information bureaus, and protective leagues."

The report of the Commissioner General of Immigration shows that the trend of immigration is now upward and is rapidly increasing and reassuming the proportions which prevailed prior to the fiscal year of 1908. During the past year, the number of aliens coming as immigrants was 1,041,570. As the later months of the year show a greater proportionate increase than the earlier, it seems likely that the ensuing year will witness a still nearer approach to the largest record so far made,—that for the fiscal year 1907, viz. 1,285,349.

The report continues:

"Of particular interest with regard to the 1,041,570 immigrants entering the country (1910) are the following statistics: Of these, 120,509 were under fourteen years of age, 868,310 were between the ages of 14 and 44 and 52,751 were 45 or over. As to literacy, 253,569 could neither read nor write and 4,571 could read but not write. These figures include no aliens under 14 years of age, which indicates a decrease in illiteracy from 29% of the total in 1909 to 28% of the total in 1910. In 1908 the ratio was 26%; in 1907, 30% and in 1906, 28%.

"The total amount of money brought to the country by arriving aliens calculated on the not altogether reliable basis of amounts shown at time of arrival, was $28,187,745 or an average of about $27 a person.

"During the fourteen months prior to September, 1912, the 1,114,989 aliens,—immigrants as well as aliens temperorarily here—brought $46,712,697. The immigrants had an average of $38 per capita in the fiscal year to July 1 and $40 per capita during the two following months.

"There is no way, of course, to determine how much of this consisted of money sent to the applicants by friends or relatives living in the United States. Concerning payment of passage, 755,453 claimed to have bought their own tickets while 274,204 admitted that they had been assisted in this regard by relatives and 11,913 that they had been so assisted by friends. According to the statement of the aliens themselves, it therefore appears that over 25% of the total number admitted were assisted to reach this country.

"It is still true that the bulk of our immigration is being drawn from the countries of southern and eastern Europe, Italy, Austria-Hungary, Greece, Turkey in Europe, and the smaller principalities adjacent, and Russia supplied about 68% of the immigrants admitted in 1910. In the year 1909, these same countries furnished 67%. This is in marked contrast to the immigration of former times.

"During the year, it was necessary to turn back at the ports, 24,270 aliens, or about 2% of the total number applying for admission. The corresponding total and percentage for the year 1909 was 10,411, or 1.1%.

"During the year 202,436 aliens left the United States. Concerning 34,043 of these, it has not been possible to secure a record of the period during which they have lived here, as they departed across the Canadian border. It appears that 13,841 were less than 14; 167,440 ranged from 14 to 44, and 21,255 were 45 years of age or over; while 136,159 had resided in the United States less than 5 years; 23,969 from 5 to 10 years; 3,877 from 10 to 15 years; 2,310 from 15 to 20 years, and 2,078 over 20 years.

"Of common unskilled laborers, 215,300 immigrated and 89,393 emigrated; as compared with 138,570 members of the skilled trades immigrating and 21,574 emigrating. These should be compared further with the figures for the fiscal year of 1909 as follows: Unskilled laborers, 174,800 immigrating and 118,926 emigrating; and skilled laborers, 87,160 immigrating and 21,919 emigrating.''

Emigration from the United States is large in volume but mostly confined to the floating labor class, whose average exodus is about 40% of the whole number of immigrants. Three-quarters of them, after leaving America do not re-immigrate, but one-fourth or 10% of the whole number come back again, so that taking the figures for 1910, 1,041,570 immigrants, 30% will sooner or later depart for good, while 10% have been here before, so that the net increase is about 600,000.

The year in which the greatest exodus took place was 1907, the year of the panic, when 711,000 returned. The panic being one largely arising out of artificial conditions created by governmental neglect, thus threw this number of men out of work who were able to get away. What its loss was to the ones who did not care to go, or could not emigrate and the native population it is difficult to calculate. What this vast army of laborers who went back could have earned for themselves and for the country had they been able to remain is also an enormous figure.

Considering the value of a wage earner as $1,700, which is the estimate of the National Conservation Commission and estimating that of the 711,000 emigrants who returned in 1907, 500,000 were wage earners, the capital loss to the country by their withdrawal amounts to some $850,000,000.

According to a special report of the Census Office, 1907, the wealth of the nation in 1904, including the value of real property, and everything having a commercial value, was $107,104,-192,410 as has been given, or 200 times the wealth of a Rockefeller. In 1900 the value was $88,517,306,775, so that at the present time it is probable that the wealth is not less than 125,-000 millions. There are some 33,000,000 wage earners, and at a calculation of $1,700, they amount to $56,100 millions, making the total wealth of the country $181,000 millions.

Of the 1,000,000 immigrants annually coming in, not less than 400,000 are wage earners, while half the remainder becomes wage earners. Their value would be $1,190,000,000 added to the capital of the country annually, and as they bring not less than $28,000,000 in money with them, the total is $1,218,000 millions, which is more than two thirds of 1% annually of the entire wealth of the country. This means, for example, that the owner of real estate worth $10,000 finds on account of immigration that the value of his property is increased at the end of a year to $10,067.

The emigration from the United States consists of those who return after coming here, and a considerable flow of very valuable emigrants into the Canadian northwest. This amounts to about 100,000 annually, mostly well-to-do farmers, and the Canadian government estimates that they bring an average of $1,000 each into the country. Assuming that two-thirds are wage earners, the loss to the United States is $213,333,333 annually, a particularly large drain owing to the high class of the emigrants, in most cases farmers who have sold their farms in America and who are going to Canada to take advantage of the rich lands and better government there.

The average return of immigrants is about 200,000, a value of $340,000,000, and as it is estimated that the total of money which they take back with money sent home by other emigrants amounts to $400,000,000, there is thus a loss of $740,000,000 from this cause.

Another loss to the country is in the emigrants of great wealth, who permanently remove to foreign countries to reside and who drain a constant income from America in addition to large capital withdrawals. Among this class of emigrants are the wealthy women who marry titled foreigners, and it is estimated that not less than $100,000,000 annually is withdrawn through this channel. Including the exodus to Canada and the general withdrawals, the country loses annually $1,053,333,333. In addition are large sums spent by our temporary emigrants, the tourists, for whose patronage an established and well organized propaganda is carried on in various foreign countries. Without the immigrants with their inbringing of $1,218,000,000 the country would suffer a heavy loss from its wealthy emigrants.

A tendency which is rapidly growing on the part of alien nationalities and races and one which is open to serious criticism is that of adopting anglicized patronymics or in many cases names of purely anglo-saxon or celtic origin. This sailing under false colors tends to debase the old and dignified stock of names and to conceal the origin and characteristics of the wearers of the borrowed plumage. It is largely resorted to for purposes of commercial and social advantages and consequently is of disadvantage to those legitimately bearing the original names.

It is a practice which should properly be frowned upon by courts within whose province it is to permit changes of names to be made.

In cases where the foreign name is unpronounceable or ridiculous, it should be permissible to alter it only to the extent necessary to make it useable, it being allowed to be in no case so changed as to conceal its origin.

The changing of names by immigrants has been severely criticized for legal reasons. The *New York Times* in an editorial published December 15, 1912, states:

Immigrants who assume the historic names of New Englanders, like Endicott, Lowell, Adams, Lawrence, or Peabody, are not only flouting their own ancestry, in which they should have pride, but they are making trouble for the courts. Chairman A. T. Clearwater of the New York State Bar Association's Law Reform Committee says:

"It is not so much the philological phase of the matter which engages the attention of the bar, as it is the opportunities for fraud, the confusion as to ancestry and descendants, the errors and perplexities arising in the search for and authentication of title to real estate, all of which seem to us grave enough to require legislative action."

Among the reasons which cause the immigrant to change his name is the disappointment which he feels when he becomes acquainted with conditions in this country and finds that the glowing prospects which he had in expectation are so difficult of realization.

America is, in the oratorical phrase, a country of unbounded possibilities, but for the immigrant it proves rather a country of will-o'-the-wisp opportunities. The immigrant with a little money in his pocket finds it gone before he gets well located and then begins the struggle for existence, a kind of a life in a swamp of immediate necessities surrounded by rainbows of opportunity wherever he turns. He remains, however, pretty well stuck in the swamp and among the schemes of a certain class of immigrant for changing his luck, is that of changing his name, which is of course merely another will-o'-the-wisp for all save a few of the more unscrupulous.

Many an immigrant finding America disappointing, is often asked why he does not go back instead of remaining here and bewailing his lot. The principal reason is that he seldom has the price of a ticket in his pocket, or if he has, he prefers to put it into some scheme in the hope of making a large sum. When it is lost, the same process is repeated as he acquires the American habit of depending on some sudden turn of fortune to lift him out of the rut.

Even should he be able to pay his fare back, he would have to return to face his relatives and former friends with the admission of failure in America which would promptly be charged against him and not against America. Even willing to endure this, he would be compelled to start all over again in the old country with its settled customs which are not adapted to getting rich quick, and where he would be at a great disadvantage on account of the spirit of speculation which he acquired in America and which he would have no means of gratifying.

Thus the immigrant, however dissatisfied and however much worse off than abroad, continues to stick to America in the hope of the stroke that will some day make him independent if not wealthy.

Even those who acquire a competency seldom return, as by that time they are Americanized and prefer not to go back to the more formal and restricted channels of European life. And in addition, having made some money they are eager to make a great deal more, an appetite which can never be appeased.

Immigration is not a German problem, and it is constantly decreasing in importance, since the number of those emigrating is much less than formerly, owing to improved conditions, while the number of immigrants is small.

According to Consul General T. St. John Gaffney, of Dresden in the *Daily Consular and Trade Report*, Oct. 2, 1911, there were 588,354 foreign workmen employed in Germany last year. Of this number, 350,000 were engaged in farming. There were 323,326 Poles, 82,092 Luthenians, 23,209 Hungarians and 39,672 Russians and Austrians.

The negro problem, too, is not a German problem, as there are but one or two in each city, usually bar tenders in American style bars, or servants; and so little is race prejudice understood that they associate freely with white people. Indeed, the negro in Germany is looked upon as a very good fellow, and held somewhat in the regard that an Indian is by the American small boy.

CHAPTER XIX

THE RIGHT TO WORK

The duty and policy of the state—Bismarck's stand—Old age pensions—
Government employment a reserve—How Germany eases the struggle
for existence—The citizen as an asset of the state—From the cradle
to the grave—Great clearing house of labor—Effect of governmental
employment—Precedence given to married men—The inevitable nature
of the prevailing rate of wages—Unemployment funds—Lack of system in the United States—The peculiar methods of the government
to get enlistments—The bright future of the soldier as seen on the
lithograph—Why 50,000 men deserted in ten years—The German
army as an educational institution—The high spirit of patriotism in
Germany—Discipline as a moral asset—The government sees to it
that the individual learns a means of livelihood—Haphazard methods
of the United States—If the Declaration of Independence were written
to-day, how would it read?—Absorption of wealth by owners of machinery—Women at work in the United States—Startling facts of
child labor—Hard conditions in the steel mills—The right to work
no more than the right to exist—The Carnegie and Rockefeller benefactions—Their true economic significance—Are they a burden instead of a blessing?—The history of over production of philanthropy
in the past—Failure of attempts to obtain more than the prevailing
rate of wages—Why $5 a day bricklayers only make $11 a week.

BISMARCK proclaimed the doctrine of the right to work as an
integral part of the policy of the German state:

"Give the workingman work as long as he is healthy, assure
him care when he is sick, insure him maintenance when he is
old. Was not the right to work openly proclaimed at the time
of the publication of the common law? Is it not established
in all our social arrangements, that the man who comes before
his fellow citizens and says, 'I am healthy, I desire to work, but
can find no work,' is entitled to say also, 'Give me work,' and
that the state is bound to give him work."

"But large public works would be necessary," exclaimed an
opponent.

"Of course," replied Bismarck. "Let them be undertaken,
why not? It is the state's duty."

The fundamental law supplemented by the Stein-Hardenberg

legislation of the second decade of the last century was the
foundation on which Bismarck stood, when his policy was outlined in 1884. Carried out with the full approval of the old
Emperor, and by conservative majorities in the Prussian legislature and the imperial parliament, this policy has had a fundamental part in the development of unified Germany. Social
insurance, industrial pensions, governmental regulation of
monopolies, the bureaucratic system in keeping politics out of
business and business out of politics, her educational system,
and the Bismarckian policy towards labor have proved the
cornerstones of German progress.

The policy has not been unaccompanied, however, with strong
opposition, and the various systems of the intervention of the
state in the relations of the employer and employee are open
to certain attacks. The social economist argues that state provision of employment, pensions, compulsory insurance and other
forms of state aid, are a tax on the thrifty for the benefit of
the unfit, thus interfering with the working out of the law of
the survival of the fittest, and undermining thrift and economy
in all by reason of the prospect of being cared for by the state
in old age or sickness.

The scheme thus tends to weaken the race as a whole. Yet
despite theories of this kind, the working out of the German
policies proceeds with generally good results. While it may
be urged that pensions for the aged encourage extravagance in
the youth, yet such pensions serve to lift a weight of anxiety
from numberless lives, enabling the task in hand to be performed with greater care and skill, than if tinctured so much
with the American anxiety that time is money.

While poverty is abundant in Germany, the violent contrasts
of pauperism is not as noticeable as in the United States and
England, where the fear of poverty, the hope of gain, and the
absence of any succor in time of necessity save that provided
or obtained by the worker himself are the sharp prods to encourage thrift.

One of the concrete proofs of the success of the present German system, lies in the decrease of German immigration to the
United States. It is now only about one-tenth the figure of
former years.

The right to work in Germany, the employment by the government of men who cannot find employment elsewhere has
not proved a social institution of much currency. Like a gov-

ernmental gold reserve, it remains unused but of great potential possibilities.

The government has not actually had to provide work to any great extent, that is Notarbeit (necessity work), but its readiness to do so can always be relied upon.

Frederic C. Howe in the *Outlook* of May, 1910, in "How Germany Cares for her Working People," states:

"Germany is not burdened with the economic philosophy which America inherited from England. Germany does not look upon the state as an unmixed evil. Germany does not apotheosize the names of Adam Smith and Ricardo; she does not believe in unlicensed individualism; she does not permit the struggle for existence to weed out the so-called weak and incompetent. Germany recognizes that modern industry has made those who labor, dependent upon other causes than their own thrift or willingness to work; they are not incompetent and unfit because they have no job. Germany has secured industrial efficiency 'by the social legislation of the state.'

"From the cradle to the grave, the state has its finger on the pulse of the citizen. His education, his health, and his working efficiency are all a matter of constant concern. The worker is carefully protected in his person from accident, he is trained in his hand and his brain to be a good producer, and he is insured against accident, sickness and old age. When idle through no fault of his own, work is frequently found for him. When homeless, a lodging is offered so that he will not pass to the vagrant class. When sick, he is cared for in wonderful convalescent homes, tuberculosis hospitals and farm colonies. When old age removes him from the mill or the factory, a pension awaits him, a slight mark of appreciation from society, which has taken in labor all that his life had to give and left him nothing more than a bare subsistence wage."

Germany provides a very efficient system of finding work. The municipal labor registries are a remarkable institution which should be duplicated in America. Mr. Howe, in the same article, describes them:

"There are nearly 400 of the labor registries in the empire. They find work for from 500,000 to 1,000,000 men and women every year. They are maintained partly by the cities, partly by private agencies. They are great clearing-houses for skilled and unskilled labor of both sexes. I visited the registries in Düsseldorf and Berlin. The latter is one of the largest and best in the Empire. It secured 120,000 positions in the year 1908. It was established in 1888 and is maintained by public authorities at a cost of $25,000 a year, and is administered by the Insurance Department. It occupies a splendid four-story building, probably a hundred feet front, on Gormanstrasse. It runs through to another street, the entrance on the latter street being to the women's department. In the center of the building is a great open hall capable of seating 1,400 persons. There were probably 600 men waiting for work when I was there. Here the men sit, grouped in sections, according to employment. When a call is received by mail or over the telephone, the men are called to the desk. The wages and conditions are explained and the men are given a card to the employer. Priority is given to the married men as well as to those first registered. On one side of the hall is a buffet where beer, cigars and food are sold at a trifling sum. There are cobblers and tailors who do odd jobs of mending. A shower bath can be obtained in the basement for a cent. There is a smaller and more elaborate room for the skilled workers and one for women workers in another portion of the building. Connected with the registry is a free dispensary and medical inspection bureau.

"These labor registries, scattered all over the Empire, are being co-ordinated, so that the surplus labor of one market can be shifted to another, while an attempt is being made to supply the demand of the farmer for casual labor.

"Voluntary arbitration courts are usually found in connection with the registries. They are made up of employers and employees, and are used for the settlement of minor trade and wage disputes. With these are free legal aid dispensaries for the aid of the working classes.

"Upwards of a dozen cities have opened up free house registries designed primarily for the working classes. House or apartment owners report to the agency, giving details as to location, rent, etc. An officer of the bureau then makes an inspection, and, if the house is approved, it is placed on the list. In some towns the plan has found much favor, so much that all other methods of renting by advertisement have been abandoned. This is a great boon to the workman, employed as he is all day at his job. It saves him the time he can ill afford to lose and enables him to find the sort of lodging he desires.

"None of these agencies creates work where no work exists.

Neither the labor registry nor the Herbergen will open the door of the factory or meet the emergency of industrial depression. They do not create opportunity; they merely attempt to find a hole for the peg, or prevent the man from losing his grip on himself during a period of waiting. Nor do they provide for the mechanic who is brought face to face with starvation for himself and his family, by reason of the closing of the factory.

"During the recent industrial depression in America the unemployed petitioned the councils of many of our cities to open up relief work. They did not want charity; they wanted work. But the cities were powerless to relieve the situation, or had no inclination to do so. Here, again, Germany recognizes that the worker has a right to work; that he has a right to expect something more than a visit from the charity organization society. 'Distress work' is very generally provided by the city. It is usually limited to the winter months. The cities disclaim any legal or moral responsibility in the matter. They do not recognize the 'right to work.' But they provide work in considerable measure, nevertheless. They distribute ordinary work so as to give the maximum of relief. They also require contractors to employ local men. Extraordinary conditions are met to some extent by development work, such as excavations, street paving, sewer construction, forestry, wood chopping and the like. Applicants must be residents of the city and must be heads of families. It is true that the work done is not of the best, and it is more costly than that done through the regular channels, but it saves the self-respect of the worker and to some extent recognizes his right to work. In a larger sense, it saves the community from the wreckage of vagabonds, tramps, and semi-criminals who are the inevitable wastage of every period of hard times.

"These are some of the means employed to prevent waste, to keep the producing power of the nation at a maximum, and to save the worker himself from the demoralizing influence of irregular employment. They stop far short of a solution of the industrial problem. The socialists have but little sympathy with these palliatives as in any sense remedial. But from the point of view of the individual, the plan is far better than nothing, although as a social programme it fails in this; it does nothing to create more jobs. And there can be no very great improvement in the well-being of the working classes until there are more jobs than men seeking them."

Mr. Howe is undoubtedly correct in his last statement. There certainly can be no very great improvement in the well-being of the working classes until there are more jobs than those seeking them. Similiarly with farmers, who must continue their present ways until there are more farms than farmers seeking them, while millionaires must remain restricted in number until there are more millions lying about than there are seekers for the same.

Mr. Howe does not indicate just where the superfluity of jobs is to come from. Certainly not from the government. Nothing is to be expected from "notarbeit" as the government pays less than the prevailing rate of wages, which will not improve the well-being of the working classes as a whole. If better wages were paid, everyone would seek work with the government.

The system of state work, however, does well in times of emergency and for individual cases. The rate of pay is very little lower than the prevailing wage, as at too low a rate, objection would be raised; similar to the objections made to convict-made goods underselling the work of the honest man; and it would be the objection of the competent against the undue competition of the incompetent. Indeed the very narrow margin under the prevailing wage, shows how little it is possible even for a government to get away from the law of the survival of the fittest, though actuated by the best of intentions. Those loudest in proclaiming the right to work, raise the greatest outcry when it is given to someone else. But Germany is aiding her workers as far as it is practicable to do so, which is one of the secrets of her progress while other nations are doing little or nothing at all.

No country has as yet actually introduced any insurance against non-employment, but it is being urged in England where the problem of the unemployed has been more pressing for years than in any other country.

The Commissioner of Labor in his report states:

"Provision for unemployment by voluntary organizations has followed the same general course of development as other forms of insurance. With the growth of the trade unions, it was recognized at an early date that proper care of persons out of work would be an efficient means of preventing such persons from underbidding the prevailing rates of wages and thereby would be an important means of maintaining an existing level.

The British trade unions in particular recognized the importance of this form of provision against unemployment; one having instituted a system of out-of-work benefits as early as 1831, and this provision was subsequently adopted in other countries, so that in all of the countries treated in the present study, such relief was found to a greater or less extent.

"The forms in which unemployment benefits are provided consist of first, a pecuniary out-of-work benefit, usually granted under many restrictions; second, a travel benefit, enabling the workman to reach localities where there are opportunities for employment; and third, a removal benefit, permitting the workman to make a permanent change in his place of residence. Some of the trade unions, notably in Belgium and France, have instituted workshops in which employment is provided for unemployed members.

"In some institutions, as for instance, the friendly societies of Great Britain, the unemployment benefit consists solely of the remission of membership dues while the member is unable to secure employment.

"Investigation of the subject of workmen's insurance has disclosed a variety of miscellaneous forms of aid in case of unemployment, and among these may be mentioned the following:

"Some of the British and Belgian societies providing relief in case of sickness, death, etc., grant their members full rights of membership without the payment of dues during involuntary unemployment.

"A number of business firms, especially in Germany, have created unemployment funds for the workmen employed in their establishments; membership in these funds is sometimes compulsory and sometimes voluntary. Most of these organizations are rather systems of compulsory saving than systems of insurance because most frequently the member is entitled only to the amounts paid in by him, together with subsidies or various forms provided by the establishment or by interest arising from a special reserve fund.

"In Italy a privately endowed organization known as the 'Umanitaris' of Milan grants subsidies on the Ghent system to labor unions and other organizations providing unemployment funds.

"A number of associations of employers in Belgium, France and Germany have collected assessments based on the number

of their employees or on wages in order to institute a fund for
the relief of the unemployed workman.

"One instance is known of a German establishment which
provides that when the workman is dismissed because of lack
of work, he becomes entitled to full wages or salary for a period
of time based \on the length of service in the establishment.

"In Germany and France a small number of private companies have undertaken to provide unemployment insurance as
a business undertaking. Although these firms issue collective
contracts, they cannot be properly classed as institutions of social
insurance. According to the information available, they have
not met with any great measure of success."

In the United States, neither the national, city or state governments make any systematic efforts to relieve the unemployed. Some cities have municipal lodging houses, where the
needy sojourner may earn a night's lodging by chopping some
kindling wood. Farm colonies appear in some places. Uncle
Sam's efforts at the relief of unemployment are chiefly connected with providing places for an army of faithful postmasters, but otherwise, he is engaged in deflecting from the ranks
of industry, a large supply of valuable workers to serve in the
army and navy.

The methods followed by the government amount practically
to a fraud on the man enlisting and the resentment which is
aroused is such that desertions reach an unprecedented number,
as will be seen.

Recruits are induced to enlist by means of booklets and
lithographs picturing the advantages of a military life. *The
Baltimore Sun* reprints matter of this kind which is typical of what is being used all over the country at recruiting
stations:

"Uncle Sam says:

" 'Why shiver in Baltimore when you can spend the winter in
the balmy air and delightful climate of the West Indies?

" 'Why feel hungry when you can get three good, square meals
a day from Uncle Sam?

" 'Why wear worn and ragged garments when Uncle Sam will
give you a complete outfit of clothes free?

" 'Why look for a job in which you have to spend all your
earnings for board, lodging, clothing and doctor's bills, with
no chance to have any fun or save anything for a 'rainy day'?

" 'A good job is looking for you. The United States navy is

looking for ambitious young men who are anxious to see the world and earn advancement.

" 'Is it not worth considering?' "

The bright side is further presented by a well written booklet, many of whose paragraphs would do justice to a get-rich-quick promoter.

"There is a fascination about a life that follows the sea, from port to port, from country to country, from ocean to ocean, amid ever-changing, ever-shifting scenes, as compared with the quiet, stationary, though commendable, life in the factory, the farm or the office.

"There is fascination about being one of the crew of a ship of the United States navy—the navy that carries the stars and stripes, the navy that produced a John Paul Jones, a Lawrence, a Decatur, a Perry, a Farragut, a Porter and a Dewey, the navy that gave birth to such expressions as, 'I have only begun to fight,' 'Don't give up the ship,' 'We have met the enemy and they are ours,' 'Damn the torpedoes, go ahead,' 'You may fire when you are ready, Gridley,'—expressions that will live in the minds of men forever."

These are only a few of the arguments set forth. It is obvious, however, that many of the arguments would not do except for cold weather. With a change of season, the recruiting offices doubtless provide themselves with slightly different literature.

Not long since a cruise was made up the Hudson with the result that many country boys, who are most easily fascinated by a life they know nothing about, were enlisted. The result of this foray was that a great scarcity of farm hands was experienced the following season throughout the region.

The same policy of using vivid colors to attract the recruit is followed for the army as well as for the navy, and in cities the recruiting officers, in spick and span uniforms, station themselves in public squares, like Salvation Army chaps, where there is a considerable floating population, and there exercise their handsomeness and talents in getting men into the army.

The results of this system of misrepresentation as to the real life of the soldier are forcibly summarized by Bailey Millard in "The Shame of Our Army" in the *Cosmopolitan Magazine* of September, 1910:

"From the year 1900, according to the actual figures and estimates of officers in the War Department, up to the end of the fiscal year ended June 30, 1910, there deserted from our new army a total of 50,000 men. This is allowing only 4,000 desertions for the past fiscal year, no report of which will be made until October, while the indications as prefigured by the number of courts martial for desertion, are that the total will be as large if not larger than for 1909. Think of it! Over fifty thousand deserters! The record would be ludicrous if it were not so tragic.

"Do we gain any consolation by looking further into the figures for 1909? Not an atom. For example, take the Sixth Infantry. From the regiment 142 men deserted, or 12.9% of the whole number. Then there was the Eighth Cavalry, with 12.7% desertions and the Fourth Field Artillery, with 10.4%. Blackest of all the records among individual troops and companies was that of Company K of the Twenty-eighth Infantry, located at Fort Snelling, Minnesota. Of the men in this company, nearly one-third became disgusted with the service and fared forth to seek other fields of usefulness.

"Here are four other companies that had high percentages of desertions last year. Company M, Sixth Infantry, 20.2%; Battery B, Fourth Field Artillery, 18.4%; Troop B, Eighth Cavalry, 17.9%, and Battery E, First Field Artillery, 17.6%.

"Other posts at which there were high percentages of desertions last year were Fort Duchesne, Utah, 15.8%; Fort Yellowstone, Wyoming, 15.8%; Fort Robinson, Nebraska, 15.6%; Fort Columbia, Washington, 15.4%.

"It is in the dog days that most men desert. Over 23% of last year's desertions occurred in July and August. A hot hike over a dusty road on a practice march in which the valiant private sees no sense or reason, a ditch to be dug under the blazing summer sun, an acre of brush to be grubbed out, or a close, smelly stable to be cleaned by the sweat of the cavalryman's brow, and there is an end to the dream of military glory.

"It is a shock to most young Americans who have enlisted in the army to taste the delights of military life to find that the most important part of their training, from the viewpoint of the post commander, is to dig ditches, wash pots and pans, wait on table, clean out stables, sweep off walks, or cut brush in the hot sun. Those were the conditions the deserters from the posts just mentioned found in the army. Soon they began to loathe the life. It sickened their souls, it humbled their pride and they ran away from the service.

"Of all the companies of white soldiers in these United States and their dependencies in 1909, there were only five from which there were no desertions."

The experience of the American enlisted man is in strong contrast to the German army conditions. As all able-bodied men must serve in the army in Germany, the government has to adopt no undignified schemes to get enlistments, and the entire point of view is different. Although formerly in the 70's and 80's, there were numerous desertions and conditions were harsh, this is no longer the case. The army is managed in the same thorough and efficient manner as other industrial and educational undertakings.

In the first place, service in the army, although compulsory for rich and poor alike, is not regarded any longer as an irksome thing. The service is an expression of patriotism, a duty discharged to the state, second only to the duties owed to one's parents. This point of view changes the entire situation and while service in the army is not a pastime by any means, it is a healthy and wholesome experience, and there are few Germans who do not look back on their time of service with pleasurable recollections.

In addition it is a moral and educational training, instilling patriotism and respect for the state and authority. The discipline received is one of the soldier's best assets in later life and though misinformed economists cry out against the vast cost of the army, it is only in a small degree, if at all, a social waste.

After the common school course in Germany, it is compulsory for the worker to attend the continuation school part of the day or evening, until the age of eighteen is reached, during and after which time a trade must be learned. The two or three years' military service occurs usually from the latter half of the twenty-first year until the age of twenty-four is reached, but it is optional to begin at 18, or in the case of one taking a college course which might be interrupted to postpone the one year of military service imposed on those taking higher courses of education, until 26.

A system thus which sees to it that the young man is properly equipped with a vocation and whose service in the army, too, adds elements of discipline and of moral and patriotic force to his make-up, is certainly superior to the haphazard system of the United States where no one is compelled to learn any vocation, where the conditions are such that the learning of a trade is made very difficult and where the needs of the army are filled by enticing young men into enlisting in a service from which so large a proportion desert, to remain fugitives from justice thereafter, without trades or any settled means of a livelihood.

Whenever conditions such as now exist in the army are seen on such a scale and over such periods of time, they become an indictment of the system. The deserters are not to blame, they are the victims of the system, the false and aristocratic organization of the whole army. The trouble begins at West Point where a certain class of young men are educated in military matters in such a manner as to transform them into snobs. They then become officers and the enlistment under their command have little or no opportunities of rising to such heights. A line of demarkation thus exists between the officer and the private. They are not comrades, but the officer considers himself a superior species and regards the enlisted man as a mere convenience or body servant. This is quite out of accord with the temper of a democratic country and is the basic reason why there are so many desertions.

The system should be overhauled. West Point should either be abolished, or admission to it gained only after service in the ranks consequent upon an ordinary enlistment, and gained by competitive examination, free to all enlisted men and free from all political influence. The heads of the army should come up through the army, and not be saddled on it by an aristocratic method as at present. While it is now possible for an enlisted man to become an officer, he labors under a stigma of having come up through the ranks instead of from West Point. This should be entirely removed. Until it is, conditions in the army will not improve.

While military service to the extent required by Germany is unnecessary in the United States, a six months' course, or even ninety days in the army for every citizen, would be a distinct benefit for all concerned.

In Germany, it is regarded as the duty of the state to see that the worker is competent in some line of work, and then to utilize every facility to protect him against non-employment and to aid him in sickness and age. That the right to work is becoming more and more a right of mankind, of a nature similar to the rights struggled for and gained by earlier generations, is coming to be more and more recognized.

Speaking at the municipal Fourth of July Celebration in Faneuil Hall in Boston, 1911, Dr. Charles W. Eliot, president emeritus of Harvard, one of the most noted of American thinkers, declared that if the Declaration of Independence were to be drawn up by the American masses in 1911, it would be a totally different document from that of our forefathers, which declared all men were created free and equal, an assertion to which he gave the lie.

The new declaration, Dr. Eliot said, would contain provisions like the following:

1. The national resources of this country, including the public health, are not to be sacrificed to secure immediate profits to a few individuals or corporations to-day.

2. More money should be spent on public education, so that new generations may become quick to deduce error.

3. Every citizen in a free state has an inalienable right to that amount of employment which will yield for him and his family a decent livelihood.

4. Every worker has a right to be insured against personal losses due to acute sickness, injuries and old age.

5. Every man has a right to the normal pleasures and employments of life and the leisure to enjoy them.

6. Land and all instruments of production and distribution of products should belong to society as a whole.

7. Every journeyman in one and the same trade, should receive the same wages. The hours of labor during a day should be the same in all occupations.

8. Methods of neighborhood buying and selling similar to those now successful in Denmark should be put into practice.

Dr. Eliot reasoned that a new declaration of independence would be appropriate in 1911, remarking:

"Is it not interesting to observe that many of the complaints made against King George III may still be made against the democratic government which succeeded that of the King."

Making comparisons, he continued:

"The spoils system creates a multitude of unnecessary offices, just as the King did.

"Tariff legislation has the same effect as come of the King's arbitrary measures to cut off much trade with the rest of the world.

"Unjust methods of taxation still prevail, and still intrenched abuses call for the exercise by the people of much patient sufferance."

Dr. Eliot voices a deep conviction, widely felt to-day, but while the efficiency of the government and its proper organization would go a long way towards the results desired, it may be noted that the right to work is an economic right and not a right of principle. Freedom, equality before the law and other natural rights involve no expense in themselves. When Dr. Eliot says that in a free state, every citizen should have an inalienable right to that amount of employment which will yield for him and his family a decent livelihood, he merely paints a desirable condition without stating a principle. He does not say who is to supply the amount of work needed, as Mr. Howe, before quoted, failed to state where the superfluity of jobs was to come from. Under the conditions depicted by Dr. Eliot, population would increase so rapidly that the inalienable right of employment and a decent livelihood would soon become impossible.

The right to work is a short and vigorous phrase. What it really means is that every man should have an equal share of work.

The absorption of wealth by the owners of machinery, or other means of production, has to-day a powerful influence in creating hard conditions for the worker, but taken with this, the standard of living is higher than in former generations, and the effort to maintain the standard of living, of the workman to maintain a democratic level or at least the semblance of equality as in former times when the population was less numerous and distribution more nearly equal, and not to sink into a definitely lower scale, taken with the competition of a rapidly increasing population, has produced the conditions which give rise to the assertion of the right to work. Such a right is gradually losing ground. Conditions for the worker are growing harder all the time, as may be seen from the statistics of the labor of women and children.

The governmental report, "Statistics of Women at Work," gives the following data:

"At the twelfth census, taken in the year 1900, the number of women in continental United States 16 years of age and over reported as bread winners, or as engaged in gainful occupations, was 4,833,630. The total number of women 16 years of age and over was 23,485,559. The proportion of bread winners, therefore, among women of that age was 20.6%, or approximately one in five."

Regarding race and nativity, the report states that of the female wage earners, there are 1,771,966 native white with both parents native; 1,090,774 native white with one or both parents foreign; 840,011 foreign-born white; 1,119,621 negroes, and 72,947 Indians and Mongolians.

According to the report, the total number of children 10 to 15 for whom an occupation was reported by the census enumeration in 1900 was 1,752,187. The report states further, that it is certain that there are a considerable number of children under 10 years of age, who are earning money regularly by labor. There are 142,105 wage earners 10 years of age. Of the total number of child bread winners, 72.2% were boys and 27.8% were girls, rather more than one-fourth. Regarding race and nativity, there are 837,402 native white with both parents native; 293,210 native white with one or both parents foreign born; 97,944 foreign-born white; 516,172 negroes, and 5,348 Indians and Mongolians. As there were 5,532,495 children 10 to 15 years of age the proportion of child bread winners therefore was approximately one in three.

This high proportion is even more disturbing than the proportion of women wage earners. Dr. Felix Adler well voices the protest which is being aroused when he says:

"I for one am startled by the fact that child labor exists at all in the United States. No doubt it exists also in other countries, but one would have inferred, in view of the temper of the American people, of their generosity, their love for children and their well-known benevolence, that it could not take root in this country. Why does it exist among a free and noble-spirited people? Why is it necessary that there should be State child labor committees and a National Child Labor Committee?"

The figures given above for child labor are now much exceeded and it is estimated that children to the number of 2,500,000 are now compelled to work.

The Wagner-Smith Commission of the State of New York found that children of even only 4 or 5 years of age were at work in canning factories in the state.

Women at work are often confronted with conditions inimicable to their welfare. In the large department stores and garment manufactures wages are so low for many employees, particularly young girls, that other means must be resorted to, to eke out an existence.   The noticeable overdressing of the female relatives of the proprietors of such establishments provides a further incentive to the girl on starvation wages to drift into an easier life. The real betrayer of the working girl is the employer who profits by the low wages paid and thus creates the conditions which lead to her downfall.

In addition to the question of the work of women and children, who should be as classes, free from the necessity of wage earning, and in addition to the low wages, harsh conditions of work exist.

Examples of this are seen in the steel industry, a highly organized business, boasted as the creator of a thousand millionaires of the three thousand in the United States.

The Bethlehem Steel Company where labor conditions were investigated by the Department of Commerce and Labor, an investigation which was confirmed by the Social Service Commission of the Federal Council of the Churches of Christ in America, found conditions justifying severe censure. Concerning the hours of labor the report says:

"Just before the strike, 4,725 men, or 51% of all the employees, worked 12 hours a day; 220 workmen had a twelve-hour day excepting on Saturdays, when their hours were either ten or eleven; 4,203 employees had a work day of ten and a half to eleven hours in length, generally with a half day off on Saturday, and 47 worked on other schedules not specified.

"Beyond, and intensifying the evils of a twelve-hour day, was the existence in many departments of a seven-day week. Twenty-eight per cent. of all employees worked regularly seven days in the week, but in addition were those who worked on Sundays as overtime, regularly. While it is claimed by the management that Sunday and overtime work is, in some departments at least, optional with the men, it is nevertheless true that foremen and gang bosses have compelled men to work on Sunday against their protest and upon pain of discharge.

"Wages," the committee says, "average less than 18 cents an hour for 61 % of the 9,184 employees, or $2.16 for a twelve-hour day. Of the balance, 31.9% earned less than 14 cents an hour, or less than $1.68 for a twelve-hour day."

Similar conditions exist in other steel plants. In the *American Magazine*, in an article "Old Age at Forty," John H. Fitch describes conditions in the United States Steel Co. in Pittsburgh.

"After nearly a year spent among the Pittsburgh steel workers in 1907 and 1908, three phases of the labor policies of the steel companies stand out in my mind as overshadowing all others; they are the factors that enter most deeply into the lives of the men: A daily and weekly schedule of hours, both shockingly long; a system of speeding that adds overstrain to overtime, and crowning all, a system of repression that stifles initiative and destroys healthy citizenship.

"To-day a large majority of the steel workers in Allegheny county work twelve hours out of each twenty-four. There are men classed as day laborers, and some molders and machinists who have a theoretical ten-hour day. But when the mills are busy these men work twelve hours and longer. The machinists work on repairs when there is a break-down, and quit when the repairing is finished. Twenty-four hours on a job is no uncommon thing. I talked with a machinist one day who had worked thirty-six hours consecutively the week before.

"Can you conceive of what it means to work twelve hours a day seven days in the week? Twelve hours every day spent within the mills means thirteen to fourteen hours away from home, for the skilled men often live half an hour's ride from the mills. It means early hours for the wife, if breakfast is to be on time, and late hours too, if the supper dishes are to be washed. It doesn't leave much time for family life, either, when the husband begins to doze over his paper before the evening's work in the kitchen is done, and when necessity inevitably drives him to bed early, so that he may get up in time for the next day's routine."

Carnegie, the philanthropist and advocate of peace, cuts a notable figure in the history of our generation. But it was from conditions such as these that he drew his wealth. As an iron master, his hand was the hand of the iron master indeed, but to-day he broadly distributes the bounty which he ground from working men and the fathers and sons of working men. He and Rockefeller, a rival in benefactions, whose wealth was chiefly derived through ruining his competitors by unfair methods rather than by direct oppression of labor, give with a lavishness never before known. A recent table of their benefactions is as follows:

CARNEGIE GIFTS

Libraries	$ 52,000,000
Pension funds	15,000,000
Carnegie Institute, Pittsburgh	16,000,000
Carnegie Institute, Washington	25,000,000
Peace Foundation	10,000,000
Scotch universities	10,000,000
Hero funds	9,000,000
Carnegie Steel Co. employees	5,000,000
Dunfermline Endowment	5,000,000
Peace Temple, the Hague	1,750,000
Polytechnic School, Pittsburgh	2,000,000
Allied Engineers societies	1,300,000
Bureau of American Republics	750,000
Small colleges in U. S.	20,000,000
County of Cambria, Pennsylvania	600,000
To fight the hook worm	1,000,000
King Edward's Hospital, London	500,000
Miscellaneous in the United States	18,000,000
Tradesmen's associations	400,000
Miscellaneous in Europe	2,500,000
Carnegie Corporation of N. Y.	25,000,000
Total	$220,800,000

ROCKEFELLER GIFTS

General Education Fund	$ 53,000,000
University of Chicago	23,309,000
Institute of Medical Research	8,240,000
Rush Medical College	6,000,000
Baptist churches	3,262,000
Baptist missions (foreign)	2,300,000
Missions (local)	2,300,000
Y. M. C. A.	3,500,000
Barnard College	1,375,000
Yale University	1,300,000
Harvard University	1,000,000
Southern Education Fund	1,125,000
Union Theological Seminary	1,000,000
Baptist Education Society	1,000,000
To fight hook worm	1,000,000
Small colleges in United States	23,000,000
City of Cleveland	3,000,000
Hospitals and medical colleges	15,000,000
Juvenile reformatories	2,000,000
Miscellaneous	20,000,000
Total	$174,711,000
Carnegie's gifts	$220,800,000
Rockefeller's gifts	174,711,000
Carnegie's lead in benefactions	$ 46,089,000

What these enormous gifts really mean, whether they are a burden or a blessing remains to be seen. To produce the interest on this amount of capital, the whole efforts of not less than 200,000 men must continually be consumed, allowing the annual earnings of a man to be one hundred dollars in excess of his expenses, giving him a value equivalent to about $1,700 of capital at 6%, the governmental estimate of the value of a workman.

The Carnegie and Rockefeller benefactions amount to vast economic machines for directing indefinitely the labor of 200,-000 men from their ordinary channels to the purposes which the benefactors select. Whether in the end this is a condition which is desirable is an open question. If all men of great wealth for the next few generations did likewise, a time would come when the burden of colleges, libraries and various foundations would be insupportable. In the middle ages, the religious orders became so burdensome through the benefactions accorded them, that they were dissolved by governments. Even to-day France has seized the property of the Roman Catholic Church and similar seizures have been made in Germany, Spain and Portugal. Too much philanthropy is thus seen to be far from desirable.

The withdrawal from its natural channels of business of such great sums of money and its devotion to education which is to a large extent unproductive, may be included among the present causes of depression. Working men are crushed under the domination of great industries that funds may be provided for these benefactions, and the right to work often becomes no more than the right to exist.

While the "Ironmaster" would not have derived from the founding of an insurance fund for the workmen from whom he drew his wealth the amount of advertising he has from the founding of libraries or the display of his name cut in the stone or on the brass tablets of so many building fronts, he would have acted with more justice and the thought would not spring so readily in the minds of the passersby that the stone and the brass should read, instead of their present inscriptions, "Carnegie Restitution."

It may be urged that conditions among workers generally, especially among the unionized trades, are not as bad, but even in these fields where the workman has succeeded in organizing branches of it thoroughly, the results are not of a very encouraging nature.

The situation is shown by an editorial in the *New York Times:*

"Mr. Thomas Scully, the general organizer of the International Plasterers' Union, made a frank admission as to the relations between wages and earnings in the trade he represents, which is extremely instructive. 'Our men are going to win,' he said. 'They receive, it is true, $5.50 a day for eight hours, but their average for fifty-two weeks is not more than $11 a week.'

"From the point of view of the working man who considers only his immediate interests, it may be just as well to earn $11 per week on a scale of $5.50 for an eight-hour day, as to earn this much by work covering more hours on a lower scale. But there is another point of view which the wage earner cannot refuse to take, without putting in jeopardy his interests as a citizen, a consumer, a payer of rent, and a participant in general prosperity. It may be assumed that $11 a week is not all the ambitious plasterer cares to earn or has use for. Obviously, however, it is all he can earn under a scale of wages which can be sustained only by restricting his average earnings to the amount named.

"He must be more or less continuously on strike, and by reducing his output of work to the least amount consistent with his views of what he should earn in the time devoted to work, he restricts building operations, discourages the improvement of real estate, makes dwellings scarcer and rents higher, so that his $11 a week is not worth as much to him as it would be if won under conditions less destructive of the general good.

"To the average mechanic it might seem like a paradox to say that at lower wages he could probably materially increase his earnings, and that if liberal earnings are his objective, the way to reach them is to fix the wage scale at a practical figure, and give up striking and contention. However, this is the truth, and it may be that by reflection he will come to a realization of it."

From this it will be seen that the plasterer, though his wages are high while he works, does not earn as much as the steel worker in a given year. All his unionism brings him is the privilege of loafing and paying higher rent. The union is thus an agency of inefficiency.

While the rise of the contractor to a position of wealth is prevented, since the contractor cannot make a profit out of his labor, he has not in reality benefited anyone thereby, not even himself.

The difficulty of the worker getting a larger proportion of profits for his work than arises out of natural causes—the relative supply of labor and capital—is thus seen to be insurmountable, and the right to work is not a right that is inalienable. Temporary expedients will not do. A thorough and systematic reorganization of the relations of labor and capital, a new fairness on both sides, coöperation, different educational systems and an efficient governmental policy must gain for the worker a fairer share than he can get under present haphazard methods.

CHAPTER XX

SOCIAL INSURANCE

Marvelous growth of insurance—An unknown force a few generations ago
—Compulsory insurance in Germany—The six forms of social insurance—The frightful waste of accident liability in the United States—
What compulsory insurance costs the Krupp Company—Germany's
program of human salvage—Important provisions of German insurance laws—What the widow receives—Shares of other beneficiaries—
No lump sums as premiums for litigation—Maternity insurance—The
wolf at the German door—Ethical effect of old age insurance.

THE world has progressed far in the last century, and its
progress is nowhere so strikingly shown as in the extension of
insurance. One hundred years ago insurance was looked on
as of a sacrilegious nature, and it was a bold and forward person who would attempt to thwart the designs of Providence in
such a manner.

To-day insurance is one of the largest factors in the social
organization, and its development in the hands of private companies has been so phenomenal that it is coming to be regarded
as more properly a governmental function.

Though accompanied by violent and complicated discussion,
the governments of Europe following the lead of Germany, are
steadily adopting compulsory state insurance in various forms,
supplementing and enlarging the work of various mutual benefit associations.

Though the governmental participation has undoubtedly
stimulated the development of all the activities of mutual benefit societies, particularly in the matter of sick insurance, the
providing of this form of mutual benefit for the entire class of
wage earners has by no means been accomplished. The only
practicable method of accomplishing this is by means of compulsory insurance, which usually carries with it the shifting of
a certain portion of the burden from employee to employer.

The United States Commissioner of Labor has investigated
the subject of state insurance, and the government has published
a comprehensive and exhaustive report on the subject, which in

common with the many highly valuable reports of the government, is readily available. In this respect, the United States is far in advance of other countries in the complete and thorough reports and investigations of a wide variety of subjects made by its experts, while their ready accessibility increases their value.

The reports cover not only the German governmental insurance systems but also those of other countries, but as Germany was the pioneer in this field, and the systems of other countries have been largely based on hers, the reports refer most frequently to that system. The subject is so great that only its salient features can be touched upon here, and the leading features of the German system will be principally considered.

The Commissioner's report states:

"Germany by its act of June 15, 1883, was the first to introduce the compulsory sickness insurance system on a national scale, and its example was followed by Austria in 1888, Hungary in 1891, Luxemburg in 1901 and recently by Norway in 1909.

"In all these countries, an effort was made to retain the sick benefit societies existing at the time when this legislation was enacted, as it was felt that local administration and self-government were necessary for the success of this system, and therefore a great variety of organizations is found in the countries mentioned, even under the uniform system of compulsion. Funds based upon geographic limits, establishment funds, trade funds, and others frequently operate side by side, though at the present time the tendency is to strengthen the funds based on geographic limits.

"The rapid development of the compulsory sickness insurance idea is demonstrated by the numerous proposals in favor of the compulsory system in various countries in which as yet, it does not exist. Thus France, Italy, Russia, and Switzerland may be mentioned as countries in which proposals for compulsory sickness insurance have been seriously considered within recent years.

"The growing importance of the subject of employees' insurance in this country, is indicated by the fact that within recent years, eight states, Connecticut, Illinois, Massachusetts, Minnesota, New Jersey, New York, Ohio and Wisconsin, and the Federal Government have appointed commissions to study methods

of compensating workmen for disability incurred in the course
of their employment.

"As a result of these activities, one state, New York, has already enacted laws of general application, while two states,
Montana and Maryland, have made provision for state systems
of co-operative insurance against accidents to workmen engaged
in mining.

" 'Social insurance' may be defined as the method of organized relief, by which wage earners or persons similarly situated,
and their dependents or survivors, become entitled to specified
pecuniary or other benefits, on the occurrence of certain emer-
gencies. The right to these benefits is secured by means of
contributions from wages, or by the fact of the insured person's
employment, or by his citizenship or residence in the country.

"The various forms of social insurance may be designated
as:

"1. Accident.
"2. Sickness.
"3. Maternity.
"4. Invalidity and old age.
"5. Unemployment.
"6. Insurance for widows and orphans.   .

"The principle of systematic compensation for losses due to
industrial accident has been long known in Europe for the
earliest examples are found in the mining industries, especially
in Germany and Austria. As these industries were the first to
be operated on a large scale, with large numbers of employees
whose life and safety depended on the care and skill of the
manager and of the fellow workmen, and in addition had a
high danger rate, it was but natural that attempts should be
made to provide in a definite manner for the relief of the distress of employees caused by accidental injuries or physical
disability.

"The industry of navigation possessed similar characteristics
and also developed at an early date, comparatively well-defined
systems of relief for disability arising from the operation of
vessels. The next industry to be operated on a large scale and
which had at the same time a high trade risk, was that of railroad transportation, and in the states of the present German
Empire, we find early efforts to make provision for railway em-

ployees on a more liberal scale than that prevailing in the manufacturing industries.

"With the development of large scale industries and the more frequent use of machine power, together with the increase in the size of industrial establishments, there was an increase in the trade risk of the industries so affected. Previous to the development of large scale production, a comparatively simple system of compensation for industrial accidents prevailed in nearly all the countries in the world, based upon the idea that a workman suffering an injury from industrial accident should be compensated by the person or persons at fault in causing the accident. The relief provided under the Civil Code in continental Europe, was more readily obtainable than that permitted under the English law, but in each case, the person liable was supposed to have committed some fault and it was necessary for the plaintiff to bring suit and prove such fault, of negligence, according to the rules of evidence prevailing in the courts of each country."

The system of bringing suits is the one in vogue throughout the United States, and as is well known, works great hardships on the injured and is subject to grave abuses.

Large employers are constantly the victims of conspiracies, while the case of an innocent victim of an accident is often defeated by perjured testimony introduced by the employer. Lawyers divide the larger part of the benefits, and the length of time taken to secure the compensation is one of the reproaches of the American judicial system.

The state of New York recently enacted a new employers' liability law, but it was declared unconstitutional by the courts and thus no practical headway has been made to correct the bad practice of the plan of compensation for accidents at present in vogue. One of its worst features is the fact that the awards by juries are irregular and disproportionate, some juries awarding more for the loss of a hand than others do for the loss of an arm, while a leg is often more highly valued than a life.

Mr. Frederick C. Howe in "How Germany Cares for Her Working People," in the *Outlook* of May, 1910, explains in an interesting way the main outlines of the system:

"Insurance against sickness has been provided since 1884. It is provided for those employed in factories, mines, work shops, quarries, transportation and other industries. Employees of public enterprises are also covered. The provisions of the law are limited to those whose wages are below $500 a year. The sickness insurance funds are of various kinds. There are local funds provided by the parishes for all of the trades within their limits. Some of the large industries have funds of their own, as do the mine owners and the contractors in the building trades.

"All of the funds provide for free medical attendance and supplies as well as sick pay from the third day of sickness. The benefits amount to one-half of the daily wages received by the beneficiary or the amount upon which his assessment is based. Benefits are continued for not more than twenty-six weeks, after which time, if the illness still continues, the burden is transferred to the Accident Insurance Fund.

"The insurance fund in Germany is sustained by the working men, the employers and to some extent by the community. Generally the employee pays two-thirds of the premium, and the employer one-third, the liability of both being ascertained by periodic reports from the employer as to the number of employees liable to insurance. The premiums are collected by stoppage, the employer deducting the assessments of the employees when wages are paid, which, along with his own share, are then transmitted to the fund.

"The administration of the funds is largely in the hands of the working people themselves, through a board chosen by the employers and the employees. General meetings are held at which all persons who contribute to the fund may come, at which meetings the delegates who have charge of the insurance are elected. About 12,000,000 persons are insured against sickness in the German Empire.

"The provisions of the law of the insurance fund against accident, cover substantially the same classes as the sickness insurance, and the method of administration is substantially the same. The employer is bound to provide insurance against accident, as in the case of sickness. Upon opening a factory, he automatically becomes a member of the trade association covering his business, and is bound to contribute to the insurance fund. This fund is managed by the executive board of the trades, which has power to classify trades and fix the danger schedule. But, better than this, the board has power to enforce rules and appliances for the prevention of accident. If a member refuses to abide by the ruling of the board, he may be fined for his neglect, or his danger rating is increased.

"By this means the employers are stimulated to an interest in safety devices, while the special knowledge on the part of the individual trade association leads to a better administration of the rules than would be possible on the part of the state. In all of these matters, the employees are consulted. They are also allowed representation on the executive board.

"Benefits under the accident insurance law are not left to judicial inquiry. The employee is not put to the expense and delay of long litigation. Even though the employee is negligent, he is entitled to compensation, unless there should be evidence that he intentionally brought the accident upon himself. Here, as in sickness, the cost of human wreckage in industry is shifted in part on the cost of production. It is passed on to the community where it belongs.

"The amount of the compensation paid depends upon the wages of the employee and the extent of the injury. If the accident wholly incapacitates the worker, he receives a full pension, which amounts to two-thirds of his yearly wage. If he is still able to work, the pension is adjusted to his earning ability. In case of accident resulting in death, an immediate payment of about one-sixth of the yearly wage is paid. In addition to this, the widow and dependent children are pensioned, the widow until her death or remarriage and the dependent children up to their fifteenth year. In this event, the annual pension does not exceed 60% of the annual wage.

"Not only is the German workman thus insured against sickness, which marks the beginning of much of the poverty of our cities, as well as against the accidents of industrial establishments, which fill the hospitals with the bulk of their patients, but practically all German workmen are insured against old age. Those whose earnings exceed $500 are not covered by old-age insurance, nor are the higher class of employees and servants. The administration of this branch is carried on by insurance societies, which cover certain sections, or by the state at large.

"All of them are under the supervision of the state and are controlled by the employers and the employees. The old-age funds are supplied by the employers and the employees, who contribute in equal shares to the fund. To this the Empire adds $12.50 towards every pension.

"The success of these insurance schemes is seen by the number of members enrolled. There were 23,679,000 insured against accident in 1908 and 15,266,000 against old age, and 13,189,600 against sickness. The total expenditures of the various funds amounted to over $183,675,000 while the funds accumulated as a reserve exceeded $521,000,000.''

In ''The German Drift towards Socialism,'' by William C. Dreher, in the *Atlantic Monthly* for July, 1911, the general results are summed up as follows:

''The aggregate revenues of the three systems in 1908 were $214,856,675 and they paid out $165,000,000 in pensions and indemnities.

''They owned invested funds amounting to $496,000,000. The contributions in the three systems have been estimated by careful statisticians at 6.75% of the wages received by the insured, of which the employers pay 3.68% and the employed 3.07%. The insurance payments have a serious effect on the finances of employers. Thus far, the famous Krupp company, in 1908, paid $807,000 in insurance money, which was in the ratio of $13.60 to $100 of net profits. Another great iron company paid into the insurance fund a ratio equivalent to $22 in $100 and another nearly $47 in $100.

''Of course such expenses in addition to heavy general taxation, must prove a serious handicap to German industry; and it is not to be wondered at that the feeling is gaining ground among the employers that they are doing enough for their help. Yet there is no indication that social reform legislation is to be checked. The bill before the Reichstag, referred to above, extends sick insurance to farm laborers and household servants, a change which will raise the burden of this system for employers from $24,000,000 to $36,000,000. The bill also provides for pensioning the widows and orphans of insured laborers at an estimated additional expense of about $17,000,000. The Imperial government has also just published a bill for establishing an entirely independent system of insurance for the protection of persons not included in the labor systems; it will apply practically to all employed persons having a salary less than $1,200.''

While Germany had in 1908 a population of 63,000,000, the number of wage earners was 16,000,000, of which 5,000,000 were women, a proportion of wage earners to population of slightly less than one in four. The United States with a population of 90,000,000 has 33,000,000 wage earners, a ratio of one to two and three-quarters.

In 1900 there were 4,833,630 women wage-earners according to the U. S. Census, and it is now estimated that the number exceeds 7,000,000, which is proportionately in excess of the number of women employed in Germany.

The impression that more women have to work in Germany than in America, is thus seen to be groundless. The German woman, working more in the open, is further more healthfully employed than the American woman, the larger part of whose work is done in closed quarters, such as factories, sweat-shops, offices, etc., and the result is shown in the more robust and vigorous physique of the German woman.

Further, the number of women wage-earners in Germany cannot be compared with the number in the United States, since such a large proportion of the German wage earning women are household servants; German domestic customs being such that families of even limited means have servants. There is no stigma attached in Germany to domestic service and the result is an abundance of competent help for the housewives and a rule of well kept homes which is almost unknown in America.

The more favorable proportion of wage earners to population is due to the fact that the German retires much sooner to live on his pension, while as a youth he begins to be a wage earner later in life than the American boy.

Owing to the German custom of contracts with employers, the profits of any gainful occupation that may be engaged in after business hours, including inventions in the line of work of the employment, go to the employer under certain circumstances. This still further identifies the interests of employers and employees, and prevents the switching from one business to another so prevalent in America. Though it discourages individual initiative, it promotes a life of ease during the evening, since the employee will hardly devote much energy to outside tasks the fruits of which go to his employer. It accomplishes, however, the object sought, of having the employees come fresh to work, with their entire energy reserved for their daily work, and not used up in outside schemes.

It will be noted that all wage earners are in three different insurance systems, sickness, accident and old age or invalidity. Thus all eventualities are provided for.

Mr. Howe, in the *Outlook*, says further:

"Aside from the positive accomplishments of the German Empire in this line of social reform, one is impressed with the seriousness with which the cities as well as the nation are considering the whole question. There are frequent conferences attended by representatives from the Empire and the various states, from the cities, the universities and the philanthropic societies. There is nothing hit or miss about it. The best thought of the university and the most energetic of city officials are constantly studying ways and means for the relief of the numerous problems which arise in connection with unemployment, with the hazards of industry, with the poor and destitute members of the community.

"Poverty has not been abolished in Germany, nor has the housing question been solved. Industrial depression takes its tribute there just as it does with us. But the impressive thing about it all is that the nation views these questions in something of the same light that it does the building of dreadnaughts, or railways, of canals, the adjustment of taxes and the building of cities.

"Germany more than any other country in Europe has entered on a comprehensive programme of human salvage. She is devoting her thought and her energy to the making of people as well as of things."

According to Oberbergrat Kratz on "German Labor Insurance," in *Deutschland als Weltmacht*, the governmental insurance system paid out in 1908 for sickness, 324,785,767 marks ($81,196,441), covering 5,655,836 cases. The management of the system cost 19,209,686 marks, which is 5.4%.

In accident insurance Germany paid out in 1908, 157,062,-870 marks ($39,265,718). The total benefits paid on accidents from 1885 to 1908 amounted to 1,615,364,647 marks ($403,841,-161).

The sickness insurance fund amounted in 1908 to 279,860,-685 marks ($69,965,171), to which must be added the reserve funds of insurance institutes which is 1,390,943 marks and also the property owned, 52,249,910 marks, a total of $83,375,383.

Some of the leading provisions of the German law are as follows:

All workmen and administrative officers, the latter provided that their annual earnings in wages or salary does not exceed 3,000 marks ($714) are insured, according to the provisions of this law, against the results of accidents occurring to them in the course of the employment, if they are employees:—

1. In mines, salt works, establishments in which ores are

treated, quarries, pits, ship yards, yards for preparing building materials and in factories, commercial breweries or smelting works.

2. In industrial establishments which include the execution of masonry, carpentry, roofing or other building work declared by decision of the Federal Council to be subjected to insurance, stone cutting, locksmithing, smithing, or well digging, and also establishments engaged in chimney sweeping, window cleaning or butchering.

3. In the administration of the post office, telegraph and railroads, and in the administration of the navy and army, including that of building operations which are carried on by these departments on their own account.

4. In the business of carting, internal navigation, rafting of wood, transportation on ferry boats and flat boats, tugging or dredging.

5. In the business of expressing and storing goods and in that of cellerage.

6. In the establishments of goods packers and loaders, goods sorters, weighers, measurers, inspectors and stowers.

7. In the work of storage, tree felling, or work connected with the transportation of persons or goods if such work is done for a commercial establishment the proprietor of which is inscribed in the commercial register.

The insurance extends to domestic and other service to which insured persons are assigned by their employers or by the employer's agents in connection with their employment in the establishment.

In case of disability compensation is rendered as follows:

From the beginning of the fourteenth week after the date of the accident:

1. Free medical treatment, medicine and other means of healing, also the facilities (crutches, supporting apparatus, etc.) to insure the success of the treatment and diminish the effects of the injury.

2. A pension as long as the disability lasts.

The amount of the pension is—

(a) In the case of total disability and as long as it lasts, two-thirds of the annual earnings (full pension).

(b) In the case of partial disability and as long as it lasts, a part of the full pension proportionate to the loss, through the accident, of the earning capacity (partial pension).

If, in consequence of the accident, the injured person is rendered not only entirely incapable of work, but also sufficiently helpless as to require attendance and care from others, the pension is to be increased to 100% of the annual earnings as long as this condition continues.

If the injured person was, at the time of the accident, already suffering from total and permanent disability, no compensation is made save that prescribed in paragraph first of this article. If such injured person has been rendered helpless by the accident as to require attendance and care from others, a pension of not more than one-half of the full pension shall be granted.

If, on account of the accident, the injured person is actually out of work through no fault of his own, the board of directors of the association may temporarily increase the partial pension to the amount of the full pension.

In the case of death, the following compensation is also made:

1. As a funeral benefit, one-fifteenth of the annual earnings, which shall be determined according to Article 10, paragraphs 1 to 4, but the grant shall never be less than 50 marks ($11.90).

2. A pension to be paid to survivors from the day of the deceased person's death. (This consists of a proportion of his annual earnings and is calculated in a complicated way according to the circumstances of the case.)

If the deceased leaves a widow or children, the pension for the widow, up to the time of her death, or remarriage, and for every surviving child, up to the completion of its fifteenth year, shall be for each, 20% of the annual earnings, but in no case is such total to be more than the husband would have received for total disability.

In the case of her remarriage, the widow shall receive 60% of the annual earnings as a settlement.

If at the time of the accident, the deceased was married but was, on account of her husband's invalidity, wholly or mainly responsible for the support of the family, the following pensions shall be granted as long as the need continues:

(a) to the widower, 20%.

(b) to every surviving child up to the completion of its fifteenth year, 20% of the annual earnings.

If the deceased person leaves parents or grandparents (ascendants) whom he was partly or mainly supporting, they shall receive until the need ceases, a total pension of 20% of the annual earnings.

It will be seen that in this system there is no possibility of the awards of large sums as in the United States, and thus no great incentives are hung up for litigation, and as the lawyers have little or nothing to do with the matter anyway, a great social waste is saved.

Indeed the companies, which under a complicated system of determining their proper shares of contributions to the funds, might be supposed to be anxious to utilize technicalities to escape their payments, are rather inclined to liberality than the reverse, and do not usually confine their payments to the pension funds to the minimum, preferring by substantial contributions over their minimum requirements, to gain the good will of employees and others in interest, with the consequent moral effect.

The idea of an American corporation paying more for anything than required by dire legal necessity, and for the sake of good will of employees, is a condition too rare to need much consideration.

The beginnings of sickness insurance may be traced further back than those of insurance against accidents or any other form of social insurance. These beginnings are to be found in the organization of mutual aid, and are not limited to any special social group. From this form of purely voluntary organization supported exclusively by the contributions of its members, there has been a steady development towards compulsory sickness insurance, strictly regulated, and in some cases assisted by the state, but the development is far from complete, and the compulsory system has, as yet, been adopted mainly by Germany and Austria. The important feature of this development has been the fact that the mutual aid society was found, for many reasons, to be the most convenient organization for the purpose of accomplishing compulsory sickness insurance. Briefly, the evolution of sickness insurance may be said to be by the following four stages:

1. Free and voluntary associations entirely unregulated by law.

2. Regulation by law, either compulsory, for all, or optional with classification of societies into recognized and unrecognized.

3. Regulation combined with government assistance.

4. Compulsory insurance.

With the growth of workmen's accident insurance systems the burden of industrial accidents has fallen less heavily on the mutual benefit societies, yet it has been found advantageous, both in Germany and Austria, to have the care of all accidents left during the earlier stages to the sickness insurance system. The advantages of such a combination are, on the one hand, the speed of relief, and on the other hand, the comparative simplicity of administration and supervision, which tends to reduce malingering. In other countries, where there is no such well-organized system of compulsory insurance, the compensation laws frequently provide for a certain waiting period during which accidents are not compensated, and the duty of furnishing relief in such cases usually falls upon the mutual benefit societies.

A study of organizations for sickness insurance shows how closely sickness is interwoven with the causes of economic distress. From the point of view of causation, it is often difficult to draw the line between sickness and accident, while on the other hand, sickness may develop into more or less permanent invalidity.

In its earliest forms, the mutual benefit society naturally gave assistance in all cases of disability, whether due to sickness or accident, and the duration of the assistance varied with the financial strength of the organization. The accumulation of actuarial data has placed sickness insurance on a definite insurance basis, and more careful differentiation between the various causes and forms of infirmity has resulted.

Nevertheless, for practical purposes of administration, it is often found of advantage not to draw the line too strictly.

One of the most recent developments of insurance in Germany is a law in reference to mining, which arose out of a disaster in a coal mine in Westphalia. The miners believed it could have been prevented by a more perfect and frequent system of inspection of the mine, and the legislation now in effect provides for the election by the miners themselves at each colliery, of their own inspectors, who examine the underground conditions at least once a month, and at the owner's expense. Thus the workmen have in their own hands the means of protecting themselves.

Quoting again from the Commissioner of Labor, he states in reference to maternity insurance:

"This branch of social insurance is still little developed in most countries and is usually combined with the general system of sickness insurance. The employment of women in industry, however, has emphasized the importance of this form of insurance and also the differences between the provisions for maternity and the provision for ordinary sickness, which make a separate treatment of this topic advisable from an administrative point of view. The two main points of difference may be stated as follows:

"First, maternity is a natural process which though calling for medical help, in modern society usually runs a normal course and requires a definite normal length of absence from work.

. "Second, also unlike sickness, it requires the absence from work for some time before the actual occurrence of childbirth. The actuarial factors upon which a system of maternity insurance must be built are different in that it concerns only the female wage earners and those only within certain well defined age periods, while the social purpose is even broader than that of ordinary sickness insurance in that it concerns not only the wage worker, but the future generation. The purpose of maternity insurance is not only that of assistance to the mother but also the reduction of infant mortality.

"The earlier efforts toward accomplishing these aims consisted in legislation regulating conditions of work of mothers for some time before and after childbirth, so as to prevent the occurrence of various diseases and accidents frequently connected with childbirth. The period varies in the legislation of different countries, usually embracing from four to six weeks. This again, unlike sickness legislation itself, in case of maternity forces a period of idleness upon the female wage earners and therefore creates a need for financial assistance."

In Italy the law proposed in 1909 contemplated an equal contribution from employer and employee of a sum equal to three quarters of the pay for twenty-eight days.

"The earliest known forms of provision for the aged are the systems of charitable relief in the form of outdoor relief and of institutional relief, although neither of these forms can be designated as features of a social insurance system. In some employments, as, for instance, that of the various government factories, pensions for superannuated or invalid employees have been customary in Europe for many years. In addition, many private establishments in Europe have been accustomed to pension aged or infirm employees after long terms of service; such pensions are often entirely paid by the employer, the purpose of the superannuation pension in such establishments being to secure continuity of service from the employees.

"The pensions just mentioned, however, have affected only a small proportion of the persons generally included in a system of social insurance. The first forms of old-age and invalidity insurance proper are found in the mutual organizations of various kinds, such as the miners' relief funds, seamen's funds, trade union funds, mutual aid societies and the like. When these organizations adopted systems of old-age or invalidity pensions it was usually without an adequate insurance basis in so far as the liabilities being secured by the assets is concerned, and at the present time, even, many voluntary insurance organizations are endeavoring to provide old-age and invalidity insurance without an adequate income in view of the liabilities.

"Under all of the accident compensation systems a fatal accident covered by the compensation law is compensated by a benefit in some form to the survivors of the insured person. These benefits usually take the form of either a lump sum payment distributed to the widows for life or until remarried and a pension to the children until a certain age is reached. It is evident that many cases will arise where the death of the insured person leaves the family in just as great distress as if the death had been caused by an industrial accident, and in many cases the family is even in greater distress because death may result after a long period of illness in which the family resources were exhausted in caring for the sick person.

"In order to make provision for the class of cases just mentioned, widow and orphan benefits were provided by the miners' relief funds in the various countries, but especially in Germany and Austria, Belgium, France and Great Britain.

"Similar provision, usually amounting to half the pension to which the deceased was entitled or was receiving, is found in the case of some of the railroad funds and seamen's funds. In Germany, at the present time, the navigation accident association which administers the compulsory accident and invalidity insurance for the seamen, conducts a system of widow and orphan insurance which is founded on a carefully considered actuarial basis. The German government now has under consideration the creation of a national compulsory system of insurance for widows and orphans, (Hinterbliebenen-Versicherung).

"In Germany under the invalidity and old-age law, in case a

member dies before reaching a pension, the survivors become entitled to the dues or contributions paid in by the insured person up to the time of his death.''

The various systems of insurance in force in Germany have proved of the greatest benefit to all concerned. The employer by small periodical payments is relieved of the harassment and losses of damage suits and the workman is free from anxiety and relieved from distress, such as the American workman is subject to through the lack of cordial relations to his employers and the failure to recognize that their interests are in common.

Students of economics consider the superior efficiency of the German workmen on the whole very largely ascribable to the systems of insurance in force. The German working people are as a class dependable and industrious. They take a proper interest in their work, are steady in habits, trustworthy and thorough. They do what they are told to do and do it well. They understand their work and are not lost the moment any new problem presents itself.

American workmen would not attempt to follow foreign plans with a metric system, but German mechanics may often be seen using original drawings in the English system of feet and inches on foreign orders in difficult engineering work.

The insurance systems lend a backbone of confidence. The wolf cannot approach the door so closely, and whatever may happen, there is a margin of financial safety, a breakwater between the worker and necessity, which does not involve charity. Thus he feels freer to devote his energies to his work and the result is efficiency, indeed the highest state of efficiency which has ever been reached by any nation.

CHAPTER XXI

TOM, DICK AND HARRY

Their principal concerns—Enormous public attention paid to sports—
The horse and the extensive record of his past performances—The
bloodlust of the spectator of automobile races—The carnage of the
racing car—The hundred fatal milestones in the progress of aviation
—The sacrifice of the lives of aviators to the humor of the crowd—
The harvest of the football field—Death on the side lines—The modern
boxing mill—Free flowing of gore though few fatalities—The baseball crank—The fascination of the game—Antique origin—Fearful
prevalence in America—Great economical wastes of the game—No
intelligence needed to be a baseball fan—Hence its popularity—Misdirected energy—The fatal celebrations of the Fourth of July—
Superfluous patriotism—The grim sport of lynching negroes—Ferocity
of this form of the lawless execution—Due largely to the law's delays
—A secret shame.

In America, a subject of the greatest interest to the general
public is sport. Tom, Dick and Harry devote a large part of
their mental energy and monetary resources to keeping track
of baseball, automobile and other sporting events.

The horse has a large circle of devotees and much study is
spent over the newspaper sheets showing his "past performances."

Every newspaper of consequence has columns, often several
pages, devoted to sporting events, and prize fighting, football,
bowling, tennis, golf, rowing, motor boat and motor cycle racing, swimming, high jumping, broad jumping, standing jumping, hammer throwing, foot races, marathon races, marathon
dancing and various other sports receive the most minute attention.

A peculiar feature of sport in America is the great number
of spectators compared with the number of those engaged in
the games. Of the spectators who assemble, often 50,000 at
a single event, few ever did or ever will practice the sport.
Their interest is in the contests, not in athletics, and in some
sports, notably that of automobile racing, a more sinister interest is manifested, the interest of seeing a catastrophe.

The public goes so far even, in its demands, as to force aviators to undertake flights in weather so dangerous that during the past season two fatal accidents resulted from this cause.

Automobile racing in the United States is carried on by professional promoters, and in their lust for money they excite an appeal to the blood lust of the spectator. Long races on roads are undertaken at early hours in the morning, and the scores of thousands of spectators are up the whole of the previous night to reach the locality and see the race. They bank the track on both sides for miles, crowding forward and it is only a narrow lane that is left for the automobilists to traverse. At their more than express train speeds, the result is that more spectators are killed than participants.

At Syracuse, N. Y., on Sept. 16, 1911, a racing automobile swerved from the track and plowed a path through the crowd, killing ten people.

"To call such outrages accidents," says the *Outlook*, "is to mock the truth. Before Syracuse had usurped the place, Indianapolis had probably the most prominent position in the rivalry for this form of slaughter.

"That bloodshed and homicide are accounted among the attractive features of such races can be shown by the method of advertising. What can Americans say of the bull-fights of Spain or the gladiatorial contests of ancient Rome, when an automobile race is advertised as follows:

" 'Shaking dice with Death. 20 Dare Devil Drivers. In Thrilling Speed Duels. The Field vs. Death—Which will Win?' and when bulletins such as the following appear:

" '6:40 P. M. Car No. 4 ran into car No. 7.

" 'Two men hurt.

" 'Come out and see the SPILL.'

"It is hypocrisy to call the ghastly results of such races 'accidents.' They are 'features,' 'drawing cards.' Those who are killed or crippled are the victims of human sacrifice to the twin gods blood lust and money lust.

"This is not the view of those who deprecate healthful, robust sport, but of those who can distinguish between what is robust and what is to the last degree brutal and murderous.

"It is time that the American people should make it plain that they are not willing to let a crowd here and there, however numerous, have its savage way at the cost of the nation's reputation. If this pandering to blood thirstiness cannot be stopped by public opinion, it should be stopped by law."

Barney Oldfield, one of the best known of the racing drivers, in *Popular Mechanics* for September, 1911, says:

"I was never famous until I went through the fence at St. Louis and killed two spectators. Promoters fell over one another to sign me up.

"The American grows sentimental about killing cattle; the Mexican prefers cattle to human beings. It is merely a matter of taste.

"I never realized my foolishness on any of these occasions until I was in the hospital with the doctors standing around and the nurses looking serious.

"While the body of Basle lay still beside his machine, women tried to cut off pieces of his clothing as a souvenir. On the day after Basle's death, ten thousand persons fought for front seats at the track.

"Many newspapers have even ceased to treat track racing as a sport. Reports of the big races are placed on the front page under a "scare," with lists of the dead and injured for the year printed in heavy type at the head of the column.

"The dignity of motor racing is gone. It has ceased to be racing, and has become merely a morbid and unelevating spectacle. It is run for money alone. Its profits are blood money."

The latest means of satisfying the spectator is the aeroplane. No more hazardous sport can well be devised. In this case the spectators have escaped injury for the most part, though a notable exception among others is found in the death of the French Minister of War, Henry M. Berteaux, who was killed by a swerving aeroplane.

Aviation scored 100 deaths on October 14, 1911, with the burning in the air of Aviator Hans Schmidt in Berne, Switzerland, while making an exhibition flight. Of the 100 fatalities, sixteen occurred in America. The 200 mark was reached October 8, 1912 with the death of Joseph Stevenson at Birmingham, Ala. While some of the deaths have resulted from the necessary risk in perfecting the aeroplane, and are chargeable to the progress of the art, by far the greater number have been due to flights undertaken for exhibition purposes and the deaths of two in America at least, J. J. Frisbie in Norton county, Kansas, and Frank H. Miller at Mansfield, Ohio, were due to the unruly conduct of spectators in forcing the aviators to ascend against their judgment.

The first of the aviators to meet death was Otto Lilienthal, of Hamburg, Germany, who fell while experimenting with a 2½ horse power aeroplane, on August 10, 1896.

Exhibition flights, like automobile racing, constitute a phase of the interest of the public in a possible catastrophe that is on a par with the taste of the population of ancient Rome. Aviators, mostly daredevil and adventurous men, work under a great nervous strain. The slightest error may turn the graceful and steady machine, which seems to fly so easily and safely, into a mass of broken sticks and wires. The public wagers its money against the aviator making such a mistake, and if he does, and though he be killed the meet goes on.

The flying men in conversation ordinarily call aviation a "game," rather than calling it aviation; as "he has been in the game only a few months," or "one of the best in the game." Truly it is a "game" when the public come to pay.

Another of the "games" the public throngs to see is the gentle sport of football. The aviator unless he meets with serious injury returns sound and whole, but every player that goes into a football field, knows that days of soreness and bruises, if not sprained limbs, broken bones or fatal accident will be his certain share, along with the "glory" of it.

The manly art of football claimed 146 victims from 1901 to 1909, while 1612 were seriously injured.

YEAR	Killed	Injured
1909	33	275
1908	10	272
1907	15	166
1906	14	160
1905	24	200
1904	14	296
1903	14	63
1902	15	106
1901	7	74

The high water mark was reached in 1909 with 33 killed, after which there was so much agitation that the rules were changed, resulting, however, in 1910 in 14 deaths with 40 badly injured, an improvement in a way. The 14 deaths resulted from injuries classified as follows:

Body blows 1
Injuries to spine 1
Concussion of brain 7
Blood poisoning 2
Other causes 3

In 1909 the injuries were of the following nature:

Critically injured 20
Broken collar bones 60
Broken noses 42
Broken legs 36
Broken ribs 26
Broken arms 24
Broken ankles 20
Broken shoulders 19
Broken wrists 8
Broken fingers 8
Broken hands 6
Broken jaws 6

The new rules under which football is now played are little better than the former ones, as far as preventing injury goes. If the professors and student body can find no way of re-organizing the game, it is one that will sooner or later have to go. There is also a darker side to football, in the fact that it is occasionally proven that the injuries are intentionally inflicted.

Bad blood develops between teams and individuals, and in the tangle of the game, old scores are wiped out and new ones entered in a way by no means polite. A game in which this is possible, is inherently defective and not good sport.

Football appeals to the humorist also. Wallace Irwin in the *New York Globe* of Oct. 14, 1911, describes the views of a creation of his, a certain "Col. Crowe of Cripple Creek," on football. "Col. Crowe" has this to say:

" 'Tain't in it with bull-fightin'. In the first place the killin' is all too harem scarem and accidental. There's plenty o' brutality, but it ain't played up so that the audience can git full benefit of it. Maybe it wasn't a first class game I seen; but it seemed to me I'd a-gone away more satisfied if more o' the injury had been did in full view of the audience. Time and again I seen 'em do the same thing—all squat down with their heads close together while the captain shouted 4—11—C. Q.D., thus givin' the secret signal for who was to be killed— next y' knew some young man was left for dead in the field, while them assassins scampered away from the scene o' the crime as merry as kangaroo colts. Now, I ain't raisin' no objections to murder, if it's included in the rules of the game; but as long as the audience pays a dollar to git in and twenty-five cents extra for the privilege of carrying a flag, I claim it's their right to be in on all the fun. If somebody's got to be killed, let it be did out in the open where everybody can see it. Though I ain't got much use for a Mexican, ordinarily I must say they're lots greater artists than us when it comes to a public slaughter house event.''

''You mean you prefer bull-fighting to football?'' I inquired, shocked.

''It's more square and above the table,'' said Col. Crowe. ''When a Mexican goes to a bull-fight, he goes with the expectation of seein' something or somebody killed. He's never disappointed. And what's more, the killin' is played up into a big draymatic spectacle. The bull, the horses, the bull stickers are all marched out to the music of a brass band. The horses and five or six assorted toreadors are slaughtered in full view of the audience, right under the grandstand. Then when the bull is all lathered up into a glorious state of peevishness, the chief sticker steps forth into the center of the arena and they fight it out. If the toreador kills the bull, the audience yells, 'Bray-vo, toreador!' But if the bull kills the toreador, the audience with equal enthusiasm yells, 'Bray-vo, bull!' It's a cinch game. Whichever way y' play it y' git what y' want—a gory sacrifice.''

''Do you think the object of the sport is a gory sacrifice?'' I asked, more horrified than before.

''Well, ain't it?'' inquired the colonel. ''You'll generally find that the public payin' from two bits to two dollars for their ticket, is goin' to be disappointed if they don't see somebody hurt. Hence sports. The object of a bull fight is to kill the bull; the object of a football game is to kill the half-back; the object of an aviation meet is to kill the aviator, the object of a melo-dray-ma is to kill the villain; the object of a baseball game is to kill the umpire; the object of a prize fight is to see a 400-pound white hope beaten hopeless by a six-ounce fireman from Pueblo.''

A sport which is an innocent amusement, compared with football when the number of fatalities is considered and one which also arouses great interest, is the pastime known as boxing.

Boxing at present is considerably under the ban. The fact that it is a brutal and degrading sport for both spectator and participant, has at no time been so clearly recognized, and in most states, forms of it are illegal if not entirely forbidden. Newspapers condemn it and those formerly its best friends now see the error of their ways. Persons who formerly journeyed all the way across the continent to witness such contests, are no longer as enthusiastic as they were. Boxing, in fact, is under a cloud, a dark cloud as it were, a strong, heavy "smoke," and its days appear to be numbered.

Loss of interest in boxing has, no doubt, been one of the causes of the recent enormous favor of baseball, a sport which for all concerned is the most interesting and least dangerous of any that has a great following. Although an average of but 8 or 10 persons a year are killed, their deaths are rather of an accidental nature than the more or less necessary outcome of the game itself.

Baseball is the great American game. It was evolved in its present form, in the early part of the last century, though its rudiments reach back into antiquity. The excavations and decipherings recently made at Boghaz-Keni, in Northern Syria, by Prof. Winkle of Berlin and Prof. Hogarth of London, show the game being played by Hittites, with gourd masks; the umpire being King Subbi-Liliman, who reigned in the eighteenth century B. C. Balls and bats somewhat similar in construction to those in present use are shown.

Forms of baseball exist in many countries, but as played in America, its form is such as to be of the greatest interest to spectator and public. It is a game of great adaptability, and though usually played by teams of nine on a side, it may be modified to suit almost any smaller number of players, and as it requires no specially prepared ground, no individual implements, a single bat and ball serving all the players, and no special costumes or paraphernalia, it is the most economical game that can well be devised.

It may be played, too, at almost any season of the year, except in cold weather, and at any hour of the day, while the duration of the game, usually about two hours, may be varied to suit circumstances.

The players need have no particular skill, as long as the opposing teams are about evenly matched, and its demands on the players do not involve over-exertion, since periods of rest are afforded between runs.

For the spectator the game is open and easily followed, while interest is continuously maintained with frequent intensifications.

Baseball brings its devotees into the open air, and it is a sport of almost ideal nature, the only drawback being the rather large number of players requisite and the necessity of an umpire, with frequent altercations over his decisions, and, in its professional forms, of the over development of the part of the pitcher, whose skill becomes so great that the batter has great difficulty in hitting the ball, and the game loses in action, becoming merely a spectacle of the pitcher and catcher throwing the ball back and forth.

Baseball as played in America is, at some time or other, a sport engaged in by every boy, so that it is a game that is understood and one in which, of the vast audiences that assemble to view it, every spectator has been at some time a participant. It is, however, a man's game, pure and simple, as women take very little interest in it, much less than football, while women with practically no exceptions do not play the game at any period of their lives. The sudden exertions of strength and quickness required put it beyond their physical powers.

Yet even as good a game as baseball is in itself, it has yet been made a sort of national nuisance by the American tendency to overdo a good thing. The followers of the game become so absorbed in the results of the various series played between the clubs of different cities each summer season for the championship of the country, that their conversation becomes a burden to others not affected with similar interests.

Such enthusiasts known as "fans" when unable to attend the game itself, or when it is being played in another city, congregate in great numbers before newspaper bulletin boards, and spend hours watching the returns from various parts of the country, impeding street traffic, though otherwise acting in a harmless manner, a welcome contrast to the activities of those who attend football games and afterwards in their exuberance of spirits, wreck theaters and parade the streets shouting half the night, or more, and exhibiting various evidences of rowdyism.

No subject, however important, receives the amount of public interest shown in baseball. If the fate of the universe hung on the result, there could hardly be more attention paid. Only on election nights do greater crowds collect before the newspaper bulletins, and then less out of real interest in the election

than merely through general common consent and curiosity.
To the baseball enthusiast, life has but one great interest, and
beware the critic of the game. If he does not believe in baseball, he is "not a true patriot" and "no good citizen." Expressions of this kind are actually used by intelligent business
men in defending their interest in baseball.

And enthusiasm for baseball is no respecter of persons. It
seizes on rich and poor, employer and employees, capitalist and
office boy alike, and the attention given the subject is so great
that practically every normal citizen is compelled to take more
or less interest in it, while the number of those who attend
regularly runs into the millions.

The professional players receive salaries of three to ten thousand dollars a season and the names of the most popular are
as familiar as those of celebrated persons in any line of endeavor, if not more so. The players of the teams in the championship series at the end of the season receive large sums for
but a few games, the players' share of four games of the 1912
series being $147,571, or from $2,500 to $4,000 each, according
to circumstances..

The amount of money expended in admissions to the game,
the half days lost from business and the amount of energy devoted to the subject in reality constitute a national waste of
large proportions. The best that can be said of baseball is
that it is not accompanied by gambling, and although the clubs
are managed for private profit, a singular thing when the public nature of the institution is considered and when football is
quite free of any touch of commercialism, it being run by the
schools and colleges and played strictly by amateur players,
while baseball is only played by professional players to any
large monetary returns; it has remained a clean sport. Occasionally politics gets in and dirties it up a bit, as in the distribution recently of the tickets of a championship series to speculators and bartenders of a certain political faith and the consequent mulcting of the public. Boxing seems to have drawn
to itself most of the crooked work in sports, leaving baseball
clean.

The baseball fan is not noted for his mental attainments as
a rule. He is not proud of being a fan, neither is he ashamed
of it. He is so thoroughly a fan that fannism is a part of his
existence and he cannot understand the attitude of the critic.
He really believes that something is wrong with those uninter-

ested in the game, or at least that they are not as perfectly normal as they should be.

Baseball enthusiasm is jealous, however. The fan has no other passion. He is not a student of the drama, nor does opera arouse him, and a philanthropic concert is Greek to him and gladly so, for there is no excitement to be found in them, and the excitement of the contest is what he lives for. He does not seek to make converts, but the fellowship of the mania is the apotheosis of democracy. Well may the philosopher envy the expectancy of the fan when he meets another and they are going to the game, though he may be saddened that so much energy is expended to no useful purpose.

The ethical aspect of baseball, the immoderate attention to a series of contests which prove absolutely nothing once they are completed, the vast concern over a thing of no real moment, is well treated in an editorial entitled "The Baseball Craze" in the *New York Evening Journal,* Oct. 14, 1911, an influential newspaper noted for the moral tone of its editorials:

"The excitement in America over baseball is similar in character to the excitement in Spain over the bull-fight, and in the Argentine over the game 'Pelota.'

"It is not agreeable to throw cold water on any kind of enthusiasm. But the *Evening Journal* wants to remind young men especially that it is extremely harmful to concentrate interest on something that some other man is doing.

"It is all very well for a baseball pitcher or catcher to concentrate every ounce of energy on the achievement of some baseball deed.

"For that achievement means his success.

"But when young men put their minds day after day, on the minute details of a baseball game, worrying over the failure of this player, wildly enthusiastic over the success of another, that is a very bad thing for the youth commonly known as a 'baseball fan.'

"If you are one of the hundreds of thousands of baseball maniacs, remember this:

"It is quite likely that twenty years hence you will be one of the average failures.

"And it is quite likely that some young man of your own age very near you at this moment will be one of the exceptional successes.

"You will be one of the average failures, because you will

have devoted your most intense concentration, attention and interest to baseball or something else that cannot help you.

"And the young man near you, no better equipped than you for success, perhaps, will pass you in the race because at this moment while you are thinking and yelling about the 'national series' he is thinking, studying and concentrating upon something that will be of value to him and contribute to his success twenty years from now.

"No young man can do two things at a time with all his energy. You cannot be a baseball fan with all of your energy and at the same time be something else.

"No man ever made his real success unless the most intense interest that he had in life. was concentrated upon that success. Don't deceive yourself with the idea that you attend to your work very well and that the wild baseball enthusiasm does no harm. The baseball mania gets your real concentration and your work gets what is left, which is not much.

"If you can learn to look at baseball in the same way, if you can transfer to your own work, to your own acts and efforts each day, the intense concentration and interest which you now devote to the baseball game, to the names, acts and efforts of uneducated, largely worthless and rather uninteresting professional baseball players, your chance of success in life will be improved."

The enormous energy devoted to baseball and other sports in America, while not an active evil in itself, is a great loss when it is considered what might be the results were this energy devoted to real progress.

Another evidence of misplaced energy is found in the method of celebrating the Fourth of July. During the last nine years, some 1,719 persons lost their lives in this way. The *New York Sun* in an editorial, "Elimination of Superfluous Patriotism," on August 30, 1911, says:

"It is only within the last five years that a serious effort has been made to correct the abuses in question. Ten years ago those who protested against them were treated generally as anti-patriots, if not as traitors. But the majority had no notion of the enormous amount of injury done, and did not stop to think of it. Thanks to the *Journal* of the American Medical Association, the facts have been made so plain by now that even the hardiest patriot cannot explain them away or pretend that such licentiousness is a necessary or desirable part of the

education of young Americans. In the last nine years, our
boisterous way of celebrating Independence Day has been the
cause of 1,719 deaths and 37,410 injuries.

"Up to five years ago, the ordinary patriot was apt to defend
the explosive method of celebration upon the same plea as saner
critics defend football and other rough games. They had to
admit that some of the consequences were unfortunate, but considering the large number of persons engaged, the death rate,
they argued, was not after all very high. It was a question,
they said, whether the lives lost and the property destroyed
were not amply compensated by the spirit of patriotism aroused
throughout the country. And then they pointed out that it
was a great day for the boys, and that we must not forget that
we, too, used to be young—and so forth.

"But this sort of sentimentality could not stand against the
figures. In 1903, 406 died in the agonies of tetanus as a result
of wounds received on the Fourth of July; 60 were killed outright or died of their injuries, and 4,449 were hurt—some of
them blinded, some suffering the loss of limb, others the loss
of a finger or two, etc. The consequences were too appalling
to be ignored and at the last the more sensible of the patriots
began to be ashamed.

"In the last few years the demand for a safer celebration
has spread rapidly and we do not remember that this year any
of the papers protested against the regulation of fireworks and
firearms. This year there were altogether only 57 deaths and
1,603 injuries. Eleven of the deaths and 483 of the injuries
were caused by firearms, 5 deaths and 114 of the injuries by
toy cannons, but most of the deaths and most of the injuries
were due to the infamous giant cracker."

The following table, taken from the *Journal* of the American
Medical Association, gives the casualties for the last nine years:

Year	Killed	Injured	Total
1903	466	3,393	3,859
1904	183	3,986	4,169
1905	182	4,994	5,176
1906	158	5,308	5,466
1907	164	4,249	4,413
1908	163	5,460	5,623
1909	215	5,307	5,522
1910	131	2,923	3,054
1911	57	1,603	1,660
Total	1719	37,223	38,942

The victims of the Fourth of July celebrations are not the only ones due to carelessness and folly. The hunter in America flourishes as nowhere else. In Germany the hunter must take out an expensive license to hunt, and must then hunt only over certain fields, set forth in his license. In America, the hunter hunts at his own sweet will and the result was 113 deaths during the season of 1910, a large increase over the usual figures. In 1912, 92 were killed; 1911, 100; 1909, 87; 1908, 57; 1907, 82 and in 1906, 74. The deaths are mostly due to carelessness in handling of guns, inexperience, and the mistaking of men for deer and other game. Carelessness is an outcome of the thirst for hunting, a form of blood lust so evident in the automobile racing and football exhibitions.

The lack of restraint and tendency to violence which manifests itself in sports is exhibited in far more sinister forms in the taking of human life in various ways.

The *New York Evening Sun* in an editorial August 16, 1912, states:

"According to the American Prison Association's committee on criminal procedure, homicidal crime in the United States has increased 450% since 1889, and the ratio of convictions is less than 10%.

"In Germany the ratio of convictions is 95%. Homicidal crime in the United States, according to the same authority, exceeds the total of that of any ten civilized nations outside of Russia.

"Nearly thirty persons are murdered every day in the United States, not including Alaska and the island dependencies. Not one out of four murderers is brought to trial, and out of twenty-five brought to trial only one receives a death sentence. Ten thousand homicide crimes are committed in the United States each year.

"In Chicago alone, in 1909, 118 homicide crimes were committed; for the same time in London 20 of the same kind of crimes were committed, and London is four times the size of Chicago. New York City last year had 119 cases of homicide. These figures are appalling and call for a close searching of hearts by the American people.

"We are no less civilized than European nations. What then underlies this terrible discrepancy in crimes involving human life?

"One cause, undoubtedly, is the more general practice of

carrying firearms, and the greater license in this respect permitted everywhere in the United States as compared with European peoples. Local laws, such as those now in effect in New York state, against bearing deadly weapons, have not the full backing of public and private opinion. This state of opinion has led to laxity in the enforcement of the law.

"From the earliest times Americans were accustomed to have and bear arms openly; in fact, the right 'to have and bear arms' is set down in the Constitution of the United States as one of the inherent rights of the people. It was considered one of the necessary protections in a new and unsettled country. It did not refer, of course, to any right of private vengeance, but rather enumerated an ancient privilege that had never been questioned.

"The conditions of other countries in this respect was radically different. Feudalism, for instance, minutely prescribed the classes who could bear arms, and named the kind of arms. The selling of arms to the general population of other countries has been jealously guarded by governments."

The carrying of firearms, however, is but a superficial indication of graver underlying causes. No man shoots to kill another, no matter how many revolvers he has at hand, unless there is in his heart an uncontrolled disregard of human life and disrespect of law. The knowledge that so few murderers are punished produces the disrespect and consequent absence of fear of the law, while lack of training in school and at the home, absence, in short, of civilizing influence, is largely at fault for disrespect of human life. Our school system while teaching much arithmetic and geography teaches but little respect for the rights or even the lives of others.

A thoroughgoing tightening of the bands of discipline is needed all along the line, and the inculcation of respect for the law in those who make the law and in those who obey the law. Disrespect for the law starts with legislators who enact foolish and impossible laws, it exhibits itself in executives who connive at violations of the law and recklessly pardon criminals in great numbers, and it continues in the citizens who evade and violate the law for personal advantage and gratification. The law, however, can rise no higher than its source and its source is the people. Respect for law and safety lies in education and in the creation and enforcement of a healthy public opinion, of the enforcement of the will of those who are sound against the will of those who are unsound.

Another form of what amounts to depravity is found in the numerous lynchings which occur throughout the United States. While lynching is not an organized crime and while there are no habitual lynchers, its frequency over all parts of the country show a primitive respect for law and order, to say the least. In recent years the ferocity of lynching has increased and burnings at the stake and unspeakable mutilations take place.

A table for the sixteen years from 1884 to 1900 shows the number of lynchings to have been 2,516. Of these, 2,080 were in the southern states and 436 in the north. The proportion between blacks and whites was as two to one, 1,678 being negroes and 801 white men.

The proportion of black men is rapidly rising, however, which is accounted for by the fact that lynchings of white men for horse and cattle stealing in the west were formerly more common than they are to-day. Of the 2,516 lynched, in the years mentioned, 2,465 victims were men and 51 were women.

A list of the causes of lynching in the sixteen years mentioned is very interesting. It shows a range all the way from throwing a stone and eloping with a girl to murder and assault. The principal causes are divided as follows:

Murder, 980; attempted murder, 24; alleged murder, 28; robbery and murder, 8; assault and murder, 6; suspected of murder, 18; assault, 514; attempted assault, 77; alleged assault, 22; horse stealing, 115; cattle stealing, 22; unknown cause, 92; no cause, 10; race prejudice, 49; by whitecaps, 9; by vigilantes, 14; living with white woman, 1; enticing away servant girl, 1; bad reputation, 8; unpopularity, 3; arson, 93; robbery, 38; outlawry, 48; keeping saloon, 3; and voodooism, 2. Altogether, 112 motives are assigned for the overriding of the law by the wrath of the mobs. Several men were lynched for writing letters to white women, one for asking a white girl to marry him and several for quarrels with white men.

There has been, however, a decrease in the crime, for in the ten years from 1900 to 1910, the number of lynchings was only 904.

It is a crime, however, which is a direct outcome of governmental inefficiency, and the distrust of seeing the law administered with celerity and dispatch is the direct incentive to mob law.

There appears to be, however, running through civilization in America, a strain of ferocity, which may be an effect derived in some way from the climate or configuration of the land or its substance. The Indians preceding white men, seemed to have a ferocity greater than that of other savage races in other parts of the world, and though mostly good natured, the Americans are subject to sudden strokes of vengeance and retribution which the barbarities of Russia and the cruelties of the Spanish inquisition do not surpass. This extends even to legal punishments, and there are in force laws in certain of the American states in reference to the sterilization of certain classes of convicts which are of such shameful and horrible nature that it is inconceivable to really civilized men how such laws could have received any consideration at all, much less being put in force, by legislatures of white men. Nothing more fiendish than these laws can well be imagined, yet they have been enacted in a number of states, among which New York and New Jersey are the most recent recruits. The public is probably too little aware of the monstrous legal barbarity, which, however, has had the sanction of the Supreme Court of the United States, it being declared within the police powers of the states to perform such mutilations.

CHAPTER XXII

CUTTING OUT THE MIDDLEMAN

How the middleman robs the isolated customer—The greatest crime of modern times—How combatted abroad by consumers' unions—How great organizations of consumers reduce prices—Why such organizations are lacking in the United States—How they may be established—Extravagant characteristics of Americans—Boasted lack of culinary skill on the part of American women—Poor household management—Why matrimony fails to cope with modern conditions—Spending a dollar like a millionaire—Thorough schooling of the European housewife—Compliments at meal times—How consumers' unions are organized abroad—Over 2,000 branches in the German union—The curse of soup in cans—Operation of consumers' union—The bulletin and its contents—How orders are placed—Advance orders—Arrangement and business methods of a consumers' union store—Pre-Christmas dividend —Removals—Courtesy and equal service—How such unions may be established in the United States—Starting one in a small way—Consumers' clubs and discounts—System of brass money—How prices could be reduced—Present tax on cash purchaser eliminated—Why the ten cent stores can sell so cheaply—How to save high rents of stores —A new purchasing system—Supply depot for staples—A complete store with discounts to members—Incentives to club managers—Small clubs of consumers managed by women as a new occupation—Communal kitchens—Ethical effect of reduction of cost of living so effected—Political significance of consumers' organizations—The startling extent of the extortion of the middleman.

PERHAPS the most conspicuous example of the lack of interest which the American public takes in its own affairs as compared with the European public, is in the absence of consumers' unions or purchasing organizations, which so materially reduce the cost of living to their members, particularly in England, Germany and Switzerland.

The collective action of such groups, the cohesion and interest taken by their members in them, is wholly lacking in America, where the organized body of middlemen has taken advantage of conditions and obtained such a power and dominance that the prices of commodities have risen to the levels of extortion.

Consumers' unions in the countries mentioned have grown to great proportions, and have proved of enormous public service. The bitter opposition which they have encountered from tradesmen goes to prove their great value.

It will be interesting to point out the essentials of the organization of consumers' unions and to indicate how they may be established in the United States, both on a large and small scale, in the latter case by women of even ordinary business ability.

There are a number of important reasons for the existence of consumers' unions abroad, which do not obtain in the United States at present. Abroad there is a greater tendency to organize and support active co-operative societies of all kinds. This is characteristic of a more mature civilization than prevails in America and is also perhaps a characteristic of European peoples, Americans being of a more individualistic nature.

The American also looks less closely at his small expenditures. He spends his nickels and dimes like water, buys a lot of newspapers, cigars and knickknacks and then economizes with a shoddy overcoat. The European looks more carefully to the small daily expenses which, though slight in themselves, yet which in the course of a year aggregate so much, and thus he is able to afford a larger outlay for the few items of considerable expense which occasionally arise.

A further reason for the absence in the United States of such consumers' unions is in the attitude which the American woman takes toward her kitchen, as compared to that taken by the man abroad. With large numbers of American women, it is a frequent boast that they do not know how to cook a meal, or have no idea how certain dishes are prepared, or do not know, in some cases, how to make a cup of coffee. Of this lack of culinary skill they show considerable pride, and they do not hesitate to air their ignorance. The American woman, doubtless, in thus showing her contempt for the kitchen, imagines that she is proving herself to be on a higher plane in the social scale than her sister who knows the mysteries of the preparation of food. It would not, however, appear to be unbecoming even in the mistress of a Fifth Avenue mansion, to be reasonably well acquainted with the methods of food preparation, and no one would feel that such a woman would be demeaned by knowing how properly to direct her servants in preparing the food for her family.

For the American woman of lesser advantages to eschew such knowledge, is likely to be an affectation or the result of indolence. Yet it is evident that American women are not well trained in household management. They regard it as an inferior science and as undeserving of their best attention, whereas the art of housekeeping is one that is of the first importance in the economy of national life.

The American woman is not good at purchasing supplies. The idea of going to market in the early morning hours is far from her idea of her mission on this temporary sphere. It suits her much better to take her coffee in bed and serve canned beans for dinner and to devote her leisure moments to suffragetting and writing essays as to why matrimony proves inadequate to cope with modern conditions.

It is never the boast of an American housewife to her guests that a meal has cost less than a certain sum to prepare, or that she has run her table within the week at a certain low figure. If anything, she is more than anxious to say how great the cost of the meal has been, and how expensive certain of its dishes. This is due, in a certain measure, perhaps, to the spirit of hospitality, but more to the spirit of spending a dollar largely, and in the grand manner of the millionaire.

Conditions that now exist are a sufficient answer to this system of housekeeping, a system perhaps the most inefficient that could well be devised. Abroad, the mistress of the house is thoroughly schooled in all the arts of domestic economy, and it is a matter of pride with her, to know how to prepare a cup of coffee, as well as more complicated dishes. She is likely before a friend who is a guest to boast how little the meal just finished has cost, and this does not show lack of hospitality, but is proof of the skill and thrift of the hostess, good evidence of which has just been despatched. It shows that much pains has been taken though no great expense has been gone to.

It is customary in America to compliment the hostess on the delicious quality of the meal, whether it is in reality delicious or only an assortment of snacks. This is a form of politeness which does not prevail abroad, where the housewife would resent such elaborate compliments, in much the same way that an American woman would the customary German salute of lifting the hat so low that it is upside down. It would seem to her to be over done. On the continent, the principal compliment paid the hostess is in refraining from using pepper and salt, at least openly, as such a use of condiments she takes as a criticism of her ability to properly season the food.

Many American women, will, however, boast of the excellent

results they have obtained with small expense in the way of clothes, and it is in this same spirit that the woman abroad speaks of her table expenses.

The lack of proper interest in the table is one of the chief causes of high prices of living, as the failure to utilize in an appetizing way, the cheaper but equally wholesome and appetizing foods, creates a demand for the more costly grades, which forces them to still higher levels.

The ignorance of American women in the art of food preparation, causes them to resort constantly to canned preparations, which though convenient, are both costly and unwholesome and a grave injury to the health of any family in which they are consumed to any extent. To cure the evils thus arising, we transform ourselves into a nation of pill eaters, and drug stores are among the most profitable and numerous of all American industries.

American ignorance of food preparation, caused Thomas A. Edison, the noted inventor, to say that the French could live on the foods that we waste. Mr. Edison was particularly delighted with the bread which he found abroad, which is due to the skill of the housewife and baker.

The French housekeeper, understanding the art of food preparation thoroughly, is able to combine ingredients in such a manner as to produce wholesome and appetizing dishes from materials which used singly have little culinary interest. The American woman if she knew how to make good dishes, would take pride in preparing them, and would find them for herself as well as for her family, tasty and healthful; but not knowing how to prepare them, she remains in blissful ignorance and really believes the advertisements so glaringly displayed of the tastiness of canned goods.

American women must take a greater interest in cooking, not only for its own sake, but for the good of society. Constantly increasing prices have made it necessary for her to turn her attention towards the kitchen, if she is to have any money left to buy rugs and phonographs for the parlor; and the operation of consumers' unions offers one of the simplest and most immediately applicable expedients for cutting down the cost of living.

Such consumers' unions operate on a most extended scale in Europe. In Germany, there is a central union with over 2,000 branches. There are also renting unions, for protecting the interests of tenants against house owners and landlords, while there are a large number of building and loan societies and credit unions along the same lines.

The local members of a consumers' union pay annual dues of about five dollars. The members at their annual meeting elect directors and officers to carry on the work. The officers may only act in a supervisory capacity over paid employees, or they may act as managers, making it their whole business and receiving suitable salaries for the work. The members also hold monthly meetings, and discuss the work of the officers of the union, market prices, methods and complaints.

The central body of the unions issues a weekly bulletin, or newspaper, which is a quite important phase of the movement. It gives the market prices, general news of interest to members, discussions and reports of the work of the various local unions comparing their methods and showing how improvements may be made. Numerous cooking receipts are given of a timely nature, showing how to utilize the foods in season at such times to the best advantage. It also gives information as to the condition of crops and indicates which foods are likely to be plentiful and which scarce later in the season. It tells the proper time for placing orders for foods and supplies so that the consumer may order at the most favorable moment. Not only the current prices are given, but also the probable prices at later periods of the year, based on the supplies in sight and the natural increase and decrease. This enables the consumer to determine whether to lay in supplies or wait until conditions change. It acts as an incentive to careful management and keeps the consumer constantly informed on subjects that he would ordinarily fail to give proper attention to.

The placing of orders by members at the proper time facilitates the work of the unions since it enables them to gauge the probable demand of their members and to place orders for the required amounts; thus saving any risk of over or under supply.

The unions knowing what the requirements of their members will be, are able to place orders at any time for certain amounts of various commodities, to be delivered later in stated quantities at stated intervals and agreed prices. Thus the consumer knows in advance what he will have to pay and when he will have to pay it.

A characteristic consumers' union store often consists of a large one-story building of the character of a market house, with a large open space in the center. Around the sides are arranged various counters, devoted each to a separate class of commodities, a counter for meats, one for rice, flour, etc., another for fruits, another for vegetables, another for wines and liquors and others for clothing and haberdashery, as the consumers' unions include also wearing apparel as well as foods and household commodities. Even bicycles and hardware, dishes, cutlery and kitchen utensils are included.

The consumers' unions are particularly popular with the working classes, though by no means confined to them. Since to become a member only involves the payment of the initiation fee, which is small, most of the families living in a neighborhood where there is a consumers' union store will become members of it. As there are many branches, a move only means the transfer from one branch to another of the same general union, without paying a new initiation fee.

It is customary, early in December, for the consumers' unions to declare a rebate or dividend out of the profits of the year, and this is the measure of the efficiency of the organization. It is given at that time in order that the members may have the money to utilize for Christmas purchases. The distribution is in accordance with the volume of purchases of the individual members. Track is kept of this in the method of making purchases, as each member is provided with a small book which is taken to the store whenever a purchase is made. The salesman marks the amount of the purchase in the book and this forms the record on which, at the end of the year, the amount of the customer's rebate is figured. The larger his purchases the larger will be the amount of his rebate, although the rate of it will be the same as the rate of a smaller consumer.

During the year, should the consumer remove to another part of the country, the same purchasing book may still be used. Members are also privileged, when there are different stores in the same city, to purchase at will from any of them with the same book. As the clientele of each store varies with its location, some having goods of a higher quality than others, considerable advantage may be taken of these differences.

As the local unions work in conjunction with the credit unions, the consumers may in this way obtain a certain amount of credit.

An interesting feature of the stores is that all the members have the same treatment in the selection of goods. The largest apples do not appear at the top of the barrel, nor are the goods picked over. Each purchaser takes the regular run of goods, and no one is shown any special favors, nor is any extra measure given. The consumer, indeed, being in effect a part proprietor of the store, would be the first to object to too full a measure since he would reflect that others were probably receiving the same if not greater favors. There is thus no bargaining between clerks and customers and the business is transacted with the least delay and annoyance. Indeed, a child may be sent to market with the assurance that just as good results will be obtained as would be by an adult, and in the same way, telephone orders may be given with equal confidence. This is a considerable relief to the German purchaser, who ordinarily takes particular care in the inspection of his purchases, often in butcher shops even selecting the meat and seeing the chopping performed before his own eyes, when his mouth waters for a Hamburger steak.

Among the methods whereby the system of consumers' unions could be introduced in the United States, several have considerable value. Only experience, however, will demonstrate which are the most feasible and best adapted to succeed under the conditions of American life, character and customs. It is obvious, of course, that no large system could at once be introduced with branches all over the country, so that it is essential to begin the plan in some small way. The method which finally becomes the one most followed will have to be the one that appeals most strongly to many different people in different localities, and one which excites the initiative of the members and causes them to institute it in a more or less spontaneous manner.

There can be no doubt that consumers' unions will soon appear in the United States. They are an absolutely necessary expedient for cutting down the cost of living, and the only question is what plan will prove most adaptable.

One form of consumers' union may be put in operation very readily. It involves the formation of a consumers' club and the co-operation of certain dealers in a neighborhood, a grocer, a baker and a butcher. Later a delicatessen and a drug store would be added. The club being formed, the initiation fees would serve to defray the cost of a supply of brass checks, serving as the coinage of the club, and the members would obtain, for example, eleven dollars worth of checks from the club for ten dollars in money. Used by the members, such checks would be accepted by the stores, and at the end of each business day, the stores presenting the checks they had accepted during the day from the members to the club treasurer, would receive the agreed value in cash.

The benefit to the members in such a plan would be that they would obtain a 10% reduction in the cost of their goods, while the stores would be enabled to take trade away from rival dealers, and being assured of the patronage of the club, would gain as much at the end of the year, through a larger volume of business at a lower profit as they would under the previous state of open competition. They would also be doing a cash business.

The effect of this plan is to reduce the profits of the stores not in the union, or even to wipe them out entirely, in which case a neighborhood which was first served by a large number of stores, without increasing its purchases, comes to be served by a fewer number of stores. Thus the cost of distribution, which is the only proper cost of the middleman, is reduced by wiping out superfluous stores.

Should any of the stores patronized fail to supply the quality of goods desired, the club could readily transfer its members to another store. This would prevent any deterioration in quality or service. The brass checks being a cash transaction would not only be to the dealer's advantage, but would be to the advantage of the cash customer, who under the present system must pay as much for his goods as the purchaser who obtains his goods on credit, and often never pays.

An additional cheapness would result should the grocer be relieved of the cost of deliveries, which is an item that raises the price to the consumer.

A noticeable example of the saving to customers due to cash business, sales without deliveries and freedom from bookkeeping expense and collections is seen in the great values given by ten cent stores. The application of the club check system just described would give the members a grocery, bakery and butcher shop utilizing the principles of the ten cent store plan. Stores patronized by the club would also have no need to advertise, another important saving.

Such stores could also be located in much less prominent and expensive places, saving high rents now paid for positions of advantage. The public would in this way effect great savings for itself, as owing to its carelessness as to where it makes its purchases and its tendency to save a few steps and drop into the avenue store instead of going around the corner to the street store up the block, places a high, fictitious and altogether unnecessary value on real estate, the rent of which eventually comes out of its own pocket in the costs of the articles it buys.

Prices are the greatest of commercial magnets. Department stores through lower prices draw patrons from distant parts of the city and even adjoining cities, who would otherwise purchase nearer home if not tempted to take the journey by the lower prices offered. Members of a consumers' club could be depended on to go even considerable distances to take advantage of their brass money.

A somewhat different form of organization could be effected by bringing together the proprietors of a number of boarding houses and restaurants, and establishing a central depot in charge of a purchasing agent. At the close of each day's business, the members would put their orders in for the next day's supplies, and the purchasing agent would then visit the principal markets of the city and procure the supplies in bulk for delivery to the depot, thus securing wholesale prices. For staple articles the orders would be placed somewhat in advance, which would enable the purchasing agent to act as a commission merchant in placing orders direct with farmers. Anticipating to a certain extent, the needs of the members, the depot would carry in stock certain staple lines of goods which could be drawn upon at will by the members. Starting in this manner, the club could readily be extended to include the smaller purchases of householders, and the depot could be enlarged and provided with a more complete line of goods until it came regularly into competition with stores of a similar character.

The advantage of this plan is that the purchasing agent would be free to buy where he found the best prices, and would be able to take advantage of any special inducements of sellers. Working on a cash basis, the purchasing agent would be able to secure the lowest prices.

A certain leeway should be given the purchasing agent, as to the times of purchasing certain articles, in order to obtain the best terms and he should be allowed to purchase at his discretion goods of any character, when particular bargains were offered.

The depot could be made to serve as an afternoon market for special articles at special prices, open to the members and to the public as well, but the members would be entitled to certain discounts not allowed the general public, although the prices to the latter would be considerably lower than regular commercial prices.

A considerable factor in the success of the plan would lie in the energy, experience and business ability of the purchasing agent, who should be given a good salary and a commission, as an incentive to him to build up the business of the club. It should not be difficult to secure competent men, as the club would furnish the working capital in the form of dues and cash payments and the manager of a large club would gain for himself greater profits without the risk of any capital than he would as a dealer with his own money invested in his business. He would thus be commercially the superior of any of the dealers with whom he came in contact, and consequently would not be placed at a disadvantage.

Consumers' clubs could also be organized on a smaller scale even with only five or six members. The purchasing agent in such a case could make two calls daily if necessary on the members, a morning call for the orders for the main produce supplies of the day, and a later call for smaller supplementary orders. The purchasing agent could make her headquarters at some convenient point, using a parlor for an office, and might even herself be a boarding house keeper. She should have a suitable conveyance, and collecting the orders, would then go to the most favorable market, order at the butcher's half a dozen cuts of meat, at the baker's the required bread and pastry and at the grocer's the necessary staples, fruit and vegetables; thereafter having the goods delivered in her own wagon. In this way, the dealers would not know who the customers were. Her accounts would be kept for the club, and it would be her object to derive her income from her work. With small effort she could build up a club which would be very profitable. A great saving to the consumers would result through freedom from the labor of going to market, as the purchasing agent could at a single visit, with a few extra minutes of time, do the work of all the housekeepers.

Such a purchasing agent could also, with advantage, suggest bills of fare in keeping with the season. On the afternoon round, she could deliver proposed bills of fare, to enable the housekeepers to plan the next day's fare.

In connection, also, with such a consumer's club could be operated a general kitchen, in which pies, cakes and bread of the best quality could be prepared. The impossibility of securing first class products of the baker's art under present conditions, should make such kitchens highly popular. The kitchen could also cook roasts, chickens and articles difficult to prepare at home, and the menus of the various members would be prepared with a view to having such cooked goods delivered to them at the proper hours. Such a collective kitchen, with expert help, would soon make the club practically a necessity to the members and would make it profitable to all concerned. The superiority of such a plan over the delicatessen store lies in the fact that no loss would occur through unsold orders since everything cooked would be ordered in advance, and no waste would result. This is a plan that would be of especial interest in New York and other large cities, where it could be conducted on a scale of some magnitude in an apartment house block, particularly by the arrangement of the entrances from the center of the block and a system of local telephones.

Organizations of the character indicated are lacking in the United States, largely because of the lack of initiative and collective action. The responsibility of conducting such clubs needs to be on the shoulders of the club itself, and the manager should not be expected to keep the organization together as well as to conduct its business. Women with business ability, however, looking for new occupations, should find the present time one particularly propitious for undertaking such work, and it would appear to be a form of club that could be very successfully managed by women with weekly afternoon meetings. It would be, in the large cities, a new social force, bringing together neighbors into a new contact, in a manner which does not now occur. It would certainly be a form of activity as useful as suffragette meetings, and one that would produce a much more favorable effect on the family finances.

The effect, too, would not only be financial, but also ethical, since it would serve to unify the life of the family. The wife would be more interestedly occupied with the affairs of the household, and the cheapening of the food would enable her to procure for the same outlay a better quality, or the same quality at a lower price. All the members of the family would be better satisfied, contented and better nourished for the battle of life. The family would accordingly be a stronger unit than at present, when every increase in prices operates to destroy and disrupt it.

The plans indicated, are, of course, only suggestions of the most general nature, and numerous others could be suggested, but enough is shown to indicate the great possibilities of collective action exerted in this way. The price of food to-day in the United States is not only an economic, but also a political question, and it is easy to see the great results that might be accomplished by a well organized system of consumers' unions, operating all over the country.

Our individualistic method of purchasing, in which every purchaser is the competitor of every other purchaser, and all are indifferent to the interests of the others, results in their exploitation by the middlemen, and this has reached such a point that only about one-third of the price paid by the consumer reaches the producer. This is a startling price to pay for our inefficiency and unorganized methods of purchasing.

CHAPTER XXIII

PUBLIC WELFARE

AMONG the adverse factors with which the engineer has to contend in his designing is crystallization, which is caused by long continued minute vibrations, and which ultimately makes metals so hard and brittle that they break under very small strains.

The American public itself is largely a victim of nervous crystallization. The continual annoyances to which it is subjected produce minute vibrations in the special senses. The sight is afflicted, the hearing, taste, touch and the sense of smell, and the total of the various annoyances creates a breaking strain which has endless consequences.

The term, public welfare, conjures up ideas of great public principles, issues, or large works, but the aggregate of the smaller inflictions which are endured by a long suffering public, amounts to a total far in excess of even the greatest of single questions.

Annoyances of such a character are utterly unnecessary. They should not be tolerated, being for the most part so readily remedied. Yet year in and year out the same conditions continue, and what is everybody's business, being nobody's business, such abuses multiply and are never corrected unless some strong, selfish interest finds a profit in bringing about a change.

The eye is subjected, first of all, to a multiplicity of inflictions. At night the streets are either poorly lighted, or else glaring advertisements in illumination are continually flashing on and off. These are made to create as violent an optical impression as possible, and are usually illustrative of some excessively vulgar or commonplace advertisement.

The private owners of the buildings on which these unsightly abominations are placed, derive rentals reaching the proportions of small fortunes annually. Commercial considerations thus place a high premium on setting us as glaring a nuisance as can be devised.

While the now-you-see-it—now-you-don't electric sign is one of the greatest nuisances which afflicts the sight, it is by no means the only one. Advertisements generally on signboards are crude in an artistic sense and cheap in every sense. Yet great sums are wasted annually in such devices, involving all sorts of evil consequences. Not only are the advertisements costly to erect and maintain, but they induce the public to buy goods for which ordinarily no desire would be experienced. Such advertisements are thus an encouragement to extravagance. The excessive expenditures which the public are thus tempted to make, through such glaring advertisements, cause discontent, and the ceaseless endeavor to excel their neighbors in expenditure thus stimulated is a fruitful source of social unrest.

Mayor Samuel Lewis Shank of Indianapolis, at the 1912 meeting of the New York State Agricultural Society at Albany, described this condition.

"Seventeen years ago, the father of a family paid $12 for a suit of clothes, had a $40 horse with no pedigree, a $30 buggy with steel tires, a $6 set of harness, a $35 cow which gave five gallons of milk a day, twenty-five-cent chickens which laid every day and a good watchdog which cost nothing.

"The son to-day expends $40 for a suit of clothes, $5 for shoes, $4 for a hat, $2.50 for a shirt, wears a white collar every day with cuffs, the buttons in which cost $20, owns a $300 horse with a pedigree longer than his list of relatives, $125 buggy with ball bearings and rubber tires, a $30 set of harness covered with brass, a $100 cow with a great pedigree, but who gives but half a gallon of milk at a milking, hens costing $1.25, and a dog with a pedigree, which cost $10.

"In household furnishings, to-day a $200 range takes the place of a cook stove, and a $300 rug the place of a rag carpet mat. In olden times the family went once a year to see 'Uncle Tom's Cabin,' at small cost. To-day it goes to the theater twice a week at $3. Seventeen years ago there was a family dinner with plain fare but to-day dinner is served at a big cost, served by waiters and the guests are sent home in taxicabs. In olden times nearly everything was prepared in the home, to-day it is nearly all purchased outside of the home."

Advertisements, it may be readily seen, are one of the causes of this increased era of extravagance.

Among other serious afflictions of the eye, which cause grave injury, is the method of collecting street refuse in open carts. Numberless pedestrians passing through clouds of dust, come off decidedly the worse for the experience, yet it continues as a permanent feature of city life, when it might be easily obviated by closed sanitary carts.

Street railways have a similar disregard for the sight of their patrons, in their lighting systems. The use of additional power frequently dims the lights, while at crossings and switches the lights go out entirely. This annoyance is a traditional one and in all probability will remain a fixture of street car travel.

The ear is afflicted even more than the eye. The variety and number of city noises is so great that an unrealized nervous strain is continually undergone which contributes to neurasthenia and nervous breakdowns.

Among the preventable but. exceedingly aggravating city noises is the flat wheeled trolley car. A flat wheel is caused by improper application of the brakes, causing the wheels to slide along the rails and wear a flat spot, which at each revolution makes a pounding noise. A flat wheel may readily be remedied by being put in a lathe and having its diameter reduced slightly to the bottom of the flat spot, but this involves expense, which is evidently more disagreeable to the company than the noise is to the public, since the lesser evil is always the one endured and the continuance of the flat wheel must prove it to be the lesser evil.

Another of the noises which afflicts the ear of the unoffending city dweller is the automobile horn. This nuisance is widespread and intensive. It exists in 500,000 varieties, that being, according to the latest statistics, the number of automobiles now at large. These noises range from a mild mannered croak to the shriek of a hyena, and interspersed are a wide variety of explosive sounds, caused by popping tires, exploding mixtures, muffler cutouts, back fires and pre-ignitions and the various other ills which an automobile is heir to, most of which produce some kind of a noise.

By a wise provision of nature, however, the automobile is not subject to flat wheels, otherwise life in a community of automobiles would be unendurable. The worst that an automobile can do with its wheels is to run over the bystander, or slap a loose chain against the fender.

By an equally wise provision of nature, trolley cars have not adopted horns, remaining content with bells and flat wheels. There are many things, thus, which the city dweller has to be thankful for.

Another nuisance which is confined to the larger cities is the shouting of extra editions of newspapers. Particularly in New York is this infliction systematically practiced. The custom is for two or three leather-lunged, rawhide-tongued newsboys, some twenty-five or thirty years of age and strong enough to lift the Flatiron building between them, to suddenly invade a street, making night hideous with their cries. They seem well satisfied if they sell a single penny paper for five cents for each block shouted-up, for the public is pretty well immune, having long since discovered in most cases, that the contents of the newspapers so sold have appeared in earlier editions the same day, or relate to some minor occurrence in a distant city.

The customs of newspapers in getting out extra editions and special extra editions on the slightest pretext has destroyed any interest in them. It is the old cry of wolf too often repeated.

Another curious phenomena of newspaper publication is the timepieces used in the press rooms. Judging by the hour dates on the papers, these clocks must be from three to six hours ahead of all other clocks, since the four o'clock edition is usually on sale before noon, while the final edition or eleven o'clock edition may still be read in daylight. The calendars in the weekly and monthly periodical offices are not to be outdone by the newspaper press room clocks. They are, indeed, even more forehanded, for it is a very backward Saturday paper that cannot be purchased on Thursday and a poor Christmas number that is not on the news-stands before Thanksgiving day, and forgotten by Christmas.

Compared with the eye and the ear, the nose of the city dweller, at first glance appears to get off very lightly. It is true that the odor of politics is regularly much and evilly in evidence, but this is an old and familiar smell.

The automobile again furnishes considerable nasal diversion, with its exhaust, largely due to the carelessness of chauffeurs in regulating and cleaning their motors, and in the failure to use a good quality of oil.

The sense of smell, however, finds a more annoying enemy in the tobacco habit, so widely prevalent in America. Although many street railway companies forbid smoking, except on the "four rear seats" the smokers are apparently illiterate when it comes to counting seats. Many lines go further and forbid entirely the smoking or carrying of live cigars, but they fail to make any provision as to dead ones, which are vastly more offensive.

The ventilation of street cars and other public conveyances in America is a fearful and wonderful thing. Either the blasts of the Arctic are blown through, or the car becomes an amateur black hole of Calcutta. Any systematic plan or idea of ventilating cars is utterly beyond the furthest reaches of the imagination of a traffic manager. On street railways any intelligence that a conductor might exhibit is dispensed with by the fixing of the heating and ventilating devices before the car starts out, and the conductor is as helpless as a passenger to make any change.

While each individual suffers but a portion of each day, and will not take the trouble to object to the imposition which springs from the carelessness and greed of the companies, the total amount of inconvenience and discomfort endured by the traveling public, and the number of cases of disease incubated in the cars is enormous. It could all be remedied by a little sharp, united action, but there appears no prospect of any such millennium.

The nose of the city dweller also suffers from the method of collecting garbage which so offends the eye. The garbage remains in exposed cans on the sidewalks until the garbage cart comes to scatter part on the street and take what is left to the dumps. The latter is an unsavory locality, but one that is wholly unnecessary, as cities may make it a source of profit by the erection of refuse destruction plants. Garbage dumps are a menace to the public health and ruin whole sections of the city. Indeed, taking into consideration public dumps, slaughter houses, chemical factories, metal foundries, tanyards, rendering plants, cellar gratings, garbage cans, beer saloons, dirty gutters and other sources of vile odors, a large proportion of every city is uninhabitable and highly disagreeable and dangerous. With proper regulation this need not be the case.

Perhaps the most intolerable condition which can exist in any city is that created by a garbage gatherers' strike. While according to the venerable proverb, the water is never missed until the well runs dry, it is far truer that the garbage is never violently noticeable until it is not missed. When the garbage men strike they are realized to be among the most absolutely necessary members of society.

The installation of refuse destruction plants is a highly desirable reform. From the sanitary point of view it is the only satisfactory solution of the problem of city refuse disposition. Careful research both in this city and abroad has proved conclusively that disease is spread through the use of refuse dumps for any kind of city waste. The decomposition of garbage causes offensive and poisonous odors to be emitted. Flies in millions cover the dumps, feeding on the decaying matter and carrying away germ laden matter in the particles of filth on their feet and bodies, which are deposited upon the food and skin of human beings when the flies light upon and crawl over them. Thus the harmful germs enter the human system and contagion spreads the disease. Refuse is sure to contain some disease germs. Poor families frequently do not call in a doctor until the patients have been ill for a long time, and all clothing, paper, etc., near them is apt to become infected. This infected stuff when thrown on the dumps is sure to be picked over by other poor people, in spite of the most careful regulations to the contrary, and the new possessor of his family is almost certain to become infected. Beds and bedding are frequently thrown away after a patient has recovered from a contagious disease, without proper fumigation, and these are morally certain to fall into the hands of the poor, spreading disease among them. If ashes could be kept clean there would perhaps be little danger to health from disposing of them at fills and dumps, but as household ash always contains some garbage, it should also be burned to make it entirely innocuous.

There are still other sanitary reasons for the use of this system. Ashes carried alone in carts cause dust to fly about to the detriment of people's lungs, eyes and clothing, while separately collected garbage emits odors, and is apt to drip infected, unclean fluid in the streets. The collection of both ash and garbage in the same carts is advisable, since the ash absorbs the moisture and both dust and drip are eliminated. Rubbish, ashes and garbage can all be collected at the same time in the same carts, reducing expense. Filled land, made up largely of mixed refuse, is liable to cause spontaneous combustion when built upon, adding a fire hazard of a dangerous sort. The health and welfare of a city, which should be its chief consideration, require that all refuse should be purified by burning before finally being disposed of.

Destructors produce steam and clinker, which in most cases can be sold at a good profit. Roughly speaking, a destructor burning ordinary garbage will give steam enough to light the city streets, thus saving the amount paid for this purpose. Or it will heat the city or run the water works, including the average amount of pumping. The vitreous clinker makes a high grade of building concrete, paving slabs or brick.

Modern engineering methods enable the refuse destructor plants to accomplish their work and to consume their own gases and smoke, so that no nuisance whatever results. The system of destructors is far superior to any other means of refuse disposal and its adoption by all cities would prove a great sanitary improvement.

The sense of taste of the American, both of the city and the country dweller, suffers together with his other special senses. To deceive the taste, a complicated chemical industry has grown up, which resorts to the uses of a wide variety of drugs and chemicals as adulterants. It is indeed difficult to obtain any kind of food in the United States which is not subjected to adulteration or treatment at some stage in its progress from the producer to the consumer, and although national and state laws of a stringent character exist, they do not seem to effect the remedies desired.

The public itself is very careless and even when, in accordance with the law, the label of a food article bears the notice of the presence of a chemical or an adulteration, the purchaser does not either take the time to look into the matter, or does not understand the true meaning of the long, technical name given to the adulterant or preservative.

The carelessness of the public in respect to its own health needs to be remedied before any substantial improvement can be expected from the manufacturer and dealer in foodstuffs. The American exhibits the utmost carelessness in regard to his food, not only as to its purity and quality, but in the way it is prepared and served, and the strange juxtapositions that he makes in his bill of fare.

It is the custom of the American to eat fresh bread and old meat, the latter shipped halfway across the continent and held in cold storage, perhaps for several months. The bread, however, is always hot out of the bakeries which are located in convenient places. Freshness, however, seems to be the only quality demanded in bread, for if it is not eaten when fresh it can never be eaten. The bakeries are almost without exception operated in an unsanitary manner and the system of inspection of bakeries is either lacking or totally inadequate. For the most part they are located in basements with little or no ventilation, and they are by no means inviting looking places. Recent disclosures of traffic in rots and spots, that is eggs which have long since passed their period of sanitary usefulness, go to show what ingredients are employed by the bakeries in the manufacture of bread and pastry. The latter is usually very cheap, which is not to be wondered at when the nature of its contents are known.

Hot bread is admittedly one of the most injurious of foods, yet Americans not content alone with bread still warm from the bakeries, are fond of biscuits, taken right out of the oven, and of a leathery-like disc of bread like material known as a pancake or griddle cake, eaten as soon as possible after leaving a hot plate or iron and saturated with syrup manufactured with acids deviously. This mass is washed down with ice cold water, after which the American feels ready for the day's business.

To top off his dinner, he takes a dish of ice cream, followed by hot coffee. The disorders of the stomach thus produced affect the teeth and result in the art of dentistry reaching a high state of development. The American dentist has a great reputation, but while his skill is commendable, the state of affairs which gives rise to that skill is by no means one upon which the public can be congratulated.

If Americans followed the custom abroad of having slaughter houses in every city, and of eating fresh meat and stale bread, there would not be so much prosperity among the dentists and the undertakers and the American would be a different person in many respects.

The art of cooking is almost an unknown art in America. Owing to adulterated foods, the cook gets a bad start, and but little effort is made to catch up with the procession. In cities where great chains of restaurants have sprung up, cooking is carried on in wholesale and destructive manner and palatable foods are made an impossibility.

America suffers too, from the fact that her foodstuffs grow too rankly, and lack the fine flavor which the European foodstuffs have in their natural state.

The climate and the nature of the soil, together with a high state of agricultural skill, the inheritance of generations of husbandmen, all combine to give European foodstuffs a fine flavor. The cattle too, feeding on a finer quality of grass and grain, provide meats of a better flavor. Added to this is the fact that cooking is thoroughly understood. The European table thus becomes far superior to the American, and faring better, he takes more time to enjoy his food. Owing to the natural inferiority of American foodstuffs and the prevalence of adulteration, the American cook should be more highly trained and the American should devote more time to his meals. The contrary, however, is the case.

The appetite of the American must be tempted with artificial condiments. One of the most noticeable of the table appointments is the bottle of catsup. What this really contains is the most profound culinary mystery that has ever remained unsolved, but veritable rivers of it are consumed in the effort to make the food, tasteless in itself and poorly prepared, even slightly palatable. The American usuallly eats because it is time to eat, rather than because he looks forward to the meal with anything like feelings of agreeable anticipation, and when it is time to eat he usually eats as quickly as possible in order to get through with a bad job.

He appears to have little or no concern as to what he puts

in his mouth or the temperature of the mixture, so long as it has a noticeable temperature.

It is in the saloon that the American finds the most devious of all the combinations which he puts into his mouth. The liquors which are dispensed, in spite of stringent laws, are concoctions of the most dangerous chemicals, either mixed in the saloon cellar or "blended" by the "rectifier" of spirits. The term "rectifier" is one of the most respectable frauds that exists. The rectifier makes it his business to mix spirits with whiskey, he rectifies the spirits, that is to say, practically raw alcohol, with some whiskey, and while he rectifies the spirits, what he does to the whiskey had better be left unsaid. At best it is a legal adulteration, but with great frequency, the product is an illegal mixture of spirits, coloring and flavoring chemicals and a modicum of whiskey, which while itself pure, may be of a very inferior quality. This mixture of the rectifier's reaches the saloon where the saloon keeper subjects it to his own skill as an adulterator, as a means of increasing his profits, and the liquid that the gayly inclined citizen finally puts in his mouth is a product of chemistry, with but a distant relation to the art of distillation.

It may be said, and quite apart from any suggestion of prohibition, that anybody who drinks anything except beer in an American saloon is a dupe and a fool, and the drinker of beer, while he may be getting a pure beverage, gets one overcharged with alcohol and of a very inferior if not unwholesome quality, often stale and invariably served at a temperature, not as regulated by law as in Germany, but too cold for healthful assimilation, and purposely so to disguise the taste, which would often be intolerable if served at the proper temperature.

The only drink in America, whose purity is assured, is the whiskey that is bottled in bond. One or more government officers are always on duty at every distillery and after the whiskey is distilled, it is immediately placed in barrels in an adjoining warehouse in charge of the government officer. Here it remains under bond in the barrels until it is properly aged, and it is then released by the government on the payment of the tax. The barrels then go to the rectifiers, but in the "bottled in bond" whiskey, the whiskey is poured into the bottles before being removed from the warehouse, and the government stamp is placed over the cork and neck of the bottle, so that the consumer knows not only that the whiskey is pure but also knows when it was distilled and when it was placed in the bottle. Although pure, its quality will depend on the skill of the distiller and the nature of the ingredients, the fame of Kentucky whiskey being attributable, for example, to the excellence of the water used in making the mash, it being from springs in a limestone formation.

It will never be safe to drink anything in an American saloon until every drink is served from an original bottle bottled in bond. The patron of a saloon under ordinary circumstances not only ruins his health, but in doing so acquires a taste for the raw concoctions he consumes, so that a drink of genuine liquor seems tasteless and flat. Stringent laws exist against refilling bottles of whiskey and if anyone cares to see a saloon keeper turn pale, let him order a drink of any well known brand from a half emptied bottle, and then hold it to the light in comparison with a bottle of the genuine with which he has provided himself. The difference in color shows the adulteration and means a term in prison for the offender if the case is pushed. The greed of the saloon keeper, however, is so great, that these grave chances are constantly being run, and it is thus that the law is powerless to effect a remedy in such a manner. Only by taking hold at the source can adulteration be stopped.

Only less noxious are the drinks served at soda fountains. What mixtures of chemicals these may be, is only known to the trade. Too often they contain alcohol and an unwholesome combination of acids and flavors. The same is true of "ice cream" as served in "ice cream parlors." The demand for cheapness by the public and the rapacity for profits on the part of druggists and confectioners who cheat in candy as in "ice cream" exposes women and children to conditions as harmful as those met by men in saloons. What remedy there is to be for this is difficult to forecast. It certainly will not be feasible for ice cream to be bottled in bond or for candy to have a government stamp on each lump; while an honest race of druggists and confectioners is equally impossible. More stringent and better laws and better control of the sources of manufacture are needed and an extension of the system of bonded warehouses for manufacturers of foodstuffs. Greater care on the part of consumers is also desirable.

Of a far more sinister aspect, however, is the adulteration of drugs, perpetrated largely by the small druggist. It is almost incredible, the cheapness and murderousness of the adulteration practiced. In prescriptions, the druggist will use an adulterated or diluted article or ingredient, or will, as cases in court frequently show, substitute other ingredients, which change or weaken the effect intended by the physician and confusing his treatment of the case, frequently result in the death of the patient. And the profit derived by the druggist from such substitution is usually a most trifling amount. Cases have come up in which willful adulterations were systematically practiced which yielded but a quarter of a cent profit, yet which frequently resulted in the death of children from a dangerous disease.

Among druggists the betrayal of trust of common honesty with which they are charged, is not perhaps any more prevalent than in any other field of business life, but in their cases the results are far more serious.

The dispenser of drugs is far too mysterious in his operations. He retires behind his high partitions and compounds in secret his mixtures, charged with life or death for the invalid, who has no more protection against the greed and rapacity of the druggist than afforded by the latter's flimsy conscience. More publicity should attend the compounding of prescriptions and the physician should himself be made responsible for seeing that the druggist does not poison the patient.

The high screen should be done away with and prescriptions compounded in the presence of the purchaser. The prescriptions should be written in an understandable way, and the purchaser should see that the amounts called for and the ingredients prescribed were actually put into the prescription.

The possession by a druggist or a drug manufacturer particularly, of adulterated drugs should be made a felony, for the only object that can be in view in having such adulterations in his possession is to cheat, and a cheat of this character is the meanest, most despicable and dangerous of all cheats.

The carelessness of the public in what it eats and drinks has a most serious effect on the nation as a whole. Poor and adulterated foods result in poorly nourished systems and bad teeth, which in turn throw a further burden on the weakened stomach. The whole body suffers from the digestive disorders and with the brain no longer clear and active, the individual becomes stupid, bad tempered, erratic and loses initiative and energy. All business suffers, and a population so afflicted neglects its rights and listens more readily to demagogues and charlatans.

Swindles of all kinds flourish, respect for law and order declines and a condition of disorganization and anarchy approaches. The whole body politic is poisoned by the bad foods which poison the individuals and the ability of the individual to secure good food is correspondingly lessened.

These conditions affect most the native population, but as rapidly as immigrants become Americanized, they are affected in a similar manner.

Superintendent Maxwell, the head of the New York public school system, is authority for the statement that foreign born children and the children of foreign born parents have better memories than American children. This he ascribes to a better condition of the teeth and the digestion, the result of the continuance of the foreign dietary and customs on the part of the parents.

Upon becoming Americanized, however, in the second and third generation, the children become so thoroughly imbued with American ideas that they are ashamed of everything connected with their foreign origin and even refuse to learn the language of their fathers. All the old healthful customs are forgotten or tabooed and the new Americans are soon in the habits of the natives and suffer equally from carelessness and waste.

Twenty years ago we were receiving a much higher class of immigrants than at present, for as time passes and economic conditions in America approach those of foreign countries, the better class of immigrants which we once had are no longer attracted and the flood becomes of a lower and lower quality. As even the children of these low classes of immigrants are superior in memory and study to the native Americans now and to the American born children of our former high class of immigrants, it will be seen that when the present immigrants' children have become Americanized in the next generation, a very low grade of pupils will result. As a consequence, this country will no longer be able to hold its own with foreign countries which employ better methods of nourishment and which are being drained of the inferior elements of their populations, thus leaving room for the better classes to expand. America is already suffering from such conditions and is losing ground in the international contest. A new point of view must be taken and the individual must learn to guard his own health better, both as a duty to himself and to his country.

As to the fifth sense, the sense of touch and feeling, much of the foregoing also applies. To the experienced American, the word touch carries in addition, most unpleasant meanings, as he designates borrowings by that name and when he has been relieved of his valuables by a pickpocket, he also has occasion to use the word touch. It has thus most uncomfortable associations, and when the sense of temperature is included, no improvement is had.

Subjected to a climate of quick and sudden changes, one day hot and the next day cold, the American had added to his unwholesome nourishment, unwholesome weather. An untold amount of sickness and death results from these changes and lack of preparation for them, as well as great nervous strains.

Women dress too lightly in order to be fashionable, and they must draw on their nervous force merely to keep warm. If they do wear warm clothing, it is in the shape of expensive furs, often heavy coils around the neck, which serve more for purposes of adornment than for protection against the weather.

Men dress with somewhat more intelligence, but they have a weakness not for warm furs around the neck, but for stiff collars, cold in cold weather and hot in hot weather and about as uncomfortable a neck adornment as could possibly be devised. The discomfort of this article of apparel is added to both by the irritation of getting it adjusted, and by the condition to which it is reduced by the laundries. These institutions employ chemicals in their operations to such an extent that linen and other garments are quickly rotted out. Whether the collar and shirt manufacturers control the laundries is not known, but if the object of the laundries was to promote the business of the collar and shirt makers, they could scarcely be more successful in their destructive tactics. This is an abuse of a nature difficult to rectify and can only be accomplished by rigid inspection.

In the street cars, the companies provide little or no heat and passengers taking long rides are subjected to the greatest discomforts, not alone from the freezing cold but from overcrowding, and draughts through the cars from doors opened by the alighting passengers and left open by the conductors.

Half frozen on the cars, the American overheats his houses, especially with steam heat, which produces a dry atmosphere. The transition from overheated rooms to cold cars is thus all the more injurious. Sleeping rooms are also artificially heated, a practice about as inimical to health as any that could be invented.

The American is subjected not only to a multiplicity of annoyances, discomforts and dangerous impositions and inflictions, which may be particularly classified with reference to each of the five special senses, but also to a large variety of impositions which affect not only one sense, but all the senses collectively and simultaneously, and if there were more than five senses, means would speedily be found of harassing them, by the horde of exploiters and selfish interests which confound at every turn.

The public is robbed, beaten and insulted on the streets at all hours of the day and night, and at every turn there is some scheme to defraud and deceive. Yet one of the most effective measures of the European police for the protection of the public is entirely ignored here, and that is the system of the registration of residence. In a European city, every one is required to have his place of residence on file with the police. To fail to do so is a crime in itself. Thus at any moment the police can lay their hands on any person who may be desired. This is a powerful deterrent of crime.

The European police system is vastly superior to the American system, and the certainty with which it works is so well understood that the offender does not take the chances or have the opportunities of the American criminal. It is an almost invariable rule that a criminal is located within three days; for if an individual himself does not report his residence, the landlords of both his old and his new residence must report the change within three days, as otherwise they would be liable for punishment. As this includes hotels, a scrutiny of entries discloses any discrepancies, which are speedily investigated. Even should the criminal hide himself, when he comes out again later on, he will betray himself by his report of where he previously lived, whether it is true or false. As all discrepancies are investigated, the criminal has a hard time, and generally makes for the boundary, where he again has a hard time to slip through.

In America, criminals are located by the police especially in the larger cities almost as readily as in Germany, but not perhaps for purposes of apprehension so much as for purposes of graft. The criminal by a substantial payment goes his way and the police and their superiors, the men higher up, profit. It was recently estimated by a noted underworld expert, Jack Rose, in the *New York American,* that the New York police collect upwards of $16,000,000 a year in graft paid them by gamblers, women of the street, pickpockets, swindlers, burglars and the like for immunity from arrest. Jack Rose it was who arranged for the murder of the gambler Herman Rosenthal, engaging Lefty Louie, Gyp the Blood, Dago Frank and Whitey Lewis for the purpose at the instigation of Police Lieutenant Becker, whose partnership in his gaming house was about to be exposed by Rosenthal. The assassins themselves divided $1,000 for the deed, but had they refused to commit it, they would probably have been "framed"; that is to say convicted on a trumped up charge. The principal law used by the police in "framing" is that against the carrying of concealed weapons, and the very simple process of a policeman dropping a revolver into the pocket of an arrested person which is thereupon "found" on his person suffices to convict, often for a long term of imprisonment in the case of a professed criminal. This law is like many others of the stripe ostensibly passed for the protection of the public but in reality for the purpose of tightening the clutches of the grafter on the criminal.

The partnership of the police and criminals is a sinister manifestation of disrespect for law which could not exist were the political system such that the public could express its will, instead of being helplessly entangled in the hoopskirts of an antiquated constitution.

Our system is to blame, and no remedy will be of any permanent good except the remedy of a reorganization of the system.

In Germany, where the governmental system is such that the police must carry out the will of the people, graft is unknown and the criminal cannot count on any immunity of any kind. He draws his issue directly with society, and large and small, has little hope of escape, which is in itself a powerful deterrent.

Knowing the certainty of the police, the administration of the law becomes much more readily carried out. For example, if an automobilist is guilty of a violation of the speed laws, he is not then and there arrested and confined for the night, but his number is taken and a couple of days later he is informed by postal card when and where to appear in court. The bicyclist, too, must carry a number on his machine as well as upon his person, and they must agree or else he is summoned too. These numbers on the wheels, through being of different colors and shapes on different backgrounds, and of different types of letters, indicate thereby the city from which the wheelman hails, which further simplifies the police work.

Individuals on being discovered guilty of a minor infraction also simply give their addresses and evidence to establish their identity, being then allowed to go, to be summoned later to court.

The police officer, too, is expected to take cognizance of violations of the laws, and does so. If he sees a smoking automobile, he reports its number of his own accord, not overlooking it as the American policeman does. Similarly, any violation which comes to his attention is marked in his report book in the presence of the violator and no erasures are permitted to be made in the book, which must be turned in every night. For each of such summons or "arrests" the officer in some towns receives as much as eight cents reward. This is not enough to excite his cupidity but in the course of a busy day will buy his cigars and drinks. The violator is duly summoned to the police station where he pays his fine, from twenty-five cents up, unless he objects and demands a court proceeding when the officer must come to appear against him.

The fines being small, the offender usually settles without further ado. The certainty of the fine and the consequent annoyance of being summoned, and the certainty that the officer will report the next violation he sees, has a very salutary effect and creates a respect for the law which does not obtain in the United States where fines are so large that a long legal struggle ensues with loss of time to the officer and all concerned if attempts are made to enforce minor ordinances.

The result is that the American is constantly subjected to annoyances and impositions which the European, living under a better system, entirely escapes. The total effect of this is seen in the faces of the men. At sixty, they have an appearance of age which is not seen in the European for ten or more years later. The American works under a nervous strain caused not only by the irritation to which he is subjected, but by his spasmodic and hurried method of work.

American women are out to spend all the money their husbands can get hold of, and the efforts of the husbands to keep them in idleness and to supply them with the luxuries of life, helps to wear out the American long before his time. Abroad, the woman is always seeking to do for the husband and to make life easy for him, just the contrary of the situation in America. The result is that the European husband is relieved of many cares and is able to continue his work vigorously later in life, and to be able to retire on a competency, which would have been spent had he had an extravagant and foolish wife.

Should a citizen have a complaint to make against a public servant, he finds at the police station a complaint book in which he writes his complaint. The entries in this book duly come to the attention of the higher police officials and suitable action is taken promptly, so that the citizen when he makes such a complaint knows that it will receive proper attention.

The post office stations are similarly provided with complaint books, and any irregularity or negligence suffered by a citizen is promptly looked into and rectified if the complaint appears in the complaint book. These books are often in charge of the officials against whom the complaints are lodged, and they are compelled to perform the unpleasant duty of turning in the complaints against themselves. This in itself acts as a strong incentive to close attention to duty, particularly as the German public is by no means backward in asking for the production of the complaint book.

In the United States, if a complaint is made, after a long interval, the person making the complaint secures a lengthy and complicated looking document with numerous blanks to be filled out. The amount of work which this involves causes it to be postponed indefinitely, and so the complaint never amounts to much. In police circles the complaining citizen is put to much inconvenience and loss of time by being invited to appear and identify the offending officer, which, if the latter has removed his mustache or otherwise altered his personal appearance, is by no means easy to do. The police stand together in a clannish manner when one of their number is invoved in any difficulty, and if it is of a serious nature, apparently the whole resources of the department are exerted to save the offender. In a recent New York case, eight policemen were accused of perjury in giving evidence to clear a brother officer. This spirit is inimical to public welfare, yet it is a condition which cannot without great difficulty be overcome.

The readiness of the public to make complaints abroad results in a much more efficient administration of the law. The police officer is compelled to attend to his duty and to take cognizance of violations. The public consequently is much less imposed upon and a great many nuisances prevalent in America, especially on the streets, are not in evidence.

The use of open gratings on the sidewalks for the purpose

of ventilation is not allowed for one thing, abroad. This is a nuisance particularly noticeable in the summer when pedestrians already partially overcome by the heat, encounter blasts of foul, hot air, full of dust and other foreign matter, blown up out of the gratings. The absence of regulations in this matter shows a curious respect for women. A particularly great imposition is practiced by contractors and constructors for foundations and buildings. They occupy half the streets for months, with building materials and supplies. It is customary even to place large steam boilers and hoisting machinery and engines in the street, which cause inconvenience to traffic for long periods, while the sidewalk is removed and platforms erected which are on a higher level, so that the public passing such a building, has the alternative of climbing the steps and taking chances on the platforms over the excavations, or of making a detour in the open street amid vehicles which are dodging around the steam boilers, lime beds, concrete mixers and piles of structural steel and bricks. What right the erector of a private building has to encumber the street and inconvenience the public is not clear, nevertheless, it is a firmly established custom. It could be ended, however, with very little trouble by proper ordinances.

Another nuisance of a similar character is the presence of vacuum cleaning engines on the streets with hose running up into the buildings, and a worse form of this nuisance is the engine which pumps blasts of sand used to clean off the surfaces of buildings. These particles of sand fall to the street like snow and do great injury to the eyes of the passers-by, but nevertheless they are constantly in evidence.

There is much temporizing with nuisances in America, where the law is not regularly enforced with any degree of vigor, being only spasmodically put into effect. This is particularly noticeable with offenders of the streets. The push cart peddler is at times allowed to rest in security, while at other times he is harassed with no end of severity.

In their treatment of another class of offenders of the street, the police, actuated by a vacillating public sentiment, follow a course of conduct which results in graft, dishonesty and injustice. Americans lack the moral courage to deal with this subject in a direct and simple manner, and allow hypocritical moralists to make laws which while they sound well, are utterly impossible of execution. The result is that the offenders, who are more offended against than offending, are hounded out of localities where they tend to segregate and are driven into the midst of uncontaminated neighborhoods, and from there back to the streets, where they are exploited by the police until the reformers stir matters up again, when the scattering process begins all over. This social ulcer, instead of being properly treated as abroad, is thus continually being pumped back through the veins of the social organization, until the extent of moral and physical contamination which results from the false, cowardly and hypocritical attitude for which professional reformers are chiefly to blame, reaches an appalling total. One instance of the policy, shown in the abolition of the army canteen with the consequent frequenting by soldiers of the illegal resorts near-by, has this result: that the proportion of disease of a certain character among American soldiers is 19.7 cases in 100, while in the German army, the similar proportion is only one-tenth as great.

These figures are taken from a petition of two hundred and seventy-five of the foremost medical men in the country addressed to Congress in the interests of a bill to restore army canteens, since without canteens the soldiers cannot be properly protected from the situation.

"The venereal peril," says Surgeon-General Torney, in his latest report, "has come to outweigh in importance any other sanitary question which now confronts the Army, and neither our national optimism nor the Anglo-Saxon disposition to ignore a subject which is offensive to public prudery can longer refuse a frank and honest confrontation of the problem."

There has been a steady increase in the class of diseases "so that the admission rate which was 8.46% in 1897, has now reached the enormous figure of 19.7%." A comparison with the figures of some of the European armies will show how grave the case is.

	Percent.
American	19.7
British	7.6
Austro-Hungarian	5.4
French	3.5
Prussian	1.9
Bavarian	1.5

Now as the petitioners observe, it is not the soldier alone who has to suffer.

"Our army is very largely composed of young, unmarried

men. When they marry, they should become the fathers of healthy children, and so add to our population, vitality and success as a nation. But the fact is that among those who have contracted venereal diseases in the army, a considerable proportion will be sterile, others will be characterized by many abortions and their living children will be defective, blind and diseased. What the sorrows of their infected wives may be we know in part, the rest can only be surmised.''

When conditions such as these exist in the army, where individual cases are promptly treated, it may readily be seen what appalling conditions must exist in private life, where concealment, lack of proper medical attention, quack doctors and other causes produce long continued invalidism and widespread propagation of the diseases.

The American public in its failure to deal directly and honestly with ''the most ancient of professions,'' commits a crime against itself whose consequences infect the present and will infect the coming generations. The suffering, disease, despair, degeneracy, imbecility, insanity and suicide which compose the failure to deal with the sources of infection, and the hypocritical attitude on the whole question enforced by preachers and false moralists, are a terrible indictment of our civilization. Well may the individual suffer the consequences of his indiscretion, but the sins of the fathers are visited on the children, and surely the coming generations should not be condemned to the fate in store for so large a proportion of its numbers, to gratify the sanctimoniousness of a handful of professional moralists. This is inefficiency, not of men or machines, but the inefficiency of lack of moral courage, of fair dealing and frankness and common honesty.

CHAPTER XXIV

DOMESTIC RELATIONS

The complicated question of divorce—Its great increase—Largely due to economic factors—The home no longer a small factory as in former generations—Present necessity of women leaving the home to do work that was formerly done in the home—Is the increase of divorce beneficial?—One marriage in twelve ends in divorce—Ethical effect on children—Lack of control of parents over children—Lack of discipline—Failure of school discipline—Unpreparedness of young men and young women for the certain discipline of the world—Wrong examples set by parents and school teachers—Superficial education.

THE problem of divorce in America is one of great complexity and of the greatest importance. The stability of the state rests on the family, and tendencies which weaken the family ties undermine the foundations of the state.

But though divorce has increased greatly in the United States in recent years, there are many important factors entering into the subject, and whether the increased frequency of divorce denotes a weakening of the ties of the family, or is an index of other conditions is a much controverted subject.

Undoubtedly divorce has lost much if not practically all of the stigma it carried half a century ago, due to the weakening of religious authority. It is therefore a more freely sought remedy and consequently occurs with much greater frequency, which continues the process of diminishing the stigma.

A second important cause of divorce is the great economic freedom of women, due to the transfer from the home to the factory of much work formerly most economically done in the home. A century ago, every home with its spindle and loom was a small factory. Mother and children labored vastly harder and longer than they would now in a factory to accomplish the same result. Thus economic factors accentuated the family bond. To-day, the woman doing the same work outside the home, is much freer than in those days. She may choose a husband with greater deliberation and if she is not happy in the union, she may return to her work more readily.

The family, to-day, thus stands on its own feet, so to speak,
and the increase of divorce under the circumstances is no cause
for alarm to anyone, save the bigot and the ignorant, since it
represents only the normal tendency to disunion; the eruption
of domestic sores that formerly failed to come to the surface.

The tendency to continue in the married state is just as great
as formerly, but the opportunity of escaping it is more freely
presented, so that the increase in divorce does not mean that
the family is being undermined, but simply that those who
would, under previous conditions, have remained nominally
married, now separate. The discontented family is eliminated,
so that under present conditions the number of contented families is proportionately larger than formerly.

The Department of Commerce and Labor in its report, "Marriage and Divorce, 1887-1906," gives the total number of marriages for the twenty years at 12,832,044, an average of 641,-
602 marriages per year. In the decade ending 1870, the annual average of divorces was 11,207, while in the decade 1890-
1900 the average was 55,502. Thus of every twelve marriages,
one ends in divorce.

A curious similarity in proportions may be observed in that
one man in twelve in New York City is buried in the potter's
field. Thus what may be termed potter's field marriages are,
according to the government reports, two and one-half times
as great as formerly. The divorce rate annually per 1,000
married couples is 4, while in 1870 it was but $1\frac{1}{2}$ per 1,000.

The darker side of divorce is in its influence on the children.
Differences between the parents may be settled by divorce and
the effects ended, but the effect on the children, the future citizens of which the state will be composed, affects the state more
than it does the parents.

On one side the state and the children, on the other, the con-
tentions of the parents, and in a larger view the interests of the
latter are of less permanent consequence.

The children of divorced parents can have little respect for
the parents they consider in error, and respect for the injured
parent is less than would have been the respect felt had no divorce occurred. And not only are the children themselves affected, but their friends and companions are infected with the
spirit, and a lack of respect for parents is created, which ultimately shows itself in lack of respect and discipline for all authority.

Parents in America have less control over their children than in perhaps any civilized country. Parents allow their children to become "smart" which quickly develops into a disrespectful attitude. The theory that the rod hurts self respect of the child, is so widely held that in the schools corporal punishment has been abolished. The results are far from gratifying. Indeed the parents by a too free and too early development of the idea of allowing the child to follow its own sweet will, have lost all discipline, and a condition of disrespect, freshness and disobedience now obtains, both at home and in the school.

Derelictions, depredations and incivilities are excused by the phrase, "boys will be boys." If this idea is extended, we shall soon be excusing other matters with the phrase, "rowdies will be rowdies."

From insignificant little beginnings of this kind, the college youth in all his grandeur takes his origin, who later in his enthusiasm, both in college and military schools, makes gentlemen and officers of his fellow students by standing them on their heads, throwing them in pools of water, tying them to railroad tracks and other direct methods, and who also, as an ardent dramatic critic, frequently wrecks theaters and finds himself incarcerated for a too vigorous style of expression.

Thus the discipline of the future citizen manifests itself. Under the method followed, the individual comes to have no respect for himself, allowing himself extravagances of all sorts, and being obstinate, self willed and arbitrary, while as a citizen, he does not respect the rights of others and is otherwise lawless if not criminal and in large bodies is of the sort that makes mobs and lynchings.

A growing tendency on the part of persons of means to have their children privately educated by tutors and governesses, rather than in the public schools, also has the effect of lessening discipline, as there is absent in such training not only the discipline of the teacher whose position is independent of the pupil, but also the discipline which emulation of others enforces.

The usually inadequate if not insignificant wage paid by those who can well afford to pay a proper wage creates disrespect and ill feeling between the parent and teacher as well as between teacher and child, making the system one from which good results cannot be expected to flow. It is in reality the duty of the state to supervise such private education, and to see that only competent teachers are employed, teaching suitable courses and paid suitable salaries. A system of licensing private teachers should be instituted and it should be illegal to pay them less than a minimum wage. It is to the interest of the state in the highest degree to see that those who are to be masters of wealth should be properly educated and not be permitted to be held aloof in such a manner that their education, at the hands of governesses earning a few cents an hour shall make them unfit for the responsibilities which they must ultimately assume, if not likely to use their wealth against the interests of the state.

A long and complicated train of evils flow from divorce. In its proper place it is a useful remedy for worse conditions, but like morphine or cocaine, it is a remedy that for a nation may become a noxious habit.

As Supreme Court Justice Benedict, of Brooklyn, remarked in denying an application for separation based on slight provocation:

"When marriage proves a failure to persons who do not look upon it as an obligation and duty, they are prone to hasten to the courts to obtain a dissolution or relaxation of the ties which they voluntarily assumed, but which their own selfishness has rendered irksome. Alimony and counsel fees are but poor substitutes for honor, love and respect, and often serve to still further separate couples who should be reunited."

The disrespect which children show for parents, springing thus from a laxity in the relations of the family, indicates a growth of so-called individuality, or a form of selfishness in which the sole object of the individual's solicitation is the individual himself.

This spirit is very noticeable in America, and is the basis of divorce and the disrespect of children for parents; for the parents being selfish do not respect their children, and breed disrespect in them in this manner. Race suicide, or the disinclination to make personal sacrifices for the sake of children is the first disrespect for the child. So often being undesired and a burden, the child grows up in an atmosphere of indifference at least, and the parent further will not exercise his own moral force to properly discipline the child, as the disciplining of children requires a certain exertion and stamina of character which the parent is too selfish or indolent to manifest.

It is easier to allow the child to exercise its own initiative, and then to get rid of the problem by sending it to school.

But when an undisciplined child goes to school, in which

the teachers are mostly young, underpaid women, whose minds are on any subject except the disciplining of children, its condition is not much improved.

The child sees in the teacher, an example of a woman dressed as fashionably as her means will permit, if not much more so, and as the child has seen similar extravagance in the home, it soon falls in the way of the rest of its immediate world, and the final result is a superficial education, acquired under duress and chiefly for the purpose of show, while a thorough digestion of any subject is left to somebody else.

This lack of thoroughgoing education is largely responsible for the numerous contradictory characteristics developed in our social organization. It makes the greatest difference in the world to the American whose ox is gored, and whenever our personal interests are touched our fine theories curl up like leaves in furnace.

We are all unanimously in favor of regulating our neighbors, but are quick to object to sumptuary legislation when our own spigot is threatened.

We boast of our patriotism, but we leave the graves of our great men practically neglected.

We claim that ours is the land of liberty and equality, but there is no land where there is greater inequality between the rich and the poor, and the just and the unjust.

We are loud in our praise of the square deal, but it takes a search warrant to find anybody who ever got one.

We do not permit teachers to use corporal punishment in schools, yet there is no country in which child labor is so greatly exploited.

We object to vivisection, but we practice sterilization.

We send invalids abroad for cures, but shut out incoming health seekers.

We decry charity, yet more money is spent on charity than anywhere else.

We seek after the truth, but do not recognize it unless it is spoken by those of the great names.

We proclaim the dignity of the law, but the small culprit has a hundred chances of going behind the bars to the financier's one.

We organize cat and dog cruelty prevention societies, yet we murder more human beings in traffic and the industries than any other civilized nation.

We multiply eugenic clubs, yet nowhere is race suicide so prevalent.

We are quick to criticize, but pray to be delivered from "knockers" and "cranks."

We champion individualism, yet we permit numberless trusts and labor unions whose principal purpose is to stifle individualism.

We think we are leading the world, but it only appears so because we have almost lost a lap.

We shout for arbitration of the disputes of Europe, but we are only too anxious to sidestep the Hague when it comes to our own propositions.

Altogether we have a most admirable comprehension of what others should do to improve our own lot, but very little enthusiasm for improving the lot of others.

CHAPTER XXV

EDUCATIONAL SYSTEMS

THE state, being composed of its citizens, is a resultant of
what its citizens are. It can rise no higher than its source, and
the nation will always be what its citizens make it.

But the state, as a whole, guided by the wisdom of its wisest
citizens, controls its own destiny and progress, in that it can influence and form the character of its future citizens as it will.

The fate of a nation thus depends on what it makes of the
raw material of citizenship which humanity provides, and the
great progress which Germany has made in the last half century is due particularly to the influences which have surrounded
the children who have grown to be the citizens of which the
nation is now composed; while the failure of other countries to
equal her progress, if they have not fallen behind, has been due
to failure to utilize to the highest degree the materials of citizenship.

This is most acutely evident in the case of England, which
has finally been forced to adopt plans of social improvement,
such as pension and insurance systems, after they have been in
force in Germany for a generation.

England having been content merely to build Dreadnaughts and heavy ordnance, now finds that Germany is fortified with an unrivaled educational system, among the fruits of which are the ability to design and construct engines of war of much higher efficiency while her trade mechanisms are such that she readily outdistances other nations. She has built her success upon the impregnable foundations of education and is thus a generation ahead of all her competitors.

England sees itself now forced to begin a nation-wide campaign of education after realizing her disastrous defeat, at a cost of millions of money annually, in competition with other advanced nations, particularly Germany. It would be the part of wisdom for England to model her educational undertakings on the lines which have proven so successful for Germany.

The statistics of illiteracy of the leading nations of the world show at a glance the unrivaled results of the German system.

The number of illiterates per 10,000 of population is as follows:

```
Russia .........6170 in 10,000 or 61%
Italy ...........3130 in 10,000 or 31%
Austria-Hungary .2570 in 10,000 or 25%
Belgium .........1020 in 10,000 or 10%
United States.... 770 in 10,000 or  7%
France ......... 400 in 10,000 or  4%
Great Britain.... 100 in 10,000 or  1%
Denmark ........  20 in 10,000 or one-fifth of 1%
Sweden .........  10 in 10,000 or one-tenth of 1%
Germany .......    5 in 10,000 or one-twentieth of 1%
```

Thus it appears that proportionately there are twenty times as many illiterates in Great Britain and one hundred and fifty-four times as many in the United States as in Germany.

It will be noticed that Austria-Hungary has a very large proportion of illiterates. This is due to the Slavonic element of the population, mostly found in the southeastern portion, the northern or Germanic part of Austria having a very low percentage of illiterates. Practically all the Slavonic and allied races show a high degree of illiteracy. Among the smaller countries, the figures are as follows: Bulgaria, 52.7%; Servia, 61.6%; Rumania, 75%, while other Balkan states, Turkey and semi-oriental districts, from which we expect large immigration in the near future, are even more illiterate. Such enormous influx will debase still further our national standards which have suffered so much already from the uneducated hordes which have come out of lower Russia. The principle of exclusion which has proven so valuable on our Pacific shores must be applied to the Atlantic seaboard if we are not to be submerged in this flood of undesirables. The danger of the yellow peril, to the gravity of which our brothers in the west had so much difficulty in arousing the country, is now duplicated along the Atlantic by a peril out of the near-East no less menacing and far more insidious because appealing in a way characteristic of the races, for sympathy and succor from oppression. It is well to care for the lepers of ignorance, to afford them their measure of relief and justice, but it is not well to contaminate ourselves in the process.

The educational system of Germany is simple, thorough, and of the highest efficiency. It is controlled by the government, through a ministry of education at Berlin, and subordinate boards in the various states, and it is thus a single organization unit. Control of education throughout Germany thus being vested in a single source of authority, there is no conflict of authority and no disproportionate results.

The salient features which make the German educational system what it is under this central system of control and supervision are principally discipline, the interests of the students in their work, ethical instruction, thoroughness and the utilization of the knowledge gained.

The ideal of German education is to make the individual a good citizen, to teach him that his duty is towards the state rather than to himself. German education has thus in view the creation of an efficient state, rather than, as in America, the development of the individual as an individual. This ideal is expressed in the motto, *"Alle für Ein, Ein für Alle,"* that is, "All for one and one for all."

As a matter of fact in making the individual a good citizen it is first necessary to make him a good individual, so that in principle, the German ideal is that of applied individualism. The creation of an efficient state can only follow the creation of efficient citizens.

German industrial progress is also a matter of education. To support 65,000,000 people on an area less than two-thirds the size of Texas, a population increasing by 900,000 a year requires the utmost economic and social foresight. The exercise of Spartan principles and Prussian drill is necessary, leadership of the highest quality, skill and discipline, all are requisite to cope with the necessity.

With greater natural resources, Germany would probably be less advanced than to-day, as, for nations like individuals, too rich a heritage is likely to prove demoralizing.

German discipline is a national trait. It is one of the springs of character of the race, and it manifests itself at the outset of the child's career, where in the home, a condition of discipline prevails that would seem harsh and unnecessary to an American. But in after years, if not at the time, the child appreciates the great value this discipline has been to him, and continues the heritage to the next generation. For Americans to acquire anything like German discipline, is doubtless an impossibility, even if desirable. Each people has its own traits. Strict discipline is not and is never likely to be an American trait, though all Americans freely admit that more discipline would be a better thing for them. Yet they take no particular steps towards that end.

Discipline is obedience to orders, and as repetition gains facility, discipline is more or less a matter of drill, of continued practice, and this drill is one of the keynotes of German educational success.

As pointed out by the late Louis J. Magee, a prominent engineer and organizer, familiar with German conditions, in the *Engineering Magazine:*

"Another element which makes for efficiency in German life and, of course, plays a great rôle in the school routine, is discipline. The average German is certainly not more mentally alert or convincing than an American in an analogous position. But the national attitude of mind is friendly to order, clearness, organization and precision. Germans are taught respect for existing arrangements; the subordination of the member to the body; regard for duly constituted authority as designated in rank and title. This comes somewhat from military régime; but long before Germany had a well organized army, it had a well organized home. The child's obedience to its father came first of all. The child is not only punished for disobedience, but is trained in a certain code of manners and correctness of formality which, under similar conditions, our children are expected to pick up for themselves. Such training may not prevent the subject from becoming a boor, but it will lay the foundation for system; obedience to the orders of the next above, obedience to the laws. This produces a normal type.

It may interfere with individuality, but it does not seem to hurt the intellect or weaken the energies.''

After discipline, a feature that is an outgrowth of ancient customs is a powerful factor in German educational success. Not less than two hours a week are devoted to religious instruction in the schools of all classes.

In older times, the schools were founded for no other purpose, and the present allotment of time is a persistence of that custom.

To an American the teaching of religion in the schools would seem an impossible, if not an astonishing condition. It would be utterly repugnant to a large portion of the most intelligent of the community who have no longer any religious beliefs. The separation of church and state is a cardinal principle of American institutions.

In effect, however, the German system accomplishes the same result, as far as those believing in religion is concerned, and there are great contributory advantages. The school buildings are apportioned according to the religion of the parents into Protestant, Catholic and Hebrew, and each receives its two hours of weekly religious instruction from a minister of its own faith, one competent to give the instruction best suited to the conditions.

These ministers teach religion in the schools, just as the professors teach mathematics, and the German youth thus acquires a moral training as well as an academic one. In America this is left to the discretion of parents, but as church going is very laxly observed by Americans and as the Sunday schools are not attended by a class of boys most in need of instruction of an ethical nature, the result is that the great majority of American citizens have grown to man's estate without any definite training of character. Thus their lines of duty toward the state are unformed, and they raise no protest against graft and inefficiency in the government. They are citizens made at haphazard, and their patriotism begins and ends with applause in theaters when a national air is played or a flag waved by some cheap comedian.

The results of the German plan prove the great superiority of a system which forms character as well as habits of study.

A system of religious instruction would be difficult to apply in America owing to the three hundred and odd religions in vogue, most of them promulgated by hairbrained fanatics for interested reasons. The Americans, however, though showing such a diversity in religions are practically united in the worship of a single constitution originated by theorists and never an instrument deserving any considerable part of the respect it inspires. The Christian religion, the result of centuries of development at the hands of the cleverest men the world has ever produced, and destined to endure, is by the numbers of its competitors in America seen to receive far less unanimous support than the constitution, the work of a few cursory experimenters, which they supposed was constructed to last indefinitely, but which it is now seen must give way to a better system.

The system of religious instruction, together with the discipline and home training, gives the German child an extremely different point of view in regard to its school work. Greater willingness to study is seen and the lesson is learned from a desire to know it rather than merely as a task to be gotten through with as quickly as possible.

German thoroughness is another foundation of the school system. This is, to a certain extent, a trait of character too, but it is also a system. The child at play is instructed in the best ways of playing, and this attention to detail permeates the whole system. When he is graduated in any department, the German knows that department thoroughly.

All this has not been accomplished, however, without development and reforms, and perfection has by no means been attained, but the German system is to-day being copied all over the world, and is the model referred to when any proposed changes are under discussion anywhere. Of a former defect of German education, the limited number of brilliantly educated men, with no intermediately educated class, another quotation may be taken from Mr. Magee's article:

"It is everywhere evident that the Germans are no longer satisfied with a few hundreds of famous scholars, a few thousands of professional men—and then a drop almost down to the three Rs. They are wisely grading off their material. They have many different standards as to what constitutes an educated man. Then they try for 99% efficiency under whatever standard the subject may properly belong. Even housemaids, butlers and chimney sweeps may receive in special schools all the correct fundamental preparation for their humble careers."

A feature of German educational methods, of the greatest

importance, is the utilization of the education received and the connection made between school and work. The average American boy gets a certain amount of education, and then is turned out to shift for himself, while the principal use he makes of his education is to forget as much of it as possible as soon as he can.

The German system does not abandon the boy when he leaves school, but keeps in step with him, continuing his education until he has mastered some means of earning a livelihood.

W. H. Dooley in "German and American Methods of Production," in the *Atlantic Monthly* of May, 1911, describes the system.

"The average American thinks that the success of Germany is due to low wages and long hours of work. This is not true, for, if labor is cheaper there, coal is dear, machinery dearer and imported raw material pays a tax. The industrial supremacy of Germany is the effect of definite and deliberate political action. Thirty years ago the German statesmen realized that the nation was inferior to the American and English in natural resources and natural ingenuity; this inferiority forced upon their attention the value of thrift and of education, and thrift was multiplied by capital and education multiplied by industrial efficiency.

"The German government has solved its educational problems in a more satisfactory way than any other country. According to their scheme of education, every worker in a profession, trade or commercial pursuit, must have not only a general education, but technical preparation for the particular work selected by him. In the United States we believe in the same policy, but apply it to those entering the professions only, disregarding the great mass—95%—that leave school at fourteen.

"Germany insists that every child be under educational influence till the age of eighteen. The child leaves the common school at fourteen. He may go to work, to a higher school and prepare for college, or to a technical school. In America he may leave school at fourteen and is not obliged to attend any other school.

"The Germans act on the principle, admitted by everybody who knows or cares anything about education, that the way to secure a good training for the mind is not to end the school life at the most plastic period, fourteen years of age, or in the case of foreigners as soon as they can pass an examination, but to insist that every boy shall spend a certain number of hours a week under educational training and sound teaching until he reaches manhood. There is less "cramming" and instruction is slower, more thorough, more reasoned, than it can be under our American system of hurrying children through the school. For we must remember that our young men in industrial plants are nothing more than mere machines; they exercise no independent thought any more than the spinning frames or the machine lathes, and the result is that they become deadened.

"The German government supports continuation schools, called *Forbildungs Schule* (go on building) for boys above fourteen to continue their instruction after leaving the regular day schools. Attendance upon this school is obligatory in most places for the boy until he is eighteen years of age. The weekly period of instruction is ten hours, of which three hours come on Saturday morning from 9 to 12 o'clock, and three hours each on two work days, from 9 to 12 in the morning, or from 4 to 7 in the afternoon. This arrangement of hours can be changed to suit the needs of the employer. No instruction is given after 7 P.M.

"The instruction is adapted to the needs of the various trades. There are classes in arithmetic for machinists, loom fixers, etc. The terms used in the class room savor of the shop and the mill. What is three-fourths of $25\frac{1}{2}$ does not mean so much to the foundry man as a problem like this: If a copper casting weighs $25\frac{1}{2}$ pounds and the specific gravity of iron is three-fourths that of copper, what will the casting weigh if made of iron? Then again, the same problem would not interest the textile worker, unless it involved mill calculations. Working people have minds of a distinctly concrete order. They have intensely practical aims when they come to school, and are unwilling to study systematically an entire subject as they did in the common schools. They demand that the instruction shall lead directly to the specific things they are dealing with in their work. The German continuation school adapts its methods of instruction to meet the needs of the working people.

"To give an illustration—the Munich Continuation School for Machinists' Apprentices offers the following subjects: Religion, machine shop calculations and bookkeeping, business correspondence and reading, the study of life and citizenship, mechanical drawing, physics and machinery, materials and shop work. The subjects of instruction are in the closest possible connection with the requirements of the machinists' trade.''

The distinguishing characteristics of the German educational system may be summed up in the word efficiency. To obtain the greatest amount of benefit possible to be obtained in the objective and central control, discipline, willingness of the pupil, ethical instruction, thoroughness and continuity are the features most in contrast as compared with the American system.

The German system to be thoroughly understood and appreciated, needs to be described in some detail, but particular comparisons with the American system need not be carried out as the latter is well understood. In order to understand the present status of the highly developed German system, a short historical review of its origin and gradual growth is necessary, and the following matter from the author's article, ''The Educational System of Germany,'' which appeared in *American Education*, May, 1911, covers the ground in a condensed form.

''The Christian religion preserved the ancient culture through the dark ages, during which the church was the only provider of education. It was but natural that great weight should be laid upon the teaching of religion, and in fact at the very beginning the object of teaching was to spread religion. The language of the monks was Latin and consequently Latin was the medium through which all education was to be obtained.

''The 13th and 14th centuries brought about a change from clerical to worldly methods due to the development of cities, the prosperity following in the wake of commerce and trade, and the power and influence of the citizens. With this increase in importance of citizenship and the growth of these communities, the necessity of town schools was felt, and these were established on the lines of the cloister schools for preliminary education only, but in the long run did not satisfy the demand for education, so that Latin was altogether abolished and the German language and alphabet took its place for public and business education.

''This may be considered as the foundation of the common schools of Germany. Naturally, after the establishment of this educational system, the demand for higher education was bound to come. This desire was largely influenced by Luther's translation of the Bible into German, Guttenberg's invention of the printing press and the general advancement of science. The realization of higher education was marked by the founding of the University of Leipzig in 1409. As the preliminary educational system resulted in the foundation of universities, so the universities on the other hand, influenced betterments in the preparatory methods.

"Compulsory education was now suggested and finally the state took in hand all matters of education and this was the beginning of the system of general higher education which led to the establishment of the present Gymnasium, which long held sway as a preparatory school for the university.

"It is endeavored herein to outline the courses of study as provided by law as a standard. It would, however, not be within the scope of this article to discuss the educational system as a whole with all its additions such as excursions to the woods, to the country, to museums, etc., in the lower schools; special classic performances in leading theaters for the middle schools; or, for instance, educational tours of a duration of ten or more days for the university. Neither shall much be said of the system prevailing at the universities, which allows the student to attain his education at as many universities as he wants to, thus giving him the advantage of hearing lectures by the different prominent professors on the different subjects.

"In consequence of the rapid advancement of science and the desire for further research, the theories of the ancients were not so strictly accepted, and recourse was had to the universities, to independent thought, and to the investigation of natural phenomena. Copernicus, Galileo, Kepler and Newton had already advanced their new theories; Columbus, Vasco de Gama, and Magellan through their discovery of new worlds, had widened the scope of vision and Ratke and Comenius worked out theories for teaching from a new point of view, which, however, could not immediately be put into effect because of the unrest consequent upon the 30 years war.

"Frederick Wilhelm I of Prussia, in 1717, finally inaugurated the system of compulsory education, and founded 2,000 new schools. In 1794, the general law of the state laid down fixed rules for the entire system of Prussian schools. The following are a few paragraphs which may illustrate its nature:

"Paragraph 1. Schools and universities are state institutions which have in view the teaching of young people in useful knowledge and science.

"Paragraph 9. All public schools and educational institutions shall be under the direct supervision of the state, and are subject to visitations and inspections at all times.

"Paragraph 29. Where no endowments exist for a public school, the expense of the institution must be borne by all the male heads of households regardless of the number of children which each family may have.

"Paragraph 34. The cost of maintenance of school buildings and dwellings for teachers must be borne by the inhabitants of the district as a common burden.

"Paragraph 43. Every inhabitant who is not able or does not care to employ private tutors for his children, must send them to the public schools when they have attained the age of 5 years.

"Paragraph 46. Instruction must be continued until the child, in the opinion of the school authorities, has acquired that knowledge which the average sound minded individual, according to his or her standing, is supposed to have.

"Paragraph 50. The exactions of compulsory education must not interfere with the health of the pupil so that it might in any sense become dangerous to his well being.

"The business and professional men, the artists and the artisans in the early part of the 19th century already felt the need of a higher public education due to the rapid development of industry and technique, and a school was established called the Real Gymnasium which ranks with the gymnasium as a scientific school and which lays special stress on modern languages, mathematics and natural science.

"Through the efforts of the great pedagogue, Johann Heinrich Pestalozzi, in the first half of the 19th century, the public school took its proper position, inasmuch as it became its province not only to teach the necessary elementary branches but also to awaken the spiritual forces of the pupil so that independent, confident and logical action might result. To relieve the strain which was put on the pupil by his spiritual education, he introduced the now highly developed system of gymnastic exercises. The pupil of Pestalozzi, Frederich Froebel, founded the "Kindergarten" system which now is known the world over.

"Upon the establishment of the present German Empire in 1871, the entire school system, and particularly as applied to the common school (Volks Schule and Buerger Schule) was again improved and in 1872 Prussia regulated the educational system, and among other things introduced an intermediate school, which is an extension of the Volks Schule. In this intermediate school, or Mittel Schule, one foreign language, additional mathematics, and some of the Real Gymnasium branches are taught. Consequently Germany now possesses the following educational institutions:

"Volks Schule (no tuition) or Buerger Schule (with tuition fees), Mittel Schule, Real Schule, Ober Real Schule, Real Gymnasium, Gymnasium and Universitat.

These schools may be divided into three categories: The lower school system, the upper school system and the universities.

"The system of lower education comprises the Volks Schule, Fortbildung Schule and the Mittel Schule.

"The compulsory education law requires that the child enter the school in the calendar year in which it reaches the age of six years and continues through a training of at least eight years of schooling.

"The Volks Schule and Buerger Schule comprise eight terms of one year each, aggregating from 22 to 32 hours of study per week. During the first period, religion, German, arithmetic, singing and gymnastics are taught, in the second period, drawing and object lessons are added, and in the third period geometry, history and physics.

"The Mittel Schulen or intermediate schools are intended for such pupils who desire a somewhat higher education than can be had in the Volks Schulen and who expect to better fit themselves for industrial and commercial life. Such schools continue six terms of one year each, subsequent to the first three years of the Volks Schule. The course of study during the first year, to which 24 hours per week are devoted, covers religion, German, arithmetic, singing and gymnastics. To these are progressively added geometry, botany, physics, geography, history, French or English and drawing, so that finally during the last term, 32 hours per week are devoted to this list.

"It must further be noted that there are a number of city schools, particularly in the industrial districts, in which the courses of the studies embrace a combination of those of the Volks Schule and Mittel Schule. In order to equalize the educational advantages as between the pupils of the upper and lower classes, all cities and many large towns are provided by the communities with so-called Fortbildungs Schulen, which constitute an extension of the Mittel Schulen and in which German composition, arithmetic, mathematics, physics and drawing are taken up, and also such branches as enable the pupil to better follow commercial and industrial pursuits. Two to four hours per day and two or three days per week are devoted thereto, and the course extends over a period of three to four years.

"In order that graduates from the last named schools may later in life be enabled to acquire additional instruction of a higher order, the so-called Volks Hoch Schulen were established in 1898, in which lectures were given during several months of the year, principally in the larger cities. The course of study at the Berlin Hoch Schule for instance comprised the following lectures for the year 1900, viz:

"On the effects of the newer remedies and drugs; on the constitution of the universe; the prevention of sickness in daily life; Greek sculpture; on germs, causes of disease and its prevention; our atmosphere and its compositions; the origin and prevention of nervous diseases; the earth and its history; the life and works of Goethe.

"This is a six weeks' course for which a nominal fee of one mark (25 cents) per evening is charged. Two thousand attended this course. At another course in Leipsig, the attendance was 10,000.

"Similar courses of study are provided for in country districts and which usually extend through a period of five months for men and three months for women. In these schools, the subjects taken up vary from year to year.

"The system of higher education comprises the Gymnasium, the Real Gymnasium, the Ober Real Gymnasium, Reform Schule, Real and Hoehere Buerger Schule. These constitute two groups, the Gymnasiums and the Real Schulen. The distinction between the two groups is as follows:

"The Gymnasium group comprises the Gymnasium and the Ober Real Schulen, in all of which the courses extend over a term of nine years and differ only in that in the Gymnasium, Greek and Latin is taught, in the Real Gymnasium Greek and Latin are omitted and French and English substituted and in the Ober Real Schule these modern languages, additional mathematics and natural science are substituted for Greek and Latin.

"The Real Schulen group comprises the Real Schule, the Reform Schule, and the Hoehere Buerger Schule, which all cover a six years' course.

"The courses of study in the Gymnasium group, and to which 25 to 31 hours are devoted per week, are with the exceptions and substitutions noted above, religion, German, Latin, Greek, French or English, history, geography, mathematics, natural science, penmanship and drawing.

"The Ober Real Schulen, in which the ancient languages are entirely eliminated, are intended to prepare the student for the technical and commercial professions.

"The greater number of these schools are located in the Rhineland province, the great industrial district.

"The Real Schulen group have a six years' course only, but the course may be continued in the Ober Real Schulen by completing the three upper grades of the latter. The student who has completed a nine years' course in any of these schools, is entitled to admission to the universities.

"Much stress is laid upon gymnastics throughout the entire course in these upper schools. Two afternoons in the week, not devoted to studies, are reserved for this purpose.

"The courses for the higher education of German women cover a term of nine or ten years, which compares with our high schools and colleges in purpose, and in the kind of education attained in them.

"Some of the higher schools for females are private and others are state schools, but all are under state supervision. To these courses may be added, in order to fit the German women for academical study, a four years' course patterned or selected from the course of the Ober Real Schule.

"The German universities, in consequence of their historical development, occupy a conspicuous position among the universities of the world. This also holds good for the technical universities and the other scientific institutions of Germany. The universities do not merely serve for acquiring the highest education in scientific matters, but are at the same time centers for independent research; their libraries, laboratories, collections, observatories, etc., are consequently fitted up not only to meet the requirements of students, but are intended to give instructors and young experimenters the means and assistance for furthering the development of science in all its branches.

"This sphere of university activity finds important extension in the work of the academies and learned societies which are organized and supported by the state. The state academies are all situated in university towns and members thereof are qualified to deliver lectures in the universities.

"The immediate purpose of the universities is to give instruction in science, theology, law, medicine and philosophy. The philosophical faculty, which originally had the task of preparing students for entry in the upper courses, now covers a very large field. Languages, natural science, chemistry, mathematics, pedagogy, political economy are some of the principal branches taught.

"The principal representative of the university is the rector, who holds the office for one year and is elected by the professors among their number. The business of the various faculties is transacted by the deans who are similarly elected by the regular professors of each faculty. The body of instructors for science consists of regular professors and private tutors in addition to which are lecturers and assistants. The students matriculate at the university and are enrolled in one of the faculties. Only those are fully qualified to matriculate who have the certificate from one of the nine years' course upper schools (Gymnasium, Real Gymnasium, Ober Real Schule). Foreigners must produce a certificate of a corresponding standard. Students may also be enrolled in the philosophical faculty under less exacting conditions. Besides this, certain branches admit Hoerer (listeners) to the lectures.

"That there are a great number of women in Germany in higher education is not understood in this country, probably for the reason that the greater application of the male students takes away attention from them. Women are not satisfied merely to complete the academic courses, but take the university courses of four years or more leading to degrees. In the winter semester of 1911, the women students were 4.8% of the whole number of matriculated students, some 4,532 attending the universities, of which 2,795 were full fledged students and the balance listeners. The former had been through the regular preparatory courses required of the male students while the listeners were subject to the same requirements as the men listeners.

The subjects pursued by women students during the semester mentioned above were philosophy, philology, and history, 1,563 students; mathematics and natural history, 504; medicine, 582; political economy, 67; law, 39; dentistry, 27; pharmacy, 8; Protestant theology, 5.

"All faculties confer the degree of doctor and the theological faculty also covers the lower degree of licentiate. The securing of such a title is not, as a rule, the aim of the students, as alone it does not qualify him for the state service. Besides the purely academic examination for the degree of doctor, state examinations are held for the principal professional callings and ecclesiastical examinations for the theological. To be admitted to a theological, legal or higher grade of teachers' examination, it is necessary to take a course of study of three years at the university as a fully matriculated student. For the medical profession, the period of study has been lengthened to five years.

"Following is a list of the German academies and universities:

"Academies:

"Berlin, established, 1700; Goettingen, 1751; Muenchen, 1759; and Leipzig, 1846.

"Universities:

"Heidelberg, established 1386; Leipzig, 1409; Rostock, 1419; Greifwald, 1456; Freiburg, 1457; Tuebingen, 1477; Marburg, 1527; Koenigsberg, 1544; Jena, 1558; Wuerzburg, 1582; Giesen, 1607; Kiel, 1665; Halle, 1694; Breslau, 1702; Goettingen, 1737; Erlangen, 1743; Berlin, 1809; Muenchen, 1829; Strassburg, 1872; Bonn, 1880 and Muenster, 1902 (founded as an academy 1771)."

The German educational system overlooks no department in which activity in later life must be exercised. Training is divided into three principal branches; industrial, commercial and technical; industrial for the worker, commercial for the business man and his assistants, and technical, for the engineering, chemical and similar branches.

The *Journal of Commere,* Oct. 25, 1911, reports an address by Herr Dr. Knorck, of the Commercial Schools of the Berlin Board of Trade, describing the progressive and thorough methods of the German Commercial educational movement.

"The practical German teaching which has been handed down from the guilds and corporations of the Middle Ages, according to which the apprentice came into the closest social and business connection with his master and teacher, has had a part in its modernized form in the successes which the German merchant has won in the world's markets. His present occupation was backed by the thoroughness of German scientific education, which, since the middle of the last century, has clearly recognized the social problems of to-day, by the establishment of commercial and economical schools, and has developed them systematically. Professional education and commercial teaching, practice and theory worked together in Germany to create a mighty army of clever mercantile employees, and a chosen host of far-seeing merchant masters, who are not afraid of the greatest enterprises in the trading world at home or abroad. The state municipalities and the commercial unions supported this far-reaching economical culture to their utmost ability.

"Practical experience is as always, regarded in Germany, as the most important foundation of professional training. After a certain all-around education has been attained at the elementary or intermediate school, the future merchant usually begins the practical training at once, which, in keeping with ancient custom, lasts three years. For those who have passed through the intermediate schools with their six classes, who have, that is, received a certificate of one year military service, sometimes two to two and a half years are regarded as sufficient; even those who have the graduating certificate of the higher, nine-class school, and therefore have the right to go to the university or technical university, must submit to this long practical training. A long practical course extended over several years is even required, quite apart from the general education, before one can attend the German commercial colleges.

"As to the practical training, the German commercial code imposes certain definite duties upon the employer in his relation to the apprentice. He is obliged to see that the apprentice is (1) initiated into all the commercial business of the firm. He is to (2) conduct the education of the apprentice, either personally or by means of a capable representative. (3) Thoroughness and method should prevail throughout this training, which ought not to be encroached upon by services of a secondary nature. The principal is expected to watch over the moral conduct of his apprentice and encourage him to attend the continuation school. He has likewise to look after his physical welfare. Those who have forfeited the rights of citizenship are not retained as apprentices.

"No intelligent and successful merchant in any land to-day, will be found to deny for the coming generation of merchants, the necessity of theoretical and scientific education along with practical training. The apprentice ought thus to be trained to clear reasoning, and the knowledge and skill gained by him in business will be widened, organized and deepened.

"What means are tried in Germany for this purpose and what are the results? All masters are obliged to allow all apprentices sufficient free time to attend a publicly recognized professional or continuation school. At the same time, the industrial code gives the town authorities the right of compelling all male and female commercial apprentices up to the age of 18 years to attend school. These authorities are thus allowed, though not compelled, by the imperial law to maintain compulsory professional and continuation schools.

"The courses in these professional schools, to which those of the Berlin Merchants' Corporation also belongs, corresponds generally to the practical apprenticeship, namely, three years with six hours a week. Very few courses exceed this number of hours, those of the Berlin corporation with eight hours and those in Saxony with twelve being exceptions.

"The curriculum contains the following subjects: Shorthand, which has been almost universally adopted; general commercial instruction as the basis and introduction for the entire sphere of commercial knowledge, which is contained in practically every course; office and correspondent work are usually connected with this; and the all important commercial arithmetic is included in each year's curriculum. Commercial and economical geography has been almost everywhere introduced as an obligatory subject, while everybody is in agreement as to the fundamental significance of bookkeeping and civics.

"The question over which there is most dispute is whether a foreign language should be introduced into the course. This is naturally as good as impossible in a six hour course. In Berlin, with our eight hours, we have made one foreign language (English or French) compulsory; three hours being allotted to it."

The former idea of Germany as a country of soldiers, black forests, violins, castles, professors, beer and dreamers is now being sharply revised. It is seen that the rest of the world has less to fear from German military ambitions than from its army of scientists, engineers, scientifically trained directors of industrial enterprises and highly educated commercial agents. That she possesses such an army as the latter is due to her educational system, particularly the technical schools and universities. The great value of these is described by President Hadley of Yale University, who in his address, "What the United States has to Learn from the Technical Training of Germany," delivered before the Brooklyn Institute of Arts and Sciences, and based on personal study and observations while he was lecturing before the universities in Germany, said:

"There are two great points in the German educational system which must impress every one—the use of the technical training and that of the military training of the people. The children are forced to go to the elementary schools for a time, and during that part of their education, they are kept out of the shops and factories. They, however, receive instruction in the rudiments of shop and factory work."

Dr. Hadley laid particular stress upon the growth and usefulness of the technical schools in Germany during the last half century. Before the spread of these schools in Germany, he said, the Germans were considered an idealistic and sentimental people.

"To-day they are intensely practical," he said. "They are, indeed, more practical than the Americans. They have become a military race. Their ideals are technical. They value things for their value in dollars and cents or for the social position which these things give their possessors. The Kaiser has been a ringleader in bringing about these changes in the views of life entertained by his subjects.

"Our good technical schools are rare. The graduates of our technical schools get most of their training in the shop, on the farm, or in the mine. In Germany, the best part of the student's training is received in the schools. The objects of the system in the German schools are two—to develop the individual and advance the welfare of the country by teaching the students what will best advance the interests of the country.

"The attitude of public mind in Germany and America to the respective educational systems is significant. In this country it is regarded as an accident if a man who has been taught the theories of commercial life in the schools succeeds when he begins his active career. In Germany it is considered an accident, if success comes to those men who have not been trained in the schools, and an accident that should not be repeated.

"Is it any wonder that England is complaining that the German business men, who are trained in the technical schools and are thorough students of the conditions they confront, are driving the English traders out of the neutral ports? If such methods succeed in commerce they will succeed in all things. Individual action cannot contend successfully with the united front of the Germans in the long run.

"I believe there is developing in this country, the spirit of organization. There has been a tendency to crowd the technical men out. We are beginning to profit from the lessons of Germany and her education system, giving our men good training in all lines adapted to practical life."

An account of the technical educational system of Germany, briefly describing its principal feature is as follows, taken from the author's lecture, "Engineering Education in Germany," as given at the eighteenth annual meeting of the Society for the Promotion of Engineering Education, at the University of Wisconsin, June, 1910:

"After the great struggle from which the German states gained their independence, at the termination of the Napoleonic War in 1815, the economic conditions of Germany had reached the lowest ebb. At that time the German states had but a small population left, owing to the undeveloped state of commercial industries and the devastation due to this long struggle. In England, at that time, the steam engine had begun its triumphal progress and opened up the country's richness in iron and coal.

"It was recognized in Germany that the country could only be lifted economically through the expansion of industrial activity. Two ways led to this end; the practical way, taken by pioneers like Krupp, Borsig and Siemens, working quietly and uninterruptedly to replace the former state of handicraft by organized industry; and the theoretical way, adopted by the government, of placing industry on a scientific basis by the establishment of technical schools. That permanent progress in competition with other countries could only be built up satisfactorily on such a foundation is proven by the recent developments in chemistry and electricity, as well as in heat-engines and in engineering in general.

"The beginning of the German technical schools dates back to the middle of the nineteenth century. Nearly all of the technical colleges originated, however, from the so-called Mittel Schulen (intermediate schools), and only after they had, by continuous effort, obtained a high standing, did they obtain charters as Technische Hoch Schulen (technical universities). As an example, the Berlin Technical University was formed by the union of the Architectural School founded in 1779 and the Commercial Acadamy or Trade School, founded 1821.

"The aim of the technical university is expressed in the first paragraph of the constitution of the Berlin Technical University, which reads as follows: 'The aim of the technical university is to furnish a means for higher education for the technical professions, in civil and industrial service and in commercial undertakings, as well as to cultivate the arts and sciences so far as they come under the head of technical instruction.' Every technical university has departments for separate studies, and in each are divisions for architecture, civil, mechanical and electrical engineering, chemistry, metallurgy and mining; natural sciences and mathematics. There are some of these universities which have special departments, as electro-chemistry, marine engineering and aerial navigation, forestry, agriculture, etc.

"The great development of technology made necessary the opening of a great number of new courses in all the technical schools. The most recent new course is that in aerial navigation, thus helping to make a positive science of this means of transportation.

"Germany at present has eleven universities, established and chartered as technical universities as given below:

"Berlin, established 1799, chartered 1799; Stuttgart, 1829, 1862; Dresden, 1828, 1851; Carlsruhe, 1825, 1865; Darmstadt, 1836, 1868; Aix la Chapelle, 1870, 1870; Brunswick, 1745, 1877; Munich, 1827, 1877; Hanover, 1831, 1879; Danzig, 1904, 1904; and Breslau, 1905, 1905.

"A certain prescribed preliminary education is necessary to qualify the student for admission to the technical universities. There are three classes of attendants: the regular student, the so-called 'listener' and the guest. Those who wish to enter as regular students must have had a nine-year course of instruction at one of the Gymnasiums, Real-Gymnasiums or Ober-Real-Schulen, and must have graduated therefrom by taking the so-called 'Abiturienten' examination. This nine-year course cannot be entered upon until after the student has passed through a three or four year course in the lower schools, so that if he enters the latter at the age of six, he will be at least nineteen years of age before he enters the technical college, since he must also put in one year at practical training in regular manufacturing plants.

"In the Ober-Real-Schulen ancient languages have been entirely eliminated from the course of study and more time is devoted to modern languages, natural sciences and mathematics, the whole course being especially arranged for preparing the student for the technical professions. The majority of these Ober-Real-Schulen are found in Prussia, there being 42 as against 69 in Germany, and as stated, the greater number of these schools are located in the province of Rhineland, the great industrial district.

"The practical experience prescribed for these students covers at least one year, for mechanical and electrical engineering, in pattern shops, foundry and machine shops. Two years are frequently voluntarily devoted, part of which is spent in construction in the field.

"As military service in Germany is compulsory, being generally a two or three year service, it might be stated here that those who have graduated from any of the three schools referred to are required to serve only one year in the army. Many students first absolve this military service before entering the technical university. As the regular course in these universities consists of eight semesters (four years) it will be observed that the graduate from the university will have reached the age of at least twenty-four years.

"Technical universities confer first the degree 'Diplom Ingenieur' (always abbreviated as 'Dipl. Ing.'). The certificate of graduation always qualifies the graduate to enter upon a further examination for the degree of 'Doctor Ingenieur' (abbreviated as 'Dr. Ing.'). This degree may also be conferred as an honorary title in recognition of work done in a technical line.

"A graduate having the degree 'Dipl. Ing.,' must, if he desires to enter the federal service, give notice thereof to the state within six months after graduation, and, if engaged, after state examination, he is made 'Regierungs Bauführer.' After being in service for four years, he may take a promotion examination for 'Regierungs Baumeister,' and eventually may reach the top of the service.

"The 'listener' can only be qualified to enter the German Technical University after graduating from one of the six-year courses in the Pro-Gymnasiums or Real-Schulen. The distinction between Gymnasium and Real-Schule is as follows: To the former belong the Gymnasium, with a nine-year course, and the Pro-Gymnasium with a six-year course. To the second class,

or Real-Schulen, belong those in which Latin is included, namely
the Real-Gymnasium and the Real-Pro-Gymnasium. The term
in the former is nine years and in the latter six years. To this
group belong also such as include no Latin course, namely, the
above named Real-Schule with a nine-year course, and the Real-
Schule with a six-year course. The graduate from such schools
with a six year course, need also serve but one year in the army.
A preliminary course of from three to four years in the lower
school precedes the courses in these six-year or upper schools.
This graduate is termed 'Einjahriger,' with reference to the
military service, and the graduate from the nine-year course
alone is referred to as the 'Abiturient,' (one who has made the
Abiturienten examinations).

" 'Listeners' may also be those who have graduated from a
Technische Mittel-Schule or College, such as the Technicum,
Maschinenbau-Schule, Baugewerk-Schule, Kunstgewerbe-Schule,
etc. These listeners are usually men of riper age, who have
already been engaged in practical work and who wish to acquire
additional knowledge in their special branches of work. They
therefore choose but certain lectures, usually extending over
'from two to three years.

" 'Guests' are those who have had an academic training or
such other persons who would not be regularly entitled to enter
as listeners; they can attend only a limited number of lectures.

"Instruction in these technical universities is in the form of
lectures, exercises, shop and laboratory work (upon which much
stress is laid), and visitation of manufacturing plants. Large
experimental shops and libraries serve as auxiliaries for instruction. For instance, at the Technical University at Darmstadt,
there is a library of 800,000 volumes, while that of the Berlin
Library amounts to far more than one million volumes.

"As is the case in all German Universities, the student may
attend the lectures to any extent that he may choose, and no roll
is called. It is the intention to make of the student an independent thinker. The attendant is supposed to have reached
the age of responsibility at the time he enters the university,
having passed through the many grades of upper and lower
schools, and having passed through the military service and con-
formed to the strict regulations of the manufacturing establishments. In all of these, strict discipline is the watch-word. The
student is allowed to attain his scholarships at as many universities as he desires, thus getting the advantage of the dif-

ferent methods of prominent professors in the different subjects.

"Many students do not take the examination and these receive a certificate of attendance showing the semesters which they attended, as do also the listeners and guests, who are not qualified to take the examination.

"In addition to the technical universities, there are also numerous other technical institutes, such as the Polytechnicum, Technicum, Baugewerk-Schule, Kunstgewerbe-Schule and Maschinenbau-Schule, all of which are classified as technical middle-schools or colleges. The number of these is far greater than that of the technical universities, and admission to them is not so much restricted. The degrees which are obtainable by the students of these colleges are those of mechanical engineer, electrical or mining engineer, etc., and some of these colleges confer the degree of Maschinen-Techniker, Electro-Techniker, etc. There are also a number of minor technical schools, all of which are important factors in making up the present high efficiency and high standard of the industries of modern Germany.

"It should always be considered the sacred duty of the promoters of engineering education to instil in the minds of students and to keep before the engineering profession in general, the fact that no great headway can be made as long as the belief is prevalent that we know it all and cannot learn from others.

"Having discussed the system in vogue in Germany for educating the engineer and fitting him for his profession from both a theoretical and practical standpoint, I will compare the German and American engineers as to standing as well as to their efforts at seeking further knowledge. To expand his knowledge, the German engineer not only serves in a professional way with engineering concerns in Germany, but also gathers experience by so serving with such concerns in foreign countries. The question of salary is, for this reason, not considered by him of first importance. America is usually his Mecca, for he recognizes the fact, impressed upon him by German professors, that much information may be gathered there and particularly from American practice. We find this custom encouraged by the government, as well as by the manufacturers and technical societies. It cannot be emphasized too strongly that the rising German engineer does not refuse to believe that much may be acquired from the methods and practice in foreign countries.

"For this very reason we find that not only the German manufacturer, but also the individual engineer, eagerly subscribes for foreign technical papers which they thoroughly study and for the study of which they are thoroughly equipped as indicated by their educational training above cited. This stands out boldly as compared with the custom in America, where the engineer rarely peruses a technical paper published in a foreign language.

"While it is believed here that most literature of importance is translated, it is, nevertheless, a fact, that the subjects of greatest importance, particularly where higher theories are treated, are seldom translated into the English language. The reason for this is that few American engineers who are masters of the foreign language care to undertake the task, while foreign engineers do not find it necessary, as they understand the original publication. It is also true that most translations fall short in every respect of being equal in value to the original.

"During my ten years of experience and observation in this country, I have found that the American engineer is too apt to take up the first technical work at hand on any special subject and adopt for his work or scheme the ideas or practice suggested therein. It is sometimes claimed that the American engineer is a thorough specialist, but this is not generally true, as he is apt to jump from one line of work to another when there appears to be an inducement in the shape of greater financial gain. In Germany, it is with great difficulty that an engineer can take up some other line of work because of the customs prevailing there which must guide his actions. Such proceeding is not looked upon favorably, as he would not be considered as having sufficient practical experience in the new line, and if attempted it would be at a financial loss for a few years at least. A 'jack-of-all-trades' is usually supposed to be a master of none. Bearing this fact in mind, it is quite apparent why we have in this country so many failures in connection with engineering undertakings, such as bridges, dams, locomotives, prime movers, and entire industrial undertakings, etc., as compared with the number and magnitude of such failures which occur in Germany.

"A fact which is beginning to dawn upon us is that we must look to Germany for originality and economies or efficiency in engineering propositions. In this country, a proposition which involves the expenditure of two million dollars for development purposes would not be looked upon favorably. Such a project was the high speed Marienfeld-Zossen line equipped near Berlin some years ago to obtain a speed of 125 miles an hour. German manufacturers for their mutual interest, similarly united in developing gas engines of large capacity. More recently, promoters and manufacturers, with the assistance of the government, united to develop the art of aerial navigation. A great handicap in America is the desire of manufacturers and others who should foster engineering education, to standardize their products for the purpose of greater financial gain. This is undoubtedly a disadvantage so far as the promotion of the engineering profession is concerned.

"The standing of the American engineer in his profession and in the community cannot be compared with that of the German engineer in his country and we need not seek very far for an explanation. All education receives proper recognition in Germany and the engineer is placed on a social plane with the doctor, the lawyer and the army officer, etc. His compensation, as compared with that of mere mechanics, is proportionately higher than in this country, so that he is naturally able to occupy a higher plane. The chiefs of departments as well as the consulting engineers and manufacturers, all work in harmony with the subordinates or assistant engineers, designers, etc., and are not loath to give credit to whom credit is due for any new designs or creations.

"The engineers and assistants are all employed under term contracts, and the law prescribes what notice must at least be given to terminate the employment. This ranges from one to three months. It is common practice to engage even assistant engineers for terms varying from one to five years, whereas in America, the unjust practice prevails of laying off such employees as though they were mechanics or laborers, practically without notice, and as soon as the important engineering work is completed.

"One prominent concern is known to have laid off about one hundred men on a Christmas Eve without giving any notice whatever. It is, therefore, not surprising that a great many well trained engineers drop their profession at the age of thirty years or thereabouts and enter upon vocations in which they may be assured of greater returns. This necessitates the employment of new and younger men when new propositions are at hand, and such men require again to be trained for their duties.

"This state of affairs is directly chargeable to the engineering profession itself in neglecting to bring about reforms in the customs and remedying of such evils. In Germany the conditions incline the engineer to stick to his post through life and the engineering concerns and manufacturers reap the benefit of his accumulated experience and knowledge."

The system of engineering education in Germany is such that a large number of original researches and technical books result. The engineer, to obtain the advanced titles of Doctor of Engineering, Regierungsbauführer and Regierungsbaumeister and other titles in respective branches must do original work or prepare original theses on the technique of his respective branch. The papers are usually of such high quality as to readily find publishers and thus a body of original literature on every technical subject is built up, which is of the greatest value to the industry. A large number of technical books are published and the total of these with the theses of the advanced engineers amounted in 1910 alone to 10,400 volumes, while the total publication of all technical works throughout the world, including the foregoing, amounted to only 15,540. These figures do not include periodicals. The technical works of the English speaking nations in that year aggregated but 2,100 while the French published 2,000.

It will be seen that an enormous amount of highly valuable scientific and technical material is constantly appearing in German which is not available to those who do not understand the German language.

As comparatively few native American engineers and technical men are acquainted with German, it will be seen why our manufacturers are lagging so far behind and how costly ignorance of the latest improvements is proving.

Engineers not only do not know German but do not know the importance of knowing it. A certain engineer, even, in addressing the American Institute of Electrical Engineers, made the astonishing assertion that not one graduate in 10,000 had any real use for German. At another meeting of the society a paper on the subject of high voltage generators was discussed and it was wisely argued that generators of a certain voltage were not practicable, although for five years, just such generators had been in successful operation in a number of continental plants, and some of much higher voltage had been installed.

An amusing sidelight on this exhibition of ignorance and incompetency soon shone forth from a London periodical which, in equal innocence of German progress, announced that such generators (those of the lower voltage) were soon to be built in America, and that further interesting developments were in prospect.

The three wise men of Gotham are certainly put to the blush by the plight in which these eminent engineers find themselves through their ignorance of the German language.

The enormous cost to the public of the ignorance of our engineers in regard to advanced German practice is too frequently demonstrated. The writer had the good fortune to be connected with a prominent engineering undertaking for the generation of electric power, and before the plant was entirely completed had occasion to make a report on the efficiency of the plant which showed that an annual saving in operating expenses of $200,-000 could be made by the adoption of German methods. When such methods were actually put in operation the saving proved to be even larger. A saving of over $1,000,000 in the construction cost of the plant could have been effected had the engineers in charge been at the outset familiar with good German practice, which of course is not to be had from books alone.

The value of German methods is better understood by some Englishmen than by Americans, as the following, which is a quotation from a speech delivered in the British Parliament, shows:

"One of our greatest failures is that less than one per cent. of our engineers and officers understand the German language so that everything we wish· to know of German progress must come to us second-hand in insufficient and delayed translation; to-day we are at a point where Germany is able to build ten ships against our one; we have to learn to imitate Germany."

Germany does not despise American progress or seek to belittle and obstruct it, but in fact is only too anxious to take advantage of all American advances. The American Institute in Berlin exchanges publications of value with the Smithsonian Institute and ·promotes the translation of all works likely to be of value to German progress.

One of the results of the German system is seen in an analysis of the awards of the Nobel prize. As is well known, the

Nobel foundation is based upon the will of Dr. Alfred Bernhard Nobel, the Swedish engineer, chemist and inventor of dynamite, who died in 1896, leaving an enormous fortune.

Each of the five annual Nobel Prizes is worth $40,000. They are awarded for the most important discoveries or improvements in (1) physics, (2) chemistry, (3) physiology or medicine, (4) for the most distinguished work of an idealistic tendency in the field of literature and (5) for the best effort toward the fraternity of nations and the promotion of peace.

In some cases the prize is divided between two competitors. The following list summarizes the awards given up to 1911. The number of recipients of prizes and half prizes is given followed by a figure in brackets showing the value in full prizes:

Germany, 16 (15); France, 12 ($7\frac{1}{2}$); England, 7 (7); Holland, 3 (2); Italy, 4 ($2\frac{1}{2}$); Switzerland, 4 ($2\frac{1}{2}$); Sweden, 3 ($2\frac{1}{2}$); Denmark, 2 ($1\frac{1}{2}$); Spain, 2 (1); United States, 2 (2); Austria, 1 (1); Belgium, 1 (1); Norway, 1 (1); Russia, 1 (1), and Poland, 1 (1).

Two societies whose whole purpose is the promotion of peace, have each received a full prize, making a total of fifty full prizes divided among 62 competitors.

The German prizes have been as follows: Physics, 3 ($2\frac{1}{2}$); Chemistry, 6 (6); Medicine, 4 ($3\frac{1}{2}$); and Literature, 3 (3). Thus Germany has received in full prizes twice the aggregate of the next competitor, but it has received no prize for peace; the prize records in physics, chemistry and medicine being largely the result of the splendid system of educational training. The United States has but two prizes, one for physics and one for peace. In the last award, however, that of 1912, a third prize, in medicine, has come to the United States.

The German educational system is constantly under scrutiny, and its creators adopt any improvement of value that is evolved. A late feature of importance is the idea of exchange professors, which is being carried out between German and American universities and which is proving of great value to both countries.

To those who are familiar with various educational systems, the superiority of the German system is obvious. It is being adopted in whole or in part by many other countries and the education of the world in the near future is likely to be largely along the lines of the German system.

CHAPTER XXVI

THE REMEDIES

IN considering the evils which affect the United States, beginning with the most obvious, the defective political system, and continuing through the long list, the one which upon analysis appears to be the basic factor in present conditions, is the educational system. If that be remedied, the remedying of the others will follow in time.

America is pausing now, like a spendthrift who by accident first runs his fingers to the bottom of a supposedly bottomless pocket. The chilling idea that our national resources are not boundless; the realization that we are getting down to par with other nations; that our national existence is open to the same dangers and threatened by the same causes that give concern to other nations, is upon us in all its grim reality.

Like a youth, a few months out of college, who sees that the world is not his walnut after all, to crack as he will, America is passing into a new era, one of more or less gravity and certainly of less enthusiasm. America is face to face with the serious business of being a sorely tried nation among sorely tried nations, with every problem to meet and solve that other nations face, and no longer the most favored of lands. While its opportunities are still boundless, its duties are more sharply defined, and the discipline of existence has laid its hand on the nation, as it lays its hand on each individual as he comes to man's estate.

America's most pressing problem is education, for education is the fountain head of all national progress. Educational standards must be raised, a more efficient system of control evolved, and moral training must be included. The conscience of the coming generations must be developed, for conscience is as capable of development as any other faculty.

The principal office of government is to enforce a relation of justice between those composing it or under its jurisdiction. This is a highly complicated and costly operation at present, and is the principal burden of civilization.

Every individual must work many weeks of each year to meet the cost of enforcing just relations between his neighbor and himself, a toil which savages escape by being ready to risk their lives in defending themselves from injustice.

Proper moral training cannot fail to greatly reduce the total of unjust, careless and neglectful acts; the prevention and punishment of which make government so costly. Conscience is thus the greatest of all economic and social factors, the greatest single item in the composition of civilization.

Next in importance in educational reforms, must be the continuation of education until the individual has a means of earning a livelihood at his command, not the discarding of studies at an early age, and an aimless drifting around into some unsuitable occupation. The state owes itself the duty of seeing that its coming citizens are put on the right road. Training must be compulsory up to the age of 18, and the learning of some trade or profession obligatory.

A system must be devised, also, for securing for each occupation a ratio of apprentices proportionate to its demands, and a method for discouraging the influx into the professions of those whose abilities are better suited for the trades. America is crowded with incompetent lawyers, bad doctors, poor teachers and underpaid clerical people, who might have much more profitably been good mechanics and famous carpenters.

The whole development of the nation, now becoming more and more a manufacturing country, will depend upon the establishment of better relations between business men among themselves, and between them and their employees. The capitalist must realize that the welfare of the business man is of the highest importance, that the prosperity of a country is largely determined by the body of business men it contains, a country having a large proportion of active, bright, aggressive and ambitious business men, all striving for new results and perfections of every kind, will outstrip a country in which love of ease and lack of progress characterize its business men; in which factories are allowed to run themselves, customers considered a necessary evil and the best hours spent in the refinements of pleasure.

In massing itself in large trusts, capital exterminates the business men of the country. It reduces them to the level of employees and dries up the springs of initiative, and capital in consequence, reaps a low rate of interest, whereas distributed in the hands of a numerous body of business men, it would be put to much more effective uses.

The small business men who fall victims to the trusts disperse in three directions. Some still unwilling to give up their independence, struggle along in other lines by hook or crook, too often by crook; others become employees of the trusts and the third class become commercial derelicts, picking up whatever living they can or becoming minor wage earners in some clerical capacity.

Thus one of America's greatest assets must be better conserved, her business men, for they are cleverer than the wage earners and are keen, driving forces of progress, not merely the cogs in the wheels. They employ the bulk of the labor and being closer to labor are less oppressive as employers, besides furnishing, by not being at too great an interval away from labor, an incentive for the ambitious wage earner to look forward to the time when he will be able to join their class.

The relations of employers and employees must undergo a radical change of tone. Means must be found of identifying their interest more obviously. If either the employers or the employees stop to consider the matter, it will readily be seen that their interests are identical, though this is a point of view not usually taken. Neither can exist without the other and the respective positions they hold are determined by a multiplicity of factors which are largely controlled by natural laws. The employer who gets the most out of his men will succeed best in the end, but the most cannot be gotten out by driving, and the employee who gets the most out of his employer will succeed best, but getting the most out of the employer is not accomplished by grudging work and dynamite domination.

Labor troubles frighten capital away and the wage earner must force out of that left, a wage which he might readily exceed if his conduct encouraged new employers to come in competition for his labor.

Although invention, by giving capital control of the "implements of production," the favorite phrase of the socialist, has greatly altered the conditions under which labor is performed, this altered condition is not permanent. In the last century, owing to the triumphs of invention, vast savings have been effected, and the world is much wealthier than in previous generations. This great increment of wealth has been accumulated by the trusts, but measures will be taken to prevent its further accumulation in their hands, so that a better diffusion of wealth will take place, particularly as the new wealth which will be increased by future inventions will come into competition with existing wealth, to the benefit of the wage earner. Natural laws which govern the proportionment of profits between capital and labor in accordance with their respective supply cannot be permanently overcome. With capital plentiful, the banks full of money and laborers scarce, the laborer will receive a larger wage, but with capital scarce, and banks having little on hand to lend, with laborers very numerous, the wage of the laborer will be smaller.

Under modern conditions, the wage earner enjoys a vast propaganda as to his rights and privileges. A constant and proper effort for the betterment of his condition is being made by politicians seeking his vote, by societies of various sorts, by his own unions and by the more progressive employers. With all these agencies working for him, it is reasonably certain that the workingman will receive his just proportion of profits. Yet beyond the gains that are fought for and won for him, he should receive an additional liberality, simply because it will pay. The prosperity of all depends on the prosperity of the worker, and in contributing to his welfare, the welfare of all is advanced.

In the immediate future, the most feasible scheme of betterment is in continuation education, and in the three forms of social insurance, accident, sickness and old age. To relieve the worker of hardship and anxiety is to enable him to devote himself with greater effect to his daily task.

A thoroughly organized effort should also be made to establish a system of distribution of labor, so that the idle workers in one part of the country may be transferred to the places where employment is to be had. At the same time, immigration should be scattered properly, both for the benefit of the immigrants and the country. These are duties which the government owes to its citizens.

Vitally necessary is a better understanding between employers and employees, and the capitalist, as indicated, must take a more progressive and wholesome attitude towards the employees of capital, those who work in capital's interest, the business men. The destructive system of American banking must be fundamentally reorganized.

Capital which is managed with liberality and foresight accomplishes vastly more for itself and for the welfare of the country than capital directed in the usual hardshell "show-me" spirit which dominates at present.

Inventors must be given a square deal, business must get a fair opportunity, and the spirit of initiative and encouragement must pervade capital as well as all branches of commerce to accomplish the results that should be accomplished.

A better understanding must be brought about between capital and government, for under present conditions, the same distrust and animosity and antagonism which characterize the relations of labor and capital, extend to capital and the government. The employer is a step above the wage earner, the capitalist a step above the employer, and the government a step above the capitalist, but here the vicious circle begins again, because the government is the wage earner en masse; very imperfectly expressed but nevertheless the voice of the people and the voice of God.

The government as it now exists not only is an imperfect expression of the will of the people, but in many respects is an actual distortion, for capitalism, in a spirit of insubordination, has sought to control the force by which it must in the natural order of events inevitably be controlled, the will of the people, for the will of the people is all powerful and the only power, and if its admonitions are deliberately and contumaciously rejected, it may turn and with a single act of confiscation level on a fatal day the exploitation of generations and of centuries.

The government as it is now constituted is a house divided against itself. The law makers and those who execute the law are some serving the public and some capital, and the government thus commands no respect and accomplishes nothing. In desperation it tears at the structure of business and creates distrust and alarm, but at the same time its efforts are not regarded as being made in good faith, and are seen to affect no good result.

Trusts are neither broken up nor allowed to work the benefits of which they are capable. In order to handle the great business undertakings which modern conditions demand, great corporations are necessary. They are economically good and produce results in efficiency which the small organization cannot rival and the trust can serve the public better than the smaller dealer. The true interest of the public is in drawing the monopolistic fangs of the trust, but at the same time preserving its useful features, and if our system of government were a good one, this result could be accomplished. But the lack of competent and faithful officials, the presence of untrained politicians and official favorites, and the lack of singleness of purpose in the government undermines its efforts and a chaotic condition exists, which must soon be remedied if we are not to encounter far more serious conditions than any we have thus far had to contend with.

At the root of the matter is the canker of inefficiency. Everywhere, in every department of public life, with only sporadic exceptions, the wrong thing is done and inexperience and in· competency flourish in the graveyard of prosperity. There is not an industry, not a factory, store or shop, that does not halt at the prospect of uncertainty and agitation. The nation is cursed by politics and burdened by the great twin evils of business in politics and politics in business. The will of the people is strangled by an antiquated system, by incompetency, bad faith and the disgraceful struggle for personal advantage indulged in by office holders. Instead of officials who when assailed in office, tender their resignation and thus throw into confusion their detractors when their motives are questioned, we have a stripe of office holders who cling to office to the last extremity and destroy respect for themselves and for the office they hold.

Above all is the pernicious and outrageous sacrifice of the interests and welfare of the people for the sake of partisan politics. Nero is said to have played the fiddle while Rome burned, but he certainly could not have played it more industriously than our office holders play politics while prosperity is vanishing in smoke.

At this time, when the most vital of business questions is before the public, the determination of the fate of the great corporations, there is absolutely no hope of an immediate solution. The whole fabric of business is shaken; doubt, uncertainty and stagnation prevail and no solution of any kind is in sight. All must wait while ruin overtakes, that the interminable processes of our political system may spin themselves out in their accustomed way; still further delayed by the unconscionable struggle for political advantage among groups of office holders who style themselves political parties.

At times we have a president of one political complection, and with remarkable fortune, a congress of another. It would

be an unthinkable thing under such circumstances for them
to consult the welfare of the country first and act in concert in the emergency, and divide the credit afterwards. Instead, however admirable the legislation which Congress may
enact, however patriotic and charged with public welfare it
may be, no president of another group of office holders could
dream of lending his approval to it; and knowing this, the patriots of congress can fairly revel in admirable legislation, which
they would not dare to pass if they thought it would be approved. Thus is politics played and the president "put in a
hole." And as for the president, who imparts in his messages
information to congress as to the condition of the country, which
they know more about than he does, we may be sure that however wise and beneficent may be his admonitions, a congress
composed of a rival group of office holders will never lend an
ear to it.

Each side will, however, endeavor to extract as much political
credit from the situation as possible and seek to cover their
opponents with the greatest possible discredit; but of honest
effort for the welfare of those on whose earnings they fatten,
there will be little or none.

Why should not remedial legislation be made possible in an
expeditious manner? Why should there be such interminable
delays? Who benefits by it? Not the public, certainly?

The directors of the great oil trust meet daily. No question
in its policy or business can arise in any part of the world which
cannot be settled in twenty-four hours by the highest authority.
Yet in our government, the trust question has not been settled
in twenty years, and there is absolutely no legal question of
vital importance that can be settled by the government in less
than three or four years. Why should a corporation have a
better system than the government? Why should it be efficient
and the government inefficient?

The question always comes back to the nature of our political
system. We live under a constitution which is ineffective and
antiquated, which was formulated by men of wealth in the interests of what is now known as "interests" and not as was so
speciously promised, in the interests of the people.

It is a constitution which proclaims the right of life, liberty
and the pursuit of happiness, but which makes living so costly
that one man in twelve is buried in the potter's field; it provides that no cruel or unusual punishment shall be inflicted,

yet daily men are being made eunuchs in state prisons, a bar-
berous custom tolerated in no other civilized nation under the
heavens and a reproach to humanity; it is a constitution which
guarantees liberty, but under which there is less liberty than
possessed by the subject of any constitutional monarch of
Europe. It is a constitution which divides with scrupulous
care the departments of the law's making, the law's execution
and the law's interpretation, but under which the president has
powers greater and more autocratic than any king in Europe,
and in which the judiciary has greater power than is to be found
in any similar body, yet in which the laws delays are a denial
of justice nowhere else exhibited. It is a constitution which
provides a government of laws, but under which lawlessness is
widespread and rampant, and it assumes to be a system of no taxation without representation; yet it creates a class of representatives who instead of attending to the people's business, are chiefly
concerned in exploiting their constituency, in continuing themselves in office and in utilizing public distress for political advantage. The constitution subverts the will of the people, and
it is an antiquated and imperfect system. It should be reorganized and made an instrument of progress, of liberty and of
equality. This is the duty that the public owes itself, a duty
which should not be performed piecemeal, but thoroughly and
forthwith.

Under the present system, inefficiency costs at the lowest estimate, over a hundred and ten dollars a year for each person
and for the 33,000,000 wage earners, not less than $5.75 per
week per wage earner. These are conditions, not theories!
Whose hand is in the public's pocket to this depth, and why do
we allow the disgrace and robbery to continue?

* * * * * * * *

The first whine that incompetency has to make for itself, when
brought face to face with foreign improvements, is that the improvements are not applicable to local conditions.

This is a foul excuse, the product of jealousy; it is the first
and readiest excuse of those who are lacking in energy and
initiative and who prefer sloth and ignorance to progress and
public welfare.

It is typical of the official and the hog-mannered business man
whose only idea of progress is to fatten but who must be forced
aside if any real progress is to be made.

Although it is humiliating to the jingoism of those who are

convinced that every improvement of any consequence if it does not originate in their own sphere must be deprecated and declared an absurdity and fought at every point; it is nevertheless true that the nations and individuals who make the greatest progress are those who adopt improvements whenever they are to be found and who from such points of vantage, move on to new improvements of their own, and this is true not only of nations and individuals, but also of municipalities, trade organizations and corporations.

In all departments of life, too, those who thus fight against improvements are those also who show the greatest of contradictions in their positions.

For example, government ownership of telegraph and cables is opposed, yet the government conducts the post office, and the proposition to turn it over to private capital is never advanced; municipal traction and electric lighting systems are violently opposed, yet the water supply systems of cities are in almost all instances controlled, owned and operated by the municipalities themselves; violent opposition is shown to fixing maximum prices of trust products and prevention of the monopolization of natural resources, yet the Interstate Commerce Commission by fixing rates stands between the public and railroad extortion and prevents monopolies of transportation, and while activities of the Government in the fostering of foreign trade are criticised, yet the most paternalistic of devices, the tariff, protects favored manufacturers.

These are but a few examples of the contradictions so apparent in American institutions and numberless others could readily be cited in every phase of public and private enterprise, and further not only not satisfied with refusing to look around and see what improvements are to be had, self-sufficient officials, when finally aroused, are too often to be seen going through with lengthy and expensive experiments with much loss of time and waste of money to ascertain facts which have already long been known to those who are familiar with conditions. This is a mole-like attitude which would be amusing were it not so tedious and criminally expensive.

And too often when improvements are adopted it is long after their foreign usefulness has been exhausted, still later improvements having taken their place abroad. This is a kind of second hand progress which is not much better than the original old fogyism.

It will be self evident that many of the improvements which
have been outlined in this volume will ultimately be adopted, but
only as has been the case with numerous improvements in the
past, after interminable delays and the squanderings of great
sums of money.

It should accordingly appeal to the public reason, that unnecessary delay and self interested opposition to proven advantage so obviously within reach, are nothing less than crimes
against progress and the welfare of humanity.

Why then it may be asked are such crimes tolerated?

And who is responsible?

INDEX

INDEX

Lightning Source UK Ltd.
Milton Keynes UK
UKHW011821050220
358245UK00001B/94